DATE DUE			

Critical Essays on Lawrence Durrell

Critical Essays on Lawrence Durrell

Alan Warren Friedman

G.K. Hall & Co. • Boston, Massachusetts

Library of Congress Cataloging-in-Publication Data

Critical essays on Lawrence Durrell.

(Critical essays on modern British literature)
Includes index.
1. Durrell, Lawrence—Criticism and interpretation.
I. Friedman, Alan Warren. II. Series.
PR6007.U76Z58   1987   828'.91209   86-25621
ISBN 0-8161-8755-X (alk. paper)

This publication is printed on permanent/durable acid-free paper
MANUFACTURED IN THE UNITED STATES OF AMERICA

CRITICAL ESSAYS ON BRITISH LITERATURE

Alan Friedman's introduction presents both sides of the Durrell controversy, including critics who deemed Durrell excessive in his prose and extravagant in his ideas, as well as those Durrell worshipers for whom he is undoubtedly the greatest writer of the last forty years. Friedman's view is balanced, seeing Durrell as falling short of the four "greats" of the twentieth century—Conrad, Joyce, Lawrence, and Woolf—but ultimately ranking "with those of the next order": Cary, Greene, Huxley, and Waugh.

The reviews and essays cover the whole range of Durrell's most important work in poetry and prose, including the recently published *Avignon Quincunx*, but place a heavy emphasis upon the masterpiece, *The Alexandria Quartet*. Friedman's introduction, concisely and deftly written, summarizes and evaluates the history of Durrell criticism and its practitioners, and gives us a handy checklist of major critical works.

Zack Bowen, GENERAL EDITOR

University of Delaware

CONTENTS

INTRODUCTION

Although Lawrence Durrell has been a prolific and protean writer since the 1930s, he is often regarded solely as the creator of *The Alexandria Quartet*. With the publication of its first part, *Justine* (1957), Durrell fulfilled two life-long ambitions: he attracted serious critical attention and he could finally support himself by his writing. Yet prior to that date he had published five novels, nearly a dozen books of poetry (including his *Selected Poems* [1956]), a trilogy of fictional accounts of his life on three Greek islands, a verse play, a book of criticism, and a collection of humorous "Sketches from Diplomatic Life" based loosely on his work in the British Foreign Service. His output since the *Quartet* has remained varied and impressive: two additional verse plays; two more island books; further volumes of poetry, including his *Collected Poems* (1980); a two-volume novel, *The Revolt of Aphrodite* (first published as *Tunc* [1968] and *Nunquam* [1970]), and a just-completed five-volume fiction, *The Avignon Quincunx* (1974–85). The image of Durrell as a one-novel author is, nonetheless, largely sustained by the history of criticism—as if *The Alexandria Quartet* were all, or at least all that matters. The present volume has two aims: to make readily available the best writing about Durrell's work, and to reflect fairly the controversy it has aroused.

Serious Durrell criticism essentially begins in the early 1960s when the *Quartet*, which the impoverished Durrell had reluctantly published as separate novels (1957–60), began to be seen by at least some critics as a single and substantial whole. Prior to 1960, the response to his work consisted largely of reviews and memoirs, the latter primarily accolades from writers like Richard Aldington, Henry Miller, and Alfred Perlès—close friends and boosters first, and critics second if at all. The initial period of critical response, from the late 1930s to the late 1950s, was framed by two remarkably similar paeans, from major critics, to Durrell's arrival on the literary scene. T.S. Eliot (1938) hailed *The Black Book* as "the first piece of work by a new English writer to give me any hope for the future of prose fiction," though as Durrell's editor at Faber and Faber he rejected the book when Durrell refused to expurgate it. Twenty years later Lionel Trilling*

---

*Items marked with an asterisk in the Introduction are reproduced in part or whole in the present volume.

(1959) in a review of *Justine* called Durrell "the first contemporary novelist in a long time to captivate my imagination to the extent of leading me to believe that he is telling me something new . . ." (51). Yet even beyond Trilling's encomium, the anecdotal / memoiristic approach, whose first phase may be said to have climaxed with "Hommage à Durrell" in the inaugural issue of *Two Cities* (Paris, 1959), has persisted. It is a pervasive and unsurprising, if not always helpful, response to this most self-expressive and accessible of writers. The first book about him, *The World of Lawrence Durrell* (ed. Harry T. Moore, 1962), is a miscellany of critical and personal commentary; the first important single-author overview, G. S. Fraser's *Lawrence Durrell: A. Study** (1968), is as much memoir as criticism; and the recent publication of Durrell's correspondence with Aldington (1981) complements earlier epistolary collections with Perlès (1959) and Miller (1963). Further, his authorized biography (by Ian S. MacNiven) is already well underway; and, above all, he has remained generous of his time and thoughts before an onslaught of inquiries and interviewers.

Perhaps reflecting a time of peculiarly intense stock-taking, comprehensive genre studies with titles like "The Novel Today" and "The Modern Writer and His World" appeared in large numbers in the '50s and '60s. In such works—for example, those by Fraser (1953), William York Tindall (1956), David Daiches (1958), James J. Gindin (1962), Frederick R. Karl (1962, 1966), Margaret Church (1963), Charles Irving Glicksberg (1963), Shiv K. Kumar (1963), Leon Edel (1964), Walter Allen (1965), and Anthony Burgess (1968)—Durrell (or at least the *Quartet*) gained first a foothold, then respectful attention, and finally extended discussion. Serious attempts were made to place him within one modern movement or another: stream-of-consciousness (Kumar), the psychological novel (Edel), fabulation (Robert Scholes*). But many others reacted—or overreacted—to him, as the following titles suggest, as to a phenomenon of Hollywood proportions: "Will Lawrence Durrell Spoil America?" (Gordon Merrick, 1958), "A Major Novelist" (R. W. Flint, 1959), "New Four-Star King of Novelists" (Nigel Dennis, 1960), "The Autumnal Arrival of Lawrence Durrell" (Thomas B. Morgan, 1960), "What is Wrong with Lawrence Durrell?" (Kenneth Rexroth, 1960), "Un grand talent de basse époque" (Albert Gerard, 1962), "The Novelist as Entertainer" (David Littlejohn, 1962), "One Vote for the Sun" (Gerald Sykes, 1962), "This Infuriating Little Man—Lawrence Durrell" (Ann Leslie, 1965), "The Permanence of Durrell" (Littlejohn, 1965), and so on. As Gerard Lebas put it in 1969, Durrell criticism evidences a strong "polemic tendency," one which manifests itself in overblown praise and harsh condemnation. Hilary Corke implied something similar when, in 1960, he referred to the *Quartet* "as a test case for reviewers" (65): comments were often so extreme they seemed responses to different works, or only to each other.

Perhaps the liveliest critical debate has centered on Durrell's subject matter and the intellectual acumen he brings to bear upon it. In the *Quar-*

tet he set out to write what he called "an investigation of modern love" centering, at least initially, on a character named Justine. He thus immediately invoked echoes of de Sade, George Meredith, and Kinsey. Epigraphs to the *Quartet* and his own early comments on it allude to Freud, Einstein, Georg Groddeck, and sufficient others to keep source hunters and scholars of intertextuality busy for decades. Largely self-educated, Durrell has read widely and creatively in many disciplines, and the prominent display of his learning has been viewed variously as flashy and shallow, or sophisticated and profound. His conception of relativity, for example, has been attacked as unscientific by Dominique Arban and Richard Boston. Jean-Paul Hamard, on the other hand, discusses it as a new and fecund myth; Gilbert Highet, Lee T. Lemon, and Glicksberg as a method of searching out truth; and Alfred M. Bork as something of a combination of the two: a popularizing of material basic to twentieth-century thought, a means of encouraging readers to become, as Durrell puts it, "their own contemporaries." Subsequent studies—those by Sharon Lee Brown, Walter G. Creed, and Nancy W. Lewis, among others—provide thoughtful and sympathetic treatment of Durrell's scientific thought. Durrell himself, more poet than systematic thinker, generally stresses the metaphorical rather than literal significance of his scientific analogies and allusions. In one interview, for example, he unselfconsciously and disarmingly admits to having "confused Bergsonian time with Einsteinian time" (Kenneth Young 64). John Arthos and Chet Taylor find serious contradictions in Durrell's philosophy and aesthetics, but critics seem decreasingly distressed about them. Instead, they have begun to provide useful commentary on what Durrell knows and how he uses his knowledge: Egyptian history, culture, and anthropology (William Leigh Godshalk*); the Tarot (Carl Bode* and Carol Peirce*); Gnosticism (James P. Carley*). Equally valuable and even more numerous are intertextual studies connecting Durrell to other writers: Mallarmé and Rimbaud (Alain Bosquet), E. M. Forster (Godshalk* and Jane Lagoudis Pinchin [1977]), T. S. Eliot (Bode*, Eleanor H. Hutchens, and Fraser), Cavafy (Christopher G. Katope and Pinchin [1977]), Groddeck (Alan Warren Friedman 49–50, 67–70, 142–44, 180–83), Spengler (Gregory Dickson).

Durrell's writing depends for its effects upon an elaborately ornamented prose. His diction and syntax have an exotic flavor; at their finest, they are lyrically innovative and compelling, but they can cloy at times and sound self-parodic. The style employs highly allusive and elaborate metaphors; incursions into various disciplines (physics, psychology, entymology, historicism, among others); an excess of exclamation marks and capital letters (Art, Truth, Reality, Love, etc.); as well as an addiction "to the repetition of the portentous word 'great' " (Bernard Bergonzi 37). Those who like this sort of thing usually admire it excessively; those who do not tend to condemn it. Thus, Bergonzi finds Durrell's novels, "which have been widely praised for their 'poetic' quality, tedious and sometimes absurd" (37), while Hayden Carruth (1962) deems the "lyrical structures" of the

Quartet the product of "an exquisite skill" (120, 128), George Steiner* considers Durrell's major achievement to be his exploitation of language's full resources, and Littlejohn calls him simply the best contemporary British writer of metaphoric prose. Malcolm Bradbury's "Voluptia"* is a superb representation and parody of Durrell's distinctive style.

Like his style, Durrell's characters and settings manifest multiple layers of significance and mythic echoes. Bonamy Dobrée, who concedes that the *Quartet* is a "striking experiment" (204), objects to what he considers its feeble characterization, as does Burgess (1970). Following D. H. Lawrence, Durrell has said that he wanted to raise the question "as to whether the human personality is not a selective fiction or a polite figment" (Young 64). He has, subsequently, noted that his characters have a "tendency to be dummies" (in Karl 49), or "blueprints" (Joan Rodman Goulianos [1971] 161); and self-mockingly, he makes the eponymous heroine of *The Revolt of Aphrodite* an android. As if taking their cue from Durrell himself, critics often find much to disparage in his characters. Pursewarden, Durrell's main speaker for aesthetic values in the *Quartet*, comes in for the heaviest criticism (Trilling*, Karl [1962], John M. Lennon). Even the devoted Henry Miller says in a letter to Durrell that "of all the characters in the quartet Pursewarden is the least interesting to me. . . . I never got the conviction that he was the great writer you wish him to seem. I think he'd come off better . . . if you sliced down his remarks or observations. They get sententious and tedious and feeble sometimes. Too much persiflage" (361). Karl, who is unimpressed by all the *Quartet*'s major characters, finds "much that is hackneyed" in the creation of Clea (Karl 52), a view that is shared by Bode* who calls her lifeless. H. Dare denounces Scobie—the one character who almost everyone, within and without the *Quartet*, finds appealing—as an incredible creation. Somewhat surprisingly, D. J. Enright, who dislikes Durrell's achievement generally and his characters in particular ("a group of over-bred neurotics and sexual dilettantes" [116]), praises not only Scobie but also Pursewarden as solid achievements. Trilling*, in a typically balanced reading, says that Durrell "proposes a new kind of verisimilitude" in the *Quartet*'s aesthetics built on epistemological doubt (56). He has reservations about its characters (who "stand in a peculiar negative relation to the will" [57]) but he takes as literal Durrell's Note to the *Quartet*, "Only the city is real," and he applauds the creation of Alexandria as protagonist. Dobrée agrees that "this story about the inhabitants of Alexandria is therefore a portrait of Alexandria, which 'lives' the characters" (194); and Durrell himself comments that "I have tried to see people through landscapes" (Marc Alyn 90). Somewhat overstating the case, John A. Weigel maintains that the "spirit of place" is so strong in Alexandria that for its inhabitants "there is no escape" from its domination (97), but he overlooks the characters' departure for Paris at the end and the resolution that the *Quartet* offers (see John V. Hagopian, W. R. Robinson, and Friedman 136–65). As for the setting—this unique Egyptian city whose people "have never been truly Egyptian" (Forster 6)—Mahmoud Manzaloui*, an Alexandrian with strong views about his city and how it should be represented, insists that Durrell gets it wrong; Godshalk*, who is more in sympathy with Durrellean fictionalizing, carefully examines Durrell's use of sources and maintains that Manzaloui, though "informative," is "misguided" (369). Those who offer sensitive analysis of Alexandria's role in the *Quartet* include Bode*, Ambrose Gordon, Jr., Goulianos (1969), and especially Pinchin (1977).

Detailed studies of Durrell's thought and style fail to impress harsh critics like Benjamin DeMott*, who deems the *Quartet* the work of a bad poet and second-rate thinker (462), and Bergonzi, who maintains that "the crippling weakness of the *Quartet* [is] the lack of an intelligence adequate to keep together its willfully complicated structure" (37). Numerous critics—including Matthew Proser, Arthos, Manzaloui*, Louis Fraiberg, Taylor, R. T. Chapman—consider the *Quartet* structurally or philosophically sloppy or crude, but Karl, Frank Kermode*, Lemon, Scholes*, Hartwig Isernhagen, Friedman*, among others, argue persuasively that it is, in Kermode's phrase, "an experiment of very great formal interest" (227). As if responding to the *Quartet's* various deprecators, Flint first concedes Durrell's faults to be "a slopping over of energies: metaphors run out of hand, needlessly multiplied analogies, repetitious descriptions. His humor is occasionally too heavy and his *sententiae* too obvious." But, he maintains, Durrell "is blessed with an intelligence that overcomes most of the vices of enthusiasm" (354). Carruth (1962) agrees that Durrell's writings are "the products of as much intelligence as a very intelligent man can bring to bear; and they are beautiful as well . . ." (128). Still, the debate continues as to exactly what to make of the *Quartet* and its place in contemporary letters. Thus, Flint hails it in the end as "a genuinely new kind of fictional enterprise" (354), while Enright—whose own Alexandrian novel, *Academic Year*, had roused little interest—objects that it "is neither novel nor true" (112). Martin Green* and Karl Miller pronounce the *Quartet* decadent; Curtis Cate finds its exploration of doubt and uncertainty a proper expression of modernity; Gerard considers it "une expression sinistrement adéquate d'une société blette" (29); and Robinson argues that the *Quartet*, "a new kind of novel, the novel of imagination, in which the sensibility works conjointly with and is strengthened by the intellect . . . [,] confutes established cliches about alienation and dehumanization as the artist's, and man's, inescapable condition in the twentieth century" (67–68). Agreeing that the problem may be that of the age more than that of the writer, Pinchin (1977) maintains that Durrell's copiousness and lack of constraint render him out of key with his time: "His readers get angry with Durrell— for overblown action, for a patronizing vision of the female and the oriental, for the need to write a masterpiece of size" (199). For all its infelicities of thought and style, however, the *Quartet* is increasingly acknowledged to be a mature and enduring achievement. George P. Elliott*, who details numerous weaknesses he finds in it, nonetheless concludes that it is "first-rate . . . a good romantic novel [that] surely merits the acclaim with which, for a variety of reasons, not all of them good, it has been greeted" (89–94). Such a view seems generally to be carrying the day.

The notion of romance—connotative of love, mythic plotting, and exotic landscapes—is central not only to the *Quartet* but to Durrell's interaction with the world he inhabits. As the titles suggest, his love affair with places and their *deus loci* infuse his early books of poetry, *A Private Country* (1943) and *Cities, Plains and People* (1946); his five island books; his travel writing (collected as *Spirit of Place* [1969]); and his major fiction: *The Alexandria Quartet* and *The Avignon Quincunx*. Born in the Himalayan area of India and sent to school in England at the age of twelve, Durrell lived a fragmented, peripatetic existence—London, Paris, Athens, the Greek islands, Argentina, Yugoslavia, Cyprus—before settling in Sommières in southern France in 1957. He has lived there ever since. In the '30s he had rejected the bleakness and sterility of what, in *The Black Book* (1938), he denominated the "English Death," for the warmth and color that one reviewer refers to as his "Mediterranean kaleidoscope" (Philip Toynbee 20), and then found the pattern of settlement and flight harshly recurrent. He fled Greece (whose loss he felt like "an amputation" [*Prospero's Cell* 131]) ahead of the Nazi invasion, then the intellectual and moral deadness he encountered first in Argentina and then in Yugoslavia, and finally the civil war on Cyprus in the '50s. Places first enticed and inspired him, then they frustrated and repelled him, threw him back on his own devices: "I am, and I remain, an expatriate. That vague sense of exile has never quite left me. But at the same time it has meant that I can feel at ease anywhere, given a minimum of sunshine. The expatriate carries his country with him, inside him: everywhere belongs to him, because he belongs to nowhere" (Alyn 24–25). He sought, as he puts it in the 1951 poem, "Deus Loci," a "natal shrine / landscape of the precocious southern heart," but found it only occasionally and then briefly. What he calls his "islomania" ("a rare but by no means unknown affliction of spirit [that causes its victims to] find islands somehow irresistible" [*Marine Venus* 15]) coexisted with claustrophobia and deracination. His quest for a life in harmony with the spirit of its surroundings has largely defined his sense of himself: "in Greece you feel the pagan world is very close. Where I live now, in the South of France, you feel something equally strong—you feel Nostradamus, the Provençal singers, the intense savagery, and a different sort of mysticism. In Dorset, where I was living last year, the Druids were pretty close, I thought" (Young 66–67). The gap between quest and fulfillment expressed in terms of landscape created a tension in Durrell that has inspired his finest writing.

For some, like the reviewer who condemned Durrell's "lazy reliance on place to do the work of thought" (Francis Hope 143), both Durrell's attitude toward his surroundings and the writings it produces are mere romantic exoticism; but most critics agree that Durrell's sense of place represents a great and enduring strength. Thus, Lawrence Clark Powell calls *Prospero's Cell* (1945), Durrell's first island book, "a Mediterranean prose-poem to rank with *Fountains in the Sand, Sea and Sardinia,* and *The Colossus of Maroussi*" (Powell i). *Bitter Lemons* (1957), winner of the British Duff Cooper Prize, is almost universally acknowledged a success. For Friedman* it is "by far his best" island book (51)—for some it is his finest achievement altogether. His non-Greek island book, *Sicilian Carousel* (1977), is his weakest—"a peculiarly perfunctory book" that "shows Durrell's talent in tatters" according to Peter Porter (87)—because in it his role is reduced to that of a tourist: "So Sicily never comes alive for the reader, unlike Corfu, Rhodes, Cyprus, Egypt and Greece" (Goulianos [1977] 18). As Jan Morris, who finds the Greek island books written "with an exquisite expertise," says of Durrell, "He is too good a writer, too good a traveller, for [the tourist] merry-go-round. We do not want to see Lawrence Durrell traipsing up to the night's hotel with the rest of the exhausted Carousellers: we want to eavesdrop upon him sitting among the lemon-trees on his own terrace above the sea, discussing philosophy and the meaning of words with ancient beloved sages and nubile friends" (78). Yet even *Sicilian Carousel* has its admirers, those who find it a worthy successor to the Greek island trilogy: Michael Malone deems it a mature achievement "by an artist who has the selectivity to see and the style to describe what he sees as well as any prosodist currently writing" (92), and Paul Fussell, who dislikes what he calls Durrell's "pretentious and badly written novels" (24), maintains that *Sicilian Carousel* "superbly captures the spirit of that place and does so with a generosity of imagination rare in any writing . . ." (25). While greatly admiring the work of both Durrell and Fussell, I am inclined to ask, along with Morris, "What possessed [Durrell] to suppose that he could honour his art from the seat of a tourist bus on a week's tour of the antiquities?" (79). His most recent island book, *The Greek Islands* (1978), is a cultural / historical survey combining travelogue, documentary, and personal experience. In it Durrell returns to the world he loves best and creates a lavishly illustrated and "entrancing book [that] will whet the appetite of readers who have never been to the isles of Greece and will stir nostalgic memories in those who have" (Henry Wilkinson Bragdon B3). Certainly it is Durrell's Greek islands, his Alexandria ("the most various and colourful [city] I could remember"), and, to a lesser extent, the Avignon of his recent series that endure for most readers. It is entirely appropriate, then, that when a Lawrence Durrell Society came to be established in 1980 its publication was entitled *Deus Loci* and its biannual conference "On Miracle Ground."

   Durrell's major fictions since the *Quartet, The Revolt of Aphrodite* and *The Avignon Quincunx,* inevitably provoke comparisons with the earlier work. They too offer exotic settings peopled by improbable characters; multiple fictional and narrative layerings; a mixing of memory and desire in the meeting of retrospective and quest narrative structures; extensive mythical and metaphysical speculation on the nature of the universe and its creator, on the ego and personality, on the enterprises of being, becoming, and creating; a harsh critique of western civilization and values; and an erotically charged prose style whose evocations and allusions overtly echo and invoke the *Quartet*. Critics tend, in fact, to dismiss *Revolt* as "persistent, unashamed self-imitation" (Bergonzi 37), and only a few studies have subjected it to serious thematic analysis. The most interesting include Tone Rugset's* approach via numerology and cosmic harmony; James A. Brigham's treatment of Durrell's women; and Reed Way Dasenbrock's* focus on death as theme. Few other aspects of this novel, it seems to me, are as likely to provide fruitful ground for further study.

The *Quincunx*, a far more substantial achievement, has only just been completed. Its underlying conception derives from an ancient mystical design formed by placing one object, usually a tree, at each corner of a square and one at the center. The name for this pattern, according to the seventeenth-century writer Sir Thomas Browne, results not only from "the Quintuple number of Trees, but the figure declaring that number, which being doubled at the angle, makes up the letter X . . ." (175). That is, diagonals connecting the corner trees create one V (Roman numeral for five) atop another, thereby forming an X (Roman numeral for ten)—so that the five trees double themselves to make ten. Further, what Browne calls "the sacred letter X" (222) may be rotated to produce a circle, the geometrical sign of perfection; and, as a form of the Greek cross, it has come to symbolize Christ. Understandably, then, the quincunx is traditionally seen as having spiritual properties: Browne finds it everywhere in the ancient and natural worlds, and attaches great significance to that fact.

Durrell's Avignon series exploits the properties of the quincunx both in its five-part structure and in its thematic allusions to the Knights Templar, the richest and most powerful military force in Europe until the early fourteenth century. At that time, King Philip of France and Pope Clement V conspired to destroy them for motives that are not entirely clear: out of fear of their power, independence, and perhaps heterodoxy, out of a desire to seize their wealth, or perhaps both. In the event, the Knights Templar, for reasons never satisfactorily explained by historians, surrendered without a struggle, and no treasure was ever found. According to the legend Durrell evokes, the still lost treasure—which, depending on the different versions, is either a great cache of gold or the Holy Grail—is buried at the center of a quincunx located near Avignon, the home of Pope Clement during the schism with Rome. Durrell conceives of Hitler as seeking the treasure in order to establish a new knightly order on it and thus insure victory and world domination. At the climax of *Quinx*, the *Quincunx*'s final book, Durrell's surviving characters—from both this series and earlier fiction— gather after the war at the Pont du Gard, the ancient Roman aqueduct outside of Avignon, to unearth neither gold nor Grail but, as at the end of the *Quartet*, the possibility of beginning anew.

The *Quincunx* has much to offer eager Durrell critics, many of whom are doubtless already at work. I anticipate extended studies of its complex narrative and fictionalizing self-reflexivity; its treatment of mysticism and Gnosticism (an area of study Carley's* ground-breaking essay initiates), of heresy and the Knights Templar, of eroticism and violence, of its linkage of early fourteenth and mid-twentieth centuries; and its relationship to the *Quartet*. Most early reviews of the *Quincunx* sound like early reviews of the *Quartet*. They remark on "a lush combination of fantastic characters, opulent landscapes, and weird rites set once again in his favored Mediterranean world: Provence, Venice, and Alexandria" (James Meehan 3145); his "opulent lexicon, his flamboyant asides, his rich, easy style and his bright local aperçus" (Julian Barnes 378); a prose "ringingly evocative, full of character and possibility . . . a troublesome and often exasperating book . . . with a wealth of atmosphere" (Anne Tyler* 37); "an elaborate tapestry of event and character [by a writer who] unsettles and enchants" (Samuel Coale 60)—and then deem the *Quincunx* a mixed success, an interesting failure, or a paler, "less fiercely characterised" *Quartet* (Barnes 378). There are, nonetheless, extreme reactions: reviewers who hail the *Quincunx*'s author as "a novelist of genius" (Alberto Manguel 12) and others who find it "puerile to adolescent" (Harriett Gilbert 28). Serious studies like Carley's* are just beginning to appear and to define the major concerns.

A controversy of such diversity, intensity, and duration as Durrell's writings have provoked suggests that he has "arrived"—or at least that the *Quartet* has—though exactly *where* remains at issue. He has declared that he has reached the end of a writing career spanning more than half a century and that he is preparing to retire to a Tibetan monastery in France, but even if this is true his proliferating critics are far from having taken his achievement's full measure, and much further still from agreeing on its dimensions. There are, I think, two main reasons for this: much of his work is only just making its presence known and felt, and his idiosyncratic style is inherently controversial and unsettling. My own prognosis is that heated debate concerning the quality and success of Durrell's work will continue for quite some time, and that eventually a consensus of sorts will emerge. He will then be deemed to rank not with the truly great British novelists of the century—Conrad, Joyce, Lawrence, Woolf—but with those of the next order: Cary, Greene, Huxley, Waugh, writers of distinction and enduring interest and worth.

ALAN WARREN FRIEDMAN

University of Texas

Works Cited

Aldington, Richard. "A Note on Lawrence Durrell" (1959). In *The World of Lawrence Durrell*, edited by Harry T. Moore, 3–12. Carbondale: Southern Illinois University Press, 1962.

Allen, Walter. *The Modern Novel in Britain and the United States*. New York: Dutton, 1965.

Alyn, Marc. *The Big Supposer: Lawrence Durrell*. Translated by Francine Barker. London: Abelard-Schuman, 1973.

Arban, Dominique. "Lawrence Durrell." *Preuves* 109 (March 1960):86–94.

Arthos, John. "Lawrence Durrell's Gnosticism." *Personalist* 43 (1962):360–73.

Barnes, Julian. "Trick or Treat." *New Statesman* 96 (22 September 1978):377–78.

Bergonzi, Bernard. "Stale Incense." *New York Review of Books* 11, no. 1 (11 July 1968):37–39.

Bode, Carl. "Durrell's Way to Alexandria." *College English* 22, no. 8 (May 1961):531–38.

Bork, Alfred M. "Durrell and Relativity." *Centennial Review of Arts and Sciences* (Michigan State University) 7, no. 2 (Spring 1963):191–203.

Bosquet, Alain. "Lawrence Durrell ou l'azur ironique." *Nouvelle Revue Française* 14 (June 1966):1116–23.

Boston, Richard. "Some Notes on *The Alexandria Quartet*." *Delta* 23 (February 1961):33–38.

Bragdon, Henry Wilkinson. "Durrell's Sun-dappled Isles." *Christian Science Monitor* 13 November 1978. B3.

Brown, Sharon Lee. "Lawrence Durrell and Relativity." *Dissertation Abstracts* 26 (1966):7310.

Browne, Sir Thomas. "The Garden of Cyrus; or, The Quincunciall, Lozenge, or Net-Work Plantations of the Ancients, Artificially, Naturally, Mystically Considered." In his *The Religio Medici and Other Writings of Sir Thomas Browne*. London and Toronto: Dent, and New York: Dutton, 1925.

Burgess, Anthony. *The Novel Now: A Guide to Contemporary Fiction*. New York: Norton, 1968.

———. "Durrell and the Homunculi." *Saturday Review* 53 (21 March 1970):29–31, 41.

Carruth, Hayden. "An Inversion of the Accepted." *Saturday Review* 44 (7 January 1961):28.

———. "Nougat for the Old Bitch." In Moore (1962), 117–28.

Cate, Curtis. "Lawrence Durrell." *Atlantic* 208 (December 1961):63–69.

Chapman, R. T. "Dead, or Just Pretending? Reality in *The Alexandria Quartet*." *Centennial Review* (Michigan State University) 16, no. 4 (Fall 1972):408–18.

Church, Margaret. *Time and Reality: Studies in Contemporary Fiction*. Chapel Hill: University of North Carolina Press, 1963.

Coale, Samuel. Untitled Review of *Constance*. *America* 148, no. 3 (22 January 1983):59–60.

Corke, Hilary. "Mr. Durrell and Brother Criticus." *Encounter* 14 (May 1960):65–70.

Creed, Walter G. *The Muse of Science and "The Alexandria Quartet."* Norwood, Penn.: Norwood Editions, 1977; Folcroft, Penn.: Folcroft Library Editions, 1978.

Daiches, David. *The Present Age in British Literature*. Bloomington: Indiana University Press, 1958.

Dare, H. "The Quest for Durrell's Scobie." *Modern Fiction Studies* 10, no. 4 (Winter 1965):379–83.

DeMott, Benjamin. "Grading the Emanglons." *Hudson Review* 13, no. 3 (Autumn 1960):457–64.

Dennis, Nigel. "New Four-Star King of Novelists." *Life* (21 November 1960):96–109.

Dickson, Gregory. "Spengler's Theory of Architecture in Durrell's *Tunc* and *Nunquam*." *Deus Loci: Proceedings of the Lawrence Durrell Society* (1981):272–80.

Dobrée, Bonamy. "Durrell's Alexandria Series." In Moore (1962), 184–204.

Durrell, Lawrence. *Pied Piper of Lovers*. London: Cassell, 1935.

———. [As Charles Norden]. *Panic Spring*. London: Faber, 1937.

———. *The Black Book: An Agon*. Paris: Obelisk Press, 1938.

———. *Prospero's Cell: A Guide to the Landscape and Manners of the Island of Corcyra*. London: Faber, 1945.

———. *Cefalû*. London: Editions Poetry, 1947. As *The Dark Labyrinth*. London: Ace, 1947.

———. *Sappho: A Play in Verse*. London: Faber, 1950.

———. *A Key to Modern British Poetry*. Norman: University of Oklahoma Press, 1952.

———. *Reflections on a Marine Venus: A Companion to the Landscape of Rhodes*. London: Faber, 1953.

———. *Selected Poems*. London: Faber, 1956.

———. *Bitter Lemons*. London: Faber, 1957.

———. *Esprit de Corps: Sketches from Diplomatic Life*. London: Faber, 1957.

———. *White Eagles over Serbia*. London: Faber, 1957.

———. *The Alexandria Quartet*. London: Faber, 1962: *Justine*. London: Faber, 1957; *Balthazar*. London: Faber, 1958; *Mountolive*. London: Faber, 1958; *Clea*. London: Faber, 1960.

———. *Stiff Upper Lip: Life among the Diplomats*. London: Faber, 1958.

———. *Acté, or The Prisoners of Time*. London: Faber, 1965.

———. *An Irish Faustus: A Morality in Nine Scenes*. London: Faber, 1963.

———. *Sauve qui peut*. London: Faber, 1966.

———. *The Revolt of Aphrodite*. London: Faber, 1974: *Tunc*. London: Faber, 1968; *Nunquam*. London: Faber, 1970.

———. *Spirit of Place: Letters and Essays on Travel*. Edited by Alan G. Thomas. London: Faber, 1969.

———. *The Best of Antrobus*. London: Faber, 1974.

———. *The Avignon Quincunx: Monsieur, or The Prince of Darkness*. London: Faber, 1974; *Livia, or Buried Alive*. London: Faber, 1978; *Constance, or Solitary Practices*. London: Faber, 1982; *Sebastian, or Ruling Passions*. London: Faber, 1983; *Quinx, or The Ripper's Tale*. London: Faber, 1985.

———. *Sicilian Carousel*. London: Faber, 1977.

———. *The Greek Islands*. London: Faber, 1978.

———. *Collected Poems, 1931–74*. Edited by James A. Brigham. London: Faber, 1980.

———, and Richard Aldington. *Literary Lifelines: The Richard Aldington–Lawrence Durrell Correspondence*. Edited by Ian S. MacNiven and Harry T. Moore. New York: Viking, 1981.

———, and Henry Miller. *A Private Correspondence*. Edited by George Wickes. London: Faber, 1963.

———, Alfred Perlès, and Henry Miller. *Art and Outrage: A Correspondence about Henry Miller*. London: Putman, 1959.

Edel, Leon. *The Modern Psychological Novel*. New York: Universal, 1964.

Elliott, George P. "The Other Side of the Story." In Moore (1962), 87–94.

Enright, D.J. *Academic Year*. London: Secker & Warburg, 1955.

————. "Alexandrian Nights' Entertainments: Lawrence Durrell's 'Quartet.' " In his *Conspirators and Poets*, 111–20. London: Chatto & Windus, 1966.

Flint, R. W. "A Major Novelist." *Commentary* 27, no. 4 (April 1959):353–56.

Forster, E. M. *Alexandria: A History and a Guide*. New York: Doubleday, 1961.

Fraiberg, Louis. "Durrell's Dissonant Quartet." In *Contemporary British Novelists*, edited by Charles Shapiro, 16–35. Carbondale: Southern Illinois University Press, 1965.

Fraser, G. S. *The Modern Writer and His World*. London: Derek Verschoyle, 1953.

————. *Lawrence Durrell: A Study*. London: Faber, 1968. Rev. ed. 1973.

Friedman, Alan Warren. *Lawrence Durrell and "The Alexandria Quartet": Art for Love's Sake*. Norman: University of Oklahoma Press, 1970.

Fussell, Paul. "Durrell Incognito." *Saturday Review* 4 (3 September 1977):24–25.

Gerard, Albert. "Lawrence Durrell: Un grand talent de basse époque." *Revue générale belge* 98 (October 1962):15–29.

Gilbert, Harriett. "Under the Skin." *New Statesman* 104 (15 October 1982):28.

Gindin, James J. *Postwar British Fiction: New Accents and Attitudes*. Berkeley and Los Angeles: University of California Press, 1962.

Glicksberg, Charles J. "The Relativity of the Self: *The Alexandria Quartet*." In his *The Self in Modern Literature*, 89–94. University Park: Pennsylvania State University Press, 1963.

Godshalk, William Leigh. "Some Sources of Durrell's 'Alexandria Quartet.' " *Modern Fiction Studies* 13, no. 3 (Autumn 1967):361–74.

Gordon, Jr., Ambrose. "Time, Space, and Eros: The *Alexandria Quartet* Rehearsed." In *Six Contemporary Novels*, edited by William O.S. Sutherland, Jr., 6–21. Austin: University of Texas Humanities Research Center, 1962.

Goulianos, Joan Rodman. "Lawrence Durrell and Alexandria." *Virginia Quarterly Review* 45 (1969):664–73.

————. "A Conversation with Lawrence Durrell about Art, Analysis, and Politics." *Modern Fiction Studies* 17, 2 (Summer 1971):159–66.

————. "Guided Tour." *New York Times Book Review* (4 September 1977):7, 18.

Hagopian, John V. "The Resolution of *The Alexandria Quartet*." *Critique: Studies in New Fiction* 7, no. 1 (Spring 1964):97–106.

Hamard, Jean-Paul. "L'espace et le temps dans les romans de Lawrence Durrell." *Critique* (Paris) 16, no. 156 (May 1960):387–413.

Highet, Gilbert. "The Alexandrians of Lawrence Durrell." *Horizon* 2 (March 1960):113–18.

"Hommage à Durrell." *Two Cities* (Paris) 1, no. 1 (15 April 1959). Special Durrell number.

Hope, Francis. "Olives and After." *New Statesman* 76 (2 August 1968):143.

Hutchens, Eleanor H. "The Heraldic Universe in *The Alexandria Quartet*." *College English* 24 (October 1962):56–61.

Isernhagen, Hartwig. *Sensation, Vision and Imagination: The Problem of Unity in Lawrence Durrell's Novels*. Bamberg: Bamberger Fotodruck, 1969.

Karl, Frederick R. "Lawrence Durrell: Physical and Metaphysical Love." In his *A Reader's Guide to the Contemporary English Novel*, 40–61. 1962. New York: Farrar, Straus & Giroux, 1972.

Katope, Christopher G. "Cavafy and Durrell's 'The Alexandria Quartet.' " *Comparative Literature* 21 (1969):125–37.

Kermode, Frank. "Durrell and Others." In his *Puzzles and Epiphanies: Essays and Reviews 1958-1961*, 214–27. New York: Chilmark Press, 1962.

Kumar, Shiv K. *Bergson and the Stream of Consciousness Novel*. New York: New York University Press, 1963.

Lebas, Gérard. "Lawrence Durrell's *Alexandria Quartet* and the Critics: A Survey of Published Criticism." *Caliban* (Toulouse) 6 (January 1969):91–114.

Lemon, Lee T. "*The Alexandria Quartet*: Form and Fiction." *Wisconsin Studies in Contemporary Literature* 4, no. 3 (Autumn 1963):327–38.

Lennon, John M. "Pursewarden's Death: A Stray Brick from Another Region." *Modern Language Studies* 4, no. 1 (1976):22–28.

Leslie, Ann. "This Infuriating Man—Lawrence Durrell." *Irish Digest* 82, no. 4 (February 1965):67–70.

Lewis, Nancy W. "Two Thematic Applications of Einsteinian Field Structure in *The Alexandria Quartet*." *Deus Loci* 6, no. 1 (September 1982):1–10.

Littlejohn, David. "Lawrence Durrell: The Novelist as Entertainer." *Motive* 23 (November 1962):14–16.

———. "The Permanence of Durrell." *Colorado Quarterly* 14, no. 1 (Summer 1965):63–71.

Malone, Michael. Untitled Review of *Sicilian Carousel*. *Harper's* 255 (September 1977):92.

Manguel, Alberto. "The Novelist as Poet." *Books in Canada* 12 (March 1983):11–12.

Meehan, James. Untitled Review of *Monsieur*. *Library Journal* 99 (1 December 1974):3145–46.

Merrick, Gordon. "Will Lawrence Durrell Spoil America?" *New Republic* 138, no. 21 (26 May 1958):20–21.

Miller, Henry. "A Boost for *The Black Book*." *Booster* (Paris) 2 (October 1937):18.

———. "The Durrell of *The Black Book* Days." In Moore (1962), 95–99.

Miller, Karl. "Poet's Novel." *Listener* 61 (25 June 1959):1099–1100.

Moore, Harry T., ed. *The World of Lawrence Durrell*. Carbondale: Southern Illinois University Press, 1962.

Morgan, Thomas B. "The Autumnal Arrival of Lawrence Durrell." *Esquire* 54 (September 1960):108–11.

Morris, Jan. "Durrell—on a Tourist Bus?" *Encounter* 49, no. 3 (September 1977):77–79.

Perlès, Alfred. *My Friend Lawrence Durrell: An Intimate Memoir on the Author of "The Alexandria Quartet."* Middlesex: Scorpion Press, 1961.

Pinchin, Jane Lagoudis. *Alexandria Still: Forster, Durrell, and Cavafy*. Princeton: Princeton University Press, 1977.

———. "Durrell's Fatal Cleopatra." *Deus Loci: Proceedings of the First National Lawrence Durrell Conference* 5, no. 1 (25 April 1980):24–39.

Porter, Peter. "Func." *New Statesman* 94 (15 July 1977):87.

Powell, Lawrence Clark. Introductory Note to *A Landmark Gone*. 1946. Los Angeles: Reuben Pearson, 1949.

Proser, Matthew N. "Darley's Dilemma: The Problem of Structure in Durrell's *Alexandria Quartet*." *Critique* (Minneapolis) 4, no. 2 (Spring-Summer 1961):18–28.

Rexroth, Kenneth. "What is Wrong with Lawrence Durrell?" *Nation* 190 (4 June 1960):493–94.

Robinson, W. R. "Intellect and Imagination in *The Alexandria Quartet*." *Shenandoah* 18, no. 4 (Summer 1967):55–68.

Scholes, Robert. *The Fabulators*, 17–31. New York: Oxford University Press, 1967.

Sykes, Gerald. Introduction to *The Black Book*. New York: Pocket Books, 1962.

Taylor, Chet. "Dissonance and Digression: The Ill-Fitting Fusion of Philosophy and Form in Lawrence Durrell's *Alexandria Quartet*." *Modern Fiction Studies* 17, no. 2 (Summer 1971):167–79.

Tindall, William York. *Forces in Modern British Literature. 1885–1946*. New York: Knopf, 1947. Rev. ed. New York: Random House, 1956.

Toynbee, Philip. "Mediterranean Kaleidoscope." *Observer* (7 February 1960):20.

Trilling, Lionel. "The *Quartet*: Two Reviews." In Moore (1962), 49–65.

Tyler, Anne. "Avignon at War." *New Republic* 187, no. 22 (6 December 1982):36–37.

Weigel, John A. *Lawrence Durrell*. New York: Twayne, 1965.

Young, Kenneth. "A Dialogue with Durrell." *Encounter* 13, no. 6 (December 1959):61–68.

Reviews

The Heraldic Universe
Christopher Middleton*

Lawrence Durrell is known as a poet whose province is the Eastern Mediterranean. His new novel, *Justine*, is a love story, set in Alexandria during the late 1930's. The publishers call the book "unconventional in form and daring in execution." But the press reviews have been much more cautious, and reactions have ranged between outright hostility and conditional surrender to what the book offers. The reviewers have differed, it seems to me, because they have not noticed how *Justine* stands in relation to Durrell's previous writings. This has even led both sides of the argument to misconstrue the book. There has been no mention, for example, of the development from *The Black Book*, which Durrell published in Paris in 1938, and from his *Key to Modern Poetry*, published in 1952. Considered in isolation, or in the wrong context, *Justine* can be misconstrued. Considered in its right context, it does begin to make sense. I want to suggest what this sense may be, and in what respect *Justine* may be considered an experimental novel. For I believe that Durrell has aimed here to create, within the framework of a psychological novel, a vision of reality that is based in myth. This means that he has considerably enlarged the range of the psychological novel as a literary form.

The experiment can be approached by watching how Durrell presents his four principal characters: the narrator, a young Irish schoolmaster; Melissa, his mistress, an Alexandrian Greek cabaret dancer; Nessim, a rich Copt; and Justine Hosnani, Nessim's wife. In the course of events, the narrator becomes Justine's lover. And towards the end of the book, Melissa becomes Nessim's mistress. These four characters are a changing configuration of various forms of love. For they show different facets of themselves as their relationships change within their configuration. Each character is kaleidoscopic, not static. And their configuration is kaleidoscopic too. The narrator writes: "I did not believe in the discrete human personality." The word "discrete" here means "separate" or "individual." It does not mean "clandestine" or "secret." In fact, the secret roots of personality are the real

---

*This review of *Justine* was broadcast on BBC radio 25 March 1957 and is published here for the first time by permission of the author.

15

objects of the narrator's investigation. He wants to shake the world of established identities apart, and to disclose the nucleus of each established identity.

In his treatment of love, Durrell does not, like D. H. Lawrence, suppress consciousness for the greater glory of instinct. For he believes, as Stendhal did, that conscious reflection intensifies love. But he does not proceed, like Proust, down the treacherous labyrinths of pure reflection. For the characters in *Justine*, sex opens the Pandora's Box of the lover's whole being. Sex and reflection are simultaneous and interactive phases of a single process. Brute sex the narrator describes as a "terrible accident." Pure reflection he likens to the intellectual evil of "excessive desire to be united to God." "Anything pressed too far," the narrator considers, "becomes a sin." Now the narrator's friend, Balthazar the Cabalist, may say of Justine herself: "Sex has left the body and entered the imagination." And this may even be true in a sense of Nessim and the narrator. But these people do not, like characters in Sartre, become atrophied by their reflections. They may not be stable egos. They may not be, in the narrator's words, "discrete personalities." Puritans would think them highly irregular persons. But they are intensely alive. And they are alive on several levels of being at the same time. This vitality is not purely animal. Nor do these characters inhabit a Freudian world of the omnipresent libido. Theirs is rather the world of the German psychologist Georg Groddeck. Groddeck, one of the first practitioners of modern psychosomatic medicine, believed that the terms mind and body are not real except as concepts by means of which we may apprehend the totality of the living person. And his theory was that what we call mind and body are interdependent and interactive functions of a cosmic process which transcends mind and body. This transcendent process Groddeck called "the It." In his *Key to Modern Poetry*, Durrell devoted an entire chapter to a discussion of Groddeck's psychology. And the entry of sex into imagination, and of imagination into sex, is one of the points upon which Groddeck's psychology is most sharply focussed.

But this complex erotic cosmos, where sex and imagination come together, is in *Justine* only partially intelligible on the level of psychology. This limitation of psychology is shown in Durrell's use of a symbolism of mirrors. The mirror stands for reflection in a physical sense. But it also stands in a figurative sense for reflection as activity of mind, and for the psychological inflections of character. The visiting English novelist, Pursewarden, breaks his mirror shortly before he commits suicide. To him, the horrified Narcissus, the Puritan breach between physical existence and the reflective activity of the mind has become intolerable. He wants to penetrate to the reality behind the masks of physical existence and the reflecting mind. He wants to penetrate the mirror; to arrive on the other side of reflection; to know the reality behind the infinite psychological inflexions of self.

But the mirror shows him the one impenetrable obstacle in his way: it shows him himself as he reflects and as he is reflected. So he shatters his image in the mirror; and then he takes his life. Justine herself is psychologically inexplicable in another way. She admires her image in the mirror. She is the glad Narcissus. Her image, shown once in a triple mirror, and once again in a five-fold mirror, recalls the ancient image of the three-headed figure, which is found in Egyptian, Medieval, and Renaissance art, and which Picasso has parodied. The three heads, or three faces, represent time past, time present, and time future. The three-headed figure is the emblem of the complexities of time. Yet, beneath these psychological inflexions of Justine's being in time, and revealed in the multiple image, the narrator discerns another face. This other face is timeless. It is hidden from the psychologists to whom Justine is taken. The narrator calls it, "the mindless primitive face of Aphrodite." I shall return to this point later.

It is not easy for the four principal characters to see through any of these reflections in which they glimpse themselves. It is not easy for them to rise above the interplay of sex and imagination, and to find the "It" in which their established identities are rooted. But the narrator continues his quest. He arrives at a conception of what he calls "right attention." This "right attention" directs awareness beyond reflection and beyond the opaque confines of time and of psychology. The structure of the narrative shows what else this "right attention" implies. In the narrative, time is treated subjectively. Things, that is, do not happen in their original chronological order. They happen in the order in which they first became significant to the narrator. So there is no straightforward presentation of events in the preterite tense. Written in retrospect, the narrative often alternates between preterite and present tenses.

The present tense is also used to describe the narrator's situation on his remote island at the time of writing. Events actually separated in time overlap or overleap each other in the narrator's reflective reconstruction of the past. The narrative is the narrator's quest, not for the chronological order of past events, but for the significant and lasting pattern which these events impressed upon his mind. The narrator seeks to uncover, as he says, the "cloth-of-gold" which underlies the "sackcloth" of concrete experience. So the narrative rises clear of time to survey this significant pattern, this "cloth-of-gold." This point, the narrative's rising above time, may be illustrated by the note, in the "Consequential Data" at the back of the book, on the so-called n-dimensional novel: "The narrative momentum forward is countersprung by references backwards in time, giving the impression of a book which is . . . standing above time and turning slowly on its own axis to comprehend the whole pattern." But this does not mean that the original complexity and immediacy of the concrete experience are sacrificed. The narrator wants "to comprehend the *whole* pattern." The myriad prism of the narrator's memory reflects, then, the original complexity and immediacy of the concrete experience. This may be illustrated by the remark Justine herself makes on one of the occasions when she appears in a complex mirror: "I would try for a multi-dimensional effect in character, a sort of prism-sightedness. Why should not people show more than one profile at a time?"

This "sort of prism-sightedness" then enters the actual language of the novel. Here, for example, is part of the description of Spring in Alexandria. A scrutiny of this passage shows how mistaken some reviewers have been to view it loosely as over-written poetic prose. The imagery is concrete; but its range of meaning transcends the fixed limits of space and time which define the imagery. As these limits of space and time recede, the many dimensions of the imagery are disclosed.

> Clouds of dried blood walk the streets like prophecies; the sand is set-
> tling into the sea like powder into the curls of a stale wig. . . . The
> ghastly feluccas passing along the canal are crewed by ghouls with
> wrapped heads. From time to time a cracked wind arrives from directly
> above and stirs the whole city round and round so that one has the illu-
> sion that everything—trees, minarets, monuments and people have been
> caught in the final eddy of some great whirlpool and will pour softly back
> at last into the desert from which they rose, reverting once more to the
> anonymous wave-sculptured floor of dunes.

This language I would call emblematic: its range of concrete reference contains, or can at any moment contain, many layers of meaning. These layers of meaning are contained in the language in much the same way as the narrative itself contains cross-references backwards and forwards in time. It is a kind of heraldry, for the naked image can disclose and enclose a multiplicity of meanings. It is heraldic, like Justine's image in the complex mirror, and heraldic like the ancient emblem of the three faces of time.

In *The Black Book*, there is a sentence which shows what this heraldry means to Durrell. Here he is writing of the dawn of the human imagination; and in this dawn he sees "the Aurignacian dipping his finger in electricity and tracing the fugitive phenomena of the heraldic universe." In *Justine*, this force in imagination which Durrell called "electricity" in *The Black Book* is canalised into what I have called his emblematic language. And with this emblematic language he traces the fugitive and many-dimensioned phenomena of his heraldic universe. It is to this heraldic universe again that Durrell refers indirectly in the *Key to Modern Poetry* when he describes the realm of poetry as "the myriad domain of the psyche."

And at this point, "right attention" once more enters the picture. For "right attention" focuses the mind on the "myriad domain of the psyche." "Right attention" transforms the electric force of imagination into the emblematic language of the heraldic universe. In a recent poem, Durrell called this domain "desirelessness." So it is self-sufficient, like Plato's realm of ideas. But in the same poem he called it "a star entombed in flesh." So it is immanent in the behaviour of individuals.

In Groddeck's terms, this heraldic universe is the field of force in which the "It" manifests itself most clearly. It is the transcendant unity which underlies and controls the fugitive constellations of individual beings. In his observations on Groddeck in the *Key to Modern Poetry*, Durrell wrote "Phenomena may be individuals carrying on separate existences in space and time, but in the deeper reality beyond space and time we may all be members of one body." This remark is echoed in the note on the n-dimensional novel: "a book which is standing above time and turning slowly on its own axis to comprehend the whole pattern." The juncture of these ideas now sheds fresh light on the idea of "right attention." "Right attention" seems to me to be a new form of the bold axiom which Durrell wrote twenty years ago in *The Black Book*: "Art must no longer exist to depict man, but to invoke God."

This axiom does not mean that, in order to penetrate the time-barrier, the imagination must dehumanise itself. Nor does the axiom involve the old Romantic confusion which identifies art and religion, imagination and belief, and so deprives art of its autonomy. The axiom says that art exists to invoke God, not to depict man. But the laws of art require that this invocation shall be, in Walter de la Mare's words, "ashine with our meaningfulness, vivid with our truth, burning hot from the fire of our reality." Any work of imagination must make its range of experience vivid and meaningful in this way.

The narrator of *Justine* describes his Alexandria as a "joint"; it is an electrified point of synthesis between widely opposite extremes, as well as a "joint" in the sense of a nasty place. The extremes of experience may be telescoped into the passions and reflections of the four lovers. It may also extend to cover such various figures as the grotesque protozoic Scobie; Mnemjian, barber, pimp, and spy; the one-eyed reptilian Capodistria; the furrier Cohen, transfigured in his foul death; and Clea in her humility and gentleness. The direct impact of these characters throws into bold relief the opalescent complexity of the four principal characters. This shows that the invocation of Durrell's old axiom has a wide range in terms of concrete experience. On the other hand, things and persons may speak for themselves; they may be independent of reflection; and they may be graphic, self-significant entities. On the other hand, as I have already suggested, the narrator may reflect all things and persons so prismatically that his vision is not single but multiple. The sharp satiric image of Scobie, for example, and the account of the duck-shoot, belong to the first type of graphic representation. The complex images of Justine herself and of Alexandria belong to the second type of multiple representation. But Durrell's use of metaphor controls both extremes of this range of experience. And so once more these extremes may meet in the service of "right attention." For at certain points the graphic and the multiple types of representation interlock, and produce the emblematic language of the heraldic universe. It is at these points that psychology stops. Psychology and its terms of reference may express most graphically those facets of the myriad domain of the psyche which are circumscribed by the complexities of time. But the quest of the meanings at the roots of the psyche, the quest of the meanings that are timeless, requires other terms of reference. These are the terms of myth. And Durrell's language does at points override the existing barriers between the language of the psychological novel and the language of myth.

Another glance at Justine will show how Durrell moves from the psychological to the mythological level of discourse. At first the narrator is at a loss to describe Justine. He resorts to slick images, like "she gazed about her like a half-trained panther." In fact animal imagery is used to describe Justine seven times in the first eighty-six pages. Simultaneously, the narrator uses a book about Justine, written by her first husband, in order to define her character in psychoanalytical terms. But then suddenly the animal imagery recedes, and psychoanalysis fails. Justine is neither animal nor purely human in her ways. The myth now begins. The narrator discovers that the psychic disturbance which imprisons Justine in her imagination, and which causes her analyst to diagnose nymphomania, is the same force which compels her time and again to commit, as he says, "the divine trespass of an immortal among mortals." It may not surprise us to find that this prisoner of her imagination should resemble the psyche as it is defined by Carl Gustav Jung: the self-sufficient psyche, "which, in the play of its images reflects not the world but itself, even though it may use the forms of the world of sense in which to manifest its images." But it is fully consistent with Durrell's idea of the primacy of myth that Justine should prove to be something more. On the psychological level, as the narrator writes, her face is "famished by the inward light of her terrors." But on the mythological level alone, her true identity is revealed; and here Justine's face is "the mindless primitive face of Aphrodite."

It is in the image of Alexandria that further forms of myth are shown. Justine is the quintessence of this image; for of all the flora of Alexandria, she as Aphrodite is the most mythologically rooted. In his treatment of the image of Alexandria, Durrell appears to have telescoped two ancient mythic images into a single modern one. The two hero-types of the classical Mediterranean world are Odysseus and Aeneas. And Odysseus and Aeneas are radically distinguished. Odysseus is not essentially connected with a city, but Aeneas is essentialy connected with the city of Rome. Odysseus is Goddess-haunted; he is a wanderer in the myriad domain of Aphrodite. But Aeneas rejects the Goddess, as he rejects Dido in order to fulfil his destiny in founding Rome. Odysseus is the wandering hero of the Quest; Aeneas is the hero of the Established Order. In the classical Mediterranean world, their destinies run in opposite directions. But what Durrell has done in Justine is to integrate the world of the Quest with the world of Establishment, to integrate the world of the Goddess with the world of the City. He explores then the dimensions of the Goddess-haunted world as these appear in the perspectives of the City. His city is an Alexandria sunk deep in Mediterranean antiquity; for here, like the cave-men of Lascaux, the children mark the walls with the prints of their hands, to avert the evil eye. But it is also the modern Alexandria of the sybarite, the child-prostitute, and the skeptic. The mythic foundation of events is found in Joyce too, of course, and in the later novels of Thomas Mann and Hermann Broch. But this integration of the mythic images in *Justine* has a special significance in Durrell's heraldic universe. It shows how deeply modern man is committed to the confines of the modern city: to its confines of violence, defilement, and despair. But it shows also how modern man is committed irrevocably to the timeless and unconfinable, to the mindless primitive Aphrodite, who is herself the emblem of his myriad soul. The odyssey may be made within the framework of the City; but it is undertaken in the service of the Goddess. And he who undertakes the odyssey must choose whether this Aphrodite shall be a thorn embedded in his flesh or a star entombed there, awaiting his call to rise from the dead.

Justine is an experimental novel. As an exploration of experience at hidden levels it seems to me to be descended in a direct line from that Inferno of the 1920s, Djuna Barnes' novel *Nightwood*. I may have overestimated some of its ambitions. But this possibility still cannot obscure its richness of atmosphere, its strength of line, its independence of vision. These qualities show a direction of thought which Durrell laid down in the *Key to Modern Poetry*. For here he suggested that the modern imagination has turned away from materialistic psychology and theories of causation, and has turned toward new Romantic and mystical spheres of perception.

Justine is actually the first novel of a series. One cannot tell if Durrell will continue to explore this no-man's-land between the frontiers of psychology and myth. It may be asked: has he come through at all? Can the poet as novelist really become the visionary, the seer, the "man without qualities"? Can he master that sense of play which liberates Romantic expression from the foggy frustrations of pathos? Can he achieve that Olympian detachment which alone objectifies entirely the passion for the singular, the visionary, the irrational? Above all: can the skeptical mind focus upon this age sharply enough to discern and to create a mythology of this age? These are some of the questions with which the reader of *Justine* will find himself confronted after the Alexandrian dust has settled and the lovers have gone.

Lawrence Durrell   Kenneth Rexroth*

1 (1957)

One of the best, and certainly one of the most civilized writers in English today is Lawrence Durrell. He has written a couple of superlative travel books, literary essays, miscellaneous belles-lettres, four volumes of poetry, and novels which are quite unlike any other fictions of our day—at least until they produce imitators.

I enjoy Durrell's poetry more than that of anybody else anywhere near his age now writing in the British Isles. In fact, only McDiarmid, Muir and Read appeal to me as much. It is a poetry of tone, the communication of the precise quality of a very precious kind of revery—animalism and skeptic faith recollected in tranquillity. Wallace Stevens wrote with the same emotional subject matter, but his poetry is cooked and strident in comparison with Durrell's easy relaxation. Again, he is gifted with a gentle, unselfconscious eroticism very rare in our nasty and Puritan world—never nastier than among our most advanced émancipés.

The poet who has influenced Durrell most is probably the Greek poet Cavafis, the only homosexual writer in history who was not ridden with guilt. Durrell's loves and adventures have been more normal and less random, so that he is saved from Cavafis' heart-rending nostalgia for vanished and vanishing fulfillment. He seems to have come naturally, by easy, heterosexual means, to the kind of tolerance of the painful heart that must have cost Cavafis a lifetime of very disagreeable trouble. No one writing verse today can better evoke a scene, a place, a room, a situation, the body of a woman, alive at just that fleeting moment that it lived, with all the meaning of its present and all the pathos of its vanishing. Again, no one can better bow over unspeaking, resonant strings. Durrell's overtones and references would be destroyed by notes. It is just a haunting flavor of Gibbon's Theodora that counts in Durrell's poem to a modern intellectual tart of the same name—lurking in the background with her rumors of bear pits and brothels, like some evanescent herb dimly sensed in a production of morels stuffed with *brochet*. What glitters in the foreground is the gold fleck in the living girl's eye—recorded forever.

Stevens may have liked to think he approached art as the late Aga Khan might have approached a race horse, a *pâté truffé*, a girl or a Chateau Ausone of the year of the comet. Actually, his approach was more that of a New England insurance executive. Durrell is so convincing as a good European he comes close to being a good Levantine. And it is all done simply, with never a mirror—the best kind of legerdemain, without a stick of apparatus. It's not for nothing that he wrote two poems years ago which are still

*Reprinted from *Assays* (Norfolk, Conn.: New Directions, 1961), 118–30.

the best ever written in Basic English. The ancestor is Horace. Someday, when the world has calmed down, maybe we will again realize that Horace was the perfect artist he was considered by less troubled times. Right now, Lawrence Durrell is the only person I know who has the indomitable guts to walk in his footsteps.

Just before the war Durrell wrote a novel, *The Black Book*. Nobody who ever read it ever quite got over it. It is the story, told from the inside, of a bunch of thoroughly wretched characters—intellectuals seeking exquisite debauchery. It gets just the right tone. It is so perfect, so dead-pan, you have to think it over before you realize that Durrell himself didn't really mean it. Now lots of people have portrayed the evils of musical beds. I believe quite a few novels nowadays deal with this and related subjects. By and large, scratch a pornographer and a furious Puritan emerges from the tousled bedcovers. Above the bidets of *The Black Book*'s disgraceful boudoirs is written in a fine Spenserian hand: "Durrell was here"—there is only the gentle echo of Epicurean malice.

Justine is at least the equal of *The Black Book*, from the comic irony of its title to the tour de force of a tour de force that is its style. It is an imitation of what the French call a *récit* of a weak, pretentious schoolmaster and amateur of the sensibility, who is very busy writing fine writing about his ridiculously self-conscious amours. But the take-off on fine writing is itself fine writing—very fine writing indeed, and the two qualities, the real and its satirical mirror image, are so blended and confused that the exact nature of the "aesthetic satisfaction" is impossible to analyze. Proust managed this sometimes, as in the absurd scene where his hero uses pages to describe the maneuvers by which he managed to spy on Charlus in the lumber room. Durrell is so much more economical; Proust, delighted to discover a spark of humor rising in his humorless mind, usually worked his jokes to death.

Once again Durrell has turned to Cavafis—in fact, *Justine* is almost a novelification (like a versification but backwards) of Cavafis' poetry. It is not just an evocation, but a bodily conjuration of Alexandria—soft, sweet, corrupt and crazy like some impossibly cloying tropical fruit. Shanghai . . . Alexandria . . . Tangiers . . . only our time has produced these sanatoria with the luxury rooms full of uprooted rotting infants and the corridors full of eyeless beggars exhibiting their stinking sores. Not only is Durrell's Alexandria so real that it envelopes you like a cloud of its own miasmas, but the people—even though we see them through comic distorting mirrors—are more real than real. The realest of all is the proverbial tart with a heart of gold. Both Durrell and I have been taken to task by the same British critics for imagining that this type of girl actually exists. He certainly makes her very convincing. I doubt if he just thought her up. Like all hearts of gold, she dies as pathetically as any Dickens girl. I doubt if the other people have hearts at all—there doesn't seem to be anything inside them but dry *râles* and spoiling orchids. But they are frighteningly like the people you know.

2 (1960)

Sitting down to write this review of Durrell's *Clea*, I have little relish for the job. For a good many years now I have been a devoted, persistent fan of Lawrence Durrell. When *Justine* came out I wrote a very laudatory review for *The Nation*. It seemed the promise of a thoroughly adult job. The characters were a distasteful crew, but certainly they were grownups; the plot was as complex as any of Conrad's, and since the succeeding three novels were announced as treating the same cast through the eyes of three different characters, the whole project promised to be a fabulous network of motives, false motives and imaginary motives. The style was saturated with a whimsical, self-mocking irony, "fine writing" making fun of itself. Altogether, I felt on sure ground when I prophesied a big work by a mature man, one worthy to be set alongside Ford Madox Ford's Tietjens series, the promise of a novel which would be fit reading for a male over thirty-five. Certainly, there aren't very many such. Now, at least this one male over thirty-five is a disappointed man.

What happened? In the first place, I think a purely mechanical mistake. Durrell sold *Justine* before the rest of the work was completed, and for the next three years had to produce a book a year against an inexorable deadline. Maybe Dickens or Dostoevski could do this; they hated it and groused about it, but they produced masterpieces that way. It is obvious that Durrell could not. Times have changed. Writers are far more self-indulgent and temperamental nowadays—they are artists, and rigorous business arrangements upset them. Durrell felt frustrated and hemmed in. Each year he put off writing and then wrote carelessly, perhaps even defiantly. What had been complex and subtle and ironic turned into something flimsy, schematic and flashy.

Plotting, which at the start was careful and wise, became sensational. It not only became sensational, it became frivolous and irresponsible. Perhaps it makes a good hot item for the paperbacks to suggest that the Egyptian Copts and the Jews are in a plot with the Nazis to betray the Arabs and British in Egypt and Palestine—but this is the kind of yarn we associate with Talbot Mundy, not with a serious writer. It is all too easy to envisage a young Egyptian officer in charge of a border post reading that book between hours of duty. This kind of childish meddling with the lives of the innocent should be left to "Steve Canyon" and "Terry and the Pirates." The word for it is cheap—as well as dangerous. One step more and the word is malicious.

The writing has decayed in the same way. Pain and disaster emerged at first from the necessary relationships of the characters; in the later books it is applied from the outside. Clea's disaster with the fish-gun is not tragedy, it is sensationalism, on a par with the highly sophisticated sadism of the pseudo-high-brow French and Italian movies. Furthermore, its gratuitousness shows; they do this so much better in Japan where sentimental agonies have a long tradition of great skill. Gone too is the subtle mockery of fancy writing. The narrator of *Clea* has decided that now he can really "write," at last he is an artist. You won't get far in the book before the horrible suspicion sneaks over you that Durrell agrees with him. I'll take De Quincey.

What is wrong with this writer? He has terrific talent, he is no longer a young man, he has learned all the lessons there are to learn. Is it an incorrigible Bohemianism? Perhaps. I went back and reread *The Black Book*. All the Alexandria tetralogy is there, writ small. It is one of the first and best books of its kind—that long spate of tales of the life and loves of the Underground Man that have become the characteristic literary fad of the last twenty years. It is a tale of a wretched warren of loathsome characters, and like Dostoevski's manifesto, *Letters from the Underworld*, like *Les Liaisons Dangereuses*, like the life and letters of Baudelaire, its moral point is that all such people can do is debauch, in rotten frivolity, the ignorant and trusting innocent. This, in a sense, is the point of the first of the kind, the immensely fashionable parent of the whole genre, that other *Justine* by Sade. The trouble with *The Black Book* is that you can never be sure of Durrell's intention. Did he know what he was doing? How close is he, really, to his characters, the closeness of the artist who understands all, or the embroilment of the participant who understands nothing?

In his preface to the new edition of *The Black Book* Durrell speaks of it as an attack on Puritanism and identifies it with the genre of *Lady Chatterley's Lover*. But *Chatterley* is not an attack on Puritanism at all. It reeks of Puritanism and crippled, self-conscious sex—and of the personal spites and ill tempers of Lawrence as well. Only an adolescent, recently escaped from the Epworth League, could think of it as a pagan manifesto of sexual freedom. So too, *The Black Book* is a tour de force of ingrown Puritanism, and so too, I am afraid, is the Alexandrine tetralogy.

While the four parts of the novel were coming out, Durrell published *Bitter Lemons, Esprit de Corps, Stiff Upper Lip*. These are all concerned with his own life as a diplomatic representative of Great Britain. They all have the same fault, a blissfully unconscious, but none the less absolute ethnocentrism. In *Bitter Lemons* the Cypriots are happy childlike innocents, misled by "demagogues" and the "envenomed insinuations of the Athens Radio." It never occurs to Durrell that they might just want to be free of the British. Only the most unworthy motives are ever ascribed to either the Turkish or Greek leaders, who are always portayed as "outside agitators," interested only in advancing themselves at the expense of naïve and friendly schoolchildren. The English, on the other hand, are seen as silly, bumbling, out of date, but oh so sane and wholesome and always concerned only with the good of the charges that God has entrusted to them. We've heard all this before; in fact, we can hear it almost any day when a Southern Congressman is sounding off, and what day is one not? *Stiff Upper Lip* and *Esprit de Corps* are unforgivable. They are written in the most dreadful imitation of P. G. Wodehouse, a favorite author of Durrell, by his own admission. (He reads him in *Bitter Lemons* during negotiations with the Cypriots over their freedom.) It is a bad imitation and so vulgar it makes your flesh crawl. These two books of purported humor explain much about what happened to the splendid plan announced in *Justine*. Possibly, carefully read, they explain everything. British diplomats are noble and silly, Indians, Negroes, Egyptians are sly and rascally children, uniformly portrayed in terms of a Soho pickpocket—the only "native," you feel, reading these disgraceful books, Durrell has ever known personally. This, of course, is not true; he has lived most of his life in the Levant. What is wrong with him? What is wrong with Englishmen?

Meanwhile he has published something else. Grove Press has brought out his *Selected Poems* and there are rumors a *Complete Collected Poems* will be along eventually. These are great poems, lovely, temperate, with every subtle cadence so carefully controlled, so excruciatingly civilized. They reek of the Levant at its best, with all of its best reeks. There is little self-consciousness in them, and little Puritanism, but lots of the weary sensuality and fleshy joy of Greek and Turkish and Egyptian life and love and food and drink. These poems, not *Justine*, really transfuse into the pale British bloodstream the wistful lewdness and wisdom of that great bad Greek, the poet Cavafis, who was one of the most consummate evil livers in all literature. Durrell's poems avoid Cavafis' more lurid sin, but they perfectly transmit his smile and his impeccable taste. I think the poems answer the question, "What's wrong with this initially so ambitious work?" Closeness, or embroilment? Durrell is an old and loyal friend of Henry Miller. So loyal in fact that he recently edited an anthology presenting poor Henry as a Thinker; it would seem that Durrell really believes Miller thinks. This is a fine friendship, well tested through almost thirty years, and it is not fortuitous. Like Henry Miller, Durrell is suspiciously like some character in his own fictions.

3 (1960)

In 1938 Lawrence Durrell sent the typescript of *The Black Book* to Henry Miller, asking his opinion of it, and telling him to pitch it into the Seine when he had read it. Miller took it to his own publishers, the Obelisk Press, who immediately published it. It has been a "banned classic" ever since. It is hard to understand, reading it today, why it should ever have been banned in the first place. T. S. Eliot, Cyril Connolly, everybody who was anybody in those days, greeted it with shouts of joy. Eliot called it "the first piece of work by a new English writer to give me any hope for the future of prose fiction." Although it has a few common colloquial terms for human anatomy and physiology scattered through it and its subject is a sort of hall-bedroom sexual rat race, it is about as salacious as a VD clinic.

It is the story of the denizens of a cheap rooming house in South London, that illimitable expanse of faceless squalor that covers many hundreds of times the acreage of the city that the Upper Classes and the international world of tourism and business know as "London." The two most human people in the cast are foreign students, the rest are lumpenintelligentsia. They are the underemployed or unemployable, devoid of all skills, too poorly educated to be of any good to others, with too much education for their own good.

It is the story of typical representatives of a class who are habitually terrorized by sex, and who therefore use it habitually as an instrument of terror. Sex does not frighten them because it is sex, but because it is humane. If wine, or music, or good food were as important as humane sex is to humane living, these too would occupy the center of attention. Good food, of course, as an instrument of *humanitas* does not terrify any Englishman of any class. Unless he crosses the Channel he never has an opportunity to encounter it. But sex is inescapable. In one form or another, as they say, it persists in raising its head. The characters of *The Black Book* can't cope with it. It obsesses them and frightens them. Their response is a kind of disheveled misery.

It is a study of the etiology of one, and the commonest, kind of Bohemianism. We forget that there are at least two kinds. Mimi's friends in Puccini's opera are the first kind, young artists on their way up. They have the arrogance of young genius. They are poor and immoral. At the end of the story they are mostly very successful, and Mimi is dead. But while it all lasted, they had a good time—love, wine, food, music. This kind of Bohemian is an under- or unemployed intellectual who gives up most of the necessities of the poor so he can enjoy some of the luxuries of the rich. But there is another kind, by far more common, the upstart product of a lower-middle-class Puritan background who discovers himself unable to compete with the world of civilized men which he is trying to enter. This demoralizes him. He rebels. He reads erotic books. He tries pederasty, at least in his imagination. He neglects to shave and often to wash. Above all else he is frightened. This is the character who forms the pattern for most of the people in *The Black Book*. Dostoevski called him the Underground Man. He is a debauched Puritan, an unwisely paroled shopkeeper.

It is the story of a group of people suffering from incurable spiritual malnutrition, and by "spiritual" I mean "physical"—fleshly. These are nervous systems which can never do anything but starve. The joys of life are as unassimilable as crushed rock. Above all else, these are people who cannot assimilate one another. Humaneness is the fine art of enjoying other people. Each of these people is utterly alone, not one knows there is anybody else out there.

All this sounds as if *The Black Book* was not very enjoyable reading. Certainly Dostoevski's *Notes from the Underground* is one of literature's more disagreeable experiences. On the contrary, *The Black Book* is often even funny. It is in the tradition of "bitter comedy," like Jonson's *Volpone* or Machiavelli's *Mandragola*—but then, I suppose, so is Dostoevski's book, in a sense. It is more than just the comic form. I can't imagine anyone less like Mark Twain than Durrell, but in almost everything he writes he shares one salient and splendid characteristic with Mark Twain—he so obviously has such a good time writing. Some of the passages in *The Black Book* are a young author's "fine writing," later to be parodied by Durrell himself in *Justine*, but, unlike so much of this sort of thing, they are never self-consciously written. They flow out of youthful scorn and pity and out of just plain enthusiasm with the newly mastered ability to write. This creates a kind of audience participation, a stylistic excitement not unlike the excitement of jazz.

The dominant mood of *The Alexandria Quartet* is a comic overcivilization. Its world is peopled exclusively by provincial avatars of Oscar Wilde, Whistler, Mercedes d' Acosta, Princess Polignac, Ida Rubenstein, Diaghilev, Nazimova—in other words, a seedy Edwardian glamour, long since vanished from Europe, and gone off to the backlands of the Levant to die. The book smells of something I for one have never smelled, that fascinating substance so popular in the novels my Aunt Minnie read, patchouli. *The Alexandria Quartet* is saved from comedy by its sad irony. If it weren't for its irony it would be a kind of chic, reader-flattering Ouida. . . .

As George Elliott has pointed out, *The Alexandria Quartet* is romantic to the core. It would be like d'Annunzio if d'Annunzio had had good taste. Everybody is frightfully high class. Even the servants and tramps have an *Arabian Nights* grotesquerie. In *The Black Book*, everybody is low class, the lowest class of all, the homeless upstarts of the lower middle class. The tragic wastrels of Alexandria are sometimes foolish, sometimes silly. The characters of *The Black Book*, in their dirty socks and rayon combinations, are ridiculous. What redeems them is Durrell's own youth—because he has, in abundance, one of the rare, sterling virtues of youth, an all-devouring, all-forgiving angry pity. As Robert MacAlmon says in Hemingway's novel—"Oh, give 'em anger, and give 'em pity."

Durrell seems to be fascinated with the thin sentence of sense in the vast, dull mass of Sade, the notion that the most life-destroying of all poisons is guilt. Guilt flagellates the major characters of *The Alexandria Quartet* with a whip of scorpions. At least they have, most of them, something to feel guilty about. Guilt has emasculated the characters of *The Black Book* at birth. They pay the penalty but are incapable of comprehending, much less enjoying, the crime. This is certainly as pathetic a predicament as could be imagined. There is other pathos, too, of the plain old-fashioned kind. The central story of the book, the vacuous debauching of the vulgar dying waif, Gracie, by her witless debaucher, Gregory, is a kind of malicious parody of the tragedy of Mimi and her lover, the *La Bohème* of hobohemia. It may be sickeningly sentimental in a perverse way, but it is one of the most unforgettable tales in modern fiction.

What makes *The Alexandria Quartet*, of course, as everybody knows,

is its structure. It is a tour de force of multiple-aspect narrative. Durrell
has said, in several interviews, . . . that he had never read Ford Madox
Ford's *The Good Soldier* or his Tietjens series. I don't doubt his word, but
find the fact astonishing. It would seem that Ford occurred spontaneously
to all three interviewers. Certainly he occurred to me. I know of no modern novelist more like Durrell. Very likely he had read Conrad, and possibly the complex, cobwebby novels which Conrad and Ford (then Hueffer)
wrote together. Maybe he just naturally thinks that way.

The Alexandria Quartet is a big job, with lots of room to maneuver.
The Black Book is a volume of about three hundred pages with a small and
rather ambiguously defined cast of characters. Yet *The Black Book*, too, is
a carefully braided indirect, direct, and third-person narrative. Much of it
is cast in the form of a diary by the lamentable Gregory. Circling over and
under and around this narrative is another, equally immodest, diary-like in
form and substance, purportedly the direct utterance of Durrell himself (he
uses his own name). Consequently, the image of the characters is always
unstable, they merge and go out of focus and return in altered form. The
writing wanders off and explodes in amateur surrealist fireworks, and when
it returns, the pattern of the characters has changed again. Gregory himself
never appears in the flesh. Durrell is part of the time writing in the same
dismal London rooming house, part of the time he is recollecting in replete
and guiltless tranquillity in rainy, wintry Corfu (or is it Crete?).

What is important in all this counterpoint is that Durrell, as first-per-
son narrator, gets slowly sucked into the moral world of his shoddy diarist,
whom, incidentally, he has never seen, and then, as imperceptibly and gra-
tuitously, escapes. The book ends like *Ulysses*, with an invocation to the
existential flesh of the wife in bed beside him, in Greece, on a rainy
morning.

The characters in Durrell's first novel are somewhat like idiot brothers
and sisters of those in his new one. Their doom is less well upholstered and
attended. They are bound for Hell in a third-class carriage. Justine and her
friends are headed there in a private car on the Orient Express, but the
road is the same doom, the end is the same Hell, just a grubbier slum of
that vast city.

Actually, though they are vaguely enough drawn, the people in *The
Black Book* are a little more real, at least they are more convincing. Most
of us have relatives like them somewhere. My own parents, as a matter of
fact, were well-to-do provincial intellectuals, and, I suspect, modeled their
lives on characters like Justine and Nessim. Maybe such people really once
existed, flirting dangerously among the fine bindings, at a reception of Mrs.
Potter Palmer's, away from the crowd, in the dimly lit library, but for me
at least, their reality is impaired by "books my mother read." On the other
hand, these people reading deep books in their unmade beds in South London are all about us—they have made a number of disagreeable revolutions
in our time.

I wonder if Durrell is, even today, aware of who stands out in the book as most real, most convincing? I, for one, think the Peruvian, full of South American animality, demoralized, but still there, and Miss Smith, the African girl who is studying Middle English, but who, someday, when she has mastered the mysteries of Europe, is going back to Africa and her own race. Neither of these people is involved, nor do they need to be involved, in the interpersonal hunger strikes of the others. Soon they will pick up and go, back to a wiser world. Meantime, Lobo can never quite "make it," Miss Smith, calmly and courteously, doesn't even try. They point the moral. It is an old one. I suppose it is an anti-Puritan one, as the book narrowly escapes being an anti-Puritan tract. It is certainly a religious one. Sin is the failure of the organ of reciprocity.

The failure of reciprocity, incongruity, low life, these are the ingredients of classic comedy. So *The Black Book* is a classic comedy. This might only mean that it is a careful concoction following the recipes of Aristotelian and Renaissance cookbooks. It is so much more because it is a lyric comedy, and the lyricism is the voice of Durrell's anger and pity and enthusiasm.

Just incidentally, it is also, along with Miller's *Tropics* and a few other books, one of the first of what has become the characteristic genre of mid-century fiction—the highbrow true-confession story, the mixture of semi-autobiography, diaristic style, interior monologue, random expostulation and prose dithyramb—the artifice of convincing immodesty. The later Céline, Miller, Kerouac, even *Lolita*. Over in France, on lower levels, there are a half dozen published every month. *The Black Book* is still one of the very best.

Lawrence Durrell's
Rosy-finger'd Egypt

Alfred Kazin*

1

I have never been to Alexandria, but having read *Justine* and *Balthazar* and now *Mountolive*—the first three novels in Mr. Durrell's tetralogy—I plan never to be disenchanted by an experience of the real thing. No place on earth could be so dense with literary atmosphere and poetic suggestion as Mr. Durrell's Alexandria. In the first volume, *Justine*, there are innumerable loving touches to bring home to us "the white city . . . whose pearly skies are broken in spring only by the white stalks of the min-

*Reprinted from *Contemporaries* (Boston: Little, Brown, 1962), 188–92.

arets and the flocks of pigeons turning in clouds of silver and amethyst"; in the second, *Balthazar*, even the foreign warships in the harbor "turned in their inky reflections—the forest of masts and rigging in the Commercial Port swayed softly among the mirror-images of the water"; in *Mountolive*, "suddenly the sky line was sliced in half by a new flight, rising more slowly and dividing earth from air in a pink travelling wound; like the heart of a pomegranate staring through its skin. Then, turning from pink to scarlet, flushed back into white and fell to the lake level like a shower of snow to melt as it touched the water—'Flamingo,' they both cried and laughed, and the darkness snapped upon them, extinguishing the visible world."

Lawrence Durrell writes prose like a man seeking the maximum sensuous enjoyment from each word. It is a poet's failing—when he writes prose. Some years ago, when Randall Jarrell published a novel, he is supposed to have exclaimed, "I didn't know it was this easy!" It isn't, and even so gifted and intelligent a poet as Mr. Durrell, when he writes novels, never gets near enough to life to know what he has left out. The English ambassador to Egypt, David Mountolive, who in youth had been the lover of an Egyptian Christian, Leila, discovers that her son, Nessim, has been sending arms to the Jewish underground in Palestine. Nessim has anticipated the rise of Arab nationalism and believes that with the decline of Anglo-French imperialism, only a Jewish Palestine will be able to protect the non-Moslems in the Near East. Mountolive is deeply troubled. "Once in bed he entered a narrow maze of shallow and unrefreshing dreams in which he floundered all night long—images of the great network of lakes with their swarming fish and clouds of wild birds, where once more the youthful figures of himself and Leila moved, spirited by the soft concussion of oars in water, to the punctuation of a single soft finger drum across a violet night-scape. . . ."

"Soft concussion" is just the phrase for my experience of Mr. Durrell's novels. There are no sharp edges, no painful passions, no real losses, no hurts. People hop in and out of beds as if sex did nothing but induce gentle reflections on life; ancient Englishmen in the Egyptian police force become transvestites and are beaten to death by English sailors; homosexual dwarfs have hatpins thrust through their brains and are discovered at the end of a ball under a mound of coats on a bed; Leila's other son, Narouz, kills a hostile employee with a bull whip and goes hunting with his brother carrying the victim's head in his hunting bag; the suave and handsome ambassador is beaten and robbed by a crowd of child prostitutes. But everything is reduced to a vaguely diffused sensuousness of word and sensations; even the honest pangs of sex are muffled in the jasmine warmth and flowers of Alexandria, in words that represent the poet's effort to reach that absolute which is inherent in language itself. What is wrong with this in a novel is that it does not carry anything forward; it does not even help to create an atmosphere from which an action can follow. It is writing that exists merely to call attention to Mr. Durrell's exceptional literary sensibility, and that it does—to such a point that reading the novels is as cozy an experience as one can have these days. You know that Mr. Durrell will jog pleasantly along, more in touch with his own delightful imagination than with any of the notorious stinks, festers, sores, and dungheaps of Egypt.

2

This coziness makes a particular appeal to the kind of literary imagination that wants the exotic brought down to its own size. Mr. Durrell is a classical scholar, a man enraptured with all the ancient and poetic associations of the city, and the appeal his novels make just now is entirely understandable, even if he is writing a travelogue of Alexandria in Technicolor. Above everything else, Mr. Durrell has a way of suggesting that our grip on the external world is now so uncertain that all truth simply becomes relative to the observer. This indeed is the theme of his novels. "Fact is unstable by its very nature. Narouz once said to me that he loved the desert because there 'the wind blew out one's footsteps like candle-flames.' So it seems to me does reality. How then can we hunt for the truth?" Or as Balthazar puts it in the second novel: "Truth is what most contradicts itself in time." And in the third, after the novelist Pursewarden has committed suicide in contrition for his failure, as a British intelligence agent, to discover Nessim's plot to arm the Jews in Palestine—"Truth naked and unashamed. This is a splendid phrase. But we always see her as she seems, never as she is. Each man has his own interpretation."

This elegant skepticism is by now a familiar conception in the novel, and for at least fifty years the most interesting intelligence devoted to the novel has attacked the old conception of "reality" as something which the novelist had only to copy. But as Mr. Durrell explains in the preface to *Balthazar*, he has modeled his novels not on the Proust-Joyce method of prolonging the individual's experience of time but on the space-time continuum of relativity. The first three novels show the "three sides of space" and are "deployed spatially, not linked in a serial form. They interlap, interweave, in a purely spatial relation. Time is stayed. The fourth part alone will represent time and be a true sequel. The subject-object relation is so important to relativity that I have tried to turn the novel through both subjective and objective modes."

Unfortunately, I do not know what this means, and in his practice of fiction Mr. Durrell seems to me more adept at creating a prose-poetry about Alexandria than he is in making clear to us the kind of new vision he is trying to incorporate into his novels. To me he is a lyric writer with a highly fragmented intelligence, an innocent delight in Egyptian upper-class society, and a profound capacity for sensuous enjoyment. His mind is more independent, more genuinely reflective, than that of many contemporary novelists; but I am thoroughly convinced, after reading these three novels, that when his characters describe truth as unstable, they are really speaking, not wisdom, but for Mr. Durrell's own uncertain sense of reality. Again and again the reader of the novels suspects this, for he cannot help noting that when Mr. Durrell so sharply separates space from time he is attempting something which in the representation of actual human experience is impossible, since we do not think of space apart from time. It is to the point, too, that whereas Mr. Durrell told us that *Mountolive* would be "a straight naturalistic novel in which the narrator of *Justine* and *Balthazar* becomes an object, i.e., a character," this character, Darley, hardly appears in *Mountolive*! And Nessim's running of arms to Palestine, the situation on which *Mountolive* turns, one which is supposed to explain at last the peculiar relations between Nessim and his wife, Justine, is as improbable, artificial, and unserious a literary device as it is a political situation.

When I say "unserious," I do not mean frivolous but literary; the literary can be the enemy of literature. Mr. Durrell seems to me fundamentally a writer concerned with pleasing his own imagination, not with making deeper contact with the world through his imagination, as Proust and Joyce did. As Henry Thoreau, the Romantic incarnate, put it, "I went far enough to please my imagination." Mr. Durrell, who like Kipling was born in India, who is saturated in the warmth and freedom of Mediterranean culture, who has written with such beauty of Cyprus as well as of Egypt, seems to me the latest example of that blind adoration of the East that has been the staple of so many distinguished British writers from Kipling and Doughty to T. E. Lawrence. He has redeemed with his own sensibility the pains of imperialism, has sweetened the gall and wormwood of the East with the "perfumed sails" and "love-sick winds" of Shakespeare's Egypt. Alexandria, its very name from the great conqueror himself, its evocation of *Antony and Cleopatra*, its mingling of so many races and nations, gives a sensitive civil servant like Mr. Durrell a chance to relish the sweetness of the primitive and the corrupt, to eat his fill of the honeyed air, without every getting any closer to the actualities of real political life and real Near Eastern dirt than he ever needs to. This saturation in atmosphere, this adoration of the primitive, is the British way of escaping the puritanism and responsibility of the national life and at the same time, by paying tribute to the victims of British power, of trying to make up for the actual guilt in which even a poet like Mr. Durrell, simply by being *there*, has shared. The enchantment of these ex-official travelers with the East is one of the great chapters in British literature, and no one can read Mr. Durrell's novels without sharing in the sensuous pleasures of Alexandria. But I cannot take these novels seriously; the greatest impression they leave on me is what a good time Mr. Durrell had in writing them.

The *Quartet*: Two Reviews   Lionel Trilling*

I

Mr. Durrell is the first contemporary novelist in a long time to captivate my imagination to the extent of leading me to believe that he is telling me something new, of convincing me that he is truly interested in what he is writing about.

Justine and *Balthazar* are the first two of a series of four novels upon which Mr. Durrell is at work. The third is *Mountolive*, published earlier this year. The fourth is still to appear. The setting of the first three novels, and I should suppose of the fourth too, is Alexandria some two decades ago. Of *Balthazar* Mr. Durrell says that its "central topic . . . is an investigation of modern love," and this applies as well to *Justine*. (*Mountolive* develops certain political intrigues which are adumbrated in the first two books, but it does not abate the concern with love of the earlier volumes.)

Mr. Durrell's ability to make no bones about his novels having a "central topic" and the simplicity with which he identifies this "topic" as an "investigation" suggest that he shares something of my view that the function of the novel is to discover and inform. And if the subject of his investigation is indeed to be described as "modern love," as he says it is, then he is certainly telling us about something new and strange. No one who has formed an idea of love from contemporary American and British fiction is likely to take for granted what Mr. Durrell is writing about; no one is going to find it easy to believe that what he is investigating is really modern love. For none of Mr. Durrell's lovers has the slightest interest in *maturity* or in *adult behavior* or in *mutuality of interest* or in *building a life together* or in any of the other characteristics of *healthy relationships* which we suppose modern love to be. Tenderness plays some part in the feelings of some of the lovers, and on several occasions it is highly praised, but the lovers do not expect from each other *emotional support* or *confirmation* or a *sense of security*; they may want things still more difficult to get or give, but none of them, in order to obtain these things, enters into one of those therapeutic alliances which, under the name of marriage, passes with us for the connection of love.

Yet it is indeed love that absorbs them. Certainly it is not sex as we know it from our novels. No one raises the question of sexual gratification as such, or as a problem; nor does any woman say, "I never knew it could be like that," nor any man, "It was good for me too." There are many episodes of sexual encounter, but no descriptions of the sexual act for, as it were, their own sake; the author seems to assume that his readers can supply the details. And although the two loved women of the novel, the gentle

*Reprinted from *The World of Lawrence Durrell*, ed. Harry T. Moore (Carbondale: Southern Illinois University Press, 1962), 51–65. First published in *Mid-Century*, 1959 and 1960.

Melissa and the proud and fierce Justine, are said to be beautiful and often have occasion to be naked, we are given no inventory of their intimate charms; by their lovers, as by the reader, they are known in no dichotomy of body and spirit, and their breasts and rumps and thighs are not, so to say, detachable.

The behavior of the lovers is not controlled by respectable propriety; they use their bodies freely and are not physically faithful to each other. Yet ideas of an ultimate fidelity have great force with them, or with some of them, and their involvements with each other are nothing if not personal, having to do with their deepest sense of themselves. To such an extent, indeed, that they are all injured and some of them are destroyed by their obsessive commitments of themselves. "I realized then the truth about all love:" says the narrator, "that it is an absolute which takes all or forfeits all. The other feelings, compassion, tenderness, and so on exist only on the periphery and belong to the constructs of society and habit. But she herself—austere and merciless Aphrodite—is a pagan. It is not our brains and instincts which she picks—but our very bones." And later he speaks of the "austere mindless primitive face of Aphrodite."

But this surely is not the love-goddess known to the moderns who inhabit Westchester and Fairfield counties and Hampstead and St. John's Wood, or to the novelists who chronicle their no doubt useful lives.

If the love that Mr. Durrell describes is indeed to be called modern, it is so by reason of its affinity to love as Proust represents it. That is to say, it is obsessive, corrosive, desperate, highly psychologized. These adjectives do seem to propose a distinctively modern condition, but not the modern condition of love between the sexes. And indeed Proust in his representation of love is much closer to the classic drama of the seventeenth century than to any literary work of our own time. The same can be said of Mr. Durrell. His Justine is in the direct line of Racine's Phèdre. Her husband Nessim, in the grandeur of his worldly power and the chivalric delicacy of his conduct, is a character with whom Corneille would have been quite at ease. The interplay between passion and duty and the high moralizing of passion are the habits of the French classic stage. All the characters of the two novels, no matter what their position in life, no matter what sordidness of circumstance they may accept to further the fulfilment of their love, maintain in their conduct some element of moral heroism. The emotion of friendship is held in high regard and there is a kind of general agreement among all the characters to accord each other a grave respect. The elaborate psychologizing in which the two novels abound never has for its purpose the belittling of the person upon whom it is directed. Neither the lust, nor the pride, nor the curiosity, nor the emptiness that may instigate love, nor the pain or devastation that may result from it, are made a reason for contempt.

The affinity of the two novels with the French classic drama is confirmed by the setting of the story, although *setting* is a word which carries too much implication of the static to suggest how active is its part in the story. The modernity of Mr. Durrell's Alexandria is bound up with its antiquity of three thousand years. Almost all the characters, both the English and the Egyptian, are of the most extreme sophistication, but their modern subtlety of morality and psychology exists in a world as primitive and as barbarous, as cruel and as dangerous, as the ancient world which imagined the stories or lived out the histories from which the French classic drama drew its themes.

In a Note prefacing *Balthazar* Mr. Durrell speaks of his novelistic method in this way:

> Modern literature offers us no Unities, so I have turned to science and am trying to complete a four-decker novel whose form is based on the relativity proposition.
>
> Three sides of space and one of time constitute the soup-mix recipe of a continuum. The four novels follow this pattern.
>
> The three first parts, however, are to be deployed spatially . . . and are not linked in a serial form. They interlap, interweave, in a purely spatial relation. Time is stayed. The fourth part alone will represent time. . . .
>
> The subject-object relation is so important to relativity that I have tried to turn the novel through both subjective and objective modes. The third part, *Mountolive*, is a straight naturalistic novel in which the narrator of *Justine* and *Balthazar* becomes an object, i.e. a character.
>
> This is not Proustian or Joycean method—for they illustrate Bergsonian "Duration" in my opinion, not "Space-Time."

This is rather more forbidding than it need be, and rather too much like those profound statements of their intentions that even excellent painters have taken to writing for their catalogues. The method of *Justine* and *Balthazar* may be described much more simply. The narrator is an English schoolteacher and unsuccessful novelist (we do not know his name, Darley, until it is mentioned toward the end of *Balthazar*); he is the lover of Melissa, a cabaret dancer, and also of Justine, the brilliant, haunted wife of Nessim Hosnani, a Coptic banker of enormous wealth and great sensitivity. The narrator's observation of events is supplemented by that of Arnauti, Justine's first husband, who has published a novel about their marriage and her neurosis, and by that of Pursewarden, an English novelist of some distinction. Three novelists in a novel is no doubt much of a muchness, but it is rather fun than otherwise. The narrator also has available to him the diaries of Justine and of Nessim, not to mention the special knowledge of the physician Balthazar and of the saintly painter Clea. The purpose of this plethora of historians is not to play the quasi-philosophical game (very dull it is) of contrasting and opposing points of view, and, so far as I can see, not to serve whatever scientific-aesthetic purpose Mr. Durrell announces in the Note I have quoted from, but to suggest the difficulty of ever knowing (especially in love affairs) what has actually happened and what people's

motives really are; the understanding that prevails at one moment is replaced or modified by the understanding that comes with new information,
and the true explanation of an event virtually never comes at the time of
its occurrence. This does indeed have an aesthetic effect in that it proposes
a new kind of verisimilitude and, by instructing the reader that he must be
careful to accept no statement at its face value, involves him in the story in
an especially active way. It is not true, as Mr. Durrell seems to suggest in
his Note, that his first two novels do not move through time. Their movement through time is certainly not simple, but neither is it so complex or
unorthodox that we do not readily perceive the climaxes and resolutions of
a story which is in the highest degree dramatic and weighty.

II

Now that I have read the third and fourth of what Mr. Durrell calls
the *Alexandria Quartet*, *Mountolive* published earlier this year and the recent *Clea*, I think I know what disquieted me. It is that all the novels,
and the *Quartet* as a whole, stand in a peculiar negative relation to the
will. . . .

The will, of course, cannot be dismissed out of hand, and the artist
cannot (alas?) do without it. At the end of Mr. Durrell's *Quartet* the novelist Darley, who clearly bears some close surrogate relation to the author,
having long failed to write in a way that pleases himself or anybody, is at
last able to know that he has achieved salvation, that he is at the great moment of "an artist coming of age"—as bold as that, quite as if we had
reached the end of *Sons and Lovers* or *A Portrait of the Artist as a Young
Man*, or any of the scores of lesser *Bildungsromane* of the 1920's. No, the
will is not easily got rid of, neither in the novelist nor in his characters.
One of the chief dramatic elements of the *Quartet*—it is fully disclosed in
Mountolive—is the great Coptic political intrigue in which Nessim Hosnani
is involved; in a remarkable love scene, Nessim, who has failed to win Justine in marriage, does at last overcome her resistance and draws her into a
passionate involvement with him by telling her of the plot and making her
party to it; she is captivated by his display of will.

Yet the very will itself becomes an element of the World-as-Represen-
tation. The actual political meaning of the plot has no great weight with
Justine; for her the real value of the enterprise lies in its danger—the
threat of death makes love and sexuality the more intense. And it may be
said in general of the acts of the will in the *Quartet* that they are drained
of their literalness, of their directness and force, that they are informed *as
if* they were real, the actors being conscious of the *as if*. Ideals of loyalty
and responsibility suffuse the *Quartet*, and have reference not only to persons but to nations—it is striking, indeed, how important the idea of the
nation is in the novels, and how much feeling the characters direct to entities as large as Egypt, England, France, and Greece. Leila Hosnani, the

mother of Nessim and Narouz, loves the young David Mountolive not only because he is charming, but because he is English, and he loves her because she is for him the soul of Egypt. Even the outrageous novelist, Ludwig Pursewarden, who has conducted a lifelong war against English culture, is committed to his nation, and even his friend, Pombal, of the French foreign service, falls in love with defeated France at the same moment, and in much the same way, that, after a career of sexual athleticism, he for the first time falls in love with a woman.

But even the idea of the nation is absorbed into the general *as if*, and succumbs to the prevailing unreality of the objects of the will—was any English ambassador ever so little concerned with the actualities of diplomacy, with the facts of power and intrigue, as Mountolive? As any reader of the *Quartet* is likely to conceive of the will, it is a peculiarly European faculty, which has found its modern expression in Protestantism, Romanticism, and the ideals of the middle class in its classic period—it is highly moralized, giving the greatest possible value to individuality as far as it can be thought of as one's own, seeing the world as the great stage which has been readied for the significant behavior of the hero: all our notions of tragedy depend upon our conception of the will. But the tragic European will simply cannot function in the *Quartet*, if only because the locality in which its action takes place does not submit to being made into the great stage of the world. Alexandria, so far from being a stage, is itself the protagonist of the action, a being far more complex and interesting than any of its inhabitants, having its own way and its own rights, its own life and its own secret will to which the life and the will of the individual are subordinate.

The intensity of the personal existence of the city derives in large part from its history, and history is a felt presence in the *Quartet*, conceived of as a tendency of happening in which human will may indeed assert itself, although to little avail. Mark Antony is virtually one of the dramatis personae of the novels; in *Clea*, Darley and Clea make love on the tiny island which Clea believes to be the one to which Antony fled after Cleopatra had brought about his ruin by her panic at Actium; the music under the earth that was heard when the voice called "the gods desert Antony" still reverberates in the city, and not only because it is the subject of one of the most famous poems of Cavafy, the Alexandrian poet who is made to figure in the *Quartet* as the city's soul become articulate.

What we of Europe and America call the past is part of Alexandria's actual present—ancient ways and the ancient people are before our eyes, and scenes that would seem bizarre and perfervid in the pages of *The Golden Bough* are of common occurrence, such scenes, for example, as the days-long mourning for Narouz Hosnani with which *Mountolive* ends, or, earlier in the same novel, the cutting-up of the still-living camels for the feast, or the religious festivals with their circumcision and prostitution booths and their possessed holy men. The ancient modes of thought are still in force—the existence of occult powers is taken for granted; scrying, second sight, palmistry, necromancy are matters of received fact with people of cultivation as well as with the primitive masses; this is the "mysterious East" of Western legend, with its belief in Kismet, or in guessed-at wills before which the will of man is of small account. And death or disablement or disfigurement can strike suddenly either at the behest of an occult or of some more powerful or beforehanded human will than one's own.

In this ancient circumstance the nature of the human personality is different from what we of Europe and America expect it to be. It is not, as I have implied, that the human virtues that we know have no existence and no appeal. Loyalty, devotion, tenderness, concern for the welfare of others are, indeed, displayed in a notable way by all the characters of the *Quartet*. "Moral" is a word that would be beyond their powers of utterance, perhaps beyond Mr. Durrell's, yet their lives are touched by considerations of goodness at every point; what is lacking is the binding force of the will which keeps steady the objects of their desire, and creates the idea of permanence and intention. This accounts for the ease and grace of their existence, for their never being torn between two possible ways of behavior, for their never displaying the harshness of moral judgment of each other. Two things only are of undoubted value in the *Quartet* and both are beyond the reach of the moral will. They are love and art—love which must follow its own laws and is not to be constrained; art which submits to no rule or purpose, existing for itself. The love that is represented in the *Quartet* is never linked to moral sanctions of any kind. The art that is imagined is without that moral urgency which is the hallmark of modern art; perhaps its paradigm is the scene in which Justine, searching for her kidnapped little daughter in a brothel, holds enchanted the swarm of child-prostitutes with an ancient romance; and the four words which, we are told, "presage . . . the old story of an artist coming of age" are "Once upon a time. . . ."

And indeed the aesthetic of the *Quartet* can best be understood by reference to the author's desire to recapture in the novel whatever charm lies in those four words, all that they imply of pleasure rather than will. It is to this end, for example, that Darley has been created to serve as the narrator of all the novels except *Mountolive*. Darley is himself a character among others and he is not held in especial esteem by his friends and lovers; he never knows everything that might be known and he is the victim of a most elaborate deception practised upon him by Justine and Nessim. Yet he does what he can, he tells what he knows. The devices that Mr. Durrell permits him to use to gather information are transparent and not always credible—the novels of other men, diaries, letters of infinite length, monologuists who are nearly as untiring as Conrad's Marlow; there are even two friends who, when he wants to evoke the image of the transvestite police-officer Scobie, are such perfect mimics that they can "do" Scobie for pages on end. It is as if Mr. Durrell were telling us that he has no intention of setting up as the novelist, of sitting enthroned like the Logos itself, in the fashion of Proust or Joyce or Mann or Lawrence. I include Lawrence because of his novels which are in the control of strict, impenetrable, universal logic; but the Lawrence of many of the shorter stories was manifestly trying to shed the weight and solemnity of his role of Genius-novelist, to speak in the voice of human intercourse, not in the voice of Art; and for that reason perhaps, among others, he is one of the literary heroes of the *Quartet*. Lawrence had his own express quarrel with the will and he sought a prose in which the rhetoric of the will was not dominant.

And this, I take it, is the prose that Mr. Durrell is trying for. I am not always of a single mind about it, but I know that it is doing a very useful thing—it is helping to save the language of the novel from Joyce. For the fact is that after reading Joyce it is very hard to take the prose of most novelists: Joyce makes it seem slack, vulgar, over-familiar. Indeed, if one reads Joyce with admiration, one conspires with him in his feeling that the presence of a reader is an impertinence, that to use language for purposes of communication is disgusting, a practice of the lowborn. Thus far had the creative will gone in pride, and the only way a novelist might again find a language was to do what Mr. Durrell has done, to take the posture of the man who begins "Once upon a time . . . ," to announce, that is, that he is going to tell a story—really *tell* it as against representing it—and that it is he who is telling it, and that he, or his simulacrum-surrogate, can only speak in his own way, as a person, sometimes high, sometimes low, sometimes businesslike, sometimes moved by wonder.

That last is important. My impression of most contemporary novels that come my way is that they say to me, "Let me give you for your file yet another instance of what you know so well, thus reassuring you of your high degree of sympathy with human frustration at no cost whatever. I will also tell you what, of course, you quite understand, how very bad The Culture is, and how it is to blame for the way people are when it isn't their own fault." Mr. Durrell's novels are much more naive, they say, "Let me tell you something interesting. Once upon a time. . . ." Some of the things he tells I listen to with one or another degree of incredulity. I don't believe in homunculi made in a bottle by Cabalists. The camels sitting quiet while they are dismembered I can scarcely credit, but why should Mr. Durrell lie about a thing like that? The prophecy and second sight and scrying are amusing to suspend disbelief in, and if I am truthful I have to confess that I was once set back on my heels by what someone read in my palm. The story of the physician Amaril and the beautiful girl with no nose (she is eventually provided with one) is implausible, but I like Isaak Dinesen. It is at least apparently true that the holy men do pierce and burn themselves without harm or pain. Maybe this is all storyteller's nonsense, the usual mystery of the East, but it consorts with my sense of the way people ought to be, in a novel at any rate—that is to say, objects of wonder. And it is in the element of wonder that Mr. Durrell's characters move, like Clea and Darley in one of their several underwater scenes, flaming with phosphorus.

I find it possible to suppose that if they were to be taken "in themselves,"as we say, that would not be so very interesting, but in their ambience of Alexandria and of wonder they exist with a quite splendid intensity of life. I make an exception of the great Pursewarden at whose wit and wisdom and charm everyone marvels—I find him a self-conscious bore, and in nothing is he so disappointing as in Darley's discovery that his bitterness is really tenderness. Mr. Durrell can do much better than that, and does, in the fierce, fluctuating passions of Nessim and Justine, in the Esau-like figure of Narouz, in the beautiful, brilliant and ruined Leila, in the canonized clown Scobie, in the general, curious vivacity of the *Quartet*.

Grading the Emanglons   Benjamin DeMott*

Henri Michaux, a barbarian who knows the road east better even than Lawrence Durrell, has some observations in one of his imaginary voyages that are worth twice the price of a NoDoz to readers just embarking on *The Alexandria Quartet*. Michaux's subject is a tribe of Great Garaban called the Emanglons which has a passion for remoteness in art. The effects of this passion are various but consistent, and evident in all quarters. Emanglon theaters are bare of greasy actors; the latter play their parts in separate buildings from which images are transmitted to the form-loving audience by mirror-play. "Some words, that come from the ceiling, are spoken in [the actors'] names." Emanglon concert halls hide the sweating musicians in the wings. As for the stuff performed: "Their music with its dying sounds always seems to be coming through a mattress. That's what [the Emanglons] like: tenuous sounds, coming from nobody knows where, fading out every second, trembling and uncertain melodies which finish off, however, in great harmonic surfaces—wide layers suddenly outspread."

The use of this report is twofold to a man who aims to make his way uncomplainingly through *Justine* or *Balthazar*. Like every subtle definition of an enlightened audience, it raises the possibility that high art always is bewildering, and Durrell's reader needs to be reminded of this possibility if he is to keep the iron in himself from page to page. Beyond this the report, which (hostilely regarded) can stand as a characterization of a whole genre of literary confusion, offers serviceable terms for the description of Durrell's unique effects. The man's "sound," for example, is by abrupt terms tenuous and dying, sudden and voluminous; much of it issues from nobody knows where. His characters in *Justine* and *Balthazar* play to mirrors and prisms, like the Emanglon actors, and are difficult to see and hear; the words spoken in their names come down from the ceiling.[1] And, at first glance, *remote*, a key critical term in the Michaux country, seems likely to be an appropriate "positive" label for Durrell's world as well.

*Reprinted from *Hudson Review* 13, no. 3 (Autumn 1960), 457–64.

What but remoteness could be expected in a work set in Egypt? Readers of Olivia Manning or P. H. Newby will call this an ignorant question, but only Egyptians will deny that the country is far away. Mosques and muezzins do not figure in the daily experience of Everyman, and the same can be said of many other items in the opening volumes of this tetralogy—a silver Rolls with daffodil hubcaps, a Babylonian barber shop, copulations of boabs, an axe murder of a camel, a bazaar where male prostitutes are tattooed, a character who spends his life travelling on ocean liners with a perfect woman called Sabina who is made of rubber ("Sabina had a wonderful wardrobe. It was a sight to see them come into the dining room"), and a man who, when asked why he is carrying another man's head in his gamebag, replies with no humorous intention: "More troubles with Bedouin labour could have cost us a thousand trees next year. It was too much of a risk to take. Besides, he was going to poison me." But in art anything can be made familiar, and if the case were otherwise, the remoteness of *Justine* and *Balthazar* would still have to be regarded as a consequence less of matter than of manner.

The chief narrator of both books is an English writer named Darley who is situated on a Mediterranean island in the company of a person called "the child." In *Justine* Darley is setting down the truth about certain people and events known to him in years spent in Alexandria; in *Balthazar* he is reviewing *Justine* in light of "The Interlinear"—a body of suggested revisions put forward by the first reader of his manuscript, a pederast named Balthazar who knows the same people and events, and considers Darley to be wanting in perceptiveness about them. The impression given by both books is that a series of related happenings of the sort described by the word *story* no doubt exists in some *ur*-text—a work that would be as valuable to Durrell's audience as a reading knowledge of Russian is to a man who wishes to know Tolstoy in the original. But in the absence of this text, the focus seems Emanglonianly dim, and the order of significance of its objects is not easy to ascertain, (*Justine* is presumably "about" the fatal lady who bears that name, but before Justine's hour arrives another fatal lady named Melissa is given much space, a circumstance which has the effect not only of perplexing the curious reader, but of dulling his appetite for fatality.) Names turn up on the page, are sung at by the narrator, and shortly disappear—for no specified reason. Then in *Balthazar* the narrator is chided for offering a mistaken explanation of the disappearances—when, as well as can be remembered, no explanation whatever had been offered. The names themselves—Pombal, Narouz, Abu Kar, Capodistria—have great piquancy, and the words spoken to and for them are remarkably fluent. But few of the messages convey much hint of what is called the real, or of any other agent capable of disturbing the taut Garabanian air of nonexistence.

Nor would it appear, to judge from the tone of the enterprise, and the dominant rhetoric, that the writer likes such disturbances. As indicated before, his stall is jammed with Gothic gimcracks: epigraphs from Sade, a stolen child, man-eating birds, poisonings, hat-pin murders, vampires, religious frenzies, houses of child prostitution, circumcision spectacles, visions, lepers, bullwhips—not to speak again of the extraordinary gallery of fatal women. (A. is consumptive and smokes hashish; B. has her fine face destroyed by the pox; C. is raped as a child; D. has an abortion and afterward a harpoon tears off her hand.) And like most barkers of this stock Durrell prefers to speak in the unreal idiom of romance. He is faithful not only to the cliché ("Truth will out," "They drifted apart") and the "short ironic" laugh and sob, but also to the breathless leading question ("And Clea, what of her?" "And Scobie, what of him?" "And Pursewarden?" "Ah, Pursewarden . . ."). And as often as not the leading questions lead only to passages of *sententiae* and *profundum* (" 'Every man,' [Justine] writes elsewhere, and here I can hear the hoarse and sorrowful accents of her voice repeating the words as she writes them; 'Every man is made of clay and daimon, and no woman can nourish both' "), or to an Expressionist tableau:

> I turned my head to look at Justine. She was holding up her wrists at me, her face carved into a grimace. She held them joined together as if by invisible manacles. She exhibited these imaginary handcuffs for a long moment before dropping her hands back into her lap, and then, abruptly, swift as a snake, she crossed to the divan where I lay and sat down at my feet, uttering as she did so, in a voice vibrating with remorseful resentment, the words: "Why Darley? O *why*?"

The aversion here revealed to palpable presences—or at least to the sort of speech and narrative line that help to create them—also appears in *Mountolive* and *Clea*, the third and fourth volumes of the tetralogy, though in these books attempts are made to disguise it. Durrell speaks slightingly of *Mountolive* as a "straight naturalistic novel"—and, in an idiom less fretted than that of *Justine* and *Balthazar*, it does tell a story rather than hide one. (*Clea* functions to restore a measure of muddle to the events that *Mountolive* sharply defines, but it too is more available as a narrative than the first volumes.) The story in question deals with a young English diplomat who is sent to a Coptic family to master Arabic early in his career. He becomes the lover of the great lady of the family, a Westernized figure who educates him not only in her culture, but to the best in European thought and art, thus releasing him from the dungeon of Englishness. Mountolive leaves Egypt to pursue his career from Moscow to Lisbon, engages in an intense correspondence with the Coptic lady over the years, and at length returns to Egypt as ambassador. The lady can no longer be his lover; she is old and her beauty is destroyed. More important, her sons are involved in an anti-British intrigue. Their machinations are first denied, then acknowledged, by Mountolive's friend Pursewarden, a character whose reputation as a writer and seer adds significance to his peculiar stance of neutrality in the struggle between East and West. And the effort to comprehend this stance, as well as to frustrate the plans of his former Coptic friends without denying the truth of his own nature, plunges Mountolive into a generativity crisis as the book ends.

The character of this crisis testifies that Durrell is attempting, in *Mountolive*, to "place" his exotic world by using it as an agent of initiation for an un-exotic head, a means by which the inhibited heart can be opened to life. And in the opening and closing scenes of the novel, discarding the mirrors in service elsewhere, he works up two events—a fish drive in the waterways near Alexandria and a Coptic wake—with a power which, though it can be described by Michaux's (again oddly useful) phrases about "great harmonic surfaces—wide layers suddenly outspread," has too reverberant and sustained a connection with violent reality to please an Emanglon audience. But as already indicated these events do not control the book's tone. The latter is established early on by an idolatrous presentation of the Foreign Office, a radiantly neat institution that in these pages seems more like fairyland, or a stainless steel kitchen in *McCall's*, than a human production.[2] And as the book develops, the fantasticating influence of the otherworldly bureaucracy is intensified by Durrell's arbitrary manipulation of his fable—a spy tale with operatic interludes.

Evidence of manipulation is everywhere visible. In *Balthazar* a Coptic rich man marries a fatal Jewess; his reason for doing so, according to the reporting intelligence of the moment, is that he is passionately in love with the lady. In *Mountolive* his reason is differently described; according to the reporting intelligence of that book, his purpose in marrying is to strengthen his hand in anti-British negotiations with Palestine. (As a Coptic, a Christian, the man believes that he will lessen Palestinian suspicion if he takes a Jewish wife.) The motives are revealed during a telephone conversation—the same conversation in each volume. In *Balthazar* the words spoken are reported as follows:

> Nessim [the rich man] took the lift up to his office, and sitting down at his desk wrote upon a card the following words: "My dearest Clea, Justine has agreed to marry me. I could never do this if I thought it would qualify or interfere in any way with either her love for you or mine. . . ." Then, appalled by the thought that whatever he might write to Clea might sound mawkish, he tore the note up and folded his arms. After a long moment of thought he picked up the polished telephone and dialled Capodistria's number. "Da Capo" he said quietly. "You remember my plans for marrying Justine? All is well." He replaced the receiver slowly, as if it weighed a ton, and sat staring at his own reflection in the polished desk.

In *Mountolive* the conversation is reported as follows:

> It was some hours later, when he was sitting at his desk, that Nessim after a long moment of thought, picked up the polished telephone and dialled Capodistria's number. "Da Capo," he said quietly, "you remem-

ber my plans for marrying Justine? All is well. We have a new ally. I
want you to be the first to announce it to the committee. I think now
they will show no more reservation about my not being a Jew—since I
am to be married to one. What do you say?"

This finagling with motives may not please traditionalists—but low-brow
Emanglons, schooled to scorn the notion that serious writers do not with-
hold information for cheap reasons, are likely to find it as much to their
taste as the mysterious music of *Justine*. And this in itself confirms the original assertion, that the ostensibly "naturalistic" parts of *The Alexandria
Quartet* are only a shade less attractive to (undemanding) admirers of remoteness than those that are ostensibly "experimental."

. . . *Justine* and *Balthazar* have interest as an indication of what
Aureng-Zebe would be like if it were rewritten by a post-Lawrentian, in
the manner of Pater, to be played underwater—and to say this is to grant
that both books possess unusual literary, or poetical qualities: but the qualities are not admirable. Durrell is chockablock with imagery, indeed the
principle of his employment of images is that of the saturation air raid of
other times—but the reader, though given opportunities to admire flames
and explosions in other neighborhoods, ultimately is numbered among the
maimed. The poetry that Durrell brings back, in short, is bad poetry—an
item which despite its power to stimulate the opportunistic is of slight
value. Again: it is claimed that Durrell has given fiction some of its old substance as an instrument of thought, that he fills his pages with intellection
of a weight and passion unequaled by any recent novelist. The measure of
truth in this contention is, as in the previous instance, not contemptible.
Novelists rarely concern themselves directly nowadays with metaphysics or
epistemology, and Durrell does concern himself with these subjects: he is,
as it were, always thinking. Regrettably, though, he is not a first-rate
thinker. The burden of intellection in his first volumes rests upon commonplace observations about the fictive nature of human life, and in *Mountolive*
and *Clea*, where most of the thinking is done by the great writer, Pursewarden, the substance of the ideas, if any, is buried in Blakeian prophetics
and Irish (or elves and fairies division) Lawrentianism. The culmination of
the argument appears in *Clea*, where thirty pages are devoted to "revolutionary" ravings like these:

> The miracle is there, on ice so to speak. One fine day it will blossom:
> then the artist suddenly grows up and accepts the full responsibility for
> his origins in the people, and when *simultaneously* the people recognise
> his peculiar significance and value, and greet him as the unborn child in
> themselves, the infant Joy! I am certain it will come. At the moment they
> are like wrestlers nervously circling one another, looking for a hold. But
> when it comes, this great blinding second of illumination—only then
> shall we be able to dispense with hierarchy as a social form. The new
> society—so different from anything we can imagine now—will be born
> around the small strict white temple of the infant Joy! Men and women

will group themselves around it, the proto-plasmic growth of the village, the town, the capital! Nothing stands in the way of this Ideal Common-wealth, save that in every generation the vanity and laziness of the artist has always matched the self-indulgent blindness of the people. But pre-pare, prepare! It is on the way. It is here, there, nowhere!

The great schools of love will arise, and sensual and intellectual knowl-edge will draw their impetus from each other. The human animal will be uncaged, all his dirty cultural straw and coprolitic refuse of belief cleaned out. And the human spirit, radiating light and laughter, will softly tread the green grass like a dancer; will emerge to cohabit with the time-forms and give children to the world of the elementaries—undines and sala-manders, sylphs and sylvestres, Gnomi and Vulcani, angels and gnomes.

The final upper-Emanglon claim advanced for Durrell is that he stands forth as an innovator, a man who is unwilling to accept the dull status quo of contemporary fictional art. And for this claim something can again be said: unlike most novelists, Durrell does put his work forward as a major literary experiment. His text is littered with methodological self-surveys in which (as already indicated) mirrors, prisms and other Emanglon props figure prominently:

I remember her sitting before the multiple mirrors at the dressmaker's, being fitted for a shark-skin costume, and saying: "Look! five different pictures of the same subject. Now if I wrote I would try for a multi-di-mensional effect in character, a sort of prism-sightedness. Why should not people show more than one profile at a time?" (*Justine*)

No, but seriously . . . you might try a four-card trick in the form of a novel; passing a common axis through four stories, say, and dedicating each to one of the four winds of heaven. A continuum, forsooth, embody-ing not a temps retrouvé but a temps délivré. The curvature of space it-self would give you stereoscopic narrative, while human personality seen across a continuum would perhaps become prismatic? Who can say? I throw the idea out. (*Clea*)

And the preface to *Balthazar* explains the experiment with precision:

Modern literature offers us no Unities, so I have turned to science and am trying to complete a four-decker novel whose form is based on the relativity proposition. Three sides of space and one of time constitute the soup-mix recipe of a continuum. The four novels follow this pattern. . . . The subject-object relation is so important to relativity that I have tried to turn the novel through both subjective and objective modes. . . . This is not Proustian or Joycean method—for they illustrate Bergsonian "Du-ration" in my opinion, not "Space-Time."

The difficulty about all this is that Durrell's remarks reflect an oblivious-ness, infrequent among true innovators, to the whole line of investigation carried on by major novelists since the beginning of this century, few of whom have been satisfied with "one profile at a time." To be sure, the problem would not matter if the books themselves were felt to be new in method or scheme, if their use of multiple points of view seemed signifi-cantly fresh. But the sense of genuine technical invention is lacking in this work from the beginning; the prime use of the methodological pronounce-ments seems to be that of encouraging innocent readers to respect as an experiment what is actually no more than a mismanagement of an already familiar narrative method.

The painful truth thus suggested is that even the invocation of Eman-glon standards, which celebrate (not condemn) confusion and monstrosities of the kind described above, fails to validate the large claims made for the author of the *Quartet* as a novelist, experimenter, seer, and baroque painter. Durrell's language has no taint of the non-fiction novelist's drab-ness, but its complications smell more of vulgar "poetical" pretentiousness than of ambitious effort to arrive at difficult, encompassing truths. His study of the illicit and the ugly is not pornographic, and is often informa-tive, but what it lays open is a scab of local self-contempt rather than the heart of a universal corruption. The possibility that his work as a whole should be thought of as a long anti-novel, a purposeful or Dada-ist mingling of styles, indicates the range of its potential interest—but the possibility is undercut by the absence of the note of amused self-awareness that lends authority to such productions. At their best his ideas *are* ideas, but since they are available elsewhere and since in his preachment of them Durrell is frequently hysterical, he does not qualify as an original or subtle mind. His belief that the need is urgent for a new formula of psychic health is unexceptionable, but since his tone is sickly and his preoccupations mean, he himself seems little more than a symptom of the wretchedness he be-moans. He is remote—this bears repeating: but in failing to comprehend that the end of remoteness is, ideally, the defeat of vulgarity, pretension, and private agony, he links himself only with the commoners of the Eman-glon tribe, whose preference for the far-out is cant.

To say this much is not to deny that *Mountolive* is a readable novel with a brilliant opening chapter, and that moments of power occur at inter-vals in all four books, and that in conception the whole work raises extraor-dinary hopes. . . . Neither is it to pretend that readable novels can be brought to general attention at present unless accompanied by volumes of notes for other novels, theories, ramshackle intellection, and murmurings from Cyril Connolly about "the spirit of Alexandria, sensual and skeptical, self-torturing and passionate." . . . But these concessions and allusions to sociology do little to support the enthusiast who sets Durrell in the com-pany of Proust or Conrad, and not much more to justify the sympathetic critic who attempts to place him honorably among the Emanglons. The terms of the latter tribe probably are narrow, precious, insubstantial—"useless for Shakespeare." But the standard they raise, as even the most reluctant and tentative testings of *The Alexandria Quartet* seem bound to suggest, is a good deal higher than lowbrow aesthetes and four-card tricks in the form of novels are ever likely to reach.

Notes

1. Durrell discourses at length in *Justine* and elsewhere about art, mirrors and prisms (see below), and it may as well be noted here that the preoccupation is monotonously apparent in his poetry. See "Eight Aspects of Melissa," "On Mirrors," "The Daily Mirror," "Je est un autre," "Nicosia," "Delos," "Channel," the first poem "At Alexandria," "Penelope," "Basil the Hermit," "Fangbrand," "Father Nicholas His Death," "In the Ionian," "To Ping-Kû, Asleep," "Letter to Seferis the Greek," the sixth "Letter in Darkness," etc.

2. The same idolatry is evident in Durrell's funnybooks—*Esprit de Corps* and *Stiff Upper Lip*, complacent chirpings about diplomats.

[From "Poetry Chronicle: The Light is Dark Enough"]

Vernon Young*

Lawrence Durrell can with some accuracy be called British. Born in India of Irish extraction (his boast), he is one of those exotics produced by Great Britain who, while enriching the "English" language, takes a less than sanguinary view of the Isles from whence his inheritance came.

> Moss walls, woollen forests, Shakespear, desuetude.
> Roots of his language as familiar as salt
> Inhaling cattle lick in this mnemonic valley
> Where the gnats assort, the thrush familiarises,
> And over his cottage a colloquial moon.
>
> "Bere Regis"

In the very few poems among all he has written which have England as their subject, reproof is stronger than nostalgia. Durrell's heartland is the Grecian Mediterranean. "Tread softly, for here you stand/On miracle ground, boy./A breath would cloud this water of glass,/Honey, bush, berry and swallow./This rock, then, is more pastoral than/Arcadia is, Illyria was." So begins "On Ithaca standing" (1937) and this is pretty much the tone and temperature of all his Ionic celebrations. The present collection makes available for the first time *all* the poems Durrell has published between 1931 and 1974. Thanks to Mr. Brigham's editing, each poem is identified

*Reprinted by permission from *The Hudson Review* 34, no. 1 (Spring 1981), 144–46. © 1981 by The Hudson Review, Inc.

by date of composition, followed by publication date. Durrell here emerges, lest anyone doubted or was ignorant of the fact, as intrinsically a poet. Written primarily for money, the notorious *Alexandria Quartet* is the grandiose prose parenthesis of a lyric talent which, if not major, has never been less than poetic. Of "development" it is idle to speak; he was from the start developed. His "Stoic" of 1971 is an echo of "Conon in Exile" of 1942, a pagan unrepentant, undeceived, self-ironic. Early in his life Durrell acquired a classical disposition, characterized at one and the same time by philosophic pessimism, sunlit serenity and an immovable admiration for the sensuous in nature and art. There he has remained, through hell and high water, through war and peace, through figs, milk and honey, with small sense of sin, sustained by illimitable images of cities dead and alive, of women dead and alive, and by a spirited gift for impersonating anyone: Cavafy, Byron, a desert father, philosophers, harlots, governors of Roman provinces, Fabre the insect man, and small boys. Durrell speaks with an eminently civilized tongue, whether he is tossing off light-verse satire of literary critics, Americans and psychoanalysis, or conjuring visions of a civilization despoiling itself. His best impartial statement of universal aspiration and disorder is "Cities, Plains and People" (1943, Beirut).

> All cities plains and people
> Reach upwards to the affirming sun,
> All that's vertical and shining,
> Lives well lived,
> Deeds perfectly done,
> Reach upwards to the royal pure
> Affirming sun.
>
> (Part XIV)

> There is nothing to hope for, my Brother.
> We have tried hoping for a future in the past.
> Nothing came out of that past
> But the reflected distortion and some
> Enduring, and understanding, and some brave.
> Into their cool embrace the awkward and the sinful
> Must be put for they alone
> Know who and what to save.
>
> (Part XV)

Durrell's lasting reputation will probably be secured by his poems of place, unsurpassed by any contemporary for their historical saturation and their exalted scenic precision: e.g., "Conon in Alexandria"—"Ashheap of four cultures,/Bounded by Mareotis, a salt lake,/On which the winter rain rings and whitens/In the waters, stiffens like eyes"; or "The Parthenon": "Man entered it and woman was the roof"; or "Near El Alamein," with its stunning last line, "Heavy with sponges and the common error"; or "Levant": "Something fine of tooth and with the soft/Hanging lashes to the eye,/Given once by Spain and kept/In a mad friendship here and sadness

/By the promiscuous sea upon this spit of sand." I'm not sure he ever wrote a better spirit-of-place poem than "Sarajevo"; certainly none that for us reverberates louder with every year that separates us from (and unites us with) the beginning of our end. My older readers may recall the last two wonderful stanzas.

> Where minarets have twisted up like sugar
> And a river, curdled with blond ice, drives on
> Tinkling among the mule-teams and the mountaineers,
> Under the bridges and the wooden trellises
> Which tame the air and promise us a peace
> Harmless with nightingales. None are singing now.
>
> No history much? Perhaps. Only this ominous
> Dark beauty flowering under veils,
> Trapped in the spectrum of a dying style:
> A village like an instinct left to rust,
> Composed around the echo of a pistol shot.

[Review of *Monsieur*]   Robert F. Moss*

While the rest of British fiction has been marching steadily backward into a sober nineteenth-century realism, Lawrence Durrell has doggedly refused to budge from his experimental, post-Proustian niche. He is endeavoring to resuscitate a dead tradition, the avant-garde movement of Eliot, Joyce, Lawrence and others, a tradition closer to us than the world of George Eliot, which is undoubtedly one reason why Durrell is a more successful steward of *his* tradition than Angus Wilson and Anthony Powell are of *their* dogged, anemic social commentaries.

The crushing supremacy of the new realism, however, seems to have retarded Durrell's reputation until the appearance in 1957–60 of the popular and critical blockbuster, *The Alexandria Quartet*. The general reader responded to its exoticism and melodrama, the critic to its bravura prose style and elaborate structure. Durrell was acclaimed a new Major Novelist at once. He followed with several works—e.g., *Nunquam, Tunc*—that unmistakably failed to confirm his new status, being little more than *divertissement*.

Durrell's latest novel, *Monsieur*, can perhaps be seen as an effort to regain his footing in the world of letters by returning to the serious, thematically weighty stance of *Quartet*. The setting is (in part) Egypt and, as in the earlier work, the characters are members of a sophisticated international set. The search for love is again a prominent theme, as are such Durrellian preoccupations as the multiplicity of truth, the salutary effects of

*Reprinted by permission of *The New Republic*, © 1975, The New Republic, Inc.

Lawrentian primitivism and the nature of the artistic process. As for the characters, the incestuous relationship of Sylvie, the heroine, and her brother Piers is, in certain ways, interchangeable with the Pursewarden-Liza affair in *Quartet*. Another cryptic, wealthy, philosophical Egyptian, Akkad, turns up to fill in for Nessim, and Rob Sutcliffe, an abrasive and tortured writer, is almost a reincarnation of Pursewarden.

Happily there are important differences. In *Monsieur* the sinister, labyrinthine melodrama is provided by a secret society of Gnostics. The mysterious death of Piers, a member of the cult, is the novel's point of departure. Considerable momentum is generated by the determined sleuthing of Bruce, Piers' brother-in-law, who seeks to wrest some explanation for the "suicide" from a handful of clues, documents left behind in the family vault, and his own recollection of a hair-raising Gnostic ceremony years before. Clearly this is a thriller formula, but Durrell gives it a high gloss—and even some substance—through his technical expertise; skillfully, he is able to fuse past and present events in his story, two disparate settings (Egypt and Avignon, where the death occurs) and two discrete religious societies (the Gnostics and the medieval Knights of Templar, who are the subject of a treatise Piers has been writing).

Durrell's ambitions reach far beyond the genre of escape fiction, but his ability to sustain them is erratic. After successfully engulfing the reader in his dark, sensuous plot, he continually inhibits its flow with long, anti-Christian sermons by Akkad, who appears to be capable of carrying out the ritual murders his sect practices by simply boring people to death. Equally lethal are the tedious, crabbed, frequently incoherent extracts from Sutcliffe's notebooks. In general the characters occupy a limbo halfway between real people and extravagant symbols.

As always Durrell's style calls attention to itself emphatically and here too the blessings are mixed. The rank, decaying beauty of the Provençal and Egyptian locales is particularly well served by Durrell's luxurious language, with its lush fertility of image. For example the ménage of Bruce, Sylvie, and Piers blooms for a time in the "quiet parentheses" of Avignon, where the "rogue wind" scatters the "olives into screens of silver-grey, supples out cypresses like fur," and rushes "to explode the spring blossom of almond and plum like a discharge of artillery." Unfortunately Durrell often lets his prose turn tropical; like dense, overgrown foliage (as he might say), it crowds out important events and obscures the characters it should clarify.

The brilliance that Durrell flickeringly displays in *Monsieur* makes its deficiencies all the more regrettable. Admittedly this is a decadent sensibility, forever crying for madder music and stronger wine, owing as much to Norman Douglas and Aldous Huxley as it does to Proust and Joyce. Still, he is an intriguing and erudite decadent; his gargoyle-like characters are distorted in fascinating poses and expressions and the baroque passageways of his plotting take many an ingenious turn.

Rather than settle for the minimal returns of crippled genius, one would like to see Durrell regain the form he displayed in the *Quartet*. At this point the gloomy obsession with death one encounters in *Monsieur* is relevant (an unhappy ending leaves most of the main characters dead, insane, or emotionally bereft). Durrell, at 62, may be experiencing the familiar intimations of mortality that are reflected in the late works of many an author. One hopes, however, that in this case the art does not die before the man.

Avignon at War   Anne Tyler*

Lawrence Durrell refers to his current project of five interconnected novels—of which *Constance* is the third and latest—as a "quincunx." He might more aptly call it the Avignon Quintet. The fact that he has avoided doing so, and thereby forestalled associations with the *Alexandria Quartet*, seems significant.

The Alexandria Quartet is arguably his finest work, and certainly his most popular. With its labyrinthine twists of plot, its unexpected facets catching light from constantly changing angles, it has remained fresh and original for over twenty years. Who wouldn't long to repeat such a feat? The Avignon books, however, rely for their surprises upon trickery. It's the reader who is tricked, and readers are not a forgiving lot.

What we accepted in the first volume, *Monsieur*, was revealed towards its conclusion to be deception—not the interesting kind of deception practiced by true-to-life characters but the self-conscious cerebral deception practiced by a writer pulling strings. It was as if, having created a successful illusion, Durrell could not resist showing how he'd done it. "Ha! Had you fooled, didn't I?" he says.

Livia, the second book, abandoned the pretense of verisimilitude and played throughout with questions of art versus reality. Were we intrigued by references to Pia in *Monsieur*? Well, there is no Pia. "It was cunning of you to make Pia a composite of Constance and Livia," a writer named Sutcliffe says in *Livia*. Sutcliffe is speaking to another writer, Blanford, who wrote a book called *Monsieur*. Blanford, by the way, has embarked upon a cluster of novels he refers to as a quincunx. This is something like those Quaker Oats boxes where the Quaker holds up an oats box that pictures a Quaker holding up an oats box, and so on into infinity.

After the intricate confusions of *Livia*—an annoying, tedious, and insulting book—it's a relief to find that *Constance* returns to a more accepted form of storytelling. Its story is that of Avignon at war—beginning with the last idyllic summer before the Nazi Occupation, ending with the ringing of the bells to signal the return of peace.

Writers still have a disconcerting way of turning up as characters here,

*Reprinted by permission of *The New Republic*, © 1982, The New Republic, Inc.

meeting other writers whom they have invented and who are therefore characters once removed—the characters' characters, so to speak. The reader, like a slapped child, has trouble resuming his trustfulness and believing in what he's told. But it's a straightforward story, nonetheless. Constance, a loyal and kindhearted young woman, loses her new husband to a freak military accident, stays on in Avignon with the Red Cross during the Occupation, and combines her voice with a few others to deliver a sort of tone poem on the atmosphere in France during World War II. These voices give us a sense of the helplessness and despair experienced by the French in the presence of the Germans. They also bear chilling witness to the French complicity in the rounding up of Jews. . . .

There are flaws in *Constance*. One is the occasional lapse of ear. Words or sounds are repeated, as if the author has not thought of aural effect:

> Poor Blanford had even gone so far as to get her a ring—she had allowed it to get to this point.

> Where might they all be now? Dead for all I knew. And the most painful evocation of all, that of Livia.

Even more of a problem is the point of view: one is first grateful for the luxurious variety, then baffled, finally discouraged. "Here in this peaceful decor had walked Goethe and Eckermann of whom [Fischer] had never heard," we are told. If we are solely with Fischer at this moment (and we are), looking through his eyes alone, how do we ourselves know there was a Goethe or an Eckermann? And there's the following, which is a prime example of the difficulties presented to the average weary reader:

> Constance's heart beat faster as she saw that the car, after crossing the bridge, took the curving narrow country roads which led through the foothills towards the villa where once Lord Galen had held court. . . . It had been taken over for the nonce as the General's residence, as well as the senior officers' mess—an arrangement which suited [the General] not at all, and made him feel more than ever slighted by the Party. He felt as if he were a sort of local concierge, for he alone lodged there, but he was forced to eat and drink and fraternise with a crew of senior Waffen S.S. officers. . . .

During the very long passage that ensues, discussing the General's mood in exhaustive detail, we're unable to concentrate fully because we keep wondering whatever happened to Constance. There she was, at the start of the selfsame paragraph, with her heart beating faster. And here's the General—not only a different character but an entirely different side in the war—and Constance appears to have vanished.

Is this to say that the novel fails? No, not completely; for it's hard to imagine any work of Durrell's that is not ringingly evocative, full of character and possibility. There is always a sense of richness in his writing. Textures, smells, and sights tumble forth; he is a master at setting the scene. *Constance* carries enough conviction so that when, toward the end of the war, a woman proposes a trip around the world and a man asks, "What world?" we nod in agreement. We can bear witness to the desolation, the waste, and hopelessness we've so palpably experienced during the course of the story.

This is a troublesome and often exasperating book, but it is above all else a book with a wealth of atmosphere, and in spite of its pretensions that atmosphere comes through with resounding clarity.

Strung Quintet   William Boyd*

> Well, squinting round the curves of futurity I saw something like a quin-
> cunx of novels set out in good classical order. . . . Though only depen-
> dent on one another as echoes might be, they would not be laid end to
> end in serial order, like dominoes—but simply belong to the same blood
> group, five panels for which your creaky old *Monsieur* would provide
> simply a cluster of themes to be reworked in the others. Get busy,
> Robin.

Thus, in a nutshell, the working model for Lawrence Durrell's latest novel sequence, *The Avignon Quintet*, of which *Sebastian* is the fourth to appear. The adumbration above, however, comes from *Livia*, the second. The speaker is Aubrey Blandford, a novelist, and *Monsieur*, the first of the sequence, was purportedly written by Blandford himself. To confuse matters further, Robin—his interlocutor—is another novelist, called Sutcliffe, who is, moreover, a fictional creation of Blandford's. At times, though, it seems that Blandford is as much Sutcliffe's creature as *vice versa*. But, of course we, the readers, know that they dance to Durrell's tune.

This will give you some indication of the complex elisions of points of view that prevail in the quintet, some sense of the tricky conflation of "fact" and "fiction." But to what end, one is entitled to ask? It is hard to construct a cogent response, for Durrell is at his most teasing and whimsical in this quintet, and makes scant efforts to guide the reader through the labyrinth of twists and turns, doublings back, and multiple identities.

"Though only dependent on one another as echoes might be. . . ." This is another vain hope, for it has to be said that anyone coming to *Sebastian* would derive precious little from the book on its own without referring back to the previous three. *Constance* is the immediate precursor, and although this new novel is named after her lover Sebastian—or Affad, to give him his Egyptian name—Constance remains at its center.

The setting is Geneva at the end of World War II. For some reason,

*Reprinted by permission of *The New Republic*, © 1984, The New Republic, Inc.

and very untypically by Durrell's standards, the city remains curiously opaque and unrealized. Much of the evocative power of Durrell's work derives from his distinctive feel for a place, his poet's ability to conjure up atmosphere and ambience, and perhaps the unsatisfactory nature of *Sebastian* is partly explained by the vague sense of locale. In any event Constance and various other characters who have appeared in the previous novels now find themselves in Geneva. Constance is a psychiatrist working in a clinic, concentrating in particular on the case of a schizoid Egyptian called Mnemedis. Sebastian, her lover, has just terminated their passionate affair and Constance repines in his absence, trying to occupy herself with her work.

Sebastian's reasons are somewhat bizarre. He is the member of a secret Gnostic society and his love affair has prompted him to renounce its vows. His apostasy, according to the rules of this sect, carries the sentence of death. Sebastian, however, has a change of heart and hurries to Egypt to renounce his renunciation. But too late. A letter has already been sent to Geneva announcing the date of his death. Sebastian's and the letter's paths cross.

For various baffling metaphysical reasons, none of the other Gnostics can actually tell him of the letter's contents. Frantic messages buzz between Alexandria and Geneva. (Fully re-embracing his bizarre faith, Sebastian is now very keen to die, a clear-eyed acceptance of death being at the center of the Gnostic creed.) Sebastian returns to Geneva. Yes, Constance assures him, I have kept the letter safe, slipped between the leaves of my Bible. And where is the Bible? Oh dear, lent to the madman Mnemedis. Mnemedis promptly escapes from the asylum, dressed as a nun and armed with two lethal carving knives.

Without doubt *Sebastian* is the least successful of the four novels in the sequence so far published, and there are, it seems to me, a number of contributing factors that explain this deficiency. First, the balance of moods is singularly uneasy. The novel skips maladroitly from vein-throbbing, romantic lyricism through turgid pontificating to a kind of high-camp grand-guignol. And when these ungainly tones of voice are combined with the hermetic obscurities of the quincunx form, the uninitiated reader is left very much in the dark. Reading the preceding volumes does admittedly make things somewhat clearer, but behind the (as it were) *ad hoc* difficulties lurks the more general metafictional tricksiness I referred to earlier. Apart from the various levels of fiction (is this Durrell's, Blandford's, or Sutcliffe's novel? Is this Durrell writing a book about a man writing a book about a man writing a book?), the original cast we encountered in *Monsieur* is transmogrified into other characters about and around whom other stories revolve. To take one example: at the end of *Sebastian* Constance meets Sylvie again. Sylvie is mad and is also the eponymous Livia of novel two. Moreover, she believes that Constance has been away in India and when they meet she utters words that echo a paragraph from the opening pages of *Monsieur*, words which she wrote in a letter to her brother Piers. What possible significance can this have? Or is it nothing more than an indication of the "organic" relationship between the novels?

Perhaps it is premature and a little obtuse to seek to understand and make demands of a work still missing its final part, but the interconnections between the novels of the quintet seem of an entirely different order than that of its sibling, *The Alexandria Quartet*. There the multi-layers and time sequences served a valid narrative role, the relativity of viewpoints nicely revealing psychological truths and ambiguities. But in the quincunx, the suspicion emerges that in the web the spider spins here complexity is being indulged in purely for its own sake—clever, glittering, intricate, but without any real strength.

Durrell, doubtless, would see this sort of reaction as typical—given the nationality of this reviewer, typically British. And to some degree his published assessments of his own critical reception in England are just. Durrell's books—raffish, vaguely decadent novels of ideas—don't sit particularly happily within any broad English tradition. His dandiness, his ornate verbal facility, his paraded symbols, and his dallying with esoteric philosophies—all ally him more with the French, with writers like Huysmans, say, or Baudelaire. Twenty-five years ago a reviewer in the *Times Literary Supplement* observed that "Mr. Durrell meets with such praise in France as to raise many a lukewarm eyebrow." Durrell hit back at this classic form of English sneer with a poem entitled "Ode to a lukewarm Eyebrow" in which he reviled the "fog-bound, Thames bedevilled fabulator" and the "cold steamed cod of thy monochromed phrasing."

But times have changed and—declaring an interest—I have never shared the condescending put-downs of *The Alexandria Quartet* and have always admired Durrell's pointed rejection of Little-Englishness and his exuberant internationalism. For all that, however, *Sebastian* takes only a few pages to become bogged down in its own pretentiousness. For example, here Constance is having a chat with a colleague:

> "If we have come to the end of this hubristic *denouement* I can't help as a Jew being deeply proud of the tremendous intellectual achievement of Jewish thought. . . . This Jewish passion for absolutism and matter has already started on the scene like a new Merlin to take up the challenge of the Delphic oracle. . . ."
>
> "Yes," she said. "I am familiar with this line of thought because of . . . Affad. . . . Unhappily we still have a need for heroes. Myths cannot get incarnated and realised fully in the popular soul . . . for reality is just not bearable in its banal daily form, and the human being, however dumb he is, is conscious of the fraud."

There are pages and pages of this sort of unreadable leaden dialogue as Durrell remorselessly compels his characters to thrash out their theories on Gnosticism, entropy, the Primal Trauma of Death, and so on. Grand ideas, admittedly, but hardly the stuff of engaging or compelling fiction, especially when presented in such unadulterated style. Reality, Constance says, is just not bearable in its banal daily form. Durrell, one feels, has similar reservations about reality in the novel, hence the evolution of a complex structure that—ostensibly, ideally—avoids the "banal" linearity of a narrative or chronology. In the discussion from which I quoted earlier, Blandford expounds further upon his idea of a quincunx.

> "The books would all be roped together like climbers on a rock face, but they would all be independent. The relation of the caterpillar to the butterfly, the tadpole to the frog. An organic relation."
>   Sutcliffe groaned and said: "The old danger is there—a work weighed down with theoretical considerations."
>   "No. Never. Not on your life. Just a *roman gigogne*."

Sutcliffe's pragmatism seems the more acute judgment. "*Gigogne*," in my French dictionary, means "nest of tables." I suspect that when we are finally presented with the full set we will applaud Durrell's tireless invention and energy and particularly admire the Blandford/Sutcliffe relationship. Whenever these two are the focus of attention the books come alive, and *Sebastian* suffers from their being too little present. Without them, its tone is either toilingly verbose, romantic-insipid, or simply ludicrous. To pursue the analogy further, in the "nest" the flaws of *Sebastian* might not be so apparent, but, set out on the floor on its own, it appears a distinctly rickety piece of work.

Links and Winks
Barbara Fisher Williamson*

"I want to saturate my text with my teleological distress yet guard its slapstick holiness as something precious," says the fictional novelist who speaks for Lawrence Durrell in *Quinx*, the final volume of his *Avignon Quintet*. What this means in practice is that although all the characters are yearning and searching for some sense of order and meaning in the world, they all frequently talk rubbish and repeatedly fall on their earnest faces. They are serious people continually mocked.

The five linked novels cover the period from just before World War II to just after it. They move from France to Egypt to England to Germany to Switzerland and include a vast and varied cast of characters. In this volume all the characters who have not been killed and who have not lost their reason during the war reunite in Avignon when it is over. They are a remarkable lot—two novelists, a psychoanalyst, a German double agent, a Cambridge-educated gypsy, a Jewish lord, a schizophrenic young woman, and an Egyptian prince.

*Reprinted from *The New York Times Book Review* 15 September 1985, 16. © 1985 by The New York Times Company. Reprinted with permission.

When the plot emerges from the interminable opening religio-literary-sexual-psycho babble of the two novelists, it centers on Constance, the psychoanalyst. In the course of the novel, she uncovers a nasty incest story about her brother and sister, finishes mourning a dead lover, gives up an infatuation with a former patient and finds at last her proper union. Bits of other plots straggle toward completion, and all join in what promises to be an illuminating and redemptive final act—the search for the oft-mentioned treasure of the Templars, a medieval Gnostic order of knights. The treasure is entombed in caves that are sacred to the gypsies and that were mined with baffling ingenuity by the Germans during the war. The caves have the shape of a quincunx, the four points of a square plus a single point at the center, which is considered a "sort of housing for the divine power," and which is also the shape formed by two conjoined human bodies. The shape, like the treasure, is teasingly referred to throughout the novels, but it never reveals its secrets.

Over and over again, patterns dissolve and systems fail. The psychoanalyst betrays professional ethics, a man whose death has been elegantly planned by the members of a death cult he belongs to is senselessly killed, the lovers who achieve mystical union never reproduce, and the novelists create this long joke of a book. The final sentence of the last volume of the quintet makes the whole 1,300-page cycle a shaggy dog story. As the narrator says toward the end, "There is no meaning and we falsify the truth about reality in adding one. *The universe is playing, the universe is only improvising!*" Another, more hilarious work of teleological distress, Rabelais's *Gargantua and Pantagruel*, ends with a similar anticlimax, when the long-sought-after oracle of the holy bottle speaks the single nonsense syllable "trinc." Although the truth never appears, the search is nonetheless worth the effort.

The sensual beauties of Mr. Durrell's text suggest a further similarity with Rabelais. Here, as in his famous *Alexandria Quartet*, Mr. Durrell writes descriptions that can take one's breath away. Avignon, ancient city of kings and popes, comes gloriously alive. The physical pleasures are the only ones that can be counted on in this world of teleological frustration.

The reliance on the physical is apparent in each volume, but the shaggy dog structure of the whole is impossible to detect if one reads only part. What makes the single volumes most perplexing is that the systems the different characters propose to give life meaning—Gnostic religion, Freudian analysis and mystical union through simultaneous orgasm—are described with such conviction and passion that they seem sufficient rather than provisional and flawed. Reading the theories in any one volume alone, one is tempted to think Durrell is silly. Reading them all, one is convinced he is wise.

Essays

Place and Durrell's Island Books

Alan Warren Friedman*

If Lawrence Durrell had written neither fiction nor poetry, he would never have become, as he has, a literary phenomenon; yet for his island books alone he would have his place among contemporary writers. For this richly evocative prose most fully and most successfully exploits Durrell's love of place, a love which, though recapturing a gilded if not golden past, nevertheless manages to avoid slipping into easy sentimentality. Places, as Henry Miller has rightly observed, have affected Durrell "as much or more than people";[1] and the motivating impetus, what is at the heart of all Durrellean imagery and design, is a passion for place that, as in this statement in a recent interview, attaches itself protean-fashion to numerous different objects: "I think the Greek landscape [Durrell is quoted as saying] is absolutely saturated by intimations of the basic type of mind that grew up in it, and in Greece you feel the pagan world is very close. Where I live now, in the South of France, you feel something equally strong—you feel Nostradamus, the Provençal singers, the intense savagery, and a different sort of mysticism. In Dorset, where I was living last year, the Druids were pretty close, I thought."[2]

In a manner apparently deriving from the "pathetic fallacy" of Romantic poetry, Durrell's landscape, usually a Greek one, corresponds to a central idea, emotion, or motif. Setting—for Durrell generally closer to a localized version of Yeats's *Spiritus Mundi* (or *Deus Loci* as Durrell calls it in the poem of that name) than to Wordsworth's "Nature"—embodies, parallels, even motivates both the intrinsic and extrinsic workings of Durrellean characters. Thus their individuality seems often suffused, subordinated to Durrell's equivalent of Wordsworth's pantheistic deity—as, on the largest scale, the various characters of the *Quartet* are dominated by Alexandria: "Only the city is real."

Prospero's Cell,[3] like Gerald Durrell's *My Family and Other Animals*, treats the years the Durrell family spent on Corfu; yet the two books are vastly dissimilar. Gerald Durrell, a child of ten when the family arrived on the island, writes mainly of his entymological escapades and of their ef-

*Reprinted from *Modern Fiction Studies* 13, no. 3 (Autumn 1967):329–41. © by Purdue Research Foundation. Reprinted with permission.

59

fects—usually disastrous—on the rest of the Durrells. *Prospero's Cell*, on the other hand, makes scarcely any reference to the Durrell family—only Nancy (N.), Durrell's first wife, is at all important, and she does not appear in *My Family*—and, rather than focusing on one small corner of the island, takes a view of this Greek world in miniature that is broad spatially and temporally.

Much more than a travel book, *Prospero's Cell* is a conglomeration of literary genres. Much of it takes the form of an artist's journal covering the period from April 10, 1937, to January 1, 1941; yet the book's spontaneity is achieved only with time and distance, for Durrell did not write it until several years later in Alexandria.[4] Something of a history, the book contains chapters with such titles as "The Island Saint" and "History and Conjecture," as well as a synoptic chronology, a brief bibliography, and a sketchy index. For the traveller, it contains vivid descriptions of the island and its people, and a useful appendix which includes, among other items, "Some Peasant Remedies in Common Use against Disease." And, finally, as its date and place of composition suggest, *Prospero's Cell* is a product of the creative imagination, a re-creation rather than simply a remembering. Its narrator (not simply Durrell, but Durrell as interpreted by Durrell) rejects the maps, tables, and statistics offered for inclusion by a helpful friend: "If I wrote a book about Corcyra," he says, "it would not be a history but a poem."[5]

Prospero's Cell, in Lawrence Clark Powell's words, "is a Mediterranean prose-poem to rank with *Fountains in the Sand, Sea and Sardinia*, and *The Colossus of Maroussi*."[6] Like its successors, Durrell's first island book employs many of fiction's techniques. For, in ways typical of his novels, Durrell here creates characters indeterminate and variable, yet of imposing stature ("It is a sophism to imagine that there is any strict dividing line between the waking world and the world of dreams. N. and I, for example, are confused by the sense of several contemporaneous lives being lived inside us; the sensation of being mere points of reference for space and time," and, "We are lucky in our friends. Two of them seem of almost mythological quality . . ." [*Cell*, pp. 11–12, 14]; an aesthetic conflict concerning the various possibilities of interpreting and re-ordering reality ("here we are," says the Count, the character of greatest and freest imagination, "each of us collecting and arranging our common knowledge according to the form dictated to him by his temperament. In all cases it will not be the whole picture, though it will be the whole picture for you." [*Cell*, p. 107]),[7] a setting vast, pervasive, and alive ("Zarian gives a discourse on landscape as a form of metaphysics. 'The divine Plato said once that in Greece you see God with his compasses and dividers,' " and, "Nowhere else has there ever been a landscape so aware of itself, conforming so marvellously to the dimensions of a human existence." [*Cell*, pp. 15, 131]); and, perhaps most interestingly, an "Epilogue in Alexandria" (where, after all, the book was written), offering the same kind of perspective shift as the Workpoints appended to the *Quartet* novels.

Durrell's intense awareness of place imposes a kind of unity on his otherwise disparate material—for he mixes his semi-literary journal with humorous anecdotes, aesthetic-philosophic discussions and meditations, more or less scholarly essays on selected aspects of the island, and the various apparatus already indicated. And the landscape and the atmosphere serve as touchstones, as controlling metaphors, for Durrell not only writes of them with often lyric intensity, but he raises them—in a manner anticipating the Alexandria of the *Quartet*—to mythopoeic significance. "Other countries," he writes early in the book, "may offer you discoveries in manners or love or landscape: Greece offers you something harder—the discovery of yourself" (*Cell*, p. 11). And because this has been true for Durrell, and because on Corfu the writing has gone well and life has been good, the "Epilogue in Alexandria" reads like the saddest of endings: the disillusionment following the loss of innocence. "In these summer twilights the city [Alexandria] lies in its jumble of pastel tones, faintly veined like an exhausted petal. . . . The last landmark on the edge of Africa. The battleships in their arrowed blackness turn slowly in the harbour. The loss of Greece has been an amputation. All Epictetus could not console one against it" (*Cell*, p. 131).

For with the coming of the war and the loss of Greece has followed the demise of love: "There is simply patience to be exercised. Patience and endurance and love. Some of us have vanished from the picture; some have had their love converted into black bile by the misery they have witnessed" (*Cell*, p. 132). And the final words of the book suggest the profundity of despair now gripping the world and its artists. "Seen through the transforming lens of memory," a deracinated Durrell writes, "the past seemed so enchanted that even thought would be unworthy of it. We never speak of it, having escaped: the house in ruins, the little black cutter smashed. I think only that the shrine with the three black cypresses and the tiny rockpool where we bathed must still be left. Visited by the lowland summer mists the trembling landscape must still lie throughout the long afternoons, glowing and altering like a Chinese water-colour where the light of the sky leaks in. But can all these hastily written pages ever recreate more than a fraction of it?" (*Cell*, p. 133).

The answer apparently is "no"—at least for Durrell the man, and his sense of inadequacy and hopeless frustration manifests itself in the failure of his marriage in Egypt during the war. As for Durrell the artist, he has succeeded perhaps better than he believes, for *Prospero's Cell* is a richly evocative book, with its many well-portrayed incidents and characters serving as a check on the tendency towards vagueness and abstraction. The inaction of the book, though an accurate reflection of the langorousness of pre-war Greece, is something of a weakness—perhaps the main one of the book. But such self-indulgence, though Durrell still gives way to it at times, becomes rarer in his more mature writings. A pattern emerges in the island books: from casual, pre-war Corfu Durrell shifts to the post-war Rhodes—with its desperate need of immediate action—of *Reflections on a Marine Venus*,[8] and then to the incipient civil-war Cypriot atmosphere of the tense and compelling *Bitter Lemons*.[9]

If being cast out of Corfu represents a fall from innocence for Durrell and his Greek world, then the re-entry into Rhodes is an attempt at lifting the guilt that has descended. Or, to shift the metaphor to the one central to *Reflections on a Marine Venus* and to much of his other writings, Durrell seeks a cure for the spiritual diseases plaguing virtually all his characters— here made manifest by the war and its after-effects. The narrator of *Marine Venus* writes of a people and a world ravaged by sickness and death, and he returns to his beloved Greece with great trepidation, as if going to visit an old, ailing friend who, he fears, may already be dead by the time he arrives. As he prepares to leave Alexandria "that spring afternoon of 1945," he thinks: "Tomorrow I should see for myself whether the old Greek ambience had survived the war, whether it was still a reality based in the landscape and the people—or whether we had simply invented it for ourselves in the old days, living comfortably on foreign exchange, patronising reality with our fancies and making bad literature from them" (*Venus*, pp. 16–17).

Durrell's own "disease" is "islomania," an ailment "as yet unclassified by medical science. . . . A rare but by no means unknown affliction of spirit," it causes its victims to "find islands somehow irresistible." And *Reflections on a Marine Venus*, Durrell adds, "is by intention a sort of anatomy of islomania" (*Venus*, pp. 15–16)—that is, in effect, an examination of the complex interrelationship of stricken moth and compelling flame. For again Durrell does not offer simply a descriptive survey of his island, but rather a probing which is at once revelatory and exploratory, at once therapeutic and self-analytic, at once a finished work of art and one prematurely made public with the skeleton of its scaffolding still lying about.

The technique is one of planned formlessness, a deploying of the many pieces comprising the Rhodian mosaic, rather than a straight-forward guide to the island or a continuous narrative of events occurring there. "If I have sacrificed form," Durrell writes in terms anticipating his technical concerns in the *Quartet*, "it is for something better, sifting into the material now some old notes from a forgotten scrapbook, now a letter: all the quotidian stuff which might give a common reader the feeling of life lived in a historic present" (*Venus*, p. 16). Like the Count in *Prospero's Cell*, Mills, an Englishman wholly a creature of Mediterranean Greece, tells Durrell the kind of portrait of the island he should write: "Not history or myth—but landscape and atmosphere somehow. 'A companion' is the sort of idea. You ought to try for the landscape—and even these queer months of transition from desolation to normality" (*Venus*, p. 36).

Mills himself aids greatly in this transition for, like Fonvisin in *Panic*

Spring, an early Durrell novel, and Balthazar and Amaril in the *Quartet*, he is a doctor not only endowed with remarkable curative power, but one who actually personifies soundness of body and mind. "It would be difficult," Durrell remarks of Mills, "to think of anyone who seemed to be such a walking certificate for good health; it simply oozed from him, from his candid face, fresh complexion, sensitive fingers" (*Venus*, p. 34). In fact, Mills, like most exceptionally healthy people, takes illness as something of an affront, a misdeed perpetrated by the patient simply, or at least primarily, to get attention.

In his Introduction to Georg Groddeck's *Book of the It*, Durrell notes that Groddeck conceived of a man's physical condition (that uneasy mean between the two abstract extremes of total health and total illness) as the outward manifestation of the internal man. Thus disease and illness are seen as expressions of a man's personal identity. To someone not totally committed to accepting his theory, Groddeck seems at times to carry it to absurd lengths—for instance, in asking an injured patient, "What was your idea in breaking your arm?"[10] Still, much of what Groddeck says can be accepted—we do, for example, tend to associate certain diseases with certain people, and see an appropriateness in *that* person's having *that* malady—especially with regard to the infirmities of literary characters. The blinding of Oedipus or of Gloucester, for instance, is clearly an objective correlative for spiritual blindness; the impotence of Jake Barnes or of Clifford Chatterley tells us something of the spiritual crippling caused by modern war and its aftermath, on the one hand, and by de-humanized technology on the other. Disease or injury strikes, at one time or another, virtually every important character in Durrell's *Quartet*, and it invariably symbolizes some major aspect of the personality it strikes.

This relationship of disease and personality has little place in Durrell's earliest writings, although there are hints of it in *The Black Book* and *The Dark Labyrinth*. In *Marine Venus*, however, Mills serves to focus Durrell's increasing interest in the subject; and he is written of in terms anticipating the subsequent involvement with Groddeck. "His diagnosis of disease," Durrell notes, "seemed somehow to be a criticism, not of the functioning of one specific organ, but of the whole man. Like all born healers he had realized, without formulating the idea, that disease has its roots in a faulty metaphysic, in a way of life. And the patient who took him a cyst to lance or a wheezing lung to think about, was always disturbed by the deliberate careful scrutiny of those clear blue eyes. One felt slightly ashamed of being ill in the presence of Mills. It was as if, staring at you as you stood there, he were waiting for you to justify your illness, to deliver yourself in some way of the hidden causes of it" (*Venus*, p. 35).

Durrell's own disease, islomania, though it is not fatal, remains nonetheless uncured. In the Epilogue to his second island book he associates it with the permanent "wound" (obviously a consequence of love) he has received from his "Marine Venus." Durrell not only rediscovers the ambi-

ence of pre-war Greece, but he helps to resuscitate it during his stay on
Rhodes—both in his work while on the island and in this book—for he correctly notes that, "by this writing," all his friends and all they have experienced on Rhodes are made forever a part "of this small green island" and
of "the greater arc" which is all of Greece (*Venus*, pp. 183–184). But though
Durrell in his work and in his art contributes to the rebuilding of a world
and a way of life, he once again fails at love—and in the Epilogue he is
once more alone with the child, with E. (Eve), his second wife, no longer
"a familiar, a critic, a lover" (*Venus*, p. 16).

The poignancy of Eve's loss, however, is far less intense than that of
Nancy in *Prospero's Cell*, since the former receives scant treatment as a
character. *Marine Venus*, like its predecessor, is richly evocative, containing several fine characterizations (especially Mills) and much good talk; but
it represents something of a falling off, for it lacks the subjective immediacy
of the first island book. The art is present, but not so artlessly deployed,
and we get only intermittent glimpses of the artist's attempting to come to
grips with the virtually intractable materials of both the creative process
and his life, of both art and love. As a consequence, where *Prospero's Cell*
seems of the very essence of Corfu (and of Durrell's persistent attempt to
understand that essence in terms of himself), *Marine Venus*, though like all
of Durrell's prose it contains vivid description and fine insights, is not so
much *of* Rhodes as simply *about* it.

The last of Durrell's island books is by far his best, for it has all the
virtues of the earlier ones and none of their failings—plus the fortuitous
advantage of a significant plot. *Bitter Lemons* (originally *Bitter Lemons of
Cyprus*) not only captures an atmosphere and a tone, a way of life and a
people, but it details and examines the destruction of the Cypriot peace
that culminates in the disastrous outbreak of civil war. The sense of place,
then, is brilliantly and appropriately subordinated to the sense of the
moment.

The book's apparatus is minimal (index, brief bibliography, and a poem
entitled "Bitter Lemons"), for against the vibrancy of the here and the now,
the intensity of the narrative, especially as Durrell counterpoints it against
the usual Cypriot languor, additional trappings would be distractingly su-
perfluous. For the same reason, the various concerns of Durrell as artist
and as man seem almost incidental, irrelevant impediments to this monolithic flux, and are thus infrequent. And yet, simultaneously, *Bitter Lemons*
is perhaps Durrell's most profoundly personal work, for it concerns nothing
if not his physical and spiritual return to the Greek world, his own quest
for the warmth denied him during a chilling half decade in Yugoslavia.

Durrell arrives on Cyprus alone and alien, almost unable to believe in
the continuing reality of the Greek world: "After five years of Serbia," he
writes, "I had begun to doubt whether, in wanting to live in the Mediterranean at all, I was not guilty of some fearful aberration; indeed the whole of
this adventure had begun to smell of improbability" (*BL*, p. 16). But after

the initial moments of strangeness, the improbable once again becomes the familiar:

A vague and spiritless lethargy reigned. I was beginning to think that successive occupations had extirpated any trace whatsoever of the Greek genius when I was relieved by the sight of a bus with both back wheels missing, lying on its side against a house. It was just like home. Three old ladies were dismembering the conductor; the driver was doing one of those laughing and shrugging acts which drive travellers out of their minds all over the Levant; the village idiot was pumping up a tyre; the owners of the house against which the bus was leaning were hanging indignantly out of their drawing-room window and, with their heads inside the bus, were being rude to the point of nausea. Meanwhile, a trifle removed from the centre of the hubbub, and seated perilously on the leaning roof of the machine, with contorted face, perched an individual in a cloth cap who appeared to be remorselessly sawing the bus in half, starting at the top. Was this perhaps some obscure revenge, or a genuine attempt to make a helpful contribution? I shall never know. (BL, pp. 22–23)

And within a week of his arrival, Durrell soon adds, "I had a dozen firm friends . . ." (BL, p. 29).

Yet re-integration, like the too-quick urbanizing of the somnolent agrarian landscape of Cyprus, is an uncomfortable bifurcating process, for the ubiquitous slogan, "ENOSIS AND ONLY ENOSIS," insistently reminds everyone on the island of the increasing intrusion of public affairs on what should normally be private intercourse. "This wonder of an Englishman who spoke indifferent but comprehensible Greek" (BL, p. 23), Durrell is readily accepted by the people he meets, and the Cypriots clamoring for their "freedom" from the British continue to proclaim their love for all the English, and especially for individual Englishmen like Durrell. Yet hatred ultimately proliferates beyond control and into impersonality, even to the point where Durrell himself is almost killed.

Actually, however, Durrell is not so much a passive victim of events as he would have us believe, for, though he attempts to dissociate himself from his compatriots, he becomes increasingly involved in the larger affairs of the island, thus automatically becoming a target for Cypriot anger and frustration. His original plan was to devote himself entirely to his own writing (and he does manage to write *Justine* while on Cyprus), but his funds dwindle and he accepts a commission "to write a series of articles on the issue [enosis] for an American Institute of International Relations bulletin" (BL, p. 121). Then he takes a job teaching English at the Nicosia Gymnasium where, as elsewhere, his British manner contrasts with Greek vivacity: "To achieve silence was impossible—a soft but persistent susurrus like a slow puncture was the nearest one could get to this—and the normal was a growling wave of chatter which rose and fell like a sea. I tried, as an experiment, sending talkers out of the room one by one, in order to see at

what stage the class became controllable. I was left at last with three students. As no corporal punishment was permitted in the school it was impossible to do more than gesticulate, foam, dance and threaten . . ." (*BL*,
p. 129).

Yet neither Durrell's essential Britishness nor his occasional condescension of tone when writing of the local inhabitants conceals his expan-
sive Philhellenism and an extroversion which overcomes many potential
barriers to friendship. Both in his tiny village of Bellapaix—where, with the
help of seemingly all the local characters, he boisterously buys and revamps
a small house—and at the school, Durrell establishes a contact of the most
significant kind with the people about him, a contact whose permanency
appears beyond question—until the acid of nationalism and terror begins
to eat away all human bonds, and the air of even the most natural of moments becomes increasingly filled with the poison of political emotionalism.
For instance, Durrell offhandedly writes of his female students that "they
were uncomfortably united in one thing, besides Enosis, and that was a
passionate, heart-rending determination to marry their English teacher"
(*BL*, p. 130). And the dualism of thought and purpose that gradually over-
whelms the island enters the school and its students: "In these classes . . .
I encountered the same shifting wind of popular opinion which hovered between anti-British intransigence and the old ineradicable affection for the
mythical Briton (the 'Phileleftheros') the freedom-lover, who could not help
but approve of Enosis as an idea" (*BL*, p. 133).

But the British make little attempt to live up to such an image, and
the youths of the island succumb invariably to hatred—for the cause is not
only just in the main, it is pervasive, intense, monolithic. And only a few
months later, Durrell, inspecting a prison containing terrorists, comes
upon two ex-students of his: Joanides, a "fat ruffian . . . , a natural come-
dian of such talent that I had been forced to expel him at the beginning of
almost every lesson," who was arrested for carrying a grenade—" 'Ach! Mr.
Durrell,' he said, 'it was just a *little* bomb . . .' "; and Paul, ashamed because he had shown "cowardice" in failing to bomb a house where small
children were playing. Durrell's comment reveals the depths of his insight
into the inner conflict of the islanders, and his hopelessness as well:

> Superb egotism of youth! He had been worried about his own inabil-
> ity to obey orders. It is, of course, not easy for youths raised in a Chris-
> tian society, to turn themselves into terrorists overnight—and in a sense
> his problem was the problem of all the Cypriot Greeks. . . . 'So you are
> sorry because you didn't kill two children?' I said. 'What a twisted brain,
> what a twisted stick you must be as well as a fool!' He winced and his
> eyes flashed. 'War is war,' he said. I left him without another word. (*BL*,
> pp. 199–201)

But Durrell does endeavor to bridge the widening chasm, for he accepts the position of Press Adviser to the British Government—a job he
held for years elsewhere—and attempts to establish communication be-

tween the conflicting nationalities. Intellectually, he is himself guilty of colonial myopia, and he sympathizes with the British rulers, who "lived by
the central colonial proposition which, as a conservative I fully understand,
namely: 'If you have an Empire, you just can't give away bits of it as soon
as asked.' I differed with them only in believing that in Cyprus we had an
issue which could be honourably compounded. . ." (*BL*, pp. 158–159). Yet
Durrell here underestimates his emotional commitment to the Cypriot
character and cause, and he over-estimates his capacity for self-blindness;
he is, on the contrary, one of the few Englishmen to recognize relatively
early in the crisis that EOKA's appeal was island-wide, that the potential
blow-up threatened not only domestic tranquility but the whole structure
of international relationships, and that to oppose vast force to the first tentative acts of terrorism would not only fail to cow the insurrectionists, it
would win them hordes of new recruits.

Durrell saw, too, that what failed for the British perhaps above all was
their sense of timing. For one thing, as Durrell learns as soon as he begins
his work for the government, the British totally lack a Cypriot policy, with
the impossible exception of maintaining the status quo at all costs. Policy
subsequently develops only as feeble reaction to mounting pressures: a
vague constitution plus partial censorship in response to a demand not for
immediate and total independence, but merely for a promise of elections
in the indeterminate future; a belated conference of the involved powers,
doomed to failure because, during the period of British ostrich-hiding, the
originally quiescent Turks had gradually developed a no-compromise posture; and, too late to do any good, a new governor, one not inherently confused and incapable of seeing that the Cyprus problem was more European
and international than colonial—" 'Why,' said my friend, and this was to
become an echo everywhere (even repeated by Makarios), 'did they not
send us such a man a long time ago?' Why indeed!" Durrell is constrained
to add (*BL*, p. 210).

On a different level, one perhaps of greater significance for the immediate purposes of this study, *Bitter Lemons* treats its subject in terms of
literature, of an aesthetic. For one thing, in retrospect at least, Durrell recognizes the artistic unity of his writings on Corfu, Rhodes, and Cyprus: *Bitter Lemons*, he notes, "completes a trilogy of island books" (*BL*, p. 9).
Beauty of landscape and natural setting, and Durrell's ability to recreate it
in a stroke, intensify progressively from book to book, from island to island:

> The dawns and the sunsets in Cyprus are unforgettable—better even
> than those of Rhodes which I always believed were unique in their slow
> Tiberian magnificence. As I breasted the last rise where the road falls
> like a swallow towards Kyrenia I paused for a minute to watch the sun
> burst through the surface mists of the sea and splash the mountain be-
> hind me with light. . . . I would start to climb the range, the sun climb-
> ing with me, balcony by balcony, ridge by ridge; until as I breasted the
> last loop of the pass the whole Mesaoria would spread out under the soft

buttery dawn-light, languid and green as a lover's wish; or else shimmer through a cobweb of mist like the mirage of a Chinese water-print. (*BL*, pp. 126–127)

But such passages of pure description become increasingly rare in *Bitter Lemons*, for what proves to be an overwhelming rush of events pre-empts both the time and the vision; and if Cyprus prior to the outbreak of hostilities embodies art and beauty—in its landscape, its people, its ambience— then that tranquil perfection is desecrated by the philistinism of shortsightedness and hatred.

And the drama that takes place—the senseless tragedy most tragic in that, Durrell insists, "it need not have happened" (*BL*, p. 128)—assumes qualities and dimensions of classic proportions: the tragic blindness of the British; the wholesale wastage of property, lives, and a wonderfully vital way of life—perhaps best emblematized by the Cypriot youths, jailed as terrorists, who incongruously complain most about "the crowded conditions [that] prevented them from studying for their examinations" (*BL*, p. 201); the obscenity of terror that smashes "the slender chain of trust upon which all human relations are based" (*BL*, p. 215); and the hopeless, hollow despair that expresses the pity felt for both self and others—"I was, I realized, very tired after this two years' spell as a servant of the Crown; and I had achieved nothing. It was good to be leaving. . . . I felt bitterly ashamed of the neglect these people had endured—the poor Cyps" (*BL*, pp. 246, 250).

But the drama lacks catharsis, the purgative cleansing which permits a stable, if mundane, moral order at last to reassert itself. Cyprus, the place, remains, but with the deaths of trust and Anglo-Greek amity what hope can arise for the future? Durrell can find none: "the mythopoeic image of the Englishman which every Greek carried in his heart, and which was composed of so many fused and overlapping pictures—the poet, the lord, the quixotic and fearless defender of right, the just and freedom-loving Englishman—the image was at last thrown down and dashed into a thousand pieces, never again to be reassembled" (*BL*, p. 242).

In the book's final episode, Durrell spends a day in the Cypriot hills with Panos, his oldest friend on the island. Except for the occasional appearance of troops, the day is idyllic: they picnic, they gather great bunches of wild flowers that fill the car, Durrell even abandons himself for a time to the cold calmness of the lagoon waters, and he makes perhaps his finest poetic image of the book: "A lizard lay asleep on the bamboo couch [in the hut by the water] looking like a Greek politician waiting for an opening" (*BL*, p. 236). But the effectiveness of the image is not in its abstract cleverness, but rather in its felt reality, in the unhappy fact of its appropriateness—at least from the British and Turkish viewpoints. The episode, then, is merely a lull, a brief respite between explosions, for Durrell has already announced his imminent departure from the island and that Panos, presumably because of his intimacy with the British Durrell, was shot dead two days after their final outing. Durrell's final gesture, the discarding of all his daughter's mementos of Cyprus, is melodramatic, but not inappropriate.

It would seem that Durrell has come full circle. *Prospero's Cell* began with an epigraph from *The Tempest*: " 'No tongue: all eyes: be silent' " (p. 11), and after *Bitter Lemons* only silence is possible. The Cypriot-Greeks had mythologized the mainlanders, seeing them as "those paragons of democratic virtue. Their idea of Greece is of Paradise on earth—a paradise without defect" (*BL*, pp. 114–115). The Greeks had envisaged a mythical Briton whose ideals were always noble, and whose actions always effected those ideals. And Durrell, for all his Britishness, had romanticized his Greek islanders and their home into embodiments of hospitality, vibrancy, vitality. Now the images, and the half-truths they depict, are shattered—not only on Cyprus and elsewhere, but within Durrell himself, who, in a revealing volte-face, several times expresses a fear that Cyprus might be invaded from, of all places, Rhodes or Crete. Now only the other half of truth—with its ugly mask of brutality, stupidity, bitterness, and despair—is all that remains. These forces have been a powerful antidote, for they have finally cured Durrell of his deep-rooted islomania. But the cure, of course, is worse than the disease, for no one but Durrell has been writing books of this kind and quality in English in recent years, and it seems virtually certain that he himself will write them no more. Thus, the price we pay for *The Alexandria Quartet* and whatever fiction is to follow is very large indeed.

In the final analysis, Durrell's Greece functions as complexly in his island books as it does in much of his poetry, and as Alexandria does in the *Quartet*: as a pervasive motif and atmosphere, as a metaphorical control, and as a concrete manifestation of his often shadowy figures. Greece, and all that it includes as both concept and place, offers a kind of comforting unity, a sense of rootedness in a vast historical context, that for the most part enables the implied poet of these works to look beyond not only good and evil, but also the optimism or pessimism one might logically expect to arise, and into the underlying aesthetic of events. Thus, Durrell the man despairs over Corcyrean loss, Rhodian desecration, Cypriot anarchy, but as an artist he suffers far more for the larger significance of these events: the violation of the True and the Beautiful. Yet here is the great consolation, for to violate a pattern is of course to imply it, and it is the permanence and strength of Durrell's Greek pattern, not the good or evil of daily events, that undergirds and inspirits his island books and transports them from the transient province of travel reportage and into the unaging realm of vision become art.

Notes

1. Henry Miller to Lawrence Durrell, in *Art and Outrage, A Correspondence about Henry Miller*, by Alfred Perlès, Lawrence Durrell, and Henry Miller (London, 1959), p. 33.

2. Kenneth Young, "A Dialogue with Durrell," *Encounter*, 13, 6 (December 1959), pp. 66–67.

3. Lawrence Durrell, *Prospero's Cell: A Guide to the Landscape and Manners of the Island of Corcyra* (New York, 1962). Hereafter cited in the text as *Cell*.

4. In a Spring 1944 letter, he says, "I've done about half of a little historical book about Corfu; tried writing in the style of a diary—you know the French anecdotal novel type of things" (*Lawrence Durrell and Henry Miller: A Private Correspondence*, ed. George Wickes [New York, 1964], p. 188).

5. As his next entry in his "journal," the narrator offers "Fragment from a novel about Corcyra which I began and destroyed [we are not told why]: 'She comes down through the cloud of almond-trees like a sentence of death, all dressed in white and leading her flock to the very gates of the underworld. Our hearts melt in us at the candour of her smile and the beauty of her walk. Soon she is to marry Niko, the fat moneylender, and become a stout shrew drudging out to olive-pickings on a lame donkey, smelling of garlic and animal droppings' " (*Cell*, pp. 20–21).

6. Introductory Note to *A Landmark Gone*, p. i. This pamphlet, privately printed for Powell, is a kind of precis, often word for word, of *Prospero's Cell*.

7. On the same page, the Count is asked to describe the kind of book the narrator *will* write of Corfu. " 'It is difficult to say,' says the Count. 'A portrait inexact in detail, containing bright splinters of landscape, written out roughly, as if to get rid of something which was troubling the optic nerves.' " A comment which could serve as an accurate blurb for *Prospero's Cell*—and much of Durrell's other writings as well.

8. Lawrence Durrell, *Reflections on a Marine Venus: A Companion to the Landscape of Rhodes* (New York, 1962). Hereafter cited in the text as *Venus*.

9. Lawrence Durrell, *Bitter Lemons* (New York, 1957). Hereafter cited in the text as *BL*.

10. Quoted by Durrell, Introduction to *The Book of the It* (New York, 1961), p. viii.

Verse Dramas   G. S. Fraser*

1

Durrell has written three verse plays, in order of composition though not of publication *Sappho, Acte,* and *An Irish Faustus*. The first is set in Lesbos, about 650 B.C., the second in Scythia and Neronian Rome, the third in a Yeatsian medieval Ireland. The language of the first is ornate and lyrical and the play is too long for performance except in a cut version. *Acte* is a much shorter play and its language, by contrast, seems deliberately harsh and abrupt, as if someone had told Durrell that plot and character are what matter in a play and that *Sappho* is too much taken up with the

*Reprinted by permission of Faber and Faber Ltd. from *Lawrence Durrell: A Study*.

lyrical expression of mood. The plot, about a Scythian captive princess and her love for a Roman general, is a grimmer one, and verges often on melodrama. The third play, *An Irish Faustus*, is, by contrast, though it pursues a dark theme as well as a comic one, serene. There is plenty of folk humour. Faustus, in the end, is playing cards in a log hut in the mountains with an old hermit, who is going to die and pass on to Faustus his final wisdom, with a rascally Pardoner, and with Mephisto, whom Faustus has earlier thwarted and tamed, destroying a gold ring created by black magic rather than use it. This Faustus is a white magician, who seeks not power but a kind of Taoist harmony with the rhythms of the universe, a harmony which is finally achieved when one learns to do nothing.

A preoccupation with a kind of repose, or quietism, as the culmination of human wisdom is central to Durrell's philosophy of life: "calm of mind, all passion spent." And some critics might feel that this is an unfortunate preoccupation for a dramatist. Drama depends on tension, and all Durrell's impulses work towards the loosening rather than the heightening of tension. Lionel Trilling notes that as a novelist Durrell seems, unlike D. H. Lawrence, for instance, whom he so much admires, not to be anxious to impose his own moral will on the reader, and in fact direct clashes of will in his fiction are rather rare. He is more interested in what people are than in what they do, and, in *Sappho*, for instance, human choice plays a very small part in working out the catastrophe, and what we remember is less the action than the penetrating discussions of why action is both inevitable and a mistake. *Acte* is a play full of violence and cruelty, with a vivid picture of the at once horrible and pathetically childlike Nero, but again what one remembers is the philosophical Petronius and his calm ruminations on his own death, and the need to accept death. *Acte* was written for the stage, and was performed in Hamburg in German translation. Working with the actors, and bearing the needs of a translator in mind, Durrell sacrificed the richness of language that characterizes *Sappho*, achieving bareness and directness and concision at the cost of a certain abruptness and baldness. The verse of this play, indeed, seems sometimes verse only by courtesy of the typesetter, as in this flat scene-ending:

> FLAVIA: I do not understand you, Uncle.
> PETRONIUS: No. It is badly expressed. Kiss me and go to bed, now.
> It is late and I am weary.

I find in these lines no scannable metre, and no rhythm other than that of very limp prose; I suppose it could be claimed that the limpness of the language mirrors that of Flavia's and Petronius's feelings.

I like *Acte* least of Durrell's three plays, and *An Irish Faustus* most. Durrell manages to create a new type of Faustus, not proud and damned like Marlowe's, not a restless, bustling modern like Goethe's, but simple, wise, affectionate, childlike and benign. He turns traditionally terrifying characters to woodcut figures in a chapbook, eternally and harmlessly playing cards. The rhythm of the play moves towards unfrightening us, to turning diabolical revelation into a winter's tale. It achieves homeliness.

2

Sappho was completed in Rhodes in 1947, published in 1950, but though broadcast on the Third Programme, and in 1959 staged in Hamburg in German, was not publicly produced in English till 1961, at the Edinburgh Festival. The post-war vogue for the verse play had by that time died down and like other Edinburgh Festival verse dramatists, Jonathan Griffin and Sidney Goodsir Smith, Durrell got a cool reception. He had written the play, he notes in a postscript, with the object of "marrying up pace, plot and poetry." He had not realized that the play was too long for practical acting purposes, and he recommends the excision of one rather interesting character, the drunken humorous poet Diomedes, in an early scene in the play and of a whole later scene in which Diomedes is consoled by Sappho as he dies, wretched because his son has been killed as a coward in mainland fighting, and because he lusts after the girl whom his son wished to marry. Durrell is wrong, simply by page-count, in assuming that these excisions alone would cut the script by a third.

Sappho, in this play, is the wife of an older man, Kreon, who rescued her from the earthquake which flooded the part of the town in which he was a merchant, and had her educated by a tutor called Minos. She is already famous as a poet, but bored, discontented, at a loose end. Her husband condones her occasional love affairs. She plays an important part in the religious life of Lesbos, wearing a golden mask, and, under the influence of drugs, speaking for the local oracle; but on one occasion she has omitted to take the drugs, and has herself invented an oracular message, advising the local hero, Pittakos, to go to war on the mainland, against Athens, largely because Pittakos is boring her and she wants him out of the way. In the war against Athens, he is being victorious, and will come home determined to abolish democracy and set himself up as the tyrant of a new Empire. Pittakos has a brother, Phaon, who for seven years has lived alone on a small island and who has taken a job as a diver for Kreon, who is anxious to recover from his sunken counting house tablets that will give him title to much of the land of Lesbos.

Phaon appears at first churlish and abrupt, but is persuaded to attend one of Sappho's poetry evenings, in which poets compete in impromptu composition and recitation (Sappho herself is handicapped in these competitions by her slight stammer). As often happens, at poetry evenings, one poet, Diomedes, is very drunk and therefore the evening is rather a shambles but, left alone together, Sappho and Phaon talk about the peace and withdrawal which Sappho seeks and Phaon has found and become lovers, though both protesting that love is not the reality they are seeking for. The aged Kreon finds them together, but is tolerant.

Pittakos comes back on the evening of a night in which Sappho must act the oracle. He is pleased with his military success, but, aware that he is no politician, asks his brother Phaon to act as his political agent on the mainland. Phaon, however, is determined to return to the peace of his small island. He has managed to retrieve, while diving, a bundle of tablets from Kreon's counting house; one of these suggested to Kreon the awful possibility that Sappho, the young girl he rescued from the earthquake, brought up, and later married, may be his own daughter by a wife he had left behind him in Egypt. Kreon consults the oracle which tells him that by law he is condemned, his property forfeited, and he is to be either killed or exiled, with his family, according to popular vote. Pittakos, now chosen tyrant, sends the now sick and dying Kreon into exile, but sends Sappho, as he had wished to send Phaon, to be his political agent in Corinth, a great mainland power whose alliance he needs.

Pittakos keeps Sappho's children as hostages. Many years pass and Pittakos's empire, his circle of alliances, increases in strength; but one of Sappho's children is killed in a hunting accident, while riding with Pittakos, and Sappho uses all her skill and cunning to join Corinth and the other mainland powers in an alliance against him. Finally he is tracked down and killed on his brother Phaon's lonely island, where he has sought refuge: betrayed by the last soldier he thought loyal to him. Back on Lesbos, Sappho, old and bitter, finds the news of this revenge dust and ashes. She embraces her surviving child, the daughter Kleis:

> Weep, little Kleis. You shall weep for both of us,
> For the whole world if you have tears enough,
> And for yourself long after you imagine
> There are no tears in the world to weep with.
>
> Then perhaps you may be blessed, only perhaps.
> Out of its murderous armament time
> May select a single grace for you to live by:
> But that we dare not hope for yet: weep, child,
> Weep, Weep, Weep.

These lines, with their fluid eloquence, suggest the general quality of the diction of the play, lyrical and asking to be spoken with a certain heightening of intonation and rhythmical sweep. In quieter passages the characters can explain their moods and attitudes, often with a certain humour or irony. They are all extremely explicit and Pittakos, in some ways the least plausible of all the characters, is extraordinarily articulate in explaining that he is a plain blunt soldier, who, knowing that he is not a master of words or contemplation, must use action to create an imperfect work of art.

All the characters are in a sense self-enclosed, acting or speaking out their own ideas of themselves. There are little ironies and reversals that make a comparatively minor effect in the ripple and suavity of the verse movement. Sappho was not Kreon's daughter: the tablets when more thoroughly inspected made this clear, but it was to Pittakos's advantage that the story should be believed. Did Pittakos love Sappho? If so, why was he so eager to send her away to Corinth? Both Sappho and Phaon are extraordinarily voluble about the beauty of silence, the knowledge of reality that lies beyond conscious thought or speech. It seems strange that Pittakos, the ruthless soldier, should grieve so much because he has had to kill one soldier, Diomedes' son, for showing funk. Diomedes himself is an odd character, drunkard, buffoon, good poet of his kind, dying in a heartbreak of self-disgust. The oracle is half believed and half not.

But the play as a whole does create an atmosphere of a lost civilization, at once primitive and lucid, of the volatile Greek temperament that combines egoism with generosity, clear-sightedness with reckless impulsiveness. The fate and actions of the characters seem to be controlled by a power that might be called Luck or Accident. They act that they may brood upon the nature of their actions; they are not so much strongly emotional as creatures of mood, discussing any new mood that comes upon them, questioning their attitudes with irony. All are introspectives, even kind old Kreon, even warlike Pittakos. Each is in a sense his own island (the very small island where Phaon has chosen to live alone is a key symbol) and the distance of all the characters, from the audience, from each other, the stances which they never relinquish, the roles which they never let go, have a cooling effect, so that we are moved by this play, but not as we are moved by Shakespearian tragedy. The cool language suggests that everything is important and trivial, monotonous and momentous, trite and ever fresh, that everything is both foreordained and arbitrary. We feel a sense of the distinguished pathos of the human situation in a certain culture, not our own, a culture partly created by Durrell's imagination, but based on his knowledge of ancient Greek history and modern Greek character.

One might say that to a northern reader, brought up on Ibsen and Strindberg, the characters of Durrell's Sappho would seem to be endlessly loquacious, like grasshoppers, and like grasshoppers strongly lacking in weight. They might seem to be all surface, to have no insides. The cool polish of the diction of Sappho reminds me, more than anything else, of some of the dialogues, in verse as well as in prose, of Landor. The characters have individuality and vivacity, each stands also for a universal or recurrent human role; but they seem to have rehearsed everything they say a hundred times, so that the laborious felicity of the expression moves us, and not the emotion expressed: the characters seem other than quite human, are art-works conversing, belong on Keats's Grecian urn.

3

Sappho is a play about a period in human history when the simple, the primitive, the perennial seem to have existed in a wonderful poise with the most civilized manners and art. Nobody in *Sappho*, not even Pittakos, is really unhappy or wicked, and that is why the effect of the play is lyrical rather than tragic. Durrell wrote *Sappho* as a poet, without the stage directly in mind. He wrote *Acte* for the stage and chose a period, that of the Roman Empire under Nero, when a corrupt civilization was confronting a raw barbarism on its frontiers. If in *Sappho* everything is fundamentally at one, in *Acte* everything is divided, including the human heart. Fabius, the hero of this play, has spent his youth in Scythia, loves the Scythian language and its poetry. As a general, he suppresses a Scythian revolt and brings as a hostage to Rome the Scythian princess Acte. She has been blinded in retaliation for Scythian atrocities, and as a girl she was raped by her brother-in-law. She tries to stab Fabius on the way to Rome, but fails, and they become lovers. In Rome, she hopes to work for Scythian independence, and makes the acquaintance of Nero, for whom she cooks Scythian broths at night in his great kitchen. But Nero is suspicious of Fabius, and Fabius's cold wife, Flavia, confronts Acte, demanding the destruction of love letters that might convict Fabius of treason. Flavia does not love Fabius (though her very coldness excites him) but she wants to preserve her social position and the future of her son, whom Nero may torture to get evidence against his father.

Petronius Arbiter persuades Nero not to kill Fabius and Acte but to leave them free to work out their own destinies. Petronius will then write their story for Nero. The two lovers do not take any obvious course, neither a suicide pact, nor a flight to Egypt. Acte goes back to Scythia to help the rebels; Fabius easily suppresses the rebellion, cuts off Acte's head and sends it back to Rome. He is now high in Imperial favour, but has become a hopeless drunkard, and his son has gone mad. Flavia relates all this in a last scene in which Petronius, at Nero's orders, is opening his veins. Petronius discusses other ways in which he might have ended the story and advises Flavia to work at living, to say yes to life, so that she may not merely die in the end but achieve death. "To become an adept of reality" is all that matters. As he is being led away to the hot bath in which he will bleed his life away, Petronius promises to tell Flavia "one story I have never told a living soul."

Acte is a play obviously influenced by Corneille, by the idea of the conflict of love and honour, of fear and courage, of passion and will. It lacks, however, the structure of a neo-classical play. Durrell becomes more interested in Petronius, the artist, and in Nero, the would-be artist, the haunted child criminal, than in his hero and heroine; Flavia in her hardness and toughness becomes, also, more alive and sympathetic to him than Acte, whose sufferings have been cruder, whose character is more simple. The tendency of the novelist to complicate, to include the frame in the picture, to suggest, like Petronius in the last scene, possibilities that are not fulfilled, a perpetual ambiguity between fact and fiction, usurps the duty of the dramatist to push a single plot through, with clarity of line.

I think that in this play Durrell was obviously restraining his taste for verbal embroidery, but without really achieving a plain classical style. The language, without being prose, is often prosaic. There are few lyrical passages. At its best, the language has eloquence, as in Petronius's last advice to Flavia:

> And you, Flavia? You have lived so much, yes,
> But you have never *worked* at life, never once.
> Said "Yes" to life, "Yes" and again "Yes."
> Like all of us you have connived with time. . . .

This, like the rest of the speech from which it comes, is excellent didactic rhetoric, probably very speakable on the stage but not poetry, in the sense in which *Sappho* shimmers with poetry all through. The language, in fact, all through, gives me an odd sense of Durrell *willing* himself to write. For once, he is without the grace and facility which are his usual triumphs and temptations. The grey, heavy, nasty world of ancient Rome, which so much suits Robert Graves's "comedies of evil," the *Claudius* books, is really alien to Durrell's lighter and sunnier temperament.

4

Durrell's third play, in order of composition, An Irish Faustus, was published in 1963. It was written at the request of a German actor who wished to play a new Faustian role. In the winter of 1966, the play became part of the repertory of Luigi Malipiero's Torturmtheater in Sommerhausen near Wurzburg, was performed over a hundred times during the season, and was critically very well received: Malipiero, who is producer, actor, and stage designer for his theatre, had already produced seven versions of the Faust legend (by Marlowe, Calderón, Goethe, Grabbe, Lenau, Vischer, and Valéry) before putting on Durrell's. The play has also, with Malipiero's company, been given a very successful performance at the small private theatre, the "House Under the Hill," at Heilbronn, where Dr Rudolf Fuchs regularly has interesting modern plays staged, with an invited audience. Writing to Durrell about his production, Dr Fuchs says: "The actors were under the direction of a brilliant stage-manager and the intimacy of a private house contributed to the success, which makes me very happy." An Irish Faustus does, in fact, seem to me a complete success both poetically and dramatically, and it also reveals Durrell's inner nature in an intimate, simple, and homely way. He *is* the Dr Faustus of this play, at least to the degree in which Shakespeare is Prospero.

The setting is a vaguely medieval Yeatsian Ireland. The play is in nine scenes (and nine, of course, is one of the magical numbers). In the first scene, Dr Faustus is instructing the young Princess Margaret of Galway in the pursuit of vision through the negative path, or in the pursuit of self-knowledge through natural analogies. Magic, he explains to her, is a kind of domestication of science. In the act of dreaming the mind, emptying itself of fixed categories, can become a field of visitation. But Margaret is curious about whether magic, when once achieved, changes only the inner self or whether it can act also on the outer world. She wonders why a man with Faustus's power and knowledge can be so calm and sensible, but immediately makes him angry by asking him about a gold ring, with magical powers of transmutation, created by a magician who had been burned at the stake, Tremethius. Faustus had been Tremethius's disciple, but had left him when Tremethius chose the path of black magic, rather than white. Faustus, however, possesses his ring. And as soon as Faustus has gone, Margaret's aunt, the fierce Queen Katherine, bullies Margaret into stealing the ring for her. Her motive, though this is not made immediately clear, is that the ring gives power over vampires, and with it Queen Katherine will be able to raise from the grave and be eternally united with her sinister dead husband, the fierce and cruel King Eric the Red. It was for Eric that Tremethius made the ring.

The second scene is one of comedy, in which a rogue called Martin is selling, in the manner of Boccaccian or Chaucerian comedy, pardons for all sorts of sins; the more outrageously he shows himself a cheapjack and mocks his customers, the more eager they are to buy. Faustus asks Martin for news of Matthew the Hermit, a solitary wise man, whom Faustus thinks of, now that Tremethius has gone, as his teacher. In the third scene, back in his study, Faustus discovers the loss of the ring. Mephisto appears to him, for the first time materializing himself, and explains that the ring was first made by Tremethius for the vampire king, Eric, who then had Tremethius burned. Its power is so awful that Faustus has been wrong to shut it up for years. He should either have destroyed it, which is very difficult, or used its powers. But the Queen, with the aid of some stolen pages from one of Faustus's magic books, has summoned Eric from the grave and given him the ring. His bloody footprints mark the chapel and the Queen has been found there raving mad.

In the fourth scene we see Katherine in her madness, describing with awful exultation Eric's satanic power over her, her obscene love for him. She goes off to seek his grave in the forest, and the others follow her, with a stake to pierce the vampire's heart. In the fifth scene, the vampire has his heart staked, Katherine agonizingly protesting. Faustus has the ring again, but what is he to do with it? He calls up spectral figures of great magicians, of whom the last is his master, Tremethius; Tremethius tells him that the only way to destroy the ring is by the recital of a very dangerous invocation called the Great Formula. A religious friend of Faustus's, Anselm, gives Faustus a piece of the True Cross, which will resist the fires of Hell itself, and preserve Faustus from destruction. In the sixth scene, secure in his possession of this holy talisman, Faustus defies Mephisto, who

wants him to use the ring, and recites the great formula, which terrifies
Mephisto even more than it terrifies Faustus. They enter together a realm
of flaming darkness.

In the seventh scene, it is morning, and Faustus's servant Paul and his
friend Anselm, the chaplain, beat on his study door and then burst in. Faustus is lying in an exhausted sleep, his hair has turned white, his clothes
have been charred to rags by the cosmic or infernal fires. But Mephisto has
gone, and Faustus is himself unharmed. The ring has been destroyed, but
the fragment of the True Cross has also been burnt to ashes (we later learn
that it was one of Martin the Pardoner's many fakes and forgeries). . . . In
the vision of destruction, to put it crudely, Faustus has found the vision of
creation, and has been confirmed in a kind of Blakean cosmic optimism.
He feels the need to renew, refresh, simplify his life and to go on a journey. Things are made easier for him by Queen Katherine, now freed from
her madness, aware that she ought to be grateful to Faustus, but unable to
forgive him for severing her forever from her demon lover, Eric. She sends
him into exile. He bids farewell to her, and to his pupil Margaret. He will
not allow Margaret to follow him into exile, but leaves her his books, which
he no longer needs. He has learned the folly of trying to control or master
the plenitude of cosmic power; one serves it best by what Wordsworth calls
a "wise passivity."

The dark theme of the play is concluded here and the last two scenes
round off the comic theme, the acceptance of humility, the ending in simple happiness. Wandering through a forest in exile, Faustus says good-bye
to his servant Paul. Martin, the pardoner, approaches him and talks amus-
ingly about his trade, telling how the more he cheats, and the more he is
known to cheat, the more he prospers, and the more people seem to benefit from contact with his forgeries. Faustus admits that Martin's forged
piece of the True Cross performed a miracle for him. They go off to visit
Matthew the Hermit, Faustus promising to help Martin in future with writing out indulgences. It will be quite a hard life, but, as Martin says:

> But it's not all work; in the evenings we could go down
> To the village tavern for a drink and a chat,
> Like weary Gods with bliss-bestowing hands as the poet says.
> And with your knowledge you could make the job really *creative*.

In the last scene, the two companions reach the log hut of Matthew the
Hermit, who had been expecting Faustus for a long time. They greet each
other jovially:

> MATTHEW: So finally it happened, my poor doctor! What happened?
> FAUSTUS: Why nothing, absolutely nothing.
> MATTHEW: Excellent; for when nothing begins to happen at long last
>   Everything
>   Begins to cohere, the dance of the pure forms begins. . . .

Matthew has known that he was not going to live till next spring, and has been waiting for Faustus, so that he can hand on to him what he calls "the thread":

> And so nothing began to happen to you. How judiciously
> Nature plans; never a drop is spilled,
> Never the slender thread is allowed to break.
> But how long it takes for one to find it out.

The thread that will be handed on will be something like Taoism, both a fulness and an emptiness of being, the sense that one co-operates best with nature by striving and worrying least. The Tao works silently; Matthew says: ". . . what I did not know / Is just how busy all this nothingness can be." Matthew tells Faustus also that, in succeeding to Matthew, in a sense he will have no duties:

> Hm. . . . If duty is what you cannot help, then I have none;
> For I am helping everything by doing nothing. I see you smile.
> I help the moon rise, the sun to set. I eat and drink.
> And, as a matter of fact, I play cards with the Pardoner.

Martin the Pardoner then enters, with a silent and polite Mephisto in a mask. They all sit down to a game of cards in which at Mephisto's suggestion they play "the old game of Fortune." Hearts, standing for Love, not Spades standing for Death, Clubs standing for Force, or Diamonds standing for Wealth, are trumps. They may well go on playing for ever.

   . . . I have given *An Irish Faustus* more detailed attention than it has received before, because I believe it is a small masterpiece, and the most coherent expression that Durrell has given of his most central beliefs. The Faust legend exists in a mixed context of Christian dualism and the humanistic, but in practice often anti-human, Renaissance desire to surpass, to excel, to move over forbidden boundaries; Marlowe's play includes both elements. Goethe's Faust, from whom comes Spengler's "Faustian man," is a figure of modern Western man defeating the Devil and satisfying God by his restlessness, his energy, his refusal to sit down and be content, his perpetual urge for self-transcendence. Durrell's Faustus is quite different from either of these. He has wished to pursue only a white magic that will put him in harmony with nature, he does not like thinking of Tremethius's black magic that produced the ring. When he is landed with the ring, he shelves it, as one shelves a problem; in the very first scene he seems to equate his magic with the *via negativa* of the mystics, the emptying of the mind of images and concepts, the making it passive, that it may be a receptacle for divine illumination. It is true that he seems to think of the Divine as the All rather than the One, as a Cosmic Power rather than as a Person, but a tendency of this sort is to be found in mystics like St John of the Cross, and this natural tendency of the mystical temperament towards a unity with Being that gets beyond any image of God as a person is one

reason why even the greatest mystics have always been regarded, by orthodox Muslims as well as orthodox Christians, with a certain suspicion: Taoism was similarly regarded with suspicion by Confucians in China, because
it seemed to counsel a useless withdrawal from the world, and to under-
mine the insistence on social duty on which Confucianism was built.

Durrell's Faustus does not, however, deny or defy orthodox Christianity. He helps to stake the vampire king to death and to heal the Queen of
her madness, casting out her unclean spirits, though he has not the power
to replace them with any holiness or grace. But the fragment of the True
Cross, even though it is burned up when he actually descends into the Cosmic Foundry, helps him to cow Mephisto. After this achievement, his
course is one of renunciation, of his worldly power and position, of his mastery over Margaret's spirit, of his magical books. He allies himself with a
humble but kindly-hearted rogue, the Pardoner, and seeks out with Matthew the Hermit a life in which outwardly doing nothing makes one a secret co-operator with the movement of all things. He is saved from the danger of damnation not through a terrible last-minute repentance or through
asserting his humanity against both God and the Devil but by a gay and
quiet submission to the cosmic order. He finds happiness or sanctification
in a state in which, as in Yeats's *A Vision*, a hair separates the saint from
the fool. But Durrell's Faustus talks not of the saint but of the sage: "A hair
separates the sage from the fool." This again perhaps shows the deep influence on Durrell of Far Eastern thought, where the figure of the saint
merges with that of the sage or teacher, and where the *sensei* teaches
lightly, in childish jokes, in unanswerable riddles.

One should note, however, that the happy ending of *An Irish Faustus*
is not quite unequivocal. The three friends at their game of cards, Matthew
the Hermit, Martin the Pardoner, Dr Faustus the Magician, are joined by
a fourth figure, the masked Mephisto. Mephisto is something like Jung's
Shadow, the unspoken element of darkness called into consciousness, for
completeness, by all bright trinities. Martin the Pardoner perhaps also is a
Jungian figure. He lies, he knows he is a liar, he says he is a liar, and yet
his forged relics perform miracles; for Jung the myths and rituals of traditional religion can never be superseded by a purely rational view of reality
since they body forth a pattern built into the human psyche. They are a
game which *homo ludens* must continue to play. Mephisto, it should be
noted, has in this play not been deliberately conjured up by Faustus but,
at a moment of crisis, has emerged as the dark side of Faustus of which
he has suddenly to become palpably aware. The use of alchemical imagery
throughout the play could also owe something to Jung's conception of alchemy (the conception, also, of the greater alchemists themselves), of alchemical processes as a metaphor for, or analogical representation of, spiritual processes.

What Durrell's Faustus seeks is what Jung calls integration; and he
achieves it through exposing himself to the most blasting awareness of the

shadow and through a paradoxical renunciation, the seeking of fulness in emptiness, of power in quiescence. Durrell seems to me to have shown, in this play, profound intuition and great artistic skill in taking ideas of the Jungian sort, so very much of our own age, and yet weaving them into a play, an art-transformation of folklore material, of which the naïve medieval atmosphere is thoroughly convincing.

Faustus no doubt partly represents a spiritual path which Durrell sees stretching ahead of him. Faustus's renunciations would mean for Durrell renunciation of his art and his fame, a breaking of his wand, as Shakespeare made Prospero break his wand, a quiet turning towards cosmic mercy. But there is a paradox. The image of Faustus or Prospero, the magician who renounces all that is gaudier or more showy in his magic, who submits, can only be created by the magician who has still his wand very firmly clutched in his hand. On the other hand, where a dark, bitter and turbulent spirit like Dostoevski creates Alyosha as an image of a simple and relatively untormented goodness he can never achieve, where the atheist Marlowe at the end of *his Dr Faustus* projects his own suppressed fears of damnation, Durrell's rational and sensible Faustus, on his small, almost shadow-theatre scale, does present in miniature an integration which, for Durrell himself, is not an inconceivable aim.

Mirror of Crises: The Poetry of Lawrence Durrell

Ian S. MacNiven*

In his discussion of Lawrence Durrell's poetry, "The Poet's Voice and Vision," G. S. Fraser writes that "When an individual poem was written does not matter much, either in relation to Durrell's biography or the development of his art." Fraser adds that this supposed lack of noticeable development, this "timeless quality," is "more often a mark of the very good minor poet than of the major one."[1] Careful reading of the chronologically arranged *Collected Poems, 1931–1974* (1980), however, clearly shows a variation in styles and the handling of major themes—love, the magic of place, death, and poetry itself—from the earliest derivative verse through the lyric and narrative poems of Durrell's pre-war and World War II period, to the more relaxed and conversational poems of his writing maturity and later years. A parallel study of Durrell's poetry and his life also reveals a profound interdependence. Fraser makes another charge, which is at once more serious and harder to answer; he claims that "The poems themselves are the expression of a temperament, rather than the history of a soul, and to say this is perhaps to define Durrell as a minor poet, though of a very

*This essay was written specifically for this volume and is published here for the first time by permission of the author.

distinguished sort" (LD 28). Yet the very title of Durrell's first commercially published collection, *A Private Country* (1943), implies both his commitment to his personal, private life and a sensitivity to the "country" he inhabits. That this country may frequently be the "Heraldic Universe" of symbol and imagination which Durrell described in 1936 to Henry Miller only reinforces the relationship of the poetry to both surface biography and internal state, to soul. The impact of Durrell's life and apparent inner state on his poetry is easily demonstrable. Another view that should be considered is the commonly held stand that his best verse was written between 1938 and 1955, and Alan Warren Friedman in *Lawrence Durrell and The Alexandria Quartet* (1970) by implication narrowed the field still further by concentrating on the two earliest Faber collections, *A Private Country* and *Cities, Plains and People* (1946).

Thus, in a re-evaluation of Durrell's poetry based on the 1980 *Collected Poems*, there are at least three main points to consider: the importance of chronology and biography; the depth of introspection revealed; and the quality of the later poetry, especially with respect to the highly praised early verse. The answers to these questions are to some extent interdependent.

We have Durrell's own claim that autobiography is central to his early poetry, and there is strong evidence that the events of his life have shaped his later verse as well. In his privately published *Quaint Fragment* (1931), the nineteen-year-old Durrell justified his poems with an apologia in "A Dedication":

> I only plead
> That I have lived them all these lonely few
> And made them personal.[2]

Some, like "Happy Vagabond / (Amsterdam 1930)," describe a specific journey, while "Inconstancy" treats a love affair: "Child, in the first few hours I lived with you, / Time beat the generous pulses of desire, / And churned the embers of a faded light to livid fever heat" (18).

If Durrell did indeed live his poems of 1931, most of that living was done under the eyes of his family in Bournemouth. There is much more evidence of intense living, along with a fairly abrupt change in style, in the eleven poems printed in 1932, after he had been more than a year in London. Gone are most of the stereotypes of Romantic diction, the sentimentalism of the "dear mute calling of the wind," the "Dreams so oft forgotten," the exclamatory "Oh!" He was young and independent in an exciting city (his mother had given him a subsistence of ten pounds per month, together with the injunction, "You can be as Bohemian as you like, but *not in the house*."[3]); he had acquired friends who took his writing as seriously as he did himself; and he was in love with the strikingly beautiful Nancy Myers, a tall, blonde art student at the Slade who was to become his wife in 1935. In "Discovery of Love" he writes:

Most merciful, since you have turned your face,
And given this perfection to my hand,
Earth has become an autumn dancing place,
And I a traveller in enchanted land;

And all the rumour of the earth's decay
Remoter than to-morrow seems to-day.

(26)

Although the "traveller in enchanted land" echoes Shelley, most of the poems Durrell published in 1932 are fairly plain in diction and seem the intentionally naïve verse of a young lover. In "Question" Durrell asks: "How can the anguished world remain the same; / The crowds still pass on unreturning feet / When we have cupped our hands about a flame?" (28).

There is also evidence in the early poetry of wide reading, of Durrell's conscious preparation for writing. "Lost," dedicated to Nancy, is headed by an epigraph from Philip Massinger, "Angels desire an alms," and a fine *carpe diem* poem carries a title from Ronsard's sonnets, "*Cueillez dès Aujourd'huy les Roses de la Vie*" (29). Experience, though, seems more important than reading in these poems. Two of the opposing impulses of Durrell's first marriage, jealousy and the desire for freedom, are prominent in the 1932 collection, *Ten Poems*. "Knowing that every lip to questing lip / Must give for answer 'Yes'," he writes in "Plea," "Pleasure is greatest pain so dearly bought, / And love unfaithfulness" (27). Nancy Myers has testified that Durrell's jealousy led to scenes of inquisition and accusation, while he reveals in "Retreat" that common panic of the ineluctably married:

I would be rid of you who bind me so,
Thoughtless to the stars: I would refrain and turn
Along the unforgotten paths I used to know
Before these eyes were governed to discern
All beauty and all transcience [sic] in love.

(31)

What is especially significant in these early poems, considering Durrell's development as a poet over the next decade, is the lack of any dominant and striking image pattern. The "autumn dancing place," the "earth's decay," "unreturning feet," and "thoughtless to the stars" are all generalized pictures without any specific reference: there is no *locus*, no individualizing identity to them. Greece was to fill this void in Durrell's poetry, give it visual and tonal impact, sensory realism, and color.

Fraser's remark about Durrell's consistency over the years is true in one important respect: in his knack of deflating his troubles with laughter. The last poem of 1932, "Ballade of Slow Decay," printed as a Christmas message, reflects his impatience with his family, his amused portrait of himself as an *enfant terrible*, and his concern over money:

> I realize that Cousin Jane is "dear",
> And that sweet Minnie has such "grace and poise",
> But why should they be planning to come here,
> When Winifred my manuscript destroys,
> And dearest little Bertie mis-employs
> His time by crying when he sees my nose.
>
> (32)

Thus grumbles Durrell about his relatives, adding the refrain, "It makes me want to stamp and make a noise: / I wish that George would pay me what he owes." In 1955 Durrell was to turn again to humor when emotionally hard pressed over the nervous breakdown of his second wife, Eve. His "Ballad of Psychoanalysis" runs through a catalogue of dreams, ending with the wry comment, "Here's the clinical picture but what can we do?" (242). "Ballad of the Oedipus Complex," published five years later, is better, and exploits the rhythms of Lewis Carroll:

> If seven psychoanalysts
> On seven different days
> Condemned my coloured garters
> Or my neo-Grecian stays,
>
> I'd catch a magic constable
> And lock him behind bars
> To be a warning to all men
> Who have mamas and pas.
>
> (255)

His 1968 first visit to the United States, "Land of Doubleday and Dutton / Huge club sandwiches of mutton / More zip-fastener than button" (290), occasioned "Owed to America." The title was a printer's slip, but Durrell was so amused by the violence done his "Ode" that he said, "Let it stand!"

Except in the later comic ballads, we have been talking so far about promise rather than polished performance: workmanlike poems selected from three private printings, poems with ideas for the most part out of Durrell's personal experience; poems not fully realized but redeemed if at all by a few fine lines. Then in 1934, after an excursion into fiction, he began to produce poetry of high quality.[4] "Tulliola" is a dramatic monologue framed by a Renaissance donné, given in a prose headnote, which recounts the discovery of a vault containing the preserved body of Cicero's daughter, "swimming in a kind of bath of precious oyle," a lamp burning at her feet. The voice of Tulliola laments her "Impalpable eclipse! / Persistent as the muzzle of a dog, / Nosing me out for ever and for ever" (33). In language that suggests Yeats's "Sailing to Byzantium," Durrell exploits the irony of the embalmer's skill in preserving the body while losing all that had made Tulliola human:

All the embalmer's poor artifice was this:
To strip me of the cogs and wheels of sense—
Those inner toys of motion,
Purse my dead lips in a kiss,
And freeze the small shell of me,
Freeze me so stiff and regimental,
Then launch me in this vault's aquarium
Upon a tide of spices.
Pity me, swimming here.
Pity me, Cicero's daughter,
Partnered by inner darkness and one solemn light.

With the cool mechanical imagery of "cogs and wheels," the "small shell" of the woman "so stiff and regimental" in the "vault's aquarium / Upon a tide of spices," he builds an unsentimental picture of mortality and loss. Although given a voice by the poet and the living exercise of swimming, this young woman is "partnered" not by gay companions but by "darkness and one solemn light." Her spices are "bitter and odorous," not the "sugar and spice" of the nursery rhyme. Despite the embalmer's astounding triumph in preserving even the color of the skin, his "artifice" mocks life because he has become an accomplice of death, stripping the body of the organs of sense. As a further irony Tulliola is floated on a "tide of spices," tides being attributes of living oceans, not dead aquariums.

From 1935 through 1937 Durrell published very little poetry: he wrote two novels, *Panic Spring* (1937, published under the pseudonym Charles Norden) and *The Black Book* (1938). This periodic concentration on fiction to the partial exclusion of verse became part of Durrell's work pattern. His residence in Greece—Corfu, Athens, Kalamata—from 1935 until the arrival of the German army in April 1941, broken only by a couple of trips to Paris and London, was of the greatest importance to both his fiction and his poetry. Durrell packed a lot of experience into his years in Greece and, directly thereafter, in Egypt. In *A Key to Modern British Poetry* (1952) he wrote: "The truth is perhaps that the English poet tends to suffer from a deficit of sexual and emotional experience. His life is not raw enough. He is sealed up among the prohibitions and anxieties of a puritan culture and this makes it difficult for him to react to real experience."[5] It would be quite consistent for Durrell to decide that "raw" experience was needed for his poetry—and then set out to find some. Durrell also quotes part of Rimbaud's creed, "un long, immense et raisonné dérèglement de tous les sens" (KMBP, 39), but notes that Rimbaud had been "badly frightened" by his "attempt on the absolute"; and in a 1974 poem, "A Patch of Dust" (which I will discuss below), Durrell examines with considerable sympathy Vincent van Gogh's derangement. Durrell rejects both the *dérèglement* of Rimbaud and the madness of Van Gogh: there is a solid Anglo-Irish side to Durrell which enabled him to search for experience outside the tabus of English society, yet still retain his psychological stability. Unlike the

French poet and the Dutch painter, Durrell has been able to work out his crises through his art and to escape intact.

The *Black Book* is unabashedly autobiographical: Lawrence Lucifer, who escapes the deadly world of the Regina Hotel and literary London for a Greek island, is in part Lawrence Durrell. Subtitled in the first edition "A Chronicle of the English Death," the novel is a prose companion to "The Death of General Uncebunke," published the same year. In both, Durrell rejects a segment of his past. "Uncebunke" is Durrell's first long poem, a work of controlled irony which chronicles the *colonial* death, the boredom and ineffectuality of the lives of Britishers abroad and of colonials retired in the mother country. The difference in the treatment of the two worlds shows that Durrell, though he sees through both, retains considerable affection for the milieu into which he was born, the Anglo-Indian world of Jullundur and Darjeeling. "My uncle" is a pompous but quixotic and even gifted man:

> Here was a ruddy bareback man,
> Emptied his blood upon the frozen lake,
> Wheeled back the screaming mares,
> Crossing the Jordan.
>
> (47)

He is highly educated, filled with practical knowledge, and humane: "Three, six, nine of the dead languages / Are folded under his lip;" and he

> Knew to shoe horses: the habits of the owl,
> Time of tillage, foison, cutting of lumber,
> Like Saint Columba,
> Could coax the squirrels into his cowl.
>
> (50)

With all this, however, he is locked in "mesmeric incomprehension," "His not to reason why, though a thinking man" (44). His innocence allows us to view him with affection: if he is incomprehending, this paragon "Devoted to the polo-pony" (45), this man "More than a spartan in tartan," his is the ignorance of the unphilosophic spirit, not of the willful Philistine. Quite possibly there is in this portrait of Uncebunke a good deal of the uncle Durrell has described fondly in a recent memoir, "From the Elephant's Back" (1982). General Uncebunke's consort, Aunt Prudence, derives her name at least from a woman Durrell grew up calling aunt, his second cousin, Miss Prudence Hughes. While Miss Hughes, at this writing still vital and vigorous in her eighties, is not the dry, dessicated "pillar of savourless salt" described in the poem, both Uncebunke's Prudence and Durrell's cousin look backward toward the past. Further, the general's wife "Ate the white lie: 'Happily ever after' " (49). She took refuge in religion, after a life given over to trivialities as much as to God: "Prudence did dip and delve in the Holy Book, / Alpha to omega angels told her the tale, / Feeding the parrot, pensive over a croquet-hoop" (48). With an ignorance as dense as the "mesmeric incomprehension" of her husband, Prudence is caught unprepared by his death: "Where is my man's address? How does he perish / Who was my relish, who was without fault?" (49). Durrell's internal rhymes and near-rhymes (spartan / tartan, perish / relish) poke fun at the apparent order of the Uncebunkes' lives; the word-magic of the poet glances ironically at the belief-magic Prudence has subscribed to and then is betrayed by. In fact, Durrell's very cleverness blunts the impact of the poem, and occasionally his images strain at philosophical effects: "Time's clock-work womb" (50), for instance.

In his best stanzas, however, Durrell unites the superficial religion of the Uncebunkes with the reality of death, real death, not simply the deadness of the society of retired colonials. There is a poignance to the harmless, decent couple, a dignity which endures despite their incomprehension of life and death:

> My uncle has gone beyond astronomy.
> His sleep is of the Babylonian deep-sea
> Darker than bitumen, defter than devil's alliances.
> He has seen Golgotha in carnival:
> Now in the shin-bone the smart worm
> Presides at the death of the sciences,
> The Trinity sleeps in his knee.
>
> (46)

In death General Uncebunke, "gone beyond astronomy," enters the timeless world of being, beyond knowledge, "the death of the sciences," and becomes part of the Godhead: "The Trinity sleeps in his knee." So much is tolerant and even positive about the Uncebunkes that it would be possible to mistake Durrell's poem sequence for tribute were it not for the teasing and the irony. Prudence is given to nostalgic musing, " 'Once upon a time was boy and girl, / Living on cherry, berry, fisherman's silver catch' " (48), and Durrell sums her up in an epigram (adapted from *Twelfth Night*) "Patience on a monument, passion on a cushion" (50). Uncebunke himself comes in for some back-handed praise: "This man . . . / A breaker of skyline, took first prize / In the regatta for men past menopause" (54). He also "Hung a harp on every weeping willow," betraying his sentimentality, and "Shot his bolt on the Gobi. / Was left in the lurch, / Then like a Roman, fell upon his sword." Clearly, Durrell's clichés lead to the mock heroic. The wheezing hymns of damp, rural chapels accompany this funeral of "A feudal death of an old order":"permit / The bromoid encomium of the harmonium" (53). "Give us to God with slim and shining handles" (55), he adds wickedly.

There is much bemused affection in Durrell's portrait of the colonial and suburban death, but the Uncebunkes were nonetheless as much dead as the victims of the English urban death pilloried in *The Black Book*. Part of the difference in tone—vitriolic in the novel, ironic in the poem—occurs because in *The Black Book* Durrell was deliberately cutting himself loose from England, a "mean, shabby little island," the England of stuffy Bournemouth and the seamy London bohemia, while in "Uncebunke" he was distancing himself from a life he had loved, from a boyhood in which he had been pampered and happy, from a life he remembered with nostalgia, although he could not in his maturity approve of it and to which he knew he could not return.

"The Death of General Uncebunke," however, functioned as a vital testing ground for Durrell's poetic development. Biblical and Shakespearean language; extravagant images in the manner of the Apocalyptic poets he had appeared next to in anthologies, J. F. Hendry, Nicholas Moore, and Henry Treece; parodies of Georgian poetry; internal rhymes and floods of alliteration; truncated grammatical structures, one-line exclamatory sentences, and staccato rhythms suited to the pulpit style of the poem. "Strike with the black rod!" (46) writes Durrell in the voice of a preacher. After "Uncebunke" there is much less discussion of Christianity, even treated ironically, a lack paralleling Durrell's own shift toward Eastern religions and philosophy. Only in "Fangbrand" (1941) does Durrell return to an overtly Christian theme, and in this poem a "missionary man" discovers "The final dualism in very self, / An old man holding an asphodel" (95)—a vision of received truth more Platonic and Eastern than Christian. Perhaps only coincidentally, many of the more spectacular tricks of prosody vanished from Durrell's poetry along with the Christianity. In "Uncebunke" he seems to have been intellectually rather than emotionally involved, and his best poetry throughout his career has been written during periods of extreme agitation, either of pain or pleasure.

Durrell's acquaintance with Greece and his close association on Corfu with both natives and fellow expatriates moved him toward his most recognizable poetic voice, his unique combination of theme, image, and tone. When he moved his bride of a few months, his mother, and his three younger siblings to Corfu in 1935, he claimed at the time that he was looking for a respite from the gloom and catarrhs of "Pudding Island," and he had heard from his friends the Wilkinsons that the island was pleasant, sunny, and cheap—the sort of place where someone with a few pounds a week could live and write in peace. There was also the attraction of Greek antiquity. His first "foreign residence" book, Prospero's Cell (1946), was to take up half-seriously the legend that Shakespeare had set The Tempest on Corfu. Durrell quickly came to feel that the eastern Mediterranean, and particularly the Greek mainland and islands, meant not merely an exotic locale of sun, olives, and "the Greek sea's curly head" (238), but also the source of European culture, rooted in Homer. And the ancient culture still flourished in the writing of Cavafy, spiritual and poetic mentor of The Alexandria Quartet, and in the work of writers who were soon to become Durrell's friends, among them Sikelianos and Seferis. For Durrell London was the outpost, the place one went to visit publishers; Paris was more exciting, the fermenting still for talent through meetings with Henry Miller and Anaïs Nin; and Greece was the muse and midwife of his poetry. "Father Nicholas His Death: Corfu," published only a year after "Uncebunke" (a poem influenced in no perceptible way by Greece), combines something of the declamatory voice and biblical language of the earlier poem with the sense of timelessness of the Greek landscape:

> Hush the old bones their vegetable sleep,
> For the islands will never grow old.
> Nor like Atlantis on a Monday tumble,
> Struck like soft gongs in the amazing blue.
>
> (66)

Landscape, real or mythological, becomes the measure, the image of man's suffering, the contrast to his mortality; and Durrell takes care to look beyond the present Greek or Mediterranean world: "Now what are your pains to the Great Danube's pains, / Your pyramids of despair against Ithaca / Or the underground rivers of Dis?" The Danube, Homeric Ithaca, or Dis: all mark regions where man has known suffering and death. Linked to the death of Father Nicholas are the psalmist of the Old Testament and the "shining ink" of the modern poet:

> Your innocence shall be as the clear cistern
> Where the lone animal in these odourless waters
> Quaffs at his own reflection a shining ink.
> Here at your green pasture the old psalms
> Shall kneel like humble brutes and drink.

The "clear cistern," the animal quaffing at his own reflection, and the "green pastures" are at once language from the Bible and from Durrell's observations on Corfu. The same combination of sources applies to another stanza of the poem, echoing Psalm 114, where Durrell describes life as a continuous cycle of birth, love, and death:

> Consider please the continuous nature of Love:
> How one man dying and another smiling
> Conserve for the maggot only a seed of pity,
> As in winter's taciturn womb we see already
> A small and woollen lamb on a hilltop hopping.

One aspect of Durrell's poetry on which the Mediterranean has had an obvious impact is his use of color. It is not surprising to find in "Father Nicholas" four mentions of blue, including "amazing blue" and "elegiac blue," along with one of green: Greece is famous for the blueness of its sea, and pastures are green in cliché if not invariably in fact. But Durrell has not always used a bright palette: in his first three years of publishing verse only twice does he stray into the rainbow spectrum, with two mentions of blue. The other colors are white (9 uses), silver (2), grey (2), and ebony (1).

Despite his move to Greece in 1935, his color chart is still fairly stark by 1938: in twenty-one pages of poetry, the dominant color is black (15), with white a distant second (7), followed by red (5), blue and green (3 each), silver and yellow (1 each). Of course, 1938 is the year of "Uncebunke," and black is the predominant color in this poem of death. During the years following 1938 his use of black dropped proportionately, while green and blue, in that order, became the most-used colors, and the Homeric "wine-dark" common. It is curious that Durrell, with his early penchant for exact meanings and often esoteric words, should stay close to the strong primaries even through 1974. A few hues beyond primary and secondary colors make occasional appearances. At the red end of the spectrum we find rufus, scarlet, rose (and rosy), crimson, coral, carmine, and pink; yellow is flanked by amber, blond, lemon, butter-yellow, and especially gold.

More important than brilliant colors or sea and island images, Durrell got from Greece a sense of the peasant life at first hand, the outhouses and wine-presses, the taste of dark bread, olives, and retsina. At Kalamai on Corfu he and Nancy lived away from family and friends for over a year in rooms rented from a poor fisherman; they shared the kitchen with their host, and saw one of his children die for want of proper medical care. In his best poems about Greek life Durrell joined his knowledge of classical history and mythology to his awareness of the present to produce the same continuity through time which Hardy projects in "The Roman Road." This appears in "Father Nicholas," where the modern Greek "Blossoms in new migrations, the whale's grey acres" (67), an image suggesting both Homer's metaphors and the kennings of Durrell's anglophone roots. In "At Epidaurus" he confirms the bonds linking the ages: "Everything is a slave to the ancestor, the order / Of old captains who sleep in the hill" (98). Before the ancient temple, "We, like the winter, are only visitors." Nature is unchanging, and so are the classical plays performed by the modern descendants:

> The earth's flowers
> Blow here original with every spring,
> Shines in the rising of a man's age
> Into cold texts and precedents for time.

In "To Argos" Durrell states exactly the modern shepherd's understanding, through his very bones, of antiquity. Of Argos, "Identified now by the scholars / As a home for the cyclops, a habitation / For nymphs and ancient appearances" (105), Durrell claims that

> Only the shepherd in his cowl
> Who walks upon them really knows
> The natural history in a sacred place;
> Takes like a text of stone
> A familiar cloud-shape or fortress.

It is the lack of meaning for the visiting moderns that Durrell laments:

> Truly, we the endowed who pass here
> With the assurance of visitors in rugs
> Can raise from the menhir no ghost
> By the cold sound of English idioms.
>   (106)

The poet's task, then, is nigh-impossible. He is all too apt to become a mere tourist, while "The modern girls pose on a tomb smiling." "And this is what breaks the heart," Durrell concludes: how to raise the ancient spirit in a modern tongue. The very difficulty has kept Durrell from seeing himself as a Mediterranean regionalist: he uses whatever *deus loci* comes to hand, but his language is that of England, his allusions range from Chaucer, Shakespeare, and the King James Bible to Hopkins, Yeats, and Eliot, and to those figures and events of Classical antiquity which have become the common domain of Western culture. It is true, however, that Durrell's muse functions best when he is close to the wine-and-olive cultures: he was unhappy during the year he spent in Argentina, disliking the country itself though not the people, and the few poems he wrote in Latin America, such as "High Sierra" and "Green Coconuts: Rio," are capable without being distinguished.

"Cities, Plains and People" (1946), the title poem of Durrell's second major collection, is at once the most consistently autobiographical of his poems and an informative prefiguring of the subsequent course of his art. He also wrote it during a period of turmoil in his private life: his marriage to Nancy had broken up in 1942 with her departure for Palestine; in 1943 Durrell had travelled to Beirut in a vain attempt to convince her to return to him; but by 1946 he was happily in Rhodes with the woman who was to become his second wife, the exciting Alexandrian, Eve "Gipsy" Cohen. The headnote following the title, "Beirut 1943," in all probability refers not to the place of composition but to the central crisis which occasioned the poem. In "Cities" Durrell attempts to sketch his development from childhood. The poem opens with the line, "Once in idleness was my beginning" (158); the "mortal boy" is "Innocent of surface like a new mind." By starting the long narrative poem with a version of the formula, "Once upon a time," Durrell has prefigured the end of *The Alexandria Quartet*, where he attributes this opening to fledgling writer Darley, who then comments, "I felt as if the whole universe had given me a nudge."[6] Is Durrell in 1946 expressing for himself his newly found maturity as a writer? I think so. The knowledge comes to his creation and sometime-spokesman, L. G. Darley, at about the same calendar time. However, in "Cities" Durrell also looks forward toward a persona of more accomplished magic: after allusions in the poem and the marginalia to many of the people and places important to Durrell, the poem concludes with the description of a Prospero

> Who many cities, plains, and people saw
> Yet by his open door
> In sunlight fell asleep
> One summer with the Apple in his hand.
> (173)

Like the boy in the beginning, Prospero is idle, but through understanding of himself and by acceptance of the Cosmos the mature man has been able to achieve the Eastern ideal of passivity, the attainment of true knowledge through receptivity rather than through Western striving: Buddha, not Goethe's Faust; Lao Tzu, not Christ. The poem details Durrell's movement from Western to Eastern philosophy and religion. The structure is circular: from idleness to idleness, from Durrell's birthplace in the East, Jullundur in India, to an Eastern state of mind as a mature Prospero. The poem prefigures Durrell's current preference for Buddhism: in 1983 he became president of a committee raising funds to build the Tibetan Buddhist temple of Kagyu-Ling near Autun in France. Nonetheless, the "Apple" in Prospero's hand, with its suggestion of Eden, represents a combination of the two religions, Christianity and Buddhism, just as Durrell's antecedents symbolize for him a meeting of East and West.

"Cities" describes Durrell's development as a poet, as well as the concurrent changes in his religious leanings. As a child Durrell "Saw the Himalayas like lambs there / Stir their huge joints and lay / Against his innocent thigh a stony thigh" (158). This passage evokes again the biblical hills which skipped "like lambs," the "slow thighs" of Yeats's monstrous "Second Coming," and the image of Jacob wrestling with the angel and having his thigh dislocated. Did the young Durrell "wrestle" with the good Jesuits in Darjeeling or rebel against the austerely religious atmosphere of his school in Canterbury, St. Edmund's, founded by the Clergy Orphan Society? According to Durrell's own recollection he did not, and he was humanely treated at both places; if he did struggle with Christianity, the conflict must have been largely internal. In this section of the poem also appears the prayer-wheel of Lamaism: Tibet, Durrell has often claimed, is his spiritual home. As he developed spiritually so too did his awareness of his calling to literature, to "the quotation of nightingales," through experience and suffering:

> To all who turn and start descending
> The long sad river of their growth:
>
> . . . .
> I give you here unending
> In Idleness an innocent beginning
>
> Until your pain become a literature.
> (159)

Like the nightingales in the legends dear to the English Romantics, Durrell's personal muse learned to sing through suffering, and these teaching sufferings he details in "Cities." Early he became aware of loss: "Those who went forward / Into this honeycomb of silence often / Gained the whole world: but often lost each other." The partings inherent in colonial life taught him anguish, while the colorful native funeral processions he witnessed, wandering alone in the hills near Darjeeling, gave him the death-consciousness vital to the poet: "Death marched beside the living as a friend / With no sad punctuation by the clock." Time and death: these essential features of his art came early to him. In *A Key to Modern British Poetry* he wrote, "If time is, as I believe, the measure of our death-consciousness, you cannot revise your concept of it without affecting our ideas of death and life" (23).

Throughout "Cities" Durrell outlines his own experiences. After life in India, "Nine marches to Lhasa" (159), he was sent to school in England, "To the prudish cliffs and the sad green home / Of Pudding Island o'er the Victorian foam" (160). Attracted to Anglo-Saxon England, to Bede, St. Augustine, and St. Jerome, had he like "mad Jerome / Made of his longing half a home from home"? Along with many references to the Bible, Durrell names or alludes to other influences: Rabelais, Descartes, Dante, Homer, Shakespeare, Blake, Wordsworth, Keats, Defoe, D. H. Lawrence, Valery, Gide. The guide is not as important, he claims, as the integrity of the search: "All rules obtain upon the pilot's chart / If governed by the scripture of the heart" (163). His formal schooling may have instilled in Durrell the teachings of the King James version, but it was the language rather than the Christianity which stuck. Some of the figures important to his development are mentioned: "Tessa," the Teresa Marbery who was to provide part of the inspiration for Justine in *The Alexandria Quartet;* Nancy, "the sad perfect wife" he was to lose ("Nets were too coarse to hold her" [165]); his first daughter, Penelope ("In her small frock walked his daughter" [166]); Dostoevsky, whose novels were in his trunk of books on Corfu in the 1930s:

> I saw them moving, the possessed
> Fëdor and Anna, the last
> Two vain explorers of our guilt,
> Turn by turn holding the taws.
>
> (168)

Earlier, Durrell had applied the word *taws* to religious flagellation, but here he sees "our guilt," his and Nancy's, reflected in the cycles of mutual reproach and guilt of Dostoevsky and his Anna. The Second World War, which Durrell saw at close hand in the harbor of Alexandria, forms a backdrop to his personal suffering: "Bombers bursting like pods go down / And the seed of Man stars / This landscape, ancient but no longer known" (172). From a flirtation with suicide the narrator is rescued by thoughts of the "Yellow Emperor" and of Prospero. Huang Ti, legendary Chinese leader of the third millennium before Christ, identified in Durrell's marginal note as

the *"first exponent of the Tao"* (169), shows the way to those who follow:
". . . his ancient heart still visits us / In Lawrence or in Blake" (171). He
has transcended earthly loss, and his sufferings have taught him wisdom:

> The old yellow Emperor
> With defective sight and matted hair
> His palace fell to ruins
> But his heart was in repair.
> . . . .
> His palms were mapped with cunning
> Life geodesies of grief.

From the Emperor's acceptance of his own suffering, Durrell learns the acceptance of the present through, paradoxically, the abandonment of hope:
"There is nothing to hope for, my Brother. / We have tried hoping for a
future in the past" (173). Finally, Prospero emerges as the embodiment of
the poet-narrator's new-found wisdom: in falling asleep "with the Apple in
his hand," Prospero rejects the mechanical omniscience offered by his book
of magic in favor of the passive inviting of wisdom. Durrell, like Prospero
in *The Tempest*, felt that he had to engage in experience, overthrow his
enemies, and then finally, when the time was ripe, he would know when
he could sit back and wait. Durrell had not achieved this passivity in 1946,
nor was he to by 1974, but his working out of the wisdom of the Yellow
Emperor in personal terms has been a continuing motif in his art. Much
more can and should be said about "Cities, Plains and People," including
the way Durrell echoes in sound and rhythm some of the writers he is discussing; the development of Duality; the imagery built around music,
places, science; but such a discussion is outside the scope of this essay. Not
only does the poem promise much that is to come in Durrell's poetry and
fiction, but it is a major achievement in itself.

   "Letters in Darkness" (1954) marks another stage in Durrell's self-
knowledge. While in "Cities" he confronted his heritage, his intellectual
development through the 1940s, and the shock occasioned by the break-up
of his first marriage, "Letters" reflects his response to a new situation: the
nervous collapse and hospitalization of his second wife. Durrell has always
been interested in medicine and psychiatry (see his "Asylum in the Snow,"
1938), and from Corfu he wrote Miller that he might take time out from
literature to become a doctor. Then with his wife Eve he became ac-
quainted at first hand with the terrors of mental illness, and the "Darkness"
in the title of the poem reflects this hidden corner of human nature, this
phantom of dreams and night thoughts:

> So marriage can, by ripeness bound,
> From over-ripeness qualify
> To sick detachment in the mind—
> Dreams bursting at the seams to die.
>   (227)

When his love is going well, the narrator ". . . lies in his love in shadowless content / As tongue in mouth, as poems in a skull" (228). However, Durrell's love has gone wrong, and in a section of "Letters" dated 3 January 1953 (which would place it after Eve's departure from Belgrade to Hanover for treatment), he writes:

> Dear, behind the choking estuaries
> Of sleep or waking, in the acts
> Which dream themselves and make,
> Swollen under luminol, responsibilities
> Which no one else can take,
> I watch the faultless measure of your dying
> Into an unknown misused animal
> Held by the ropes and drugs; the puny
> Recipe society proposes when machines
> Break down. Love was our machine.

Elsewhere Durrell has linked his life with rivers, with natural flow, but here the estuaries are choked, as the Nile is with silt, as his wife's sleep and waking are with tranquilizing drugs. The penalty is that, through this "recipe" for sanity, the bonds joining the lovers have come asunder, and they have become "unknown" to each other. Durrell does not assign fault to one side only; both have lied:

> It was so simple to observe the liars,
> The one impaled, and lying like a log,
> The other at some fountain-nipple drinking
> His art from the whole world, helplessly
> Disbanding reason like a thirsty dog.
>
> (229)

Typical of Durrell's cunning is his exploitation of puns and double-meanings: liars lying and the "fountain-nipple" suggesting at once the inspirational muses and the sensuality which was apparently a bone of contention between the "thirsty dog" and his mate. Nothing he has learned in the past has helped, for "Madness confides its own theology." Finally, Durrell goes back to the Greek wells of his young manhood on Corfu to express the scoring left on the lovers by society and the psychoanalysts:

> We bear like ancient marble well-heads
> Marks of the ropes they lowered in us,
>
> Telling of the concerns of time,
> The knife of feeling in the art of love.
>
> (230)

Consistent with his statement about having lived his poems and his claim that the poet needs experience before he can write well, Durrell sums up at the end of "Letters" the implications of his suffering and new-found understanding:

> So at last we come to the writer's
> Middle years, the hardest yet to bear,
> All will agree: for it is now
> He condenses, prunes and tries to order
> The experiences which gorged upon his youth.

This condensing, pruning, and ordering is exactly what goes on in such important poems of the 1970s as "Last Heard Of" and "A Patch of Dust," in which Durrell strives to come to terms not with his middle but his later years.

The Ikons (1966) stands as a relatively calm poetic interlude between the bitter edge of "Letters in Darkness" and the powerful later verse. Some of the poems in *Ikons* are prosy to the point of lacking Durrell's accustomed music, but among the many excellent offerings are "Congenies," "Salamis," "Troy," "Io," and the title poem itself. Images of vine and altar, eagles and bats, "ogres in dry river beds" (279) combine modern mood with ancient heritage. In "Acropolis," nearly as innocent of capitalization as a poem by e. e. cummings and in that a departure from his usual practice, Durrell mixes past and present, living and dead:

> the soft *quem quam* will be Scops the Owl
> conjugation of nouns, a line of enquiry,
> powdery stubble of the socratic prison
> laurels crack like parchments in the wind.
>
> (281)

Presided over by the bird sacred to Athena, "strangers still arrive like sleepy gods / dismount at nightfall at desolate inns," after days spent "among the tombs gnawing of mandolines." In this eerie presentation of modern life among ancient ruins, images of the inanimate coming to life proclaim the continuity of the spirit of place, of the past: mandolines "gnaw," "the fresh spring empties like a vein," while "surely the shattered pitchers must one day / revive in the gush of marble breathing up?"

"Congenies" (1963) is representative of the best poems in *Ikons*. Named for a small village near Durrell's Sommières, the poem evokes the landscape like a painter's canvas, not surprising since Durrell was then completing some of the pictures which would be shown the next year in Paris under his *nom-de-peinture*, "Oscar Epfs":

> In tones of dust or biscuit, particularly kind to
> Loaves of sunburnt soil the plough turned back,
> Is merciful to marls in their haphazard colours,
> Blood, rust, liver, tobacco, whatnot . . .
> So far so good; but then comes the king-vine.
>
> (265)

The vine *is* king in Languedoc, and Durrell peoples his landscape with the twisted plants: "Dynasties of sturdy cruciform manikins," "snopped" by the secateurs "in circumcision," "spreadeagled helpless" against walls, martyred but resurrected, ". . . left to crucify into the small green / Pilot-leaf of flame, distrustful, lame, confiding" (266). After humanizing the vines, Durrell sees the *vignerons* in terms of plants and minerals: "And the human version matches—the stock thick. / Thighs roll to the whistle and snatch of scythes. / Bonemeal grows necks of rock and teeth like dice." The past is still present, "Among these tumbled Roman wall and towers," under whose shadows vines and men have lived parallel lives in "this immensely quiet valley / Alive to the clicking of the pruners' toil." Initiated into the art of pruning by the "Old Mathieu" he described in an article for *Time and Tide* magazine, Durrell became part of the wine culture of Languedoc as he had earlier adopted Corfu's sea and olives. Again, his life informed his poetry.

Between the publication of *Tree of Idleness* (1955) and *The Ikons*, Durrell wrote little verse, being occupied with *The Alexandria Quartet* and then, due to the financial security it brought him, with the modernizing of a rustic farmhouse, the Mazet Michel. Also, he was writing plays for the innovative Hamburg director, Gustaf Gründgens. Finally, his marriage to the lovely and supremely capable Claude Vincendon was evidently a happy one. But whenever his life has been flowing relatively smoothly, some malicious god—and Durrell is too much a Mediterranean not to agree—steps in to disrupt his life. The German invasion of Greece, the neuroses of Eve, the Enosis conflict on Cyprus: each drastically altered his plans. On New Year's Day, 1967, Claude died unexpectedly after a short illness. The calm, reflective verse of *Ikons*, poems conveying a sense of personal well-being, gave way to the often anguished poems about ageing, loss, vampirism, and death in *The Red Limbo Lingo* (1971), *Vega* (1973), and *Lifelines* (1974).

Hayden Carruth, in a perceptive and often engagingly flippant essay on Durrell's poetry entitled "Nougat for the Old Bitch," finds "something almost Frostian" in his writing. "Would he be shocked to be called the Frost of the Peloponnesos or some such?"[7] asks Carruth. A fine 1971 poem, "Last Heard Of," invites comparison with Frost's "Oven Bird": both deal with "what to make of a diminished thing," as the American poet characterized the problem of ebbing life. Durrell's image is more striking than Frost's retiring bird:

> The big rivers are through with me, I guess;
> Can't walk by Thames any more
> But the inexpressible sadness settles
> Like soft soot on dusk.
>
> (320)

Durrell names other rivers which are through with him:

> . . . the mind-propelling, youth-devouring ones
> Like Nile or Seine, or black Brahmaputra
> Where I was born and never went back again
> To stars printed in shining tar.

Each river stands for a stage in Durrell's development: the Brahmaputra his childhood in India with its star-studded nights; the Thames his young manhood and early poetic efforts in London; the Seine his introduction to Henry Miller and Anaïs Nin; the Nile the maturing shocks of wartime Egypt. These rivers also imply a history of Western civilization: its birth in Indo-European languages and Egyptian culture; its efflorescence in such European capitals as Paris and London. It is no accident that Durrell names precisely these rivers as being "through" with him. But does this mean he has given up his art along with his youth? No, for he concludes,

> I am thinking of things I would rather avoid
> Alone in furnished rooms
> Listening for those nymphs I've always waited for,
> So silent, sitting upright, looking so unowned
> And working my destiny on their marble looms.

Like conversation among familiars, the tone of this poem is typical of his later verse: the deliberate "I guess," and the cliché "Alone in furnished rooms" as if to underscore that most devastating cliché of declining life, old age. Among the "things" the poet would rather not think about is surely death: the rivers are through with him, he has told us, ". . . except the one of sorrows / Which winds to forts of calm where dust rebukes / The vagaries of minds in silent poses." This river of "sorrows" must be the Acheron, the river of woe in Classical mythology. "Dust," death, resides in the "forts of calm," tombs, perhaps, or minds gone silent. The poet has not gone silent, but is still working out his destiny on the "looms" of the muses, "those nymphs I've always waited for." Although Durrell tempts us to see the nymphs as Fates weaving his destiny—"I have been washed up here or there"—in the last five lines the focus is on the poet: it is the narrator, not the nymphs, who is waiting, "So silent, sitting upright, looking so unowned / And working." In Durrell's nearly contemporaneous fiction, *The Avignon Quintet,* one of his personae, the fictive novelist Sutcliffe, is described as being "unowned," "unloved," "like an old bugle full of spit." But Durrell like Sutcliffe keeps creating; it is his fate. At the threshold of the muses / Fates ambiguity of the nymphs, Durrell exploits the possibility that these are the very real "nymphs" of physical experience he is awaiting. If these maidens are any relation to Eliot's Thames nymphs in *The Waste Land,* the "marble looms" could also refer to the pale, smooth bodies of the poet's lovers. He recognizes the shallowness of these meetings, yet he derives spiritual and artistic profit from even the most trivial. Durrell has linked his three big subjects, love, death, and poetry, to the creative media central to the image pattern of "Last Heard Of," to the inspirations he has derived from the "big rivers" and their nymphs: the stars are "printed," the very dust of mortality "poses," and the poet's written claim on destiny is woven on "marble looms."

Love, death, art: these three themes are united in "A Patch of Dust," one of Durrell's most perfectly realized poems, in which he pledges his faith unto death, his steadfast acceptance of the life remaining to him. Significantly, Durrell chose this poem to be one of the four collected under the title *Lifelines* in a privately printed pamphlet; these are lifelines for a man tormented by thoughts of suicide and death. He compares Vincent van Gogh to Johann Wolfgang von Goethe, an artist who committed suicide at age thirty-seven to a poetic genius who wrote his way out of his early temptations toward suicide to die at age eighty-two in his bed with the words "Light, more light!" upon his lips. Durrell's poem treats the artist's tightrope act, his need to survive yet at the same time to astonish; and he declares his "loyalty" to the tormented Van Gogh over the solid statesman and literary oracle Goethe.

Is the "dust" of the title and of the first line, "In all this summer dust O Vincent" (337) and in the second-to-the-last line, "All this I saw in a patch of dust at St Remy" (338), the biblical dust from which man came and to which he must return, Hamlet's "quintessence of dust," or Eliot's "fear in a handful of dust"? Very likely Durrell had all three in mind. *Dust* is a common word in his poetry, often synonymous with the biblical reference to man's mortality. Durrell comes close to both Shakespeare's and Eliot's uses of *dust* to reflect death, and in talking about Goethe, the German Shakespeare, he refers to the "Famous last words to reach the inessential," Goethe's dying phrase and a complement to Hamlet's "quintessence of dust." Durrell implies that Goethe missed the quintessence which Shakespeare and Van Gogh found. A paradox illustrates the opposition Durrell evidently saw between Goethe and Van Gogh: the dying Goethe mistakenly thought that "more light" could reverse the process of death, while the light-madness of Van Gogh drove him inexorably down the spiral of insanity to suicide, to non-light. To survive, Durrell had to avoid the errors of both.

Durrell's choice of Van Gogh as a subject, and particularly the St. Remy period of the painter's life, is significant. Durrell too has been a painter since the 1930s, although his bright gouache renderings of Mediterranean scenes are more reminiscent in style of Matisse than of Van Gogh. Durrell's own release of spirit under the influence of the Greek sun came early, and Van Gogh responded similarly to the Midi after the gloomy skies of the north. It was at Arles, only sixty kilometers from Durrell's Sommières, that Van Gogh turned to the brilliant palette of his later work; and Durrell spent many summers at Les Stes. Maries de la Mer, which Van Gogh had visited in June 1888. Why did Durrell choose the St. Remy period, between Van Gogh's marvellously productive Arles sojourn and his brief stay at Auvers, the site of his suicide? After the relative serenity of the Arles canvasses, those painted at the asylum at St. Remy are twisted, violent, nervous, unstable, almost formless. Durrell makes it additionally clear that it is the later Van Gogh he means by addressing him as Vincent, the name the artist signed to his paintings from shortly before the St. Remy days until his death in 1890. And in Durrell's life at this time despair and self-doubt oppressed him: his fourth marriage was showing signs of fracture after a mere two years; he was suffering from a painful eczema; his work on *Monsieur* was not going well. It would be a mistake, however, to overlook the humorous tone of the poem, Durrell's ability to laugh at his misfortunes once again coming to his rescue. Even the "Patch" of the title suggests the colloquial name for a clown, and the dust traces the harlequin's family line back to Hamlet's Yorick and to the "noble dust" of Alexander used to "stop a beer barrel."

No discussion of Durrell's late poetry would be complete without a consideration of the masterly handling of the image pattern in such poems as "A Patch of Dust." The key word here is *light*, which shimmers through the deliberate dichotomy of the poem: "dust" is both the opaque stopping of a bunghole and the dust-motes glinting in sunlight, "In all this summer sun O Vincent." Van Gogh's canvasses contain "the candlepower of stored light," at once a literal truth, "Like water in the humps of camels or in / Canopies of fire smouldering in volcanoes" (337), and an oxymoronic image, for how can light be stored, except in the form of energy? Soon we are given the answer: for the storage is figurative, unseen and unseeable, yet as real as the water stored in the humps of camels, as the fire hidden in dormant volcanoes, and as real as the poems and paintings stored in artists' minds. The light illuminates "Memory giving the ikon of love a morbid kiss!" The poet's loves live now in memory, just as Van Gogh five years before his death renounced the prospect of happiness through love yet lit up the world with the brilliant light of his paintings, just as the Greek peasant lights up his ikons with votive candles. The fires of love also belong to the same realm as the "stored" light.

> Bravely the poet proclaims,

> It doesn't matter; in the silent night
> Fragrant with the death of so many friends, poets,
> The major darkness comes and art beckons
> With its quiet seething of the writer's mind.

He announces a *Liebestod* in which the lover is Art: "art beckons." Art in its perfection draws the artist away from life, toward death, toward a night swirling with Van Gogh's stars. The stored light, the stored water, each stands for the energy stored in the writer's talent, energy released in the "silent night," a night made "fragrant" with the death of friends. By 1974 Durrell had lost many friends, yet it is an article of faith with him that a poet's death is never wrong, that true poets sense the right time to depart. Writer-friends who had died by the time this poem was written include Richard Aldington, T. S. Eliot, John Gawsworth, R. Romilly Fedden, George Seferis, Bernard Spencer, and Dylan Thomas. They have made death's night "fragrant" for the poet, have shown him the way into death and unto dust, to the stored stuff of mankind, to the primal reservoir of stored art.

Durrell's quarrel with Van Gogh is that he was not able to see by the light he poured into his canvasses, or to profit by the love he felt:

> But the terror for me is that you didn't realise
> That love, even in inferior versions, is a kind
> Of merciful self-repair. O Vincent you were blind,
> Like some great effluent performer
> Discharging whole rivers into hungry seas.
>
> (338)

In Van Gogh's giving of himself, both in art and light, his love was subverted, and he kept nothing back for "self-repair." Thus, in Durrell's image equation, stored light equals withheld love, let out, in the case of Van Gogh, only in his art: and so, tragically, he had cut himself off from humanity. This is Durrell's "fatal diagnosis of light, more light," the principle which had misled Van Gogh just as it had the dying Goethe. Ironically, the light which tormented Van Gogh to suicide also deluded the dying Goethe into thinking that with "more light" he could elude death. But Van Gogh was tormented in other ways than Goethe or than the poet Durrell: his "ethical strife" "signposting always desires at bay" also prevented him from achieving the "merciful self-repair" of love. Paradoxically, the excess of light which leads to the blindness of Eastern sun-worshippers can also bring truth through the realization that nothing can really be known. The recognition of blindness, ignorance, is the first step toward truth, "Because the irritation of light leads onwards / Towards blindness which is truth, an unknowing." Finally, however, the poet issues a warning: art is a "jack o'lantern to console and punish." Like the will-o-the-wisp, it may lead us to death as easily as to knowledge.

The three big words of Durrell's poetic vocabulary are art, love, and death: light stands against death, the "major darkness," yet "art beckons" the writer towards the "silent night" of death. Behind all this hangs Van Gogh's "great canvas humming like a top," and he himself becomes the embodiment of the artist who in his search for light, for knowledge, has pushed himself to the point of madness, the "companionship of angels." In his direct vision of truth, Van Gogh has cut himself off from love. Not so the poet, living with his "French whore" (338), recognizing the limitations of his advancing age and, even more important, of his increasing wisdom: "The creed of loneliness is all that's left, / And art." Like Socrates, for whom the beginning of wisdom was the recognition that he knew nothing, like the Eastern sages who moved towards passive acceptance, knowledge through unknowing, Durrell here depicts a cosmic wisdom based on duality: light leads to the acceptance of night, action ("One must act") to the restfulness of passivity, art to the embrace of death. "All this I saw in a patch of dust at St Remy / During the fatal year of 1974," Durrell concludes. The vision is the more all-containing since the images of the poem emphasize all four elements of ancient creation: Earth (dust), Air ("Famous last words . . ."), Fire (light, "Canopies of fire"), and Water (the doges of Venice, the "hungry seas"). Wryly, the poet sees himself living in loneliness and "dying of self-importance," rejecting Goethe's dying assertion that with "light, more light" death would become unnecessary, rejecting the madness and suicide of Van Gogh, yet preferring the Dutch painter's wild and bitter struggle to the solid unresting striving of the German genius. The tremendous power of "A Patch of Dust" comes from this welding of image and theme, of the elements of creation and the core preoccupations of life. No, the big rivers do not seem to be through with Lawrence Durrell yet.

What we have seen over the range of Durrell's poetry is a considerable variety in expression, a development from the derivative early verse to the conversational yet still lyrical rhythms of his major poems. Also, that Durrell has reflected certain key events and crises in the mirror of his poetry shows the importance of biography to a consideration of his art. Does the poetry as assembled in *Collected Poems, 1931–1974* refute Fraser's judgment that Durrell's poetic *oeuvre* presents the "expression of a temperament, rather than the history of a soul"? Yes, if maturing heartbreak over separation, insanity, and loss; a gradual acceptance of Eastern duality and passivity as both philosophy and religion; and an eventual reconciliation of love, death, and art constitute the history of his soul. Finally, among the poems of the 1950s, 1960s, and 1970s are enough of the top rank to show that Durrell has been capable of continued high accomplishment long after his first two Faber collections, and to make us regret that he has published little verse since 1974. But then, he has been writing *The Avignon Quintet*, and concentrated work on fiction has invariably meant little time and energy for poetry. Now that Durrell has completed his "Quincunx," perhaps we can expect some important late poems.

Notes

1. G. S. Fraser, *Lawrence Durrell: A Critical Study* (New York: Dutton, 1968), p. 29. Hereafter cited in the text as LD.

2. Lawrence Durrell, *Collected Poems, 1931–1974*, ed. James A. Brigham (New York: Viking, 1980), p. 25. Hereafter cited in context by page number in parentheses; where there are two or more consecutive references to the same page, only the first appearance will be noted.

3. Lawrence Durrell, *Spirit of Place: Letters and Essays on Travel*, ed. Alan G. Thomas (London: Faber and Faber, 1971), p. 17.

4. Durrell remarked in an unpublished interview with the author on 14 December 1983, "I wrote *Pied Piper of Lovers* [1935] to prove to my family that I was a writer. They couldn't deny a bound volume. After that they had to take me seriously."

5. Lawrence Durrell, *A Key to Modern British Poetry* (Norman, Okla.: University of Oklahoma Press, 1952), p. 101. Hereafter cited in context as KMBP.

6. Lawrence Durrell, *The Alexandria Quartet* (New York: Dutton, 1962), p. 877.

7. Hayden Carruth, "Nougat for the Old Bitch," in *The World of Lawrence Durrell*, ed. Harry T. Moore (New York: Dutton, 1964), p. 118.

Works Cited

Carruth, Hayden. "Nougat for the Old Bitch." In *The World of Lawrence Durrell*, edited by Harry T. Moore, 117–28. New York: Dutton, 1964.

Durrell, Lawrence. *The Alexandria Quartet*. New York: Dutton, 1962.

———. *Collected Poems, 1931–1974*. Edited by James A. Brigham. New York: Viking, 1980.

———. "From the Elephant's Back." *Poetry London / Apple Magazine* 2 (1982):1–9.

———. *A Key to Modern British Poetry*. Norman, Okla.: University of Oklahoma Press, 1952.

———. "Old Mathieu." *Time and Tide* 39 (6 December 1958):1464. Reprinted in *Spirit of Place*, listed below.

———. *Spirit of Place: Letters and Essays on Travel*. Edited by Alan G. Thomas. London: Faber and Faber, 1971.

———. Unpublished Interview with Ian S. MacNiven, Sommières, 14 December 1983.

Fraser, G. S. *Lawrence Durrell: A Critical Study*. New York: Dutton, 1968.

Friedman, Alan Warren. *Lawrence Durrell and "The Alexandria Quartet": Art for Love's Sake*. Norman, Okla.: University of Oklahoma Press, 1970.

An Unacknowledged Trilogy   James A. Brigham*

What's become of the early novels? *The Black Book* has been available in an American edition since 1960, and it was finally published in England in 1973. But *Pied Piper of Lovers* (1935) and *Panic Spring* (1937) have both been out-of-print for more than forty years, and nothing is being done to reissue them. Mention them casually to Durrell and he'll laugh and say, "Good God! The family doesn't talk about *them* any more!" They weren't particularly good novels: *Pied Piper* is the predictable *Bildungsroman* of a twenty-three-year-old, and *Panic Spring* presents a set of character studies loosely linked by the presence of all the characters on the same island in the Adriatic. But Professors Wickes and Weigel were incorrect when they described *Pied Piper* as "an account of bohemian life in Bloomsbury"[1] and *Panic Spring* as merely "a put-together job by a young writer who is impressed by and borrows from the best talents and minds of his time."[2] Both novels contain some fine bits of writing, as Durrell himself was aware,[3] and they should be reissued as the early work of a major novelist, for they will repay the reader interested in Durrell with glimpses of themes and character types that would be prominent features of *The Dark Labyrinth* (1947) and *The Alexandria Quartet* (1957–1960).

And they will pay another, greater dividend: the attentive reader who is not deterred as G. S. Fraser was[4] and who reads right the way through *Pied Piper, Panic Spring*, and *The Black Book* will suddenly realise that he

*Reprinted from *Deus Loci: The Lawrence Durrell Newsletter* 2, no. 3 (March 1979):3–12.

has been reading a trilogy. Taken separately, the three are so different in setting, structure, and characters that a reader might be forgiven for thinking that they have little in common; taken together, the three appear as complementary novels, panels of a triptych in which the setting changes but which are linked by small structural parallels and the reappearance of characters, and, more importantly, by textual echoes so clear that they cause one narrator to comment, "This is a piece out of another book."[5]

Pied Piper of Lovers is itself a work in three parts, with a "Prologue," and an "Epilogue" which points to *Panic Spring*. The "Prologue" neatly births the eponymous hero, Walsh Clifton, who is the half-caste son of an English father and a Burmese mother, and almost immediately disposes of the mother. Thus we are left with the Cliftons, *père et fils*, whom we meet at the beginning of Book One when Walsh is six.[6] In an early letter to Henry Miller, Durrell gave a biographical sketch which might have been a summary of the plot of *Pied Piper:* "My birth and upbringing?" he asks. "I was born in India. Went to school there—under the Himalayas. The most wonderful memories, a brief dream of Tibet until I was eleven. Then that mean, shabby little island up there wrung my guts out of me and tried to destroy anything singular and unique in me."[7] In Book One, Walsh goes to school—both the formal one run by the Jesuits and the informal one presided over by a little native boy who becomes his friend—and, at the end, has a nightmare which brings all of the events of that book together with the realisation that he is going to England and leaving India forever (pp. 150–154). Book Two opens aboard the liner which is taking Walsh and his Aunt Brenda "home," and the boy is very quickly installed in a public school which, for the most part, he doesn't leave until the death of his father at the end of this section of the novel. Book Two is important to our discussion because it introduces Ruth and her brother, Gordon, who tells Clifton, " 'You're not a damned Englander yet. [. . .] They haven't got you yet. [. . .] [I'm English.] At least that's my nationality, but I don't stand for any of the things that your Englishman stands for. And you don't . . . yet. They haven't spoiled you yet . . . ' " (p. 217), and thus introduces the idea of a spiritual sickness from which some of the characters in *Panic Spring* will suffer and which Durrell will identify as "the English death" in *The Black Book*. Book Three is really a rejection of "bohemian life in [a] Bloomsbury" which echoes hauntingly Wyndham Lewis's *The Apes of God* (1930). By the end of Book Three, Walsh has rediscovered Ruth and has begun to see England as a perverted nineteenth-century "heaven" rather than the "land of hope and glory" to which his father had once thought he was sending him. The "Epilogue" finds Walsh and Ruth earning a meagre living writing jazz tunes, and preparing to "move across the billow" (p. 371) to a Greek island from which Gordon has been writing to them.

Panic Spring opens with the voyage to Gordon's island, a voyage undertaken, not by Walsh Clifton but by Christian Marlowe, a schoolmaster who has taken a leave-of-absence to write a book on Quietism. Like the rest of the characters, Marlowe is taken to a small island in the Adriatic by Christ, a boatman with curiously Pan-like feet.[8] With such an obviously Lawrentian figure as a guide, we are prepared for the self-revelations and self-realisations that comprise the bulk of the novel. Upon his arrival on Mavrodaphne, Marlowe meets Francis and Fonvisin, Walsh and Gordon, and Rumanades, the owner of the island. The plot, such as it is, is sparse after this point: the various characters interact; Rumanades becomes ill and dies; and the rest all prepare to go their ways. But, where *Pied Piper* takes its linear progression from the biography of Walsh Clifton, *Panic Spring* is more like a collage in which several characters are juxtaposed. Each of the major figures has a chapter, and each character study makes clear the ways in which the character is suffering from a disease not unlike "the English death." Durrell originally called this novel "Music in Limbo,"[9] and a limbo is precisely what the major characters inhabit: Mavrodaphne is a point of rest from which they can analyse their own predicaments before moving on.

The structure of *Panic Spring* is not unlike the structure which Durrell would use in *The Black Book:* "I've tried," he wrote to Alan Thomas, "just for an exercise in writing to create characters on two continuous planes of life—the present—meaning the island and their various pasts. It does not progress as an ordinary novel progresses. The tentacles push out sideways while the main body is almost static."[10] *The Black Book* is composed of three quite distinct units: the present on Corfu; memories of the England which Lawrence Lucifer, the narrator, has left before the novel begins; and passages from the diary of Herbert "Death" Gregory. The whole novel is a chronicle of "the English death," which makes its point by juxtaposing characters and events from the three units to show that the disease is absolutely fatal unless one recognizes the symptoms and effects a cure by leaving England forever. "Dear Alan," Lawrence Lucifer writes in Book Two: "this is a very necessary valediction, not only to England, but, if you like to the world. [. . .] It was the temptation of the devil, the vision of the cities offered to me from an immense mountaintop. The devil! What should be more plausible than that you should be the Black Saint himself—panurgic, long-nosed, calculating bastard that you are! You were offering me, in your oblique way, the whole of England—the masques, the viols, the swans, the mists, the doom, the fogs: you were offering me a medieval death in which I could live forever, stifled in the pollen of breviaries, noctuaries, bestiaries: split silk and tumbrils, aesthetic horses and ruined Abbeys. [. . .] That is an England I am going to kill. . . ."[11] While it recapitulates the themes of the earlier novels, *The Black Book* is also and more importantly an act of ritual murder, and the third novel ends with a narrator who has passed from the death-in-life which "Death" Gregory seems to have accepted through the limbo of indecision to a new state of being in which, for the first time, he feels truly alive.

As we have seen, *Panic Spring* is structurally different from *Pied Piper*:

the elements of its plot are grouped spatially around an "almost static" core instead of being arranged in a linear fashion. There is a passage near the end of *Pied Piper* which provides a key of sorts to the structural shift in volume two of the trilogy. In the letter to his room-mate, Turnbull, which comprises the "Epilogue" to the novel, Walsh Clifton speaks of "the eternal quibble with words. Failing to express to others what you have expressed to yourself. I think sculpture is the medium in which to express. Space against Time curves and stresses, structures and dimensions. How in hell can I express the *volume* of things by daubing ink on paper?" (p. 369). The structure of *Panic Spring* is a response to Clifton's question, and so is the structure of *The Black Book*. There is a narrative progression in the third novel which parallels that of one and two taken together, but the structural mode is spatial rather than linear, and is the product of a logical progression from the biography of *Pied Piper* through the annihilation of linear time with the use of "memory" chapters in *Panic Spring*.

Just as Walsh Clifton's remarks on "the eternal quibble with words" foreshadow the techniques of the second novel, so, too, *Panic Spring* is tied to *Pied Piper* through the presence of Clifton on Mavrodaphne. Chapter VII of *Panic Spring* is devoted to "Walsh," and it may well be a chapter of *Pied Piper* which was cut out and replaced by the "Epilogue" as a more satisfactory way of ending that novel. There are more details about the life of Ruth and Walsh as described in the "Epilogue," some of which tie directly to the earlier novel. For example, Walsh's reference to the jazz tunes which he and Ruth had been writing is paralleled in detail. In *Pied Piper*, Clifton tells Turnbull, "The two which we've done while we've been here are called, respectively, 'Hold Your Woman' . . . and 'Never Come Back' " (p. 371; italics mine). In the comparable passage in *Panic Spring* there is "a cheque for thirty pounds on the mantelpiece and a letter from Garland saying: 'Do you mind selling your soul? You do it well. This last tune of yours is good. As I see it you'll be rich before long. *Ecstasy to be in Love* is still selling mildly. *But I anticipate bigger things from this one, 'Never Come Back' "* (p. 106; italics mine). Garland is also an echo from *Pied Piper*, and the Christmas card from "Gordon, Ruth's brother, with a beautiful Greek stamp" and the suggestion that Ruth bring Walsh down to "this Island" (*Panic Spring*, pp. 123–124), is a retrospective link between the two books. These links are certainly not fortuitous, and this same section of *Panic Spring* contains references to characters who will appear in *The Black Book*. For example, Tarquin, the village schoolmaster near whom Walsh and Ruth lived in England, is a "memory" character in the second novel. He is not really presented as a character *per se* until he appears as a major figure in *The Black Book*. In this way, through the presence of characters in two of the three novels, Durrell provides clear links between the volumes of his trilogy.

It might be argued at this point that, rather than being involved with a trilogy as such, we are faced with one novel which Durrell clearly felt was his first true book,[12] and that those passages in *The Black Book* which echo the previous novels simply appear because he wanted to condense his statement on "the English death" into one novel. In other words, the echoes are not intended to form any kind of summary tying the three novels together. This would be quite defensible if it were not for the details from *Pied Piper* and *Panic Spring* which appear in the third novel. Toward the end of *The Black Book*, this lengthy passage appears:

> Let us walk quietly in the declension of the season, smoke a pipe over the gate, take note of how the asphodels are doing. In the little house run over the accounts, select a book, doze over the fire, or at bedtime light the candles and start the piano hymning. It is all the same, for this is a piece out of another book. It is significant merely because Tarquin is mentioned. Over the fire and the crusader's hearth, in the smoke of pipes, Tarquin is mentioned. It is a strange immortality to be consummated here, in this cottage, drowned in flowers, under the glimmering bottoms of the books. I record it now merely to reassure myself that we are never forgotten (p. 251).

This passage echoes directly that portion of the "Walsh" chapter of *Panic Spring* in which Clifton's later relationship with Ruth is discussed and Tarquin is, indeed, mentioned:

> Walsh would go instead for a walk, dropping in on his way home at Tarquin's cottage. Tarquin was the schoolmaster.
> Sitting in the threadbare armchair, puffing his pipe, he would be again amazed at the huge, bald, gentle cranium of his host; the twists of silver at his ears. The mild eyes, almost olive-purple, with their fine lashes.

> Tarquin was interesting because he was a splendid medium: through him one could reach history. No, it was more than that, for Tarquin *was* history. The perfect refugee to whom any age was more immediately accessible than his own, he lived between the fireside and the long shelves of dusty books which fed his insatiable taste for the living death (p. 117).

The parallels between these two passages are too exact to be accidental, and the excerpt from *The Black Book* actually stipulates that "this is a piece out of another book."

The correspondences between *Pied Piper* and *The Black Book* are not as direct—or at least not as directly stated. The clearest parallels are with Book One of the first novel: there are many references to Tibet or to India in the final volume of the trilogy. While most have symbolic significance, three specific references echo *Pied Piper* quite unmistakeably.

The earliest reference is interesting because of the precise details from the first novel which it contains. "Letters with Indian stamps on them, Halma, Ludo, Baedeker, Old Moore, dripping, sequel, the green house lit with a green rain from heaven, the haggard fingers stitching a winding cloth for the morning . . ." (*The Black Book*, p. 52). The "green house lit with a green rain from heaven" is clearly "the house . . . called 'Emerald Hall' " to which the Cliftons move from Burma in *Pied Piper* (pp. 49–50). The "haggard fingers stitching a winding cloth for the morning" are the fingers of the old doctor who, with an Indian servant, "crossed the room to the bedside and started to sew a blanket about the body" of Clifton's mother the morning after his birth (*Pied Piper*, p. 28).

The next reference to the first novel, a passage much too long to quote here, contains numerous correspondences which would have to be picked out of *Pied Piper* page by page, and the catalogue would become tedious (*The Black Book*, pp. 152–153). It is a reminiscence, virtually a resume of the sights and sounds of the Indian hill country described in the first novel. The opening sentence is significant: "When the drums begin, and the opaque lightning trembles in the night sky, I become a child again, in revisited history" (p. 152). With this sentence, Durrell throws the reader back into the first novel and at the same time brings forward from that book the very presence of the Tibet which [he] employs as a symbol in book three.

The final clear reference to *Pied Piper of Lovers* in *The Black Book* is to some extent a continuation of the previous example as well as an amplification of the "brief dream of Tibet" to which Durrell referred in his letter to Miller.

> Tibet hangs like a sphinx over the revisited childhood which my dreams offer me: the craters crammed with jewelry; the hills curving up into their vertiginous flowers of snow; the dawn opening like a coral umbrella on Lhasa; the yak and the black bear the only visitors of that immense vista in time; the monasteries as remote as stars upon the hills; everything has fallen upon me in this stuffy English room with a pathos that is beyond ink (pp. 237–238).

The heroes of the trilogy—Walsh Clifton, Christian Marlowe, and Lawrence Lucifer—all experience the same sort of despair that Durrell felt before he left England in 1935, but only Lawrence Lucifer identifies their common malaise as "the English death" and prescribes a rejection of England as the cure. In *The Black Book*, Tibet becomes Ultima Thule (p. 244), the place to which the blessed are taken and a symbol of the breaking free of England. Walsh Clifton learns by the end of *Pied Piper* that England offers "a medieval death in which [he] could live forever." In *Panic Spring*, Christian Marlowe discovers the truth about England, but—having found his own form of quietism—he returns, like the troglodyte to the Platonic cave, to tell anyone who will listen what he has found. And Lawrence Lucifer narrates *The Black Book* from Corfu, the island which was clearly the model for Mavrodaphne in *Panic Spring*.

W. Y. Evans-Wentz, in his preface to *The Tibetan Book of the Dead*, states that "*The Egyptian Book of the Dead*, correctly entitled, is *The Coming Forth from Day*, with reference to the sacred Egyptian art of the coming forth from this life into another life. . . . Similarly, [the title of] *The*

Tibetan Book of the Dead [implies] a *yogic* method of coming forth into *Nirvanic* Liberation, beyond the Cycle of Birth and Death. Each of these two books concerning death thus inculcates, by its own peculiar method, an Art of Dying and Coming Forth into a New Life."[13] In a "Contributors" note to the September, 1937 issue of *The Booster*, Lawrence Durrell is said to be "now at work on *The Book of the Dead*."[14] At that point, *Pied Piper* and *Panic Spring* were in print, and—although *The Black Book* would not be published until June of the following year—the same note lists the third novel, and an excerpt from it actually appeared in the next issue. On what, then, was Durrell working? Future commentators may well discover that the whole of his prose fiction forms a multi-volumed "book of the dead." Certainly the first three novels constitute a trilogy which presents a guide to the thoughtful English reader who, having recognised that his culture is terminal, wishes to learn the "Art of Dying and Coming Forth into a New Life."

Notes

1. George Wickes, ed., *Lawrence Durrell and Henry Miller: A Private Correspondence* (London) Faber (1963), p. 3.

2. John A. Weigel, *Lawrence Durrell* (N.Y.) Twayne (1965), p. 43.

3. See his comment on *Panic Spring* in Alan G. Thomas, ed., *Spirit of Place: Letters and Essays on Travel* (London)Faber (1969), p. 38.

4. G. S. Fraser, *Lawrence Durrell: A Study* (London) Faber (1968), p. 10.

5. Lawrence Durrell, *The Black Book: An Agon* (Paris) The Obelisk Press (1938), p. 251. Hereinafter cited as "*The Black Book*."

6. Lawrence Durrell, *Pied Piper of Lovers* (London) Cassell (1935), p. 39. Hereinafter cited as "*Pied Piper*."

7. Wickes, ed., *A Private Correspondence*, p. 60.

8. Lawrence Durrell, *Panic Spring: A Romance* (London) Faber (1937), p. 32. Hereinafter cited as "*Panic Spring*."

9. See Durrell's letter to Thomas re: *Panic Spring* cited above.

10. Durrell's letter to Thomas re: *Panic Spring* cited above.

11. *The Black Book*, pp. 139–140.

12. Lawrence Durrell, "Preface" to *The Black Book* (Paris) Olympia Press (1959), p. 8.

13. W. Y. Evans-Wentz, "Preface to the Second Edition," *The Tibetan Book of the Dead* (London) Oxford University Press (1960) [1949; 1927], p. xvi.

14. *The Booster*, II: 7 (September 1937), 49.

[Durrell's *Alexandria Quartet*]   Frank Kermode*

I

[T]he major modern novel is a poem, giving the *kind* of pleasure that the vast majority of new novels do not even aim at. One of the few exceptions is Mr. Durrell's work in progress, an anatomy of love undertaken in the conviction that "somewhere in the heart of experience there is an order and a coherence which we might surprise if we were attentive enough, loving enough, patient enough," to quote its narrator. One must respect the attempt, in *Justine*, to focus the thing itself, to get something analogous to Lear tearing off his clothes, in that basic act of sex in a bazaar-booth, where the lovers lie "like the victims of some terrible accident"; and, in theory, the power of love to evolve into every species of perversity and refinement, without severing its relations with simple evil, is a wonderful theme for a book about everything. But Mr. Durrell seems not to hold on, to keep his poem on earth and be that kind of necessary angel. His angel becomes a Neoplatonic demon, his Alexandria is too Alexandrian, his fineness turns into finesse, and we become (to borrow an analogy of his own) as dulled by its battery as a chamberpot at a symposium. Consequently it seems to fall short of completeness; measure it, for this quality, by *Doctor Zhivago*. Yet *Justine* and its successors would remind us of the need for such attempts to treat, parabolically, everything, at a time when novels are merely about something, like the Foreign Office or aeroplanes or Chelsea or sin. [. . .]

II

We now have three parts of Mr. Durrell's tetralogy, and it may be possible to take a few inadequate, merely three-dimensional, bearings; always remembering that in the nature of the case these can be only relatively true, and that Mr. Durrell's is a work which sets out, like all Romantic art, to disarm this kind of inquiry. There are moments when critics, like priests, simply have to prefer their own systematizations to those of the creator, arguing that otherwise he will be even more seriously misunderstood. The publication of *Mountolive* brings us to the first point where anything useful may be said, however tentative and blundering.

Considered in itself, *Mountolive* seems to me the best novel in the series, though of course it's hard to discount the pressure of the others as one reads it. It goes over the same situation as the other two, but provides a lot of new information about the story, some of it radically altering the character of previously described persons and events. . . . But *Mountolive* is distinguished from the others by its being uniformly impressive from be-

*Reprinted from *Puzzles and Epiphanies: Essays and Reviews 1958–1961* (London: Routledge and Kegan Paul, 1962), 214–27.

ginning to end, partly, no doubt, because its narrative method involves far less merely rhetorical strain than that of the earlier volumes. There the need to produce a various and dazzling texture led to bursts of overwriting, which an author so omnisciently in love with language would in any case— given the setting—find it hard to avoid. . . . In the new book there is not this nimiety, and there is corresponding gain in control of texture and image: "the English of fine breeding and polish which carried those invisible diacritical marks, the expression of caste." The earlier novels benefit, of course, by this new, luminous strength.

However, the relation between the books is not merely that each reveals new aspects of the others; certainly there are clearings-up of mysteries, but it is all much more ambitious than that. From Mr. Durrell's prefaces, from his appendices, and from his novelist-characters, Pursewarden and Darley, we may cautiously infer something of his intentions. He claims that he is attempting "classical status": "Modern literature offers us no Unities, so I have turned to science and am trying to complete a four-decker novel whose form is based on the relativity proposition"—three volumes for Space and one for Time, the whole thing constituting "a morphological form one might appropriately call 'classical'—for our time." Mr. Durrell fears this may sound "immodest," but of course it does not, since it is not a paradox but a simple fact that, as Pursewarden says, "The classical in art is what marches by intention with the cosmology of the age." That is why our neo-classic age was also the age of deism, and, perhaps, why Greek science and Greek tragedy grew up together. The formula doesn't, in the first instance, affect the matter of the book, so that a modern work which is in this sense "classical" may perfectly well have as its "central topic" "an investigation of modern love." But whatever its central topic, a work classical in this sense is at present likely to be, in another special sense, romantic; and just as the parallel between deism and neo-classicism, though accurate, is of secondary interest only, so relativity matters less in Mr. Durrell's work than the presumptions and the iconography of romanticism. Pursewarden speaks of his "classic head and romantic heart"; his novels were structurally similar to Mr. Durrell's, which is in this way also classic and romantic. Let me try to show how romantic myth informs it.

Justine has a faintly old-fashioned, Huysmans-like atmosphere—neurasthenia, perversion, *femmes fatales*, a certain sentimentality about the artist's life, some inhibited admiration for cruelty, and beneath most of the characters the everlasting arms of some religion, usually occult. It was, I hope, pardonable to suppose that we were getting an old Agony slightly modernized—Paris transferred, two generations late, to Alexandria. But the later books add so much that we now have, almost complete, the total, "classical," romantic mythology, so that the *fin de siècle* element takes only its proper place in the pattern. This can be seen from the full development of Pursewarden. At first we saw him through the slightly envious eye of Darley, the narrator—an inferior artist. Little emerged that had any bearing upon his gifts, though there was a good deal about how *maudit*, or, if you like, Beat, he was—a born expatriate, a drunk, a whoremaster, etc. Now the dossier is fuller, though there will probably be more in the last volume about his suicide, at present presumed to have been caused by the discovery of a mistake he made in his official capacity by relying too much on the good faith of Nessim; but his blind sister is involved somehow, as we shall see. So we don't know all. This blind sister has been his lover, a bit of Byronism perhaps meant to indicate a narcissism of the sort that sets up an oscillation between an artist's inner and outer life that only an Empedoclean suicide can end. The artist's job of providing joy and unity in a world of division, his need "to bring resolution and harmony into the dying lives around him," require him to "submit to despair." Pursewarden talks and behaves like a modern artist synthesized out of all the "classical" elements. He despises Darley, for instance, because Darley likes to talk about "the novel"; all works of art are *sui generis*. He despises the bourgeois notion of "literature" ("the poor bastard is still interested in *literature*"). He mistrusts language, a corrupt medium for communicating intuition. It is Mr. Durrell in his own person who says "words kill love as they kill everything else," but he could easily have given this to Pursewarden, with whom he absolutely must agree about all the important aesthetic issues. Pursewarden believes critics to be useless, comparing the communicated work of art to "an electromagnetic change which can't be rationalized"—sound romantic doctrine. He believes that "Reality . . . is always trying to copy the imagination of man, from which it derived"—a sophistication of the basic romantic axiom. He regards the life of the artist as essentially a progress, necessarily dissipated, from one victory, the completed work, to the next, with a period of dangerous, as it were post-coital, exhaustion intervening, during which suicide is always a possibility. He honours Blake. Finally, like the Tragic Generation, he has to face his end when young. He is Mr. Durrell's impossible central artist, his major man; and he is the key to this book.

This is not a cavalier dismissal of Mr. Durrell's own statement that the central topic is modern love. He affirms the traditional association of his topic with that of modern art, as when Justine outrages Pursewarden by telling him he is hopelessly promiscuous: "for those who love poetry," he replies, "there is no such thing as *vers libre*." This remark is profoundly right, and it brings us to consider the part of Justine, who on the face of it fits even more easily into the modern romantic myth. Among the many new things we find out about her, one is of prime doctrinal importance: Darley, in the first book, had been wrong in supposing that she was in love with him; she was, naturally, in love with Pursewarden, the better artist. Justine is often associated with the "austere mindless primitive Aphrodite," the goddess who rules over the book, though of course she is also a human being, with a queer sexual history, hysterical, destructive, intelligent, vulgar at times, and devotedly Jewish. Pursewarden himself once calls her "a tiresome old sexual turnstile through which, presumably, we all must pass"; but this does not prevent her from playing a role perfectly familiar to the long line of romantic agonists. She is sometimes Cleopatra, sometimes "the girl-friend of the man whose head was presented on a charger"—Judith, or the Salome with whom Judith is easily confused—and her face, at moments, is "expressionless as a mask of Siva." In fact she is the classic emblem of the romantic image, and of its suicidal cost to the artist. Mr. Durrell may not have thought of it in this way, I confess; but in so far as three-dimensional criticism can be true I think this is; he could not have this sort of character without these implications, though, needless to say, the material doesn't look so pointedly doctrinal when you see it in the remarkably rich context Mr. Durrell has invented for it.

Finally, one more essential romantic element. The modern novelist, if he attempts greatly, is bound by indissoluble indentures to some masters, no matter whom he may choose to serve voluntarily. Given Mr. Durrell's theme, his relation to Lawrence should be of interest. In fact he makes Pursewarden a devoted though critical friend of Lawrence, and disarms us with a postcard from disciple to master, in reply to a letter accusing him of hating the dark Gods: "I am simply trying not to copy your habit of building a Taj Mahal around anything as simple as a good f-k." This was thoughtful of Mr. Durrell, but it shouldn't divert our attention from the tremendous Laurentian build-up he gives to Narouz, the brother of Nessim. Narouz isn't even mentioned in *Justine*, so far as I remember, but later we are given a most careful and memorable account of him. He is a farmer, without civility; deformed by a harelip but very strong; cruel to servants and camels but extremely pious in religion and family relationships; an exultant tamer of horses, possessor of a terrible whip, with which he controls men and animals. Narouz, at present, dominates the whole work; his growing obsession with prophetic religion has made him a political menace, and this brings about his death at the end of *Mountolive*. Narouz is an extraordinary achievement, and he is in the book primarily because of the romantic need for a genuinely primitive figure. In that absolutely primitive act of love which Darley, in *Justine*, observed in a bazaar booth, the male partner was Narouz. He abominates literature (in this, the correlative of Pursewarden) and has no place in society, being both an outcast and a power like one of nature's. He is a sort of human St. Mawr, in fact. His slow death, a dozen bullets sunk in his body, the ritual peasant mourning over him as he lies with the great whip coiled beneath his pillow, bring the work to its latest halting-place with an effect of magnificence previously beyond Mr. Durrell's reach.

Narouz, then, adds to the classical "soupmix" another indispensable romantic herb, it now has the romantic metaphysics, the romantic iconography, the romantic primitivism. The novel is, only half-secretly, about art, the great subject of modern artists; it offers an alternative nature with another physics, highly special and highly indeterminate. There remains in the whole book too much, for my taste, of the superficial mannerism of 'nine-tyish romanticism, too much that is merely *épatant;* but of the size of Mr. Durrell's achievement there seems no longer room for reasonable doubt. I seem to hear the disagreeable laughter of Pursewarden as I publicly confess to having—like many others—badly misjudged this work in its early stages.

1959.

III

Mr. Durrell has been producing a "word-continuum," "a four-decker novel whose form is based on the relativity proposition." What he now calls the "Alexandrian Quartet" is completed by *Clea;* we have three for space and one for time, though he claims that having "the axis . . . well and truly laid down" he can, if he please, "radiate in any direction without losing the strictness and congruity of the continuum." Still, the great undertaking is complete. We had already seen the events and characters in multiple pro-file, had had the pleasure of coming upon the same moments, the same gestures and sentences, from many different points of view. In the second volume the "Interlinear" of Balthazar took us between the lines of *Justine;* in the third, *Mountolive,* the narrator Darley is reduced to a mere charac-ter in a "straight naturalistic novel" that supplies further corrections to the first two, and also provides the essential political context. The possibilities of further explanation and illumination are no doubt endless, but the most obvious lacunae are filled by *Clea;* for example, the suicide of the novelist Pursewarden is fully accounted for. As one foresaw, it has to do with his love for his blind sister, rather than with the discovery that he had been wrong about Nessim's political activities. There is a parade of familiar char-acters in new guises, and from a new angle: the lecher Capodistria, sup-posed dead in the duckshoot of the first volume; Scobie, the comic English Bimbashi, now after his death the object of a popular cult; the ambassador Mountolive, in love with Liza Pursewarden; Balthazar, half-wrecked by a disastrous affair with a Greek actor; Pombal, the amorous diplomat, at last farcically and tragically in love; Justine and Nessim; and Clea, the young painter who had formerly been a somewhat minor character, once the be-loved of Narouz, and the lover of Justine and now of Darley, that the prophecy of Darley's dead mistress Melissa might be fulfilled.

Romantic putrescence is characteristic of the whole trilogy, but *Clea,* a little unexpectedly, takes on a Proustian air—the apples-of-ash taste of Proust's last volume. Once more we pay the usual visit to the child brothel with its décor of apotropoeic palm-prints; once more the perversity and cruelty of the city are exhibited; but there is more change, decay and death. Death now comes by water; and the novel is brilliantly and silently stretched out over four images of love and death by water, the first merely a picture of a child diving, the others of the accidental death of Fosca, mistress of Pombal, of the mutilation of Clea, and of a row of dead Greek sailors in an ocean pool. Decay comes in many forms; Justine has had a stroke, Nessim has lost an eye and some fingers in an air-raid; Balthazar is toothless. Only the journalist Keats, back from action in the desert, is an improved man.

Still, all things considered, anything but rapid decay would lack verisimilitude in Mr. Durrell's Alexandria. Its erotic versatility, its many faces of pain and pleasure, appear to provide him with endless matter for his purpose, which is ostensibly the exploration of modern love. Of course he holds that this topic includes all others. "When a culture goes bad in its sex all knowledge is impeded." "Culture means sex, the root-knowledge, and where the faculty is derailed or crippled, its derivatives like religion come up dwarfed and contorted—instead of the emblematic mystic rose you get Judaic cauliflowers like Mormons or Vegetarians, instead of artists you get cry-babies, instead of philosophy, semantics."

So, naturally the tetralogy is a highly erotic work—*Clea*, though comparatively simple and changed in tone, is here at one with its predecessors. . . . What one disliked about *Justine* was the over-perfumed manner, the insistence on exotic sin and fatigue, the Huysmans-like neurasthenias, the perpetual straining of the prose to produce dazzle, and the consequent bathos. This impression was strictly qualified by the ironies of *Balthazar* and the cooler prose of *Mountolive;* but with *Clea* one's doubts return. Mr. Durrell frequently writes with a genuinely Mediterranean clarity and colour, but he cannot always be lucky, and in the descriptive and in the gnomic he frequently fails. The opening paragraph of *Clea* is badly written. "The oranges were more plentiful than usual that year. They glowed in their arbours of burnished green leaf like lanterns, flickering up there among the sunny woods. It was as if they were eager to celebrate our departure from the little island—for at last the long-awaited message from Nessim had come, like a summons back to the underworld. A message which was to draw me back inexorably to the one city. . . ." "Long-awaited," "inexorably," are tired. "Like . . . as if . . . like"—none of these metaphors is more than perfunctory. And the descriptions of the city, the *anus mundi*, heartless, beautiful, ancient, polyglot, poignant, terrifying, diseased, pleasure-seeking, epicene, and so forth, come too often with an air of weariness. The passages of erotic metaphysics, whether aphorisms or dialogues incredibly protracted and literary, one comes to dread. This is true even of the well-written extracts from Pursewarden's notebooks, intended to shock us puritans. Although Mr. Durrell has performed a considerable feat in convincing us that Pursewarden was a far better novelist than Darley, or indeed than Durrell, he cannot always prevent him from seeming tiresome and jejune. Altogether there is a great deal about kisses made more passionate by remorse, there are too many unshed tears, too many people say this kind of thing: "perhaps our only sickness is to desire a truth which we cannot bear rather than to rest content with the fictions we manufacture out of each other," following the remark with "a short ironic laugh."

Yet it may be said without violence to Mr. Durrell's intention that the heart of his book is not the erotic; that it is, as I have argued before basically about art and the artist. Pursewarden is its true hero, and the new Pursewarden material is the core of *Clea*. It is all excogitated, with great persistance, from a radical Romantic myth. Mr. Durrell has put in the centre of his ambitious novel a writer capable of even more ambitious novels of exactly the same kind (and there is a third novelist, Arnauti, to give more density to this handling of the artist). The writer's problem is that the image dissolves in "the acid bath of words"; he struggles perpetually with "the failure of words" to support the image; he is a Symbolist, aiming at "the abbreviation of language into poem." His concern is with "the heraldic aspect of reality." All these new observations confirm the Symbolist position already established in the earlier books. Art is therapeutic but not didactic, and the earlier saying that the artist is concerned with joy alone, but that he must submit to despair, is here repeated. Art says nothing; it "points, like a man too ill to speak." Consequently criticism is absurd or obscene, certainly irrelevant; Clea strikes Darley only for saying he is thinking of writing a critical book. Now why Pursewarden, who writes a great deal along these lines, should think his beliefs "strange" is not clear; they are almost entirely orthodox, as derivative as his account of our "progress from the belly-consciousness to the head-consciousness." And *Clea*, readable though it is in every page, adds almost nothing to what the other books have promulgated on these topics.

Indeed, despite the shift of attention to Clea herself, there is some flagging of invention in this book. For example, the long excursus on Capodistria's black magic seems extraneous to the cabbalism of the earlier books, so well integrated with the political plot. Also, there is the feeling that we are touring determinedly round for the last look at the old faces and places. Also, Scobie isn't as funny as he needs to be. Also, there is the occasional fatigue of the prose, the too-easily evoked decadent odours.

I have blown hot and cold over his work; cold over *Justine*, hot when I saw, with three novels before me, the remarkable patience and skill with which Mr. Durrell was elaborating his chosen myth. About *Clea*, considered alone, I find it hard to be other than cold. Yet this tetralogy, for all its fatigue-failures, its pretentiousness, its power to irritate, is punctuated throughout by conceptions of astonishing force, from the love-making of Narouz in *Justine* to the dead sailors of *Clea;* and it is an experiment of very great formal interest, a highly serious contribution to modern fiction.

The Other Side of the Story   George P. Elliott*

Lawrence Durrell is quite justified in asking his reader to think of these four novels as a single book. I read *Justine* when it first came out, and liked it so much that I resolved to wait for the rest so that I could read them together. Now, having done so, I heartily recommend *The Alexandria Quartet* as a whole, whether you have read none of it or any of its parts. *Justine* is not all there till one has finished *Balthazar* and *Mountolive*, and the three together need *Clea* to round them off. This interdependence is true of any good sequence of novels. H. H. Richardson's *Ultima Thule*, that sadly neglected monument of psychological realism, is the stronger for being read as the last of its conventional trilogy, *The Fortunes of Richard Mahoney;* yet it stands alone much better than any part of Durrell's sequence could do. For these four subnovels interreflect in a way that not only is unconventional—a trivial matter—but that also makes isolating them an act of impoverishment. It is a pity Durrell published them severally; he says he wrote in a hurry, needing money—a circumstance which accounts, no doubt, for the fact that some of the prose is infelicitous to a degree surprising from one with so highly developed a style.

It is not altogether easy to get to *The Alexandria Quartet*. For one thing there is the way it has been recommended. The lushness of the adverbs in the ads and blurbs urging you on (brilliantly, hauntingly, suffocatingly) arouses the mule and you tend to balk. For my own part, when *The New York Times Book Review* was quoted as saying that *Justine* demanded comparison with Proust "since it treated also of recollected experience of love" and that Durrell is a "truly important writer," then I strapped on my greaves, pulled down my visor, and advanced with lance leveled, fearing another novel of the caliber of *Anthony Adverse*. But no, *Justine* was good; and *The Quartet* is better. To be sure, it would not be kind to press the comparison to *Remembrance of Things Past* (or to *War and Peace* or to *Don Quixote*—my God, what goes on in a *Times* reviewer's head!). But I found that the book—the style, the characters, the actions, the feel of the city, even some of the philosophizing—engaged my attention early on and never seriously let it flag.

KINSEYS IN THE PSYCHE

But there is another impediment between this novel and its reader, one put up by the author himself: form-consciousness. The obvious manifestation of this is Durrell's pontificating about what he has intended to accomplish in his book. At this enterprise he is as embarrassingly pompous and *off* as painters usually are when they write their manifestoes, and in much the same way. . . . When Durrell announces that *Justine, Balthazar,*

*Reprinted from the *Griffin* (April 1960), 2–9. © 1960 by George P. Elliott.

and *Mountolive* are the space co-ordinates of his book and *Clea* the time co-ordinate, I cock a wary eyebrow, for I (an English teacher) do not begin to understand the theory of relativity and I doubt that Durrell (a littérateur in the foreign service) understands it either. When, in the prefatory note to *Balthazar*, he says concerning the whole *Quartet* that "the central topic of the book is an investigation of modern love," I groan, for I have no taste for sociology in my fiction, Kinseys in my psyche. When he names the first volume *Justine* and prefaces each of the four with a quotation from the Marquis de Sade, my heart sinks, for I have read in the monster and found him dull. Well, maybe Durrell has in fact accomplished the irrelevancies he threatened; I neither know nor care; but I am happy to report that he has also done something first-rate. He has written a good romantic novel.

The special quality of *The Quartet* derives only in part, and by no means entirely, from its form and its form-consciousness. Most of the elements of which it is composed are old-fashioned, tried-and-true, romantic.

KIDNAPPED BY A DERVISH

The characters are wild and tormented and dingy in ways that are familiar enough to anyone who has ever enjoyed Graham Greene or H. Rider Haggard. Take Justine and her husband Nessim, the characters at the nexus of the novel's actions. He is rich, powerful, composed, and charming. She is beautiful, seductive, and intelligent; she was ravished as a child; and has already been the heroine of a novel written by her first husband, a psychoanalyst. One of the themes of the book is her search for her daughter, who apparently was kidnapped by a dervish and who probably met a fate so appalling we are more impressed by its romanticalness than shocked by its horror—she was sold as a child prostitute (in a brothel we first visit with the British ambassador to Egypt!). Nessim and Justine are indissolubly joined by their devotion to an ideal—an international conspiracy hiding behind the love affairs, and the extravaganzas staged for the highest society, and the double betrayals, and the corruption of ministers of state, and the plain broken hearts.

Oh, there is plenty here for the greediest romancer. There is an important novelist who kills himself because his blind sister, with whom he had long committed incest, falls in love with another man (our friend the ambassador, who has had a protracted affair-by-correspondence to gnaw at *his* vitals). There is a surgeon who falls madly in love with a girl in a domino; she has no nose; he makes her a nose and marries her; he introduces her to society waltzing to "The Blue Danube" in a hushed and glittering ballroom. There is an old British policeman whose transvestism gets him squalidly murdered but who is apotheosized after his death into a sort of Coptic saint. There is a prostitute with a loving heart; a proud beauty humbled and half maddened by smallpox (the ambassador is her epistolary lover); a princely, peasantish, harelipped, mystic man of action who can wield his whip of hippopotamus hide so well that one of his sports is to flick down bats from the twilight air; Balthazar, a man in middle life, shamed and nearly ruined by his infatuation for a godlike young actor whose tawdriness he despises.

A CITY WHICH REMEMBERS CLEOPATRA

And there is Alexandria itself. I had not supposed there was so much romance left in any city as Durrell finds in the Alexandria of the 1920s through the early 1940's. The mélange of races, classes, nationalities, religions, civilizations; the intrigue, the power, the mysticism and superstition; the ostentation of shameless riches, the destitution of abject disease and of bitter poverty; consciousness of vice, perversion, injustice; delicacies of relationship between individuals; exiles, and those who have never had a home; the sea, the desert; a city which remembers Cleopatra—what more could a tale-teller ask for! And Durrell (who asserts that the Alexandria of his book could not be "less unreal") knows enough not to allow into his romance-real world the slightest vestige of that deromanticizer, that power which unsavors the salt of romance—a decent, comfortable, middle-class Western family, bland to look at, all their amazing things introjected. There is scarcely a modern, or at least American-style modern, neurotic in the entire tetralogy. Here, when a woman in middle life discovers that the world is too much for her, she veils herself, retires to a garden house with a cobra for a pet, and every two or three weeks goes mad for a few days. These inward people project themselves against the world: they do what conventional neurotics wish. Maybe Alexandria really is as Durrell represents it; after all, it is no harder to believe that human beings ever created an actual city corresponding to the fictional city of *Studs Lonigan;* yet Chicago is indeed there. There is this to support Durrell's claim: the verses of Cavafy, who is called "the poet of Alexandria," fit handsomely into the strange world of this novel.

ENCAPSULATED IN EPIGRAMS

As for Durrell's philosophy, quite a lot of it appears to be there, like quite a bit of Henry Miller's and D. H. Lawrence's, *pour épater les bourgeois.* . . . However, in *The Quartet* most of the philosophy is encapsulated in epigrams composed by either Pursewarden, who is represented as being an eminent novelist, or Darley, the narrator of three sections of *The Quartet* and also a central character. Consequently, one can enjoy some of the epigrams for their own sake ("Truth is what most contradicts itself," "I am just a refugee from the long slow toothache of English life.") and one need not view them as doing much more than helping to establish character and create ambience. The most important of the philosophizing holds, with De Sade, that it is not natural to feel guilty for sexual deeds. However, Durrell is a stronger novelist than philosopher; that is to say, he puts his philosophy to the service of his fiction so that this Sade notion serves a dramatic function: the character who chiefly advances it is riven with guilt from having committed incest. Further, those personages who apparently inhabit the novel to demonstrate to us that natural sex is guiltless have no fictional density but are not much more than gay epigrams.

The special quality of *The Alexandria Quartet* (as of *Tristram Shandy*) is accomplished by something considerably more interesting than its overt philosophy: its fictional strategies.

EXCITING IMBROGLIO

Durrell's shifting of the point of view from volume to volume is the most spectacular of these, its effect being the expansion, alteration, deepening of our knowledge of what has happened. *Justine* is narrated by Darley some while after the event, not in simple chronology but according to his rather dreamlike memories. *Balthazar*, supposed to have been written a few years later, is Darley's commentary on Balthazar's commentary on the manuscript of *Justine*. Balthazar has known more than Darley about the hidden motives of various of the characters, especially of Justine and Nessim, and he adds a number of important events which serve both to prove his knowledge and to delight us; the final hiddenmost motive, however, he is ignorant of.

These two volumes are written in romantic prose, while the third, *Mountolive* (the name of the British ambassador), is told in a fairly objective, realistic third-person style. It covers, in addition to part of Mountolive's story, the same basic events as the first two volumes. In this portion, too, we get to the "real" motive behind the actions and deceptions of Justine and Nessim. *Clea*, also recounted by Darley in his elaborate prose, is a some-years-later sequel to the events of the first three and to the writing of *Balthazar*. It both extends our acquaintance of the characters and considerably alters—as the passage of time does in real life—our attitude toward the exciting imbroglio of the main actions. That is, in a way that is at once true and poignant, the actions and relationships which Justine and Nessim enter upon in order to deceive others, to mask their "real" motives, become in our minds more valuable than the cause they serve: the cause fails, the attachments have mattered and they endure in our minds. Similarly, the social importance of the characters—high Mountolive, for example, against low Darley—modifies their actions as it would in real life and modifies our reactions to them in the way of romance, but it does not determine their importance in our imagination. This is a novel; it is about secret lives. The secret life of Darley, for instance, is considerably richer than that of Mountolive and we are glad to know it well.

SARDONIC AND ASTRINGENT

But, important though this strategy of shifting point of view may be, it is no more important than the prose itself in creating the novel's flavor. Darley's prose is dreamy and evocative in a way that is wonderfully suitable to the romance of the city, the characters, the story. It is an introspective, mulling-over, conscious style of writing; and after all, compared to realistic fiction, romance is figurative and symbolic, poetic. Not that this prose is flawlessly executed: in wild and wonderful set pieces it evokes the required effects, but occasionally in the jog-trot sections, in which even romances find themselves from time to time, the prose can become a bit slick. That is to say, it produces unnecessarily special effects with rather glib means ("Amaril was an original man in his way and a bit of a dandy withal"). Balthazar's prose is scarcely to be distinguished from Darley's, and Pursewarden's—of which we get some excerpts—is sardonic and astringent but also highly self-conscious. The style of *Mountolive* is, compared to that of the other three volumes, realistic and representational. But compared to, say, C. P. Snow's, it seems mildly gorgeous, abounding with figures of speech and rhetorical elegances which not only point at the subject but also call some attention to themselves, invite our admiration. Still, the effect of this relatively ordinary prose, after two volumes of rhetorical hallucination, is to make us feel that this is what *really* happened. And then to shift back to the wavy, self-aware style in the fourth volume is to convince us that what people think about a matter may be—and here is—yet more delightful than the supposed truth of that matter.

THE GRAND STRATEGY

Shiftiness—that is the grand strategy of this novel. What really happened matters only as it is known; no one can know all of what really happened, including the author himself; reflecting upon it is one of the fascinations of life; and finally, knowing and reflecting upon what has happened becomes a part of what happened. Not many novels have been so conscious of form as this one or have used form-consciousness to so good effect. Yet, except in trivial ways such as the notes clumped at the end of the three Darley sections of the novel, the form itself does not irritate, is not there for show. It renders the matter, and finally itself becomes a part of the matter, with skill and vigor. The book surely merits the acclaim with which, for a variety of reasons, not all of them good, it has been greeted.

Lawrence Durrell I:
The Baroque Novel
George Steiner*

With the publication of *Clea*, Lawrence Durrell has completed his quartet of novels set in Alexandria. No recent work of fiction has provoked fiercer disagreement. There are critics who assert that Durrell is a pompous charlatan; a mere word-spinner and gatherer of flamboyant clichés; a novelist whose angle of vision is grotesquely narrow; a late Victorian decadent and minor disciple of Henry Miller. Elsewhere, and particularly in France, it is held with equal vehemence that the Alexandria quartet is the highest performance in the modern novel since Proust and Joyce and that Durrell is a genius of the first rank. The main source of controversy is Durrell's style. And that style is, in fact, the vital center of Durrell's art. It meets the reader like a bristling parapet when he first enters the world of *Justine*; and when he has finished *Clea*, he will realize that that style is also the inward sanctuary of Durrell's meaning. It is, therefore, with the shape of the syntax and the rare glitter of the words that one must start. . . .

The style is a mosaic. Each word is set in its precise and luminous place. Touch by touch, Durrell builds his array of sensuous, rare expressions into patterns of imagery and idea so subtle and convoluted that the experience of reading becomes one of total sensual apprehension. Such paragraphs live to the touch of the reader's hand; they have a complex aural music; and the light seems to play across the surface of the words in brilliant tracery. "The clicking of violet trams" is as complete a sensuous rendition as might be achieved by a *pointilliste* painter, breaking light into minute, precise flecks and reassembling the elements of vision into memorable design. No one else writing in English today has a comparable command of the light and music of language.

But this does not mean that this jeweled and coruscated style springs full-armed from Durrell's personal gift. He stands in a great tradition of baroque prose. In the seventeenth century, Sir Thomas Browne built sentences into lofty arches and made words ring like sonorous bells. Robert Burton, in his *Anatomy of Melancholy,* used the same principal device as Durrell: richness through accumulation, the marshaling of nouns and epithets into great catalogues among which the eye roves in antiquarian delight. The feverish, clarion-sounding prose of De Quincey is a direct ancestor to that of *Justine*. And more recently, there is the example of Conrad. In the later parts of *Lord Jim* and throughout *The Rescue*, Conrad uses words with the sumptuous exuberance of a jeweler showing off his rarest stones. Here also, language falls upon the reader's senses like brocade.

This baroque ideal of narrative style is, at present, in disfavor. The modern ear has been trained to the harsh, impoverished cadence and vocabulary of Hemingway. Reacting against the excesses of the Victorian

*Reprinted from the *Yale Review* 49, no. 4 (June 1960):488–95. © 1960 by Yale University.

manner, the modern writer has made a cult of simplicity. He refines common speech but preserves its essential drabness. When comparing a page from the Alexandria novels to the practice of Hemingway or C. P. Snow or Graham Greene, one is setting a gold-spun and jeweled Byzantine mosaic next to a black-and-white photograph. One cannot judge the one by the other. But that does not signify that Durrell is a decadent show-off or that his conception of English prose is erroneous. We may be grateful that Hemingway and his innumerable imitators have made the language colder and more astringent and that they have brought back into fiction the virtues of plain force. But they have done so at price. Contemporary English usage is incredibly thin and unimaginative. The style of politics and factual communication verges on the illiterate. Having far fewer words at our reach than had the educated man of the seventeenth and even of the late nineteenth century, we say less or say it with a blurred vagueness. Indeed, the twentieth century has seen a great retreat from the power of the word. The major energies of the mind seem directed toward other modes of "language," toward the notations of music and the symbol-world of mathematics. Whether in its advertisements, its comic-books, or its television, our culture lives by the picture rather than the word. Hence a writer like Durrell, with his Shakespearean and Joycean delight in the sheer abundance and sensuous variety of speech, may strike one as mannered or precious. But the fault lies with our impoverished sensibility.

Who is to say, moreover, that the Alexandria quartet will not lead to a renascence of prose? A number of contemporary writers are beginning to return to the great springs of language. The value of *Lolita* lies precisely in Nabokov's rediscovery of the resources of style. And the lineage, Conrad-Nabokov-Durrell, is suggestive. All three approach English from a certain distance. Conrad and Nabokov as foreigners who learnt the language, Durrell as an Irishman born in India and steeped in the Greek and French legacy of the eastern Mediterranean. Their prose has the quality of marvel and surprise which comes with personal discovery. Unlike the current hack novelists, they use words as if they had lain buried in some ancient treasure-trove.

But Durrell's style is more than a formal instrument; it carries the heart of his meaning. *Justine, Balthazar, Mountolive,* and *Clea* are founded on the axiom that the ultimate truths of conduct and the world cannot be penetrated by force of reason. Where truth can be apprehended at all, in brief spells of total illumination, the process of insight is one of total sensuous absorption. In a conceit which is the very crux of his imaginings, Durrell instructs us that the soul enters truth as man enters woman, in a possession at once sexual and spiritual. Again, this is a view which has existed before Durrell. It plays a vital role in oriental and medieval mysticism; it is at work in Dante and in the erotic metaphors of the seventeenth-century Metaphysical poets. Moreover, it is crucial in the theories of Gnosticism and the citadel of Gnosticism was Alexandria. And it is here that the example of D. H. Lawrence is relevant. The presence of Lawrence is felt through the four novels and one of the main characters is in personal touch with him. Like Lawrence, Durrell believes in a wisdom of the senses truer and subtler than that of the predatory mind. Both men see in the act of love the crucial affirmation of human identity and the only true bridge for the soul. Durrell's personages pursue each other in an elaborate cross-weaving of sexual encounter, for only thus can the ghostliness of the human spirit be given the fulness of life.

This mystique of sensual insight encompasses more than individual identity. Our entire perception of reality depends on similar illuminations (Joyce called them "epiphanies"). It is by accumulating these moments of vision, touch by exact touch, that we arrive at a grasp of the surrounding world—in this instance, at a true image of Alexandria. The long, glittering arabesques of adjectives with which Durrell surrounds objects are no mere exercise in verbal acrobatics. They are successive assaults upon the inner mystery of things, attempts, often exasperated and desperate, to trap reality within a mesh of precise words. Being equipped with a superb apparatus of sensual receptivity, Durrell is aware of the myriad movements of light, scent, and sound. He sees the world reflected in waters which are never still and tries to capture the essence of a city from the kaleidoscope of changing seasons, colors and moods. So far as Alexandria goes, he has succeeded magnificently. Durrell's Alexandria (not, of course, the Egyptian harbor-city of our ordinary acquaintance) is one of the major monuments of the architecture of imagination. It ranks in manifold coherence with the Paris of Proust and the Dublin of Joyce.

The technique of accumulated nuance, the painter returning constantly to the same scene in the changes of the light, applies not only to the portrayal of the city but also the entire plot. As in the Japanese fable of *Rashomon* and in the plays of Pirandello, identical events are recounted from successive points of view. The narrator's first impression of Justine, of the Coptic magnates in whose secretive life she becomes involved, of Melissa the golden tramp, and of the relations between Justine and Pursewarden, is submitted in *Balthazar* to ironic revision. The four volumes should be printed in the manner of loose-leaf notebooks allowing one to close earlier gaps with later insights. Nowhere in the quartet are things what they seem to be. In *Clea*, the principal narrator is himself drawn into the vortex of action. Nothing is ever wholly explained; neither the murder of Narouz—one of the great set pieces of writing in modern fiction—nor Justine's odd flight into Palestine, nor the true nature of the conspiratorial web which surrounds Nessim and Mountolive, keeping them entangled yet divided. To complicate matters further, there are three writers in the novel who are themselves characters, and even those personages who are not professional artisans of language, share something of their creator's dazzling virtuosity of style and feeling. The novel closes in midcourse, on a series of tantalizing notations of what might be further developments. This too is essential to Durrell's meaning. The true poet (and Durrell is a poet before being a novelist) knows that time and action flow like the Nile. He can show us the depth and rush of the water and throw stones into it to break the images of the moon; but he cannot arrest the river in his sieve of words. Durrell says that "the central topic of the book is an investigation of modern love." The reach of his inquiry is large and stands under the aegis of Sade and psychology at its most liberal. We find in this labyrinthine city not only the love of man and woman, but the more oblique byways of the ravenous blood. *Clea* contains, in miniature, as gross a tragedy of homosexual passion as any in Proust. Mountolive is lured into a house of wizened child-prostitutes who swarm at him like bats. Memlik, the police chief, is a delicate sadist. We encounter fetishists and transvestites, phallic rituals and private vice. The most tragic love story in the entire novel, the unendurably intense love of Pursewarden and Liza, is a story of incest. Critics have seen in this profusion and variety of sexual concern a mark of decadence. Durrell has been accused of being a follower of Swinburne and Beardsley, a purveyor of ornate morsels of erotic lore. There are one or two instances in which such a charge might be sustained. But on the whole, it is wide of the mark. Durrell must explore the ambiguities and covertness of sensual lust precisely because he believes that it is only in the fiery or desperate contact of the flesh that we can gain access to the truth of life. In his treatment, moreover, there is neither prurience nor the snigger of the eroticist. Love in Durrell has an ashen taste. When Liza burns her brother's "immortal" letters (there is here a muffled echo of the Byron legend), she illustrates Durrell's feeling that the extremity of passion brings with it utter despair. And our last vision of Justine, standing naked beside Darley's bed, soliciting the empty gestures of spent ardor, is one of total defeat. As in so many poets able to experience the fulness of sensuous life, there is in Durrell a touch of the Puritan.

But although its range of material and emotion is very great, the Alexandria quartet leaves one, at the last, with a suspicion of triviality. There lies the real problem for the critic. Why should there be at the center of this magnificently wrought fable of life a certain undeniable hollowness? There are, I think, two possible reasons.

Durrell dramatizes a wide spectrum of sensibility; but his cast of characters is of an exceedingly special kind. All these fascinating and exotic beings share a high degree of nervous intelligence; they articulate their emotions with lyric power and unfailing subtlety; they live life at a constant pitch of awareness, more searching and vulnerable than that of ordinary men. They are cut from the same fragile and luminous stone and so they reflect each other like mirrors disposed in cunning perspectives. Mirrors play a crucial symbolic role throughout the action (as they do in Sade). And it is a dangerous role; for although they multiply vision and drive it inward, they also shut it off from the outside. In Durrell even the sea is a pool for Narcissus.

The angle of vision, moreover, is rigorously private. The gusts of social and political life blow across the scene, but they are not accorded much importance. Nessim and his clan are involved in a tenebrous conspiracy to further Coptic independence and they run guns to Palestine. But we are given no clear account of what they are really up to. Between *Mountolive* and *Clea* falls the shadow of world war, and at the start of *Clea* there is an account of an air-raid on Alexandria. It is superbly written; rockets empty on the sky "their brilliant clusters of stars and diamonds and smashed pearl snuff-boxes"; the German planes are like "silver moths" moving with "fatal languor" among the "strings of hot diamonds" which spout from the batteries below. But neither the terror nor the real meaning of the action comes through. It is merely one more jeweled miniature to treasure in the vault of memory. All that Durrell touches is somehow diminished to the scale of goldsmith's work.

Now no one would be so absurd as to demand from him a novel of "social consciousness." But by severing his imagined world from the intrusions of political and social fact he makes it even narrower and more fragile than it need be. Behind the intimacies and stylistic experiments of Joyce lies the stabilizing structure of the Homeric epic. Proust buttressed his narrow and even perverse view of human conduct with a close, technical awareness of social, political, and military affairs. Charlus is no less eccentric than Nessim or Balthazar. But the Zeppelins which cruise above Paris during his nocturnal prowlings are grimly real and carry with them the weight of historical crisis. Similarly, D. H. Lawrence gave to his accounts of private experience a firm anchorage in social reality. The legend of Lady Chatterley is as narrow and private as that of Darley and Melissa; but *Lady Chatterley's Lover* is a classic study of class relations.

Because of its enclosedness and utter privacy, the Alexandria quartet is more convincing in its details than in its broad design (or, if you will, it is a series of brilliant miniatures rather than a coherent canvas). It is the marginal characters who spring most completely to life: Scobie, the finest comic invention in English fiction since *Tristram Shandy;* and Narouz, in whom massive silence becomes a kind of rhetoric. It is not so much the main plot which arrests the memory, but the digressions and minor episodes: the shadowy account of Mountolive's childhood; the affair between Justine and Arnauti, who never even appears in the quartet; the exquisite misadventures of Pombal, the French diplomat; Capodistria's recital of his experiments in black magic. As in medieval illuminations, the fringe is often brighter than the center.

But there is also a particular failure. *Clea* marks a drastic falling-off. It is a brittle, self-conscious gloss on the three preceding volumes. The long extracts from Pursewarden's notebooks are not only insufferably tedious, but they act as a parody of Durrell's own style. The episode of Clea's near-drowning is a classic exhibit of how symbolism should not be used. The ravages which time and the death of the heart have caused in Justine and

Nessim are thrust before us as stark facts. There is no attempt to render them psychologically plausible. What happened, I imagine, is this: Durrell had completed the first three movements of his quartet and sensed that he had a masterpiece in hand. When he turned to the finale, he seems to have been beset with the fear of spoiling the whole. He took no risks and wrote a series of narrow variations on earlier themes. Thus *Clea* represents a distinct failure of nerve.

Yet even when such reservations are made, there can be no doubt of the magnitude of Durrell's achievement. Anyone caring for the language and the future of the novel will have to come to grips with this singular work. We are too near the event to say with any assurance what place the Alexandria quartet will hold in future estimates of English literature. I would guess that it will stand somewhere above the range of *Green Mansions* and just below the narrow but more humane eccentricity of *Wuthering Heights*. That Durrell will have an enduring place is certain.

Lawrence Durrell II: A Minority Report
Martin Green*

These novels [*The Alexandria Quartet*] concern a group of exotic characters from different nationalities and social levels—an Irish schoolmaster, a Greek cabaret dancer, a Coptic millionaire banker, etc.—who are very involvedly involved with each other in the brilliant but depraved society of contemporary Alexandria. They exhibit every variety of extreme intellectual, religious, and sexual position—all five sexes, as the reviewers say—all characterized by profound suffering and dissatisfaction. They find each other, and themselves, very elusive and multifaceted, and what they are most sure of—Justine's love for the narrator, for instance, or Nessim's for her—always turns out to be radically ambiguous. There are very violent events, murders, suicides, rapes, spyings, but these also are not so important in themselves as for the totally different proportions and significances they assume as they are further examined. The narrator writes his account after most of the relationships have broken down, and from outside the city, but the repercussions of it all are still developing, and the second novel is a radical reinterpretation of the first, in the light of one of the characters' comments on it when he read it. And the first novel itself, *Justine*, reinterpreted what the narrator had thought he felt at the time. So the basic material of the books is not the events or people, lurid though these are, but a series of progressively more esoteric formulations of experience; there is even a good deal of quotation from a supposedly published novel by Justine's first husband, a man who never himself appears. The primary

*Reprinted from the *Yale Review* 49, no. 4 (June 1960):496–508. © 1960 by Yale University.

use of language, then, is reflective, aphoristic, rhetorical-questioning, with only occasional attempts at first-hand rendering of experience; the general movement or structure is circular, recurrent, re-echoing, which accords, of course, with the emotional and moral life of the characters, in which there is nothing certain or reliable.

In this account of it the novel sounds a good deal more like Proust than it reads. While you are in process of reading it seems almost totally original, in one sense—a bizarre re-arrangement of elements which in themselves, though not unfamiliar, are very unexpected. Critically, however, its challenge is less bewildering.

Some of the descriptions of landscape and sky have a genuine Parnassian glitter, but the writing in general does not begin to sustain such an elaborate and pretentious structure. Everything is bloated to the point of absurdity; the notes Balthazar scribbles on the manuscript of the first volume are referred to always as "The Interlinear"; a casual nickname given to one of the characters is "Lineaments of Gratified Desire"; not content with "Notes" at the end of a volume, Durrell has also "Consequential Data," "Workpoints," and "Scobie's Common Usage." The dicta, in such numbers and offered with such empressement, are never as good as they should be:

> Balthazar on Justine; "You will find that her formidable manner is constructed on a shaky edifice of childish timidities." . . . As for Pursewarden, he believed with Rilke that no woman adds anything to the sum of Woman, and from satiety he had now taken refuge in the plenty of the imagination—the true field of merit for the artist. . . . When she said to him, "You are hopelessly promiscuous, like I am," he was really angry, really outraged. "Imbecile," he replied, "You have the soul of a clerk. For those who love poetry there is no such thing as *vers libre*." She did not understand this. *"O stop behaving like a pious old sin-cushion into which we all have to stick the rusty pins of our admiration," he snapped.*

A steady diet of sentences like this makes one feel one is sickening for a bad cold. And in the events and persons there is the same air of immense sophistication, unsupported by any originality of conception or subtlety of detail. Everything is in poster colors, from the names (Pursewarden, Mountolive, etc.), to the central incidents, like Narouz's murder of Toto. (When the latter, masked and cloaked, makes homosexual advances to him, he thinks it is the beautiful Justine being heterosexual, and stabs him through the head with a hatpin, and covers the body with fur coats and goes away without discovering his mistake.) In the plot, development is replaced by mathematical complication, as Nessim turns from his wife, Justine, to her lover's lover, Melissa, or as we learn that this secret love of Justine's for the narrator was all a pretence, anyway, to conceal her real (?) love for Pursewarden. Complicatedness in place of complexity, violence in place of vigor, rhetoric in place of rendering; the whole thing bears all the marks of a daydream about a Great Novel.

As an example of the writing take this passage: "Riding beside her in the great car, someone beautiful, dark, and painted with great eyes like the prow of some Aegean ship, he had the sensation that his book was being passed rapidly underneath his life, as if under a sheet of paper containing the iron filings of temporal events, as a magnet is, in that commonplace experiment one does at school; and somehow setting up a copying magnetic field." Here one should note the repetition of "great," with the even more significant apologetic "commonplace"; which is carried on in "passed *rapidly* underneath" and "*some* Aegean ship"; this is the keynote of the Durrell experience, the insistent meaningless dramatization of everything—theatricalization. And the two main images are so external, so premeditated, so discontinuous with the situation they describe, that you feel the mortal chill of rhetoric itself. It is not Justine who looks like a Greek ship; it is the words about her, "great painted eyes." One does not have the *sensation* that the temporal events of one's life are iron filings, in a copying magnetic field; one sits down with a Poet's Handbook and thinks it up.

And yet reading Durrell is not an unprofitable experience. He clarifies and connects certain important points. But the interest of his work derives from what he aims at and what he expresses—an interest doubly vindicated by the success he is having—not from what he achieves.

What Durrell aims at is primarily—or rather originally—the kind of paganism indicated by his proposed epitaph, "Lawrence Durrell wishes you great passions and short lives." But this sensibility has had little expression for some years, and may deserve some elucidation.

At the beginning of this century there was a very general tendency among British writers to reject the middle-class Protestant moralism we can roughly identify with George Eliot and John Stuart Mill, and to seek a more relaxed, more hedonistic, less ethical approach to life. Life and love were to be practiced as arts; one was to make something beautiful out of them, something amusing, above all something amenable. The Mediterranean was the natural setting for this, because of its climate and echoes of the classical cultures, but also because of its remoteness from all the industrialism and progress and contemporaneity of England; and it so happened that it was Italy, not Greece, Spain, or Provence, that was picked on; Italy and the islands of the Mediterranean. The pilgrimage south was made by some major talents—D. H. Lawrence and E. M. Forster (though they returned to more interesting work)—and by some unlikely ones—H. G. Wells in *The New Macchiavelli*. But the really central figure is Norman Douglas, and the work that expresses the most of this movement is his novel *South Wind*. It has nearly all the elements we are to find later in other writers; the young man malingering on the verge of fornication, the middle-aged conventional British mind unable to deal with Mediterranean experience, the gathering of exotic characters with exotic names, all talking brilliantly, the classical learning and the drinking parties, the deliberately condoned and admired murder, and the implicit contrast of everything with middle-class British standards. This "pagan" sensibility was shared by people who didn't write about Italy, like Ford Madox Ford and the critic Edward Garnett, and to some extent by the writers of the Catholic Revival, like G. K. Chesterton and Hilaire Belloc; they had the same distaste for moralism and progress, the same admiration for gusto, paradox, and drunkenness, and it is not really surprising to discover that Graham Greene is a great admirer of Norman Douglas. After 1918 the trek to Italy (especially Capri) resumed, and Aldous Huxley, Compton Mackenzie, Eric Linklater, Francis Brett Young, worked the same vein. Nothing very good was ever produced in it, no doubt because it is based so largely on a rejection of responsibility and reality, and the old impulse to *épater le bourgeois*.

A good deal of the strangeness of Durrell's Alexandrian novels would disappear if they were set back forty years into this context. Characters like Gaston and Scobie and Toto, conversation like Clea's and Balthazar's, are essentially of Douglas's world. Here too you have the British mind fumbling in a Mediterranean world of much greater experience; the same expertise and disillusion about sex and sin; the same implicit contrast with "ordinary" life. The formal complexity, the continual re-discussion of fantastic events, the tone of more-than-natural experience and exhaustion, all this reminds one of Ford's Tietjens series. Ford worked with Douglas on *The English Review*, and felt about Provence (another center of "civilization," that opposite of "morality") much as Douglas did about Capri.

This interpretation implies of course that Durrell's mind is in some sense culturally retarded. But that this is so is so strikingly attested on totally other grounds that it returns as a major recommendation of the theory. *White Eagles Over Serbia* (1957) begins: "Though Methuen usually lived at his club whenever he was in London. . . . Four months in the jungles of Malaya had starved him for the sound of his own language and he was glad—yes, glad—to catch sight of old Archdale, the bore of bores, in one corner of the room." Which carries one back to one's boyhood with a rush and a jerk; and in one's boyhood this kind of thing was only to be found in old books, published for the children of the previous generation. Methuen belongs of course to the Secret Service unit known as the Awkward Shop, "the unit known to a few highly placed officials as SOq," and his colleagues and boss belong to the same club as himself. In Serbia, Methuen disguises himself as a peasant (he speaks perfect Serbian) and tramps about the mountains, sleeping in caves, reading *Walden*, trout-fishing, solving a cipher, preventing a revolt, taking part in minor battles. This is the kind of story, in all its elements, that bright British schoolboys wrote between 1910 and 1920, and duller ones between 1920 and 1930; all in imitation of John Buchan, who first perfected this objective correlative for the public school mind. The rules are simple; only gentlemen can take part, and they must have scholarly tastes, and there's a lot of climbing and fishing—no playing around with women—and in the end nobody gets hurt. The enemy—very much on the horizon—is sinister, sedentary, fanatic—

not to be thought about too much. John Buchan's period, of course, is exactly Norman Douglas's, and indeed Douglas, too, may be said to have created an objective correlative for Etonians, but his was for the outsiders, the disaffected, the too-clever ones, who didn't like games and were no use in the House. The two complemented each other; between them they are a paradigm of the pre-1914 sensibility. As a result of living so long out of England, and so much among embassy officials, Durrell's mind is a museum-piece.

But though so much of Durrell's work seems to me to belong completely to this pre-1914 world—even a "serious" novel like *Cefalu* (1947)—the Alexandrian novels cannot be explained away so easily. The depravity in them is extremer and uglier than anything in *South Wind*; the narrator's voice is more exhausted, emotionally, morally, philosophically; classical culture is no longer important; the style and structure are infinitely more pretentious.

The origin of these new elements becomes clear when one remembers *The Black Book*'s date and place of publication. It was in Paris in 1935 and 1936, the two years preceding the publication of Durrell's first novels, that Henry Miller brought out *Tropic of Cancer* and *Black Spring*. And it is of course the Paris of those novels that stands between Durrell's Alexandria and the Capri of *South Wind*: the Paris of expatriates, debauchees, parasites, paranoiacs, students, artists, and all their sightseers and hangers-on; the world of Henry Miller, Michael Fraenkel, Djuna Barnes, Anais Nin, Wyndham Lewis, etc. On the other hand, Durrell has none of Miller's perverted Whitmanism, his total acceptance of life-as-it-is, or his delight in every sight, sound, and smell, or his formlessness; he is very consciously the artist and the intellectual, and unconsciously the public school Englishman. Nor can he have known much of the real Paris he and Miller "started from," which was after all an affair of the 'twenties. Miller's books re-created a vanished world he remembered; he was himself in his forties when they came out. Durrell was in his twenties. It is another example of his curious attraction to the past. . . .

One could make the point of his 'twenties quality equally well by recalling *The Black Book*'s debt to Joyce and praise by Eliot. The non-Douglas elements can be seen as expressions of the disruption of meaning, the apocalyptic breakdown of standards and communications which Eliot made so much of in the 'twenties. There is something of the mood of "The Waste Land"—its exoticism, eclecticism, experimentalism, as well as its despair—mingled with the *South Wind* paganism. Da Capo is like a figure out of that poem, and Burbank and Bleistein would merge into *Justine* without trace. We have seen that Durrell thinks all characteristically modern verse an expression of this disruption of meaning, and he necessarily gives Eliot the central place in it. Indeed, his own poetry contains lines which seem to announce an almost identical sensibility ("Between rocks 'O death', the survivors" and so on).

Though nearer to us in time than *South Wind*, this kind of Eliotism or Paris-ism is almost equally unexpected today, almost equally left behind. The two moods, moreover, are so essentially of their time, one pre-1914, the other post-1918, that they accord very oddly together. No wonder the first reading of *Justine* is such a queer, dream-like experience. Its reviews, however, seem more dream-like at each return. Can England be really so nostalgic for the elaborate, the garish, the grand gesture, at absolutely any price? Can Dr. Leavis have been right to treat Durrell as a significant fact back in 1946?

Obviously the answer is yes. Ever since the exhaustion of the Victorian impulse, England has been experimenting with ways of taking life less seriously, morally, and more elaborately, aesthetically and intellectually. Proust has become a more British than a French author, with Durrell and Anthony Powell's novels, Pamela Hansford Johnson's recent book on him, Angus Wilson's and C. P. Snow's interest in him; because Proust did so magnificently, for France, what we want doing for us; Britain is hungry for the artist who will give *her* a world of mythical size, color, and complexity, which yet needn't be taken seriously. Durrell satisfies that hunger, however meretriciously. The American enthusiasm for him is more simple; a graduate school vision of sin and subtlety in exotic old Alexandria, where you can forget you grew up in Ohio.

But there is one book by Durrell which seems to me fascinating because it so well dramatizes the "British" mind reacting to its contemporary crisis, and particularly the mode of coöperation between the lion and the unicorn, the general and the poet, the commanding administrating official faculties of that mind, and the imaginative, creative, wayward part. This is of course *Bitter Lemons*, which tells of Durrell's life on Cyprus in 1953–56, where he became the Government's Press Representative when the troubles began in 1955. . . .

The first part of the book describes Durrell's coming to Cyprus as a writer seeking somewhere congenial to live and work for a few years. His characteristic emphases are all on the romantic picturesque: in psychology, "A Bolognese is always worth listening to on the subject of wine"; in history, "Who remembers Catherine? Titian and Bellini painted her; Bembo wrote a philosophy of love to amuse her courtiers. In the only portrait I have seen the eyes are grave and beautiful, full of an impenitent life of their own; the eyes of a woman who has enjoyed much adulation, who has travelled much and loved much." And there is the old-fashioned paganism—"topers" is one of his favorite words, and of one place he remarks, "Saint Paul received a well-merited thrashing there at the hands of the Paphiots." The prose is elegant, with many trailing dots, but never quite exact: "Circumstances gave me several unique angles of vision of Cyprus life and affairs."

He decided not to live in Kyrenia because it was becoming too like a modern British provincial city—"this crude and graceless world"—and he wanted to be where "these Mediterranean folk lived a joyous, uproarious, muddled, anarchic life of their own." So he bought himself a house in a village called Bellapaix, full of characters—topers, liars, quarrelers, half-wits—and with its social life centered round the coffee house under the Tree of Idleness. And it is obvious that not only did Durrell really enjoy his life there, but that he really made friends with the men, and knew how to manage his life among them. When he ran into people who asked to be taken seriously he was of course somewhat taken aback ("Little Lozius— 'the Bear'—was a pillar of the church and a very serious fellow altogether"). But on the whole the ethos of the place (not unlike that of a London club, after all) was genuinely congenial to him.

But of course, "Life on a small island would be unbearable for anyone with sensibility were it not enriched from time to time by visitants from other worlds, bringing with them the conversations of the great capitals. . . ." Durrell's visitants were John Lehmann, Rose Macaulay, Freya Stark, Sir Harry Luke, Patrick Leigh Fermor—a good sampling of the writers who make abroad "abroad" for the British. And he says of the man to whom he dedicates the book: "I suddenly realized that I was in the presence of the hero of *South Wind* or an early character from Huxley. He represented that forgotten world where style was not only a literary imperative but an inherent method of approaching the world of books, roses, statues and landscapes." With such people Durrell had drinking parties, exquisite food, brilliant conversation, etc. And in all this time, though he had seen "Enosis" scrawled on walls the day he arrived on the island, he had found no reason to take it seriously. The few hostile islanders he met could always be brought to profess personal friendliness to him, and even to England, by an appeal to their code of courtesy and hospitality, which he understood from long experience. His own attitude seems to have been, very naturally, to take the British administration of the island entirely for granted, avoiding offices and officials himself because of their dullness and suburbanism— "England as Wimbledon."

When visitors first began to talk to him of a crisis he replied, "I'm sure the F.O. has weighed it up," and pointed out how much he and England were loved by the peasants of his village. (It is quite a shock, at this point in the book, to realize how limitless a faith in the British government underlies such kinds of poet's skepticism, and what contempt for political issues). He seems never to have met, or even heard of, anyone who wanted Enosis at the expense of quarreling with England, much less anyone who simply hated the English. When he does meet the desire for independence later, at the Gymnasium at Nicosia, he explains it as "kept permanently at the boil by official direction, by the press, by the heady rhetoric of local demagogues and priests." His language, unconsciously, makes these latter inconsiderable, unreal figures. He explains for a page, at this point, how the Cypriots can sincerely feel a genuine desire to be governed by their own kind—and it is the first time the idea has occurred to him. A friend points out to him, when the troubles start, that Nicosia has no theatre, no bookshop, no university, etc. "These things came to me with the force of a revelation." Because, of course, he had looked only for the picturesque, the non-contemporary, the non-serious.

The British responsibility, like the Greek, he locates always outside, away from the people and the situation he knows—the noisy contentions of Athens radio and the slow workings of the Crown Agents in London; such undeniable evils as did exist were not the fault of any particular persons, but of abstract forces in the distance. In other words, he shows us a Cyprus straight out of John Buchan—the people, all picturesque and peaceful, the government, well-meaning but slow-moving, and the enemy, a black, impersonal evilness in the distance.

To a certain extent, of course, Durrell's attitudes reversed when he became Press Representative in 1955. He then deplored the lack of modern facilities, like printing presses, in the towns, where previously he had found too many; and feared an invasion by "whiskered island lunatics I knew in Rhodes and Crete," who are exactly the muddled uproarious anarchic folk he has come to the Mediterranean for. But on the whole it is striking how smooth the transition was. His epigrammatic national psychology remained appropriate—"No Greek can interpret policy in anything but personal terms." His imagination was engaged as romantically by the aristocrats of Government House as it had been by the peasants of Bellapaix; he refers to the Colonial Secretary always as "the great man," and speaks of his intimidating height and good looks, his charm and liberal disposition of an eighteenth-century gentleman; his name for the Governor is "the francolin"—"the graces of a courtier combined with the repose and mildness of a family sage"; and he thrills like a schoolboy to "the sleek old-fashioned C.O.I. cars drawn up outside the private office . . . the Secretary of State's own gleaming Rolls . . . armed with a copy of the Iliad which sorted well with his gentle and scholarly manner," and to the spectacle of "the great man" groaning and clutching his head when England's cricket score was wired to him aboard the plane taking him to Cyprus. His loyalties are as simple as Colonel Blimp's: "We for our part were filled with a quite unjustifiable elation at the trimness and expertise of Wren's little operation." And one soon realizes that he had not, never had had, any complicating sense of the Cypriots' rights in the situation, by any definition of those rights—no sense that "these muddled Mediterranean folk" might want to be taken seriously politically. When he talks of needed reforms, the two examples he gives are the Public Relations department and the Police Force; the advantage of the referendum he recommends would be time gained for a reorganization of the police and the administration, which weren't ready to face an emergency. His sympathies were the soldier's rather than even the administrator's. "Of course, the island could always be held by military force—but nowadays, with wobbling electorates at home unable to stand bloodshed and terrified of force. . . ."

At the end of the book, as Durrell visits his village for the last time, no one of the crowd gathered outside the coffee house will speak to him. The pathos and moral of this—private happiness ruined by public quarrels—are genuinely poignant. But the book as a whole has its larger pathos; that of the poet, the profounder intellectual, fitting himself so smoothly into his place in the "British" machine, moving from coffee house to Government House with no sense of strain, because without being skeptical about either, he takes neither one really seriously. Because he refuses to take anything in life any more seriously than one takes a historical novel. And the moral is something for the "British" mind as a whole, which can even now, apparently, find such a sensibility a powerful instrument of beauty and truth.

Durrell's Way to Alexandria   Carl Bode*

Durrell himself has warned us. When, as Darley, he tells his lovely blonde Clea that he has been meditating a book of literary criticism, she slaps him full across the mouth. And yet he has some reason to be charitable to the critics who want to understand his work better and feel it more deeply. After all, he himself has written such a book. Its title is *The Key to Modern Poetry*. Published in 1952, it was based on a series of lectures he gave while in Argentina on a British Council grant. In spite of its pompous title (which he may not want us to take seriously), it is a stimulating book for many a reader of poetry. And for anybody with an interest in the *Alexandria Quartet* it is an important one, for Durrell has written me that almost all the ideas of the *Quartet* are to be found there in germ form. With a single significant exception: that when he first set down those ideas he "hadn't twigged that Einsteinian time was not Bergsonian." After the *Key* came out he was, in fact, to decide that Bergson's theory of duration held little for him and that the Space-Time of Einstein was the central conception to use in the *Quartet*. The stress was to be on Relativity. Indeed the *Quartet* became for Durrell his "relativity poem."

For a better appreciation of the *Quartet* and especially its structure— the *Key to Modern Poetry* is indispensable. It is not the be-all and end-all, however. Much can be derived from his other writing. Actually, the *Quartet* is the splendid culmination of Durrell's work over a quarter of a century. The brightly decorated travel books, the crude early novels, the elegant, allusive poetry: Durrell drew on all these to create the *Quartet*. He levied on everything, it would seem, that he had ever thought to write about. He levied on his life. He appears in two guises in the *Quartet* if not

*Reprinted from *College English* 22, no. 8 (May 1961):531–38 with the permission of the National Council of Teachers of English.

three or four. He is at least the scribbling schoolmaster Darley and the wry genius of letters Pursewarden. But he is probably also Jacob Arnauti, who wrote a book about Justine, and John Keats, the crudest of journalists, who grows up through battle. In at least one sense he is the old Coptic woman Leila. Durrell also levied on the extraordinary stock of opinions and attitudes which he had previously revealed in print. Their diversity is remarkable. Among those represented in the *Quartet* are a belief in the occult, a detestation of the English (they are sexless and eccentric), love for low comedy, a preoccupation with symbols, and a tenderness toward mankind especially when it is bedeviled.

Besides Durrell's own writing there are other significant sources of clues and directions to help us comprehend the *Quartet*. They range from classical mythology to a handful of playing cards, from Freud to Eliot.

The central subject of the *Quartet* is sex, an "investigation of modern love." In kind the sex ranges from incest to nymphomania but it is always treated with sympathy. The respect Durrell shows for all human coupling prevents the *Quartet* from being sensational and emphasizes his conviction that the ultimate value of sex is what it can teach us about ourselves. Our only world is the world of self-exploration; love gives us the means.

The form of the *Quartet* is that of four books, of course, but once that has been said, there are some complications. According to Durrell himself, the first three books, *Justine*, *Balthazar*, and *Mountolive*, occupy the same general area of time while the fourth, *Clea*, is definitely a sequel. In reality, however, *Clea* for the most part moves spatially too rather than historically. Durrell also says that the third, *Mountolive*, is intended to be a straight naturalistic novel. I am not sure what he means by naturalistic; aside from some stretches of synoptic narrative at the beginning and near the end, much of the technique is that of *Justine* and *Balthazar*. But the Grand Design of the *Quartet* is a noble one.

Out of the many elements in the *Quartet* I want to concentrate—in connecting the work with its background—only on the chief ones.

First, then, something about the main male characters. Two guises of Durrell are among them. One is Darley, who tells the story. Through the experiences he alternately enjoys and suffers, he grows out of his callowness; and at the end of the *Quartet* he is, like Proust, ready to write a major work. In his other guise, that of Pursewarden, Durrell is the theorist of literature. Witty, wise, and annoying, Pursewarden speaks for Durrell and in doing so says some splendid things. Nessim Hosnani, the complex Coptic banker, is the third of the important male characters. We constantly see new depths in him during the course of the *Quartet*. Then we have a brilliant group of minor male characters. In painting them Durrell is at his best—better, frankly, than in presenting the three major ones. Old Scobie, the policeman-pederast, is a comic creation which Dickens might have given us if Queen Victoria had let him. Balthazar is an old Jewish mystic and like Scobie a sexual deviate. Narouz is Nessim's harelipped brother who turns into a religious fanatic. Pombal is a French official whom someone in the *Quartet* dryly calls one of the great primates of sex. The snakelike Capodistria is male sexuality personified; he once samples five women in an afternoon to see what the blend is like.

To one side of these men and less involved than most of them is Mountolive. Though he gives his name to a book in the *Quartet*, he is surprisingly commonplace. The role he plays is largely that of the traditional British diplomat, human enough under his Ambassador's uniform but hardly individual.

The three principal male characters are balanced by three remarkable women. One is a pale Greek named Melissa Artemis. She is in turn Darley's first love, Pursewarden's companion during his final night, and the mother of Nessim's child. Her sordid life as a cafe dancer and prostitute somehow fails to coarsen her: It is the bone-weariness of that life that makes her appealing to us. She whimpers with fatigue and the reader's heart aches. Justine Hosnani is as aggressive and powerful as Melissa is weak. She is dark, a Queen of Spades. Her perfect Jewish features and flashing eyes make her sexual conquests easy. Yet sex for her is usually a contrivance—to help her find the normal self she lost as a child when someone raped her. For all her strong lines, her vivid posturings, Justine seldom comes to life. She seldom engages us as Melissa does. Clea Montis, the golden-haired painter, is the third of the trio. She must fall in love with Justine before she can realize that she is a woman made for men. Her love for Darley, after he is done with Melissa and Justine, is noteworthy in that it turns out to be simple, natural, and a little dull. Perhaps one reason for Clea's lack of life is her absolute beauty; Pombal suggests that it would be easier for a man to make love to her if her face were covered. One other woman, older than these three, should be mentioned again. She is Leila, the mother of the Hosnani brothers. She was once Mountolive's lover and has since remained his cherished guide, turning him from a narrow public-school boy into a man of cultivation. For most of the time—and space—she stays at the edge of the *Quartet*. Her beauty has been scarred by smallpox; the veil she wears stands plainly for her withdrawn life.

These are the characters who weave, in time and space, the web of love. They vary enormously in the extent to which they come to life for the reader—and it may be presumed that Durrell realizes this. He believes, we know, that it is only through love that the real personality can be comprehended. And he believes that it is the act of love itself which is the most revealing, but he consistently refrains from describing it. Though he tried in his early novel *The Black Book*, he was no D. H. Lawrence and *The Black Book* turned out to be a sexual goulash. I do not recall that he has tried since. The *Quartet* will never be banned in Bournemouth or Boston, yet it may be guessed that some characters in the *Quartet* have lost by not being shown at love. But there is more to it than that. More than one critic has been disturbed by a hollowness in some of the characters. Though a few of them have a Dickensian vividness and reality, most do not. I have come to believe, however, that we should not look purely for realism in them but for something else—most probably, in fact, for symbolism. It contributes a new dimension, another emphasis.

I am convinced that Durrell's sources for symbolism are several. Among them is classical mythology. One of his most delightful characters has a strong suggestion of Tiresias. This is old Scobie, who comes from Greek myth by way perhaps of Eliot's *Wasteland*. He has the gift of prophecy, though inclined to discount it, and forecasts Clea's encounter with death under the sea. Scobie owns the characteristics of both sexes. Though he is male and given to false boasts of salty masculinity, he also acknowledges that he has "Tendencies" which lead him to gloat over the "mile upon mile of angelic blacks" waiting for him on the Delta and to dress like a Waterloo strumpet to tempt British sailors. Significantly, after his death he is deified. The Alexandrians enshrine him, pay him homage. He becomes El Scob, who sleeps with women to make them fertile, with men to make them potent. Suppliants stream to his most sacred relic, a bathtub. Bathing and water provide one or two more links, if tenuous ones, with Tiresias; I am thinking of the fact that a key episode in the Tiresias myth involves his sight of Athene bathing and that Scobie the sailor was long associated with the water. There is another, more somber figure in the *Quartet* who reminds us of Tiresias too. This is Balthazar, who is old, wise, and perverted. He too has something of the seer in him. A female character, much different from these old men but also with associations with classical mythology, is Melissa. Her delicacy, her pallor, her Grecian beauty are emphasized by the surname Durrell gives her: Artemis. Aside from mythology there are other souces from which Durrell draws. He hints in the *Quartet* that they include the four winds and the humors but so far I have been unable to work out their connection with any of the characters.

I do not feel this is true for the most remarkable source of symbols, the Tarot deck of cards. Eliot used them in the *Wasteland* but his use was slight compared to Durrell's. For him they are the chief source of symbolic suggestions. If we study the Tarot pack we do so at a risk not only because the individual cards and interpretations vary but also because we are enjoined from reading them for a casual purpose! So I make my own interpretations tentatively; in general I have used the studies of Paul Foster Case as my guide. The Tarot pack is divided into four suits, like the deck on any bridge table. The Wands are our Clubs, the Cups our Hearts, the Swords our Spades, and the Coins our Diamonds. Each suit has an extra picture card called the Page. For Durrell's symbolism, however, the most important part of the deck is a group of so-called Key cards which have no equivalents in our deck. On the face of each Key card is a picture with a special title. Each card corresponds to a letter in the Hebrew alphabet and each has particular associations and characteristics. Needless to say, Durrell does not model a character exactly on any one of the Key cards. He exchanges characteristics or modifies qualities. He uses the cards loosely but freely.

Perhaps the most striking example of the use of the Tarot pack is in the case of Pursewarden. For him we have not only some vital characteristics drawn from a Tarot card but even his odd name. He is to be identified with the Tarot Fool, by no means a figure of fun but a person of airy, cosmic energy. His intelligence is brilliant, his aspirations noble. As he is portrayed on the card, he carries a wand over his shoulder and fastened to the wand is a wallet, or purse. The lock on the purse is an eye; within the purse is all human experience. Pursewarden acts as the custodian of what Durrell calls "the universal human anecdote." Indeed, he sees for Durrell. And the Fool and Pursewarden are both associated with Venus and also with cultural activities. There is even such a small similarity as the fact that the Fool's coloring and Pursewarden's are both light. Capodistria is another character with remarkable resemblances to one of the Key cards, the card of the Devil. We associate Capodistria both with Capricorn and with the snake; he has the lust of a goat and the look of a serpent. The Devil's personal sign is Capricorn; in addition, he personifies serpent-power. The key to Capodistria's character is his hide-bound concentration on one half of human experience, the fleshy sexual half. This same defect he shares with the Devil. The Devil is shown as sitting on half a cube; Capo is pictured as having only half of his sight—a black patch covers one eye. In his left hand the Devil holds a burning torch upside down, a perfect image of a phallus used wastefully and not for creation.

Durrell's picture of Balthazar is another with strong Tarot resemblances. He is very probably based on the Key card of the Magician. The Magician and Balthazar are both occult philosophers, hermetic adepts; the Magician has the power of healing, Balthazar is by profession a physician. The Magician holds a two-ended phallic wand; Balthazar acts as man and woman both. A further point is that the Magician has black hair, the black of ignorance, but on it he wears the white crown of knowledge. Balthazar's hair is at first dark under the dark hat he habitually wears, then whitens when he has endured enough suffering to give him wisdom. The face under the hat, I must admit, is closer to the Devil's than to the Magician's; for the Devil and Balthazar both have goatish faces and a tuft of beard. The last of the male characters for whom I want to propose a Tarot prototype is Nessim's barbarous brother Narouz. He is suggested at least in part by the Key card of the Hierophant. The Hierophant has the gift of revelation; it gradually becomes Narouz's; Taurus is the Hierophant's sign just as it is for the bull-like Narouz. Psychologically the Hierophant represents intuition; Narouz shows intuition, though only at times and then like a man possessed. But the Hierophant remains a good priest while Narouz becomes a reckless fanatic. In his hand the Hierophant holds a golden staff; Narouz is given to holding a whip, which he wields increasingly.

About the Tarot pack and Durrell's women I am not as sure as I want to be. However, I think a good case can be made for a derivation for Clea and a weaker one for Melissa and Justine. I believe Clea is suggested by the Key card called the Star. Pictured on its face are stars and a nude woman pouring water into a pool. Water is one of the card's prime qualities; with it go associations of fish-hooks and fishing. The Hebrew letter for the card means fish-hook in fact. Here may be the origin for Clea's horrible if accidental harpooning by Balthazar. "Still waters of pain" is Durrell's "character-squeeze" of Clea at the end of *Justine*. There are other associations with water and the Star which are not painful. Water is Clea's element; she loves to swim in it. Water also stands for meditation, a plumbing of the waters of thought, so to speak. We can remember that she is more thoughtful, more meditative, than any other female character except perhaps Leila. I think there is also something of a Tarot prototype for Melissa. It is the High Priestess, whose celestial body is an eternal satellite, the Moon. In spite of her impressive powers the priestess symbolizes obedience, the quality of being "below." Like her, Melissa bows meekly to necessity. But the Priestess is celibate, while Melissa both through necessity and choice is not. I have looked for suggestions of Justine in the Tarot Key card without much satisfaction. There are some resemblances to the Empress, who is also linked with love. Both women are regal, both are highly sexed. The Empress is wise and foolish by turns as is Justine; also, she and Justine are patently powerful. However, the Empress is fruitful as well while Justine has borne a single doomed child. But regardless of whether the associations are as slight as for Justine or as considerable as for Pursewarden, the Tarot pack has certainly served to enrich the *Quartet*.

As to the setting: it is much more than a setting; that is the most striking thing about it. It is the main character itself. In its richly described changes, in its brilliant mingling of the magnificent and the mean, in its assault on every sense, it is to me the most memorable element in the *Quartet*. Durrell has rightly called the *Quartet* a Big City Poem. He fixed on Athens first when he decided to portray a city but switched to Alexandria because it more clearly had enough color to support four volumes. He writes about Alexandria like a lover. The love is natural and organic, for Durrell has always been enamored of places. Alexandria has stimulated him most, up to now, but he has also written with pleasure about other localities. Though he prefers islands, he has recorded his delight in at least two other cities, Athens and Paris. Because he feels places strongly, he also has an exceptional animosity toward those that displease him. He can find little good to say of London, for example, and contemptuously calls England "Pudding Island." . . .

Plot—and structure—must rest on the conception of time which Durrell has adapted from Einstein. Its implications permeate the *Quartet*. First and most important, the old idea of time as a flowing river is gone. The plot is no longer a stream of consequential events, with one resulting from the other and following it in chronological order. Instead the order of events is determined by which one first becomes significant to the character from whose point of view Durrell is writing. This is the proper way, to him, for literature; the other is history. If the point of view shifts, so does the order of significance of the events. Events themselves alter as they acquire new interpretations. The most notable instance is probably Pursewarden's suicide. This tragic event constantly changes its shape as we see it from the point of view of different characters and as the characters themselves learn more about it.

Though time stops its steady forward motion, it does not stand still. It moves backwards and forwards and sideways. It now moves around in space; and time becomes, as Durrell says in the *Key to Modern Poetry*, "a thick opaque medium welded to space." The place where a character stands in space becomes vital to his view of time and of events. If he moves in any direction, his world will vary. So will time and so will he. Pursewarden sums it up: "Two paces east or west and the whole picture is changed."

Two further implications of the Einsteinian approach ought to be brought out. One is that the line between the subject and the object becomes blurred. We are no longer sure that anything is objectively real. We are the ones who comprehend it, but the very comprehending changes us—and in consequence for us changes the object we have been comprehending. Absolutes are gone. In their place, in Einsteinian relativity, the observer and the thing observed mingle with one another. The other implication is also noteworthy. As Durrell says, again in the *Key*, "Another aspect of the relativity theory is the manner in which it sidetracks causality." We can see that most modern fiction pays earnest attention to causality, particularly in the form of motivation. The more that novelists know about formal psychology, the more they are apt to write about it; and to write with greater confidence. But not Durrell. He is convinced that the more we know of an event the less we can determine its cause or effect. At one point he ties up both implications by observing, "If two or more explanations of a single human action are as good as each other, then what does action mean but an illusion?"

The shifting realm of Space-Time has much that is new to most fiction. Time changes from an orderly series of moments, from Past, Present, and Future Tenses, to an enormous Present. Yet it is a present rich with the significance of the past. The past—or the only part of the past which has meaning—is the past with us now. It is our present image of a dead lover, the lingering of her perfume. If we do not see her in our minds, she does not exist. The enormous present, says Durrell, is "the impact"—and note the word *impact*—"of all time crowded into one moment of time." The Future is also involved in the Enormous Present, though Durrell shows himself much more reticent about using this implication of his idea. However, there are two or three striking cases of prophecy, and Scobie, Balthazar, and Melissa—among the more important characters—all have the gift of seeing the future at one time or another.

We have been separating plot from character for the sake of convenience. Space-Time integrates them, however, and so we need to return to character briefly. As subject mingles with object, character mingles with event. Just as Justine, for example, often affects her experiences, her experiences affect her. Love affects us most of all, especially when all is lost for it. Here Durrell's view of life, always positive and affirmative, reaches a kind of nobility. Loss, all loss, and suffering, all suffering, can teach us. Through them we can grow wise. We learn by enduring, says Balthazar, and he knows. He himself has tried to commit suicide out of his infatuation for a handsome Greek actor and then has painfully discovered his own foolishness. The silly journalist Keats, we remember, turns into a mature man by enduring the ordeal of battle. Darley too, termed by Pursewarden "Brother Ass," knows at the end of the Quartet that he has grown from an awkward schoolmaster into a writer with something to say. Clea must have her hand cut off—death for a painter—and yet with the device of metal and wood which replaces it, she can paint as never before. Of course the world of Alexandria is not uniformly rosy. Sometimes experience can bear down so heavily that it kills. No one is more innocent in spirit than Melissa, but her life and death are a wearisome struggle. No one is wiser than Pursewarden, but he learns too much and then swallows cyanide.

But experience must be bitter if it is to be wholesome. Again and again in the Quartet some physical loss appears; it stands of course for the psychic price we must pay for tuition. Justine has a stroke. Nessim loses an eye and a finger, Clea loses her hand. Nessim's mother Leila sees her beauty turn into smallpox scars. However, most of the characters endure and ultimately flourish. At the end of the Quartet Durrell has almost a Dickensian distribution of awards. Justine and Nessim are handsome again and happy; Clea is full of zest in Paris; Mountolive has pulled himself together and is about to receive the plum of ambassadorial appointments, France. Darley himself begins to write his book.

As Durrell drew from Einstein, he drew from Freud. But with fewer and less rewarding results. In an epigraph to the book *Justine* he quotes from a letter in which Freud said that he was getting used to the idea of every sexual act as a process in which four persons were involved. This conception Durrell tries to apply to the plot of the Quartet in two ways. In a few cases he draws on the Freudian idea that we all are part male, part female. In this sense the four people are simply two people in their four parts. Logically enough in a world of flux, the proportions of masculine and feminine not only vary in all of us to begin with but change under the impact of events. Justine, for example, always has much of the masculine in her and Nessim much of the feminine; but there is a peak moment when this is strikingly exaggerated. Durrell writes then that Nessim "felt her on top of him, and in the plunge of her loins he felt the desire to add to him." The second way in which Durrell tries to adapt Freud's view we see much more frequently. It is to have not a triangle of lovers but a quadrangle. One person loves another as the surrogate for the third. As Darley says once about Melissa, Justine, Nessim, and himself: "The four of us were unrecognized complementaries of one another, inextricably bound together." Often the characters themselves are conscious of this conception and use it. Nessim knowingly comes to love Melissa as an extension of Justine. Melissa urges Clea to love Darley for her after her death.

Durrell also drew on Freud for a theory of dreams. Dreams play an extraordinary part in the *Quartet*. Durrell describes them with great thoroughness. They illuminate his characters and illustrate his use of Space-Time since dreams are a notable example of things more spatial than temporal. They too blur the line between subject and object, between present and past—and future. Nessim in particular has dreams which are magnificent, cloudy phantasmagorias.

A final device which Durrell uses to create the Space-Time structure of the *Quartet* is an intricate expansion of one employed in his travel writing. There he often inserted letters, diary entries, and other material to give the reader a sense of what he called the historical present. In the *Quartet* he inserts a great and complex variety of materials, again to keep his time together. There is a novel about Justine which her first husband wrote. There are Justine's diaries. There are Darley's own drafts with Balthazar's elaborate annotations and emendations. There are long stories or reminiscences given by one character about another. There are long stories by some of the characters themselves, particularly Scobie. The device is pushed to its extreme in the last book of the *Quartet* when Clea is induced to give a four-page imitation of Scobie telling a story. Actually, the *Quartet* is like a collage, a splendid, surrealist paste-up of written materials.

Though I have now said something at any rate about plot, setting, and character, there are still a dozen things I should like to discuss. But because no magazine has unlimited space, I can only mention them here. One is the autobiographical elements in the *Quartet*. We all write about ourselves. Durrell is no exception, though he is subtler now than when he pictured himself as Campion, the painter in *Cefalû*. Another is the tall tale in the *Quartet*. Durrell has developed a lovely low-comedy sense of the grotesque—think of Capodistria's father and his rubber woman, for example, or Scobie's story of the rebellious earth-closets. Another is the relation of the theories of the psychologist Georg Groddeck to the *Quartet*. Another is the existentialism in it. Still another is the varied role of occult. Durrell believes in it and it shows itself in more than the Tarot deck. Another is the relation of the writings of the Marquis de Sade to the *Quartet*, though here I must add that I think the relation is slighter than Durrell's epigraphs suggest. Another is an exploration of Durrell's ethics—for I have seen nothing like their magnificent amorality in modern fiction. He seems to make no ethical judgments at all. Another is the effect that those two mandarins of modern literature, Eliot and Henry Miller, have had on Durrell. And there is the style, about which I have said little. It is the very stuff of the *Quartet*; this is what, more than anything else, makes the *Quartet* a poem. And the pageantry: the procession and feast of Sitna Mariam, for instance. And the recurring motifs, ranging from phrases and single sentences to whole scenes such as the dismembering of the camels. And the management of the great scenes, for instance the final one between Pursewarden and Melissa, the visit of Nessim to Memlik Pasha, the death of Narouz. The possibilities seem endless and many of them look rewarding. Here is a novelist who has created a city and peopled it for us; here is a remarkable and complicated achievement which I believe we shall long enjoy.

Curate's Egg: An Alexandrian
Opinion of Durrell's *Quartet*   Mahmoud Manzaloui*

Now that one can look at Durrell's *Quartet* more calmly, judgments are likely to be more balanced. My own impression is that Durrell's *Quartet* is neither a masterpiece, nor so inferior that it deserves the vilification some critics have given it. It is mediocre, but its mediocrity, as a total work of literature, is of an unusual kind, made up of superlatively good and execrably bad elements. The elements remain badly mixed, and do not form a compound; the closest comparisons are with the nursery rhyme boy who wobbles between being "very very good" and "horrid," and the egg that was in parts excellent. On the whole, description is masterly in the four volumes; by and large, the narrative element is flat. But the case is rather more curious: there is at least one single element which itself wavers in the same way between the highest quality and the lowest—and that is Durrell's prose style, an element that never in his other works sinks below the good. The book is therefore certainly a surprising one, especially for the minority of readers who already knew Durrell's earlier works.

Ordinarily, nothing is less rewarding than the analysis of a work into components; the uneven quality of these books forces one into this approach if one is to try to give a balanced opinion. It seems permissible, then, to look at the *Quartet* as a poem, a novel, a documentary work, and, more broadly, as a "criticism of life," before assessing it as a whole. This four-faceted diagram of the *Quartet* has no relation to its four-decker structure, or to its alleged view of life as four-dimensional; it is imposed upon one by Durrell's earlier writings.

The poetry of Mediterranean and of personal landscapes (and of the

*Reprinted from *Études Anglaises* 15, no. 3 (July—September 1962):248–60.

interaction of these two upon each other), remains, I think, Durrell's most valuable contribution to this century's literature and sensibility. Those who have been drawn to this by the *Quartet* will find the full essence if they read *At Strati's, Eight Aspects of Melissa*, or parts of the longer poem *Cities, Plains and People*. Also in Durrell the poet lay the wit-writer, ebullient, out to give his reader shock-treatment, the writer of *Mythology* and the *Ballad of the Good Lord Nelson*. He reappears in the *Quartet*, but there he has retrogressed to the fifth-form humorist of Pursewarden's occasional verse (especially in *My Conversation with Brother Ass*). At other times, in the directness of prose, he has suffered an attack of almost Miltonic elephantiasis, so that we stand politely sustaining a smile through those passages in *Clea* where the characters and, it seems, the author, are "quietly laughing" or telling long pub-crony anecdotes (*Clea*, 120–4).

The documentary prose poet of Mediterranean islands, the twin to the lyric poet, is a writer who has given the travel book a new dimension. Would there, one wondered, be a book on Egypt where—beyond the time filter which, in each case, Durrell finds necessary to place between his experience and his recreation of it—he would once again combine his love of limpid beauty and of the sheer goodness of human simplicity? As an Egyptian and an Alexandrian, I waited, and when *Justine* was announced wondered whether this was to be the expected piece.

Durrell the poetic novelist joined Henry Miller in 1938 in exploring the human regions where self-exploration and the outward-seeking sexual urge march together. In the wake of the Freudians and of Joyce, *The Black Book*, whose admitted "crudity and savagery" (to quote Durrell's preface to the 1959 edition), have so far prevented its publication in England, is a clearly original work, in its evocation of moods, its weaving of reflexions and lyric insights around anecdote, in its avant-garde freedom from the restrictions of moral convention and literary forms, but, mainly, for the total freshness of its phrases.

More recently, Durrell has widened the range of his talents still further with his *Key to Modern Poetry*. Here, besides the regulation chapters on Hopkins, Eliot, and "Poetry in the Thirties," we have four chapters of very great interest, on the limits of objective criticism, on the new conception of time and space, and on the human personality and the artistic probe into truth.

Prepared originally as lectures for a Spanish-speaking audience, and bound down to the objective facts of modern literary history, the book obliged Durrell to write in a simple, direct, expository style, and so revealed a further facet of his abilities.

Re-read today, the first ninety pages of the *Key* can be seen to form the conceptual background to the creative experiment of the *Quartet*; if the theories of Einstein and Planck are rather naïvely distorted, and homage is paid to at least one particularly fatuous literary assessment by Freud (p. 66), the twists given to scientific and pseudo-scientific theories are just those which a creative writer often gives to the non-literary trends that provide the spark which sets off his imaginative power.

To the reader who comes to the *Quartet* from the earlier work, it is the meeting point of these diverse streams, and, at first sight, a culminating-point of Durrell's literary qualities, unified in an ambitious book: a work of fiction evoking a Mediterranean port and its life, in poetic prose, and presenting a view of things derived from the modern time-space theory, and from Groddeck's vitalism and his theory of inward and outward causality.

In the execution the book is not the success that it might have been, and is not in fact the book one could have expected. The main reasons, I think, are these: that there are inherent flaws of vision in the writer, and that he has not used his talents in their full integrity, that a hive of otiose entities unaccountably swarms in, and that the work, far from having the unity it pretends to have, is used as a cumbersome holdall, and contains subterfuges to disguise its true structure, or rather its absence of serious structural vision.

On the credit side, Durrell the poet and the documentary artist gives us the magnificent set pieces, landscapes, and townscapes which are all the more memorable when they do not concern themselves with active inter-relations between human beings. The memorable passages are sometimes fragments describing place and atmosphere, a deeply evocative word or half-phrase; there are memorable paragraphs—particularly rich when they describe weather or street life—and there are the great passages which will surely find their way into the prose anthologies of the future: the description of the brothel-quarter (*Justine*, 185 ff.), the wild life of Lake Mariout (*Justine*, 213 ff.), winter in the English Home Counties (*Mountolive*, p. 95), summer memories of Agami (*Clea*, 222 ff.);—with these goes the overpowering *tour-de-force* of the lyrical air-raid (*Clea*, 24 ff.), best described in one of its own phrases, "as beautiful as it was stupefying." To these, adding to their tone more than a hint of the irony of intelligent introspection and of true empathy, the novelist attaches the nostalgia of love, separation, and disillusionment. The *Quartet* explores the mystery and paradox of human beings, who are, somehow, both monads which never interpenetrate successfully, and complementary parts of an "It" which goes back beyond all conceptualizing, all separations, and, to borrow the words of the *Key* (p. 79) (and perhaps mis-apply them) is not even a thing, but a "Way," more specifically, "a way of seeing." The juncture of novelist and thinker gives the *Quartet* its highest ambition as a work of art. The reader of the *Key* can interpret it as a novel, or anti-novel, in which the experience by human beings of each other is used to de-individualize them by showing that "character" is a "Realist" illusion, that, viewed from a point of anti-personalist nihilism, both the personality of others and one's own experiences, are variable aspects of a protean experience. In this there are only a few fixed realities. One is the depersonalized and fragmentary world of sense-experience which can be reconstituted by the self through association, and the evocation of past impressions. Another is the all-pervasive power and beauty of sex. Another, the warmth of camaraderie. To express this vision of life in narrative form is extremely difficult, since the usual machinery of character must be set in motion only to be smashed, and the straight-forward line of time, without which, in some form, the worn "narrative" can have no meaning, must be partly preserved but partly vaporized into a diaphanous volume. Mr. Durrell's plan, if it is such as I have tried to describe it, serves him well in his role of prose poet of the outer and inner landscapes; while he, up to a point, serves it excellently as a writer whose best work, whether it deals with men or with the inanimate, can be described as a verbal form of mobile sculpture.

But the schema seems to me, at the same time, to contain the seeds of its own failure. A form which attempts to represent the inchoateness of experience itself slips easily into the inchoate; a novel in which the sense of the word *character* is made to wither away, runs the risk of falling outside the area of literature which deals with the interaction and interdevelopment of human tensions, that is, it may have none of the qualities either of novel or of anti-novel. It seems to me that the *Quartet* succumbs on both counts; this is not a weakness of plan alone (though the threat of indefinite extension, which the *Author's Note* to *Clea* makes, is disturbing enough), nor of plan and texture only, but is linked with an inherent infertility that lurks in the writer's particular vision of the world. Durrell heightens the sensory and momentary to such an extent, and, concurrently, lowers the estimate of what are conventionally taken to be the "higher" ranges of human activity, that the resulting levelling, far from adding to the freedom of human perception, is almost a scuttling of humanistic values.

The levelling of philosophy and sea-bathing on to one plane may be refreshing in *Orphan Island*; in the *Quartet* it is not only a dangerous sign culturally, but self-defeating artistically; we end by losing interest, for, as it has been often said, if everything is equally important, everything is equally unimportant. The very beauty of the description of the air-raid in *Clea* depends upon a measure of dissociation with its anonymous human suffering, which, accumulating its effect through the four volumes, ends by repulsing one.

The essential shapelessness of the *Quartet* is not redeemed (as Joyce's two major works are by the underpropping of parallelism with classical works) by Mr. Durrell's ostensive schema as outlined in the *Note* to *Balthazar*. This, if compared to the text of the *Key*, is the poorest précis any author ever gave of his own vision, and if Mr. Corke's *Encounter* article had not clearly beaten it to it by several lengths, one could have called it the weakest advertisement so far of the *Quartet*.

No one can seriously believe that because Time-Space has four dimensions, a novel should have four sections. No one can take the dependence of *Balthazar* upon *Justine* for an analogy of the relationship between two dimensions of space. If the *Quartet* as a whole has as one of its principal effects the revealing of the contradictory and the amorphous in human personality, then none of its component volumes should as it stands, be labelled "a novel" in its own right; if on the other hand, you regard them each as a novel, then the *Quartet* is surely made up of five novels; its component parts, plus the total work itself. Is the dullness of outlook in *Mountolive* meant to show a world that is more objectively real than the personalized world of the other volumes? How does the writer reconcile himself to the artificiality of construction in *Clea*, with its many unlikely coincidences, and its role as a long-drawn-out dénouement to the whole? Most serious of all, has it genuinely escaped him that the volumes do not represent "dimensions" but a series of random probings into the solid of human experience? And that, unlike Proust, he does not build up the complexity of his characters by his successive revelations, but, rather, cancels them out? . . .

The originality of the architectonics and vision of the *Quartet* has been unaccountably exaggerated; what positive contribution is there which *Ulysses*, *A la Recherche du Temps Perdu*, *Rashomon*, *Citizen Kane*, and Durrell's own *Black Book* have not already made? One only that I can detect, and that is the disengagement from experience which Durrell gains by writing so much of the book in the form of letters, diaries, pages out of printed books, written commentary by one character upon another character's experience, and reminiscence of a character upon his own past. The novel is largely one of action in the pluperfect. Durrell's poetry of life is essentially one of emotion recollected in comparatively cerebral tranquillity, and this filtering technique suits it; but where the action is being related directly and immediately, Durrell's vision fails him. We are moved by the evocations and re-assessments of love, but love in actuality is, in the *Quartet*, less convincing and sometimes hardly moving at all. At the nadirs of bathos, the love-making is so perfunctory, and the description so preoccupied with its incidental adjuncts, that the anatomy of Durrell's *Ewigweibliche* seems, like a bad onion, to have no core at all.

The more sustained nature of the *Quartet* shows up weaknesses in Durrell's make-up as a writer, which, on looking back, one can detect in his earlier work. There is a failure to find any interest in normality, which drives the author into an exploitation of the fantastic, without the positive exploratory value of surrealism, and too late for the negative debunking virtue of da-daism; the comic passages (especially in *Clea*) are often quite unfunny; the changes of tone, as when passages from reports upon Renaissance magic are introduced (*Clea*, pp. 198 ff.) in a letter from Capodistria, cannot be justified; the exigencies of the narrative create flaws such as the unconvincing flatness of that lay figure, Melissa's child. With these weaknesses, goes the sheer badness of taste which sees the Beatitudes as jokes (*Clea*, p. 144), and which demolishes the dramatic effects of the writer's own narrative: Darley, diving to save Clea's life is made to say: "*I turned my toes to heaven* and returned on my tracks" (*Clea*, 250). There are outstanding vices in the *Quartet* which, on the other hand, the early Durrell is not guilty of. The most obvious is the blown-up pretentiousness of the entire schema. An author who prints his own rough notes under the title "Consequential Data"; a book studded with cheap gnomic paradoxes such as "pleasure . . . is the opposite of happiness, its tragic part, I expect" (*Balthazar*, 53), and attempts at *pensées* which sound like Dryden's Melantha practising her words for the day. A false decorum makes the author prefer not to mention Cavafis by name, but refer to him in circumlocutions such as "the old poet of the city." An affected sprinkling of words intended to evoke local colour: the *"iodine-coloured meidan"* of Mazarita is iodine-coloured because it is metalled, and a *meidan* because that is the Arabic for a square: it is a small feature-less European-type square such as you may find in Abbeville or Wigan. We miss the Durrell to whom a friend wrote, about his *The Black Book*, "No, you are not *pretending!* Hence the impact of the book, I think."

The *Quartet* attitudinizes. Its events take place in a pink and over-scented haze; everything is coloured with the *renchérissement* of traditional western pseudo-orientalism. Curiously, Durrell seems to think that his own baroque vision resembles the poignant intimacy of Cavafis, and of his own earlier poetry. His sexualizing of life and landscape descends far beneath Lawrence's mystique or Freud's clarification of life, into a mannerism which is predictable, and easy to parody. . . .

Durrell even parodies himself in a few lines that form a bad précis of his own Lord Nelson poem (*Mountolive*, 65). This falling into mannerism ought, in any fuller study of his writing, to be related to the surprisingly slipshod patches which astonish the reader in a writer who is at other times (mainly in the "set pieces" of the book) so splendid a stylist. Revolving doors are "circular" (*Mountolive*, 197), Pursewarden's "perfect white teeth" and "sad little blond moustache" (*Justine*, 141), reappear eleven pages later as the "small perfect teeth" and "neat little brush-stroke moustache" of Youssef Bey; cordite and bread are called "natural objects" (*Clea*, 113), aerial bombing is "bombardment" (*Clea*, 161 and 162), the "bottom half" of the narrator's pyjamas "were crisp" (*Clea*, 240). Similar crudities are in sentences like this following:

> A room which had housed (*if walls have ears*)
> their most secret deliberations. (*Mountolive*, 232)

> One day I caught a *tortoise* at my front door; on
> the beach was a smashed *turtle's* egg. (*Clea*, 277)

The dialogue is often unconvincing, but reaches the depths of textbook quality in long speeches (e.g. *Clea*, 53–4) or in snippets like "I have been experimenting with drugs of late, *the sleep-givers!*" (*Clea*, 57).

A comically simple instance of the blowing up of Middle Eastern reality is Durrell's over-use of the word "great": great desk, great car, great lounge, great "semicircle of boats," "huge sacred tree," "great dictionary," great domed room, great brass-framed windows, great rose-bowl, are thrust upon one in quick succession (all these particular examples are from one volume), until the mind lurches with this upstart barbarian's naïve dazzlement at the Opulent City. Even the Alexandria Corniche has become the Grande Corniche, a name it has never been given—and a curious twist in Durrell's memory.

The most repugnant feature of Durrell's style is his repetition of an ossified joke. The *tarbush* is given its proper name early in *Justine* (p. 56), but at least on five other occasions it is called a flower-pot, an inverted flower-pot, or a red pill-box, a joke that is not worth making even once. If one gives serious attention to the French and Arabic in the work—but perhaps this is not legitimate?—we find many wrong genders and forms, incorrect syntax, wrongly remembered names, forms of Arabic from non-Egyptian dialects, and sheer nonsense.

One page of *Clea* (p. 149) contains two Arabic howlers which show something more: that Durrell is a literary plagiarist, and that he is not above pulling the innocent European reader's leg. On this page he requires some names for an "immortal story," a popular Arab folk-epic, which he has just invented. He has lifted the names from page 80 of an English book printed in Egypt, J.W. McPherson's *Moulids of Egypt (Egyptian Saints Days)*, Cairo, 1941, a book which he has used again and again for details of his *Quartet* (as Mr. John Parker, of the University of Khartoum, is showing elsewhere). Durrell takes "Aziza and Yunis," and inverts their sexes to produce Aziz, a possible male name, and Yuna, an impossible female name. He follows McPherson's misunderstanding of the words of a popular song, "Hassan Abu Ali Saraq el Meeza" (Hassan Abu Ali has stolen the goat), and gives this, substantially, as the *name* of a character in the epic: "the mishaps which befell them from the doing of Abu Ali Saraq el-Méeza." This is about as reasonable as creating a Spenserian villain called Tom-Tom-the-piper's-son-stole-a-pig-and-away-he-ran. It has more serious implications. Book-knowledge is not a source that, I think, Durrell would care to admit, and the off-centered inaccuracy of vision and "invention" that this one example shows is repeated again and again in his picture of Alexandria. The writer may wish to shelter behind an unassailable subjectivism, to claim that his Alexandria, his Egypt, are parts of an entirely "personal landscape"—I have used these words several times because they were the name of the wartime poetry magazine of the Middle East to which Durrell was a distinguished contributor. If so, he is fully entitled to change, add and subtract; unfortunately, in the introductory *Note* to each of the first two volumes, he commits himself to the statement, "the city is real." Even his staunchest supporters have not interpreted this statement to mean that the reality of the city is a subjective one of his own esemplastic construction—

if it were, then Durrell's defences would be difficult to engage; let me offer that interpretation to any one who wishes to save the appearances. The fact is that, for the past two years every one of our European and American visitors has pressed us for a tour of "Durrellian" Alexandria, and Mr. Corke has hobbled to Mr. Durrell's defence with absurdities (patent, I hope, even to those who have never left their hometown) about the dimensions of Alexandria shaving-mirrors.

It was an unlucky decision of Mr. Durrell's to decide, as he seems to have, upon giving Alexandria, its inhabitants, and the *hinterland* formed by Egypt and its life, a status in his novel which corresponds to an extent with the part that Dublin plays in *Ulysses*. Joyce knew Ireland; Mr. Durrell does not know Egypt. Joyce with the gifts of a true novelist as well as those of a poet, had a firm grasp upon reality, a keen eye, an accurate memory; above all, he had the fiction writer's gift of double knowledge—perception of the outside world and insight into the inner life of the individual, with the ability to weave his creation out of the fusion of these two worlds. It seems to me that we have here a crucial difference between what we call poetry and what we call fiction, a difference more important than the surface one between "lyric" and "narrative" approach. Mr. Durrell, a master of the inner landscape, is a flounderer at the craft of welding it to the outer. From this, follows the deepest falseness of the *Quartet*. It is a falseness that is greater than the individual examples of "mistake" suggest; the mistakes, however, are surely an index of it, and it should not be necessary to point out that there are peculiar little flaws of vision and of workmanship throughout the *Quartet*, which are unconnected with Alexandria. How can the Cavafy canon be "established" by a *translation* (*Justine*, 251)? What is the "Unabridged Oxford Dictionary" (*Mountolive*, 240)? Why has Darley never seen a photograph of De Gaulle, though the time is even later than the fall of Greece to the Germans in 1941 (*Clea*, 39)? Durrell's ignorance of the Rabelaisian nature of the first troubadour's poetry, that of William IX of Aquitaine, makes his assessment comic (*Clea*, 43). The Catholic Church is preternaturally incapacitated (*Clea*, 121); while a Coptic monk takes priestly orders quite unnecessarily if he merely wants to become a religious (*Justine*, 163). Why is the British Embassy called a Legation and the Consular corps of Alexandria called "diplomatic" (*Justine*, 171; *Balthazar*, 78; *Clea*, 74)? The last "Workpoint" to *Balthazar* is a sentence torn out of its context. Why write the name of a magazine in a peculiar Anglo-French: "Values (sept)" (*Mountolive*, 60)? Is Durrell pulling our leg again when he says (*Justine*, 211) somewhat out of emotive context that "bag-and-shot talk" is "the most delightful and absorbing masculine conversation in the world"? It cannot still be the "crepuscular evening" (*Justine*, 199) after Melissa's night-club performance. Why is an independent Syria before 1939 (*Mountolive*, 140) brought in?—it cannot be one of the "necessary liberties with modern Middle Eastern history" of the *Note*, since it adds nothing to the book. And what can one make of an independent Ceylon at the same date (*Mountolive*, 163)? Does Durrell seriously think "fornication" is a Germanic word (*Mountolive*, 176)? How is the exclamation mark within brackets expressed by Clea, in the middle of whose long speech (*Clea*, 82) it occurs? Is there such a thing as a Viking "catafalque" (*Clea*, 148)? Was Mountolive's marriage (*Clea*, 279) "secret" or merely *private*: I, for one, cannot believe in a post-war ambassador of St. James's in Paris, with a blind morganatic wife. The term "Holy Office" is used wrongly (*Justine*, 223); Clea's calling her lover Darley by his surname as late as p. 255 of the last volume is peculiar.

One can add many other instances to show Durrell's careless attitude towards objective reality. If I have spent so much time on what, taken separately, may seem mere pinpricks, it is in order to show the essential falsity of description, and weakness of grasp, without reference to Alexandria and to things Egyptian. When we turn to these, we find the same shoddiness, the same slipshod planning and cavalier distortion of the truth. The very fact that, mostly, these attitudes are not inherent to the inner shaping of the novel, shows that we are not, most of the time, examining the esemplastic transmutations of a great creative writer of narrative. If this part of my criticism skims the mere surface of literature, it is because this surface is precisely where most of Durrell's Alexandria is built, and neither in documentary reality nor the depths of introspective and symbolic truth.

Is it pedantic of an Egyptian reader of the *Quartet* to find it strange that almost every Arabic word in the four volumes has a wrong form, or is misused? *Ebed* (*Clea*, 99) is a non-existent word; *Kohly* (= "navy-blue") an impossible surname (*Balthazar*, 19); *Abdul* (*Balthazar*, 36) without a genitive following it, is an Urdu barbarism, impossible in Arabic (the correct abbreviated form is *Abduh*); *tibbin* (*Balthazar*, 73) is a Syrian, not an Egyptian, form of *tibn*, and this means *straw* and not *corn*; the "legend '*B'ism'il-lah ma'sha'llah'* " of the same page is an impossible combination of words, and the translation given is wrong; *kurbash* (*Balthazar*, 86) is *kurbag* in Egypt, and *abba* (*Justine*, 163) is *abayah*. No Copt is called *Serapamoun* (*Mountolive*, 217); *Zananiri* is a surname held only by Christian families and therefore there can be no "Ahmed Zananiri" (*Justine*, 247).

To say "*Ma-a-lesh*" (*Mountolive*, 316) i.e. "What does it matter?" to the relatives of a dead man, at his funeral-wake, is the height of rudeness. Arabic verse is not noticeably "alliterative" (*Clea*, 149). There are brave attempts where Durrell has unconsciously quibbled: the "*arusas*" of *Clea* (260) are mere "dolls" and not "brides" (the word has two usages); *zaghareet* ("*zaghreet*" in *Mountolive*, 314) are happy ululations, and not keenings, mournful cries, which are "*siwat*." "Kiss of *thorns*" (*Clea*, 24) should be the "kiss of *desire*." *Surah*, in the *Koran*, is not the same word as the word for *image* (*Mountolive*, 317), and by what absurdity is the *Koran* being recited at a Christian funeral?

This last example is only one of many confusions in connexion with religion. It is part of the deliberate joke that Scobie should be sanctified by

the popular imagination of the Anfouchy quarter, and that this sanctification should contain a confused mixture of Moslem and Christian elements.
But the confusion seems (*Clea*, 82 ff.) to have infected the author's own
mind. This is not unexpected in a writer who thinks (*Justine*, 163–5) that
St. Catherine's monastery is Coptic, that the *Kalima* is part of the *Koran*
(*Balthazar*, 37), that a Moslem woman can become a nun (*Mountolive*,
152), that serious Moslem believers think God created unpleasant things on
a Tuesday (*Mountolive*, 261), that the lunar calendar can slide up as well as
down (*Clea*, 242) and who, throughout, shows Islam as a strangely Diony-
siac religion: a view he derives from knowing certain marginal manifesta-
tions, and not knowing the more characteristic ones. Of course, one does
not demand that a novelist should be learned; but there is something seriously wrong when a reader who is unfortunate enough to have a modicum
of knowledge of a country and its background of thought, finds this a positive hindrance to enjoying the novel.

If linguistics and elementary theology are thought too recondite for a
modern novelist, Durrell cannot escape so easily over topography. The
writer, again, is by all means free to alter the details of a town or of a country to suit his purposes, but he causes an artistic flaw if his changes turn a
serious situation into farce. Durrell moves the desert into the middle of the
Delta (Section IV of *Balthazar*), and he places the *eastern* desert (*Clea*,
217) immediately outside Alexandria. His characters find granite rocks on
the sea-bed off Alexandria (*Clea*, 224). In a hilarious love-scene, a blind
woman and an English ambassador take a flying leap from the Corniche to
the beach of Stanley Bay below—it is a pity that "Stanley Bay" is the only
beach-name that Durrell could remember, because it is the only beach
which had three (there are now four) tiers of cabins, one jutting out beyond
the other, so that these acrobatics would involve a jump of about forty feet
forward and thirty downwards.

Bad observation and dishonest reporting cover all the facets of Egyptian life: the water of Lake Mariout is brackish and no one would use it for
irrigation (*Mountolive*, 35); upper class women wore white, and not black,
veils (*Mountolive*, 24) when Leila was a young girl; no one, not even an
Englishman, can wear even a "light" overcoat over a dinner-jacket in Cairo
in July (*Mountolive*, 141). Where did Clea buy oranges in the middle of the
summer (*Clea*, 225)? The "little" Ramleh tram (*Justine*, 52) is an exceptionally large one. To say that in Egypt Alexandria is the "only capital [?*sic*]
which bore the remotest traces of a European way of life" is gross hyper-
bole; calling *bersim*, a staple fodder crop, a "wild clover" (*Balthazar*, 32) is
foolish and is contradicted elsewhere. Weak memory even extends to the
life of the Anglo-Egyptians and the fashionable Levantines who lie at
the core of the book. The British Summer Residence was not "new" in the
thirties (*Mountolive*, 144); no one in Egypt calls five pounds "500 piastres"
or ten pounds "a thousand" (*Mountolive*, 168–9 and 179); I doubt if Clea
would have used gold nail-varnish (*Clea*, 51)—or have regularly smoked

"silver-tipped" cigarettes (*Clea*, 57); no fashionable shop in Alexandria would have the Anglo-Indian name "Ghoshen's Emporium" (*Clea*, 212).

But other changes are made deliberately, to add *renchérissement* to the exotic glamour of the subjective Alexandria. The Levantine carnival of Alexandria, which disappeared before the first world war, is resuscitated in the Thirties, and is described as much more indigenous and spontaneous than it was—just as Agami beach is described as though it were a relatively deserted and unspoilt spot, when it is a highly organized, fashionable Levantine resort, accessible only by expensive methods of transport, and entered by a toll-road whose owners make tidy sums out of prosperous pleasure-seekers. The Coptic festival of St. Damiana is transported from the Delta to the implausible venue of Alexandria—as unconvincing to an Egyptian as a Cornish folk festival in Piccadilly Circus. I bow to Mr. Durrell's obviously intimate knowledge of the lupanars, but take leave to doubt the existence of those roving brothel booths, side by side with Moslem dervishes, at Christian festivities.

As for the "curling" streets of Alexandria (*Clea*, 13), which extend "radiating out like the arms of a starfish from the axis of its founder's tomb" (*Clea*, 63), the reader with some education does not need an Alexandrian to tell him that Mr. Durrell's much-vaunted Hellenism must have been fast asleep, and that for a Hellenistic grille-plan he has, by an unnecessary and uncouth substitution, introduced mid-nineteenth century radial planning. As he has very often substituted the crude pseudo-orientalism of the last century for direct observation, this is not surprising; though these are moments when the unreality reaches almost pathological depths: e.g. when he writes (*Balthazar*, 15) as though Leila's keeping of a pet cobra was typical of middle-aged Coptic ladies . . . and, of Narouz' funeral, "All the china and glass in the house—save for the ceremonial black coffee set which was kept for funerals was now broken up, trampled on, shivered to atoms" (*Mountolive*, 315). How I agree, as an Alexandrian, with Durrell's own sigh, "And they talk of the romance of the East! Give me the Metropole at Brighton any day!" (*Clea*, 146).

This failure to focus does not only affect the documentary aspect of the *Quartet*, but its abstract artistic integrity. What are the exact proportions of objective to personal in Durrell's city? This is never clear. When he calls Nessim's outing "the great yearly shoot" (*Justine*, 192), is the reader intended to suppose that this social event is important in the annals of the City, or only of the little group of central characters? Since he writes at one point "Justine, Melissa, Clea. . . . There were so few of us really" (*Balthazar*, 14) how are we intended to interpret the opening paragraph of Part II of *Clea*:

> To have written so much and to have said nothing about Balthazar, is indeed an omission—for in a sense he is one of the keys to the City. *The* key . . . If Mnemjian is the archiver of the City, Balthazar is its Pla-

tonic *daimon*—the mediator between its gods and its men. It sounds far-fetched, I know.

(One is not disarmed by the skittish closing sentence.)

Egyptians have ceased to be surprised at the strange contortions which the western mind goes through in its attempts, I will not say to estimate, but to avoid estimating, the true facts of the Palestine problem. But no one before Mr. Durrell had thought of the grotesque notion of a Copt who thinks that the creation of Israel is a boon to Middle Eastern Christians. Is Mr. Durrell unaware of the large number of Christians among the million Arab refugees? I suspect so, since "Arab" and "Egyptian" in his vocabulary, apparently exclude "Christian." Notice his weird sentence "Alexandria, outwardly so peaceful, was not really a safe place for Christians" (*Justine*, 153) where, if the sentence is to have any *meaning*—not the same thing as being a *true* proposition—"Christians" must be a synonym for "Western European." A *delta minus* for the way in which he contrasts Memlik with Nessim by calling Memlik "the Egyptian" (*Mountolive*, p. 264) and makes Nessim number Copts among "we the foreign communities" (*Mountolive*, 199). This is as likely as an English Old Catholic landed gentleman referring to himself as a foreigner. I cannot emphasize too strongly that the best description of the political plot of the *Quartet* is one that Durrell himself uses of it in another sense: "this pitiable political design" (*Mountolive*, 201). The only thing that saves it from being insulting, my Coptic friends agree, is that it is too far away from reality to be worth fraying one's temper over. Durrell must be the only writer of exotic romances to face the very live present with the buoyant falsity with which the Crusades and the age of Louis XIII are dealt with by "historical" "novelists."

Mr. Durrell must know that the typical Alexandria is not as introspective as he makes it. He must know, too, that the foreign element which his novel is about, that is, the prosperous Levantine one, is, essentially, a business one, and that his world is, therefore, "Phoenician" rather than Hellenic. An English visitor is free to imagine that Levantine Alexandria is a survival of the Hellenistic city: but I do not think that he is justified in imposing on others, as an objective fact, that this belief is a truth. For twelve centuries Alexandria was an Arab port, in an Arab country, with a small foreign population. For a hundred years or so, beginning in the last century, the modern city developed very much under the domination of the richer and more powerful members of a Levantine minority whose status Egyptians resent, for they, in many cases, exploited the country for their own ends, and retained their position by establishing a distorted picture of themselves as a beneficial, and even as a "traditional" aristocracy of the land. This period has now ended, but it is of it that Durrell wrote. The selectivity of an artist's imagination allows him to concentrate upon this aspect of Alexandria. In any case, the fact is that as an Englishman it was easier for him during his years here to mix with Levantines rather than with Egyptians. But for anyone with a love of Egypt and a feeling for the

English language, it is alternately amusing and insulting to find that Mr. Durrell has even taken over the "Levantinisms" of thought and expression of pseudo—or semi-European colons. Throughout, "Arab" means "lower class Egyptians" (see *Justine*, 53 and 195; *Balthazar*, 123, and *Clea*, 34). We sink into the further Levantinism of "Arab" in the grotesque sense of "Nubian" on p. 52 of *Clea*. The quaint "Arab bread" of Levantine French also appears (*Balthazar*, 35), and the influence of his characters' own speech has gone as far as to make the writer, like a Frenchman, speak of a "*port*" when he means a harbour (*Mountolive*, 286) and of a "*cocktail*" when he means a *cocktail party* (*Mountolive*, 135). "Native quarter" is apparently equated with "brothel quarter" (*Justine*, 185), but, to counterbalance Levantinism, there is the equally unattractive "burrah sahib" attitude of the Englishman out East: at least, this is I suppose to be the explanation of the "noble savage" attitude implied when Durrell writes: "*as simple as an Arab*, without precociousness, unrefined as a drinking habit among peasants" (*Balthazar*, 56). Certainly no Levantine would imagine that an Egyptian contrasts Europeans with himself by thinking of them as "white": "The emotions of white people, he [Nessim] perhaps was thinking, are odd and excite prurience" (*Justine*, 225–6).

There is a lower reach of this attitude that I cannot discuss dispassionately on the literary level, because it is too deeply offensive. I leave it for others to take up less emotionally, and give the readers the following pair of quotations without further comment—except to wonder at the otiose explaining of the simile in the second of them:

"Stop whining like an Arab" [Spoken by Nessim!] (*Balthazar*, p. 125).

He proceeded slowly, for to register an idea in a Moslem mind is like trying to paint on a wall: one must wait for the first coat to dry (the first idea) before applying a second. (*Mountolive*, p. 273)

To return to purely literary considerations, are we to admit that the picture Durrell gives is out of reach if we impugn it on purely literary grounds? and are the strong objections which most Egyptian readers feel, out of order because they are non-literary? I think not entirely. I agree that a great deal of my distaste for the *Quartet* is irrelevant by literary criteria— I am, with hundreds of thousands of Alexandrians like myself, treated as though I do not exist. Not unnaturally, I am annoyed that my Alexandria, which I regard as more real, more rooted, is dismissed; in addition, I am irritated because I seem to be the reader that Durrell forgot: did he think there was no one from the inside to riposte and to give evidence as to the tawdriness of his scenery? But over and above this irritation, and, in fact, after I have overcome it, I am still faced, as an objective critic, with an alleged description of Alexandria, which, on sheer statistical grounds, distorts the essential Egyptianness out of existence, and one by an outsider whose vision is patently out of focus, because he is dazzled by what he sees. Mr. Durrell strikes one, in fact, as a provincial who has been able, because richer Egyptians and Levantines have given him the *entrée*, to live among his social superiors for a short time, in a way he would not have found possible in his own pre-war England. The result is that he turns his parvenu experience of aristocratic glamour and plutocratic comfort into an exotic account of an *Arabian Nights* East, and a *fin-de-siècle* Mediterranean. When he talks, for example, of "the great cobweb of Alexandrian society" (*Justine*, 50), he does so because he has not known the great cobwebs of London, Rome, or New York, and is envious of Proust's opportunities in the much more exciting "cobweb" of Paris. . . .

Exile offers familiarities that home does not allow, and, beside them, of course, the freedoms that home ground excludes. Pursewarden, in many ways the writer's self-conscious literary persona, puts this well in a remark which throws light upon many of the faults and the merits of the *Quartet*: "I am always glad to get out of England to countries where I feel no moral responsibilities and no desire to work out such depressing formulations. After all, what the hell! I am a writer!" Unfortunately the position of having no moral responsibility is a weakness as well as an advantage. With the abandoning of moral responsibility, the temptation is also to abandon elementary morality. In the writer's case and, what the hell! Mr. Durrell is a writer, elementary morality includes the obligation to remain honest, not to exploit or distort for the sake of easy success. I cannot help thinking that the Durrell of the *Quartet* has succumbed to "Levantinism" in a deeper sense than the one just examined. Many Mediterranean fortune-seekers came to Alexandria in the last century, with their know-how and determination; many exploited, carved out their fortunes, and distorted facts to justify their position, and keep their situation. Mr. Durrell has come in this century, with a great deal of literary know-how and sensibility, but is the use he has made of Alexandria in his work not a parallel to the Levantine business-man's: an outsider exploiting, distorting, and emerging with a myth woven by himself around the truth, a sort of camouflaging cocoon? The rich business-man, in his *Quartier grec* villa, baroque and convoluted, may have remembered with a touching nostalgia the modest Sicilian village of his boyhood: Mr. Durrell perhaps at times, flicks through the pages of the *Black Book*, of *Prospero's Cell*, and of *Cities, Plains and People*. If he turns in particular to his theories in the *Key to Modern Poetry*, does he wonder at the long way he has come since? or does he recall the lines from another poet's work:

> Between the idea
> And the reality
> Between the motion
> And the act
> Falls the Shadow.

And if he does, does his musing ever carry him on to the very last line of that poem?

Some Sources of Durrell's
Alexandria Quartet
William Leigh Godshalk*

In 1952 Lawrence Durrell declared himself "deficient in true scholarship."[1] And in this, perhaps, we may take him at his word. Nevertheless, to counterbalance this deficiency in scholarship, he says, he has set himself to a "wide if haphazard reading." He claims to have studied anthropology in the works of Tylor, Frazer, and Rivers, psychology in Jung, Rank, Freud, and Groddeck, and science in Eddington, Whitehead, and Einstein. In the course of his lectures *A Key to Modern British Poetry*, he displays his wide reading, using an illustration from Eugene Marais's *Soul of the White Ant*, praising Francis J. Mott's little-known theories of biosynthesis, and discussing various esoteric works of theosophy.[2] Durrell obviously prides himself on both the diversity and the obscurity of his reading.

A further aspect of Durrell's reading habits is revealed in his travel books. *Prospero's Cell* ends with a brief bibliography of five books, only one of which was published in this century (1911).[3] *Reflections on a Marine Venus* has a longer bibliography in English, French, Italian, and Greek.[4] However, only three are twentieth-century studies, while six are nineteenth-century, one eighteenth, and two seventeenth. In brief, Durrell's material is not always the most recent and up-to-date.

These observations suggest the types of book which form the literary background of *The Alexandria Quartet*.[5] But perhaps the best place to begin is with those sources the author acknowledges. At the end of *Justine*,[6] Durrell has two notes to E.M. Forster's *Alexandria* and two rather obscure references to "Paracelsus." Eugene Marais is the source of a long citation in *Balthazar*.[7] While *Mountolive* has no authorial notes,[8] *Clea* has a reference to Franz Hartmann's *Life of Paracelsus*.[9] Of these three works cited, Forster and Hartmann seem to be most important.

Forster provides Durrell with both historical and religious motifs.[10] In his narrative history of Alexandria, Forster describes the Ptolemies as a "dynasty . . . interwoven with terrific queens. There is the Arsinoe whom Philadelphus married; there is Arsinoe III who faced the Syrian army at Rafa; . . . and there is the last and greatest Cleopatra, with whom the tangled race expires" (pp. 23–24). A few pages earlier, Forster had related that Philadelphus "married her sister Arsinoe" (p. 16), and thus instituted incestuous marriage among the Ptolemies. His phrase "terrific queens" found fertile ground in Durrell's mind. Justine reminds the gentle Darley "of that race of terrific queens which left behind them the ammoniac smell of their incestuous loves to hover like a cloud over the Alexandrian subconscious. The giant man-eating cats like Arsinoe were her true siblings" (*Justine*, p. 11, p. 20). Justine becomes a part of the historical past. And the distinction

*Reprinted from *Modern Fiction Studies* 13, no. 3 (Autumn 1967):361–74. © by Purdue Research Foundation. Reprinted with permission.

between time past and time present becomes blurred. Rather than a person set in time, Justine is an "exemplar" of place; she is a manifestation of the "Alexandrian subconscious," as indigenous to Africa as the very lions, "her true siblings."

Justine's religious questioning also in part depends on Forster. Describing the major tenets of Gnosticism to which Justine seems especially drawn, he begins: "Gnosticism taught that the world and mankind are the result of an unfortunate blunder. God neither created us nor wished us to be created. We are the work of an inferior deity, the Demiurge, who wrongly believes himself God, and we are doomed to decay" (pp. 75–76). These words were obviously memorable for Durrell, and they merge, imperceptibly for the general reader, into Justine's speech patterns. "I remember," says Darley, "her asking one night, so anxiously, so pleadingly if she had interpreted his [Balthazar's] thinking rightly: 'I mean, that God neither created us nor wished us to be created, but that we are the work of an inferior deity, a Demiurge, who wrongly believed himself to be God?' "[11] Later even Nessim, Justine's well-educated husband, relies on Forster for a slightly telescoped quotation from Plotinus.[12] Unfortunately, however, Nessim finds himself incapable of following the Neoplatonic path to salvation.

Some passages in the *Quartet* depend upon knowledge given in Forster for their total comprehension. The Moslem prostitute who reminds Narouz of Clea, in turn reminds Darley of "Petesouchos the crocodile goddess, no less."[13] In all probability, Durrell's chief source for Petesouchos is Forster, who says that Fayoum, where crocodile worship flourished, was developed by Philadelphus, Arsinoe's husband. Fayoum in general, and Petesouchos worship in particular, says Forster, "was barbaric and provincial" (p. 118). Durrell's reference to Petesouchos, then, helps to characterize the scene. In these various ways, Durrell weaves the separate strands from Forster into his total pattern.[14]

A close investigation of Durrell's use of Hartmann reveals—as with Forster—that his debt is greater than that directly acknowledged.[15] The notes citing "Paracelsus" in *Justine* are not to an original text of the doctor, but to Hartmann's theosophic study. For example, Durrell's definition of Caballi, only half of which he quotes, comes directly from Hartmann's "Explanation of Terms" and not from Paracelsus.[16] In the body of the novel, Hartmann provides the translation of other Paracelsian texts which Durrell put so aptly into the mouth of Balthazar, the cabalist.[17] It is also quite likely that Durrell's quotation of Boehme, "Where the carrion is, . . . there the eagles will gather," which Justine uses to catch the feeling of Alexandria, is not directly from Boehme, but from a footnote in Hartmann.[18]

But most significantly, Hartmann seems to supply Durrell with the name "Melissa" and to suggest her function in the *Quartet*. As Darley's first mistress, Melissa Artemis, "patron of sorrow," is his first introduction to Alexandria, the capital of memory.[19] In the *Quartet*, Melissa is presented both as a memory from time past and as the only hope for the future.[20] Similarly in Hartmann, Melissa has two aspects. Rhetorically he asks, "What is Melissa, but a power which exists in the Astral-light and finds its material expression in the herb Melissa, which grows in our gardens?" (p. 252). Further, according to Hartmann's theosophic definition, Astral-light "is the storehouse of memory for the great world (the Macrocosm), whose contents may become reimbodied and reincarnated in objective forms; it is the storehouse of memory of the little world, the Microcosm of man, from which he may recollect past events" (p. 41). Melissa then primarily exists in the great storehouse of memory. But physically embodied in the Primum Ens Melissae, Melissa acts as a rejuvenating agent. Of this fact, Hartmann gives several examples (p. 354).

The rejuvenating effect of Melissa in the *Quartet* is underlined by Darley: "In some curious way the future, if there is one, has always been vested in her."[21] And it is Clea who is "reimbodied and reincarnated" from Melissa, as Durrell reveals so vividly in one of his significant repetitions. At the beginning of *Justine* Darley sees Melissa "sitting in the corner of a coffee shop, alone, with her hands supporting her chin, . . . staring into her cup with a wry reflective air of amusement";[22] so at the beginning of the last novel, he first sees Clea again where Melissa had been, "gazing at a coffee cup with a wry reflective air of amusement, with her hands supporting her chin."[23] Melissa from the past becomes Clea in the future.[24]

Another type of source is the studies of Egyptian life to which Durrell went to refresh his fading memory of war-time Alexandria.[25] These studies help him fill in the romantic Eastern background of his tetralogy, and they also supply him with those minor historical characters who appear and reappear throughout. J. W. McPherson's *Moulids of Egypt*[26] furnishes Durrell with "the doyen of the guild" of circumcision, Mahmoud Enayet Allah,[27] and his "black 'Sambos' in their war paint" who "so amuse the little victims [of circumcision] by their antics and *tarturs* and other lures, that these become of the mutaharin . . . (purified), before they fully realise why they have been so brought into the lime-light, or in stubborn cases their cries are so drowned, that there is little risk of their panic spreading amongst waiting candidates for circumcision" (p. 69). Remembering this passage—or perhaps with his notes before him—Durrell describes Mahmoud's "Negro clowns with painted faces and grotesque clothes [who] used to gambol out to amuse and distract the boys, inveigling them by this means into the fatal chair where they were, in Scobie's picturesque phrase, 'hyphenated,' their screams being drowned by the noise of the crowd, almost before they knew what was happening."[28] The similarities between the passages are obvious. But Durrell links the scene to Scobie's monomania against circumcision with the old sailor's comic term "hyphenate," and emphasizes the horror of this kind of circumcision by concentrating on the individual boy. The "waiting candidates" in McPherson are forgotten.

Later in the narrative, McPherson provides Durrell with many of the details of Narouz' visit to the moulid of *Sitna Mariam*.[29] Durrell gathers these details from throughout the *Moulids*, and perhaps the best way to illustrate his method is in parallel columns.[30]

Durrell, *Balthazar*

McPherson, *Moulids*

p. 147: "Manouli the monkey in a paper hat brilliantly rode round and round his stall on the back of a goat."

p. 9: "The last monkey I saw riding a goat was arrested and dragged off. 'Manouli' [see Glossary, p. 333] and the bow-wow had appeared as happy as the onlookors" [sic].

p. 147: "Towering on either side of the thoroughfare rose the great booths with their sugar figurines brilliant with tinsel, depicting the loves and adventures of the creatures inhabiting the folk-lore of the Delta—heroes like Abu Zeid and Antar, lovers like Yunis and Aziza."

p. 79: "the Sugar Booths . . . shelves of sugar figurines, to which the general name of *Arusa* is applied, a word which means bride, and which may also indicate a doll, because the prevailing type is that of a gorgeously dressed maiden . . . marvellously arrayed in paper garments, with tinsel of gold, spangles, and the rest. . . ."

p. 80: "a very up to date model has appeared, representing a bridal chamber with mirrors and couch and the young couple. . . . I am told this is a revival of an old classic known as Aziza and Yunis. . . . Other popular examples are the heroes Abu Zeid . . . and Antar. . . , armed and mounted. . . ."

p. 147: "the famous blind preacher Hussein who stood like an oak tree, magnificent in the elf-light, reciting the ninety-nine holy names."

p. 69: "the gentle and reasonable blind Hag [i.e. pilgrim] Husein, . . . who always rounded off his homily by the ninety nine sacred names. . . ."

p. 147: "the approaching procession with its sudden bursts of wild

p. 64: "It is usual to lead up to these zikrs [religious observances

music—kettle-drums and timbrels like volleys of musketry—and the long belly-thrilling rolls of the camel-drums which drowned and refreshed the quavering deep-throated flute-music."

in which the name of "Allah" is repeated] by processions. . . . The execution of the dervishes on . . . the great tambourines . . . is startingly effective, sometimes resembling a volley of musketry. . . . "

p. 67: "Although the tambourines already referred to are the most striking instruments to be seen and heard on these occasions, . . . others are the cymbals, [and] . . . the immensely long and deep-voiced arghul . . . [which are] flutes. . . . Then in some moulid processions drums in great variety vie with the tars,—for instance in the day zeffa of Sidi Abdel-Rahim where the immense camel drums and others of the kettle type are a sight to see as well as an experience to hear."

p. 147: "From the throat of a narrow alley . . . burst a long tilting gallery of human beings headed by the leaping acrobats . . . of Alexandria, and followed at a dancing measure by the long grotesque cavalcade of gonfalons, rising and falling in a tide of mystical light, treading the peristaltic measures of the wild music—nibbled out everywhere by the tattling flutes and the pang of drums or the long shivering orgasm of tambourines struck by the dervishes in their habits as they moved towards the site of the festival. 'All-*ah* All-*ah*' burst from every throat."

p. 67: "Sometimes wandering minstrels, or professional strolling musicians cut in . . . : of these the *Alexandrian* acrobats who act as forerunners to most big zeffas are a picturesque and harmless instance."

p. 65: "The dervishes on these great occasions of course appear with their insignia and colours, and may to a great extent be recognised by these and by the inscriptions on the *gonfallons*." [Durrell here modifies and repeats an earlier passage; see above.]

pp. 60–61: "the reiterated calling on the name of God, Allah!" "the actual utterance of Allah! Allah! Allah!"

These parallel passages reveal Durrell's process of selection, condensation, and transmutation. Although in the above examples most of the material is drawn from Chapter III, "Moulids, Their Devotional Side,"[31] Durrell takes images and ideas from various parts of the *Moulids*. Relieved of their original context, the images are molded into a new, typically Durrellian, scene. Words and phrases like "elf-light," "mystical light," "peristaltic," "orgasm," add a combined physical and spiritual depth—"a sort of religious materialism"[32]—lacking in McPherson. Also the comparison shows how Durrell modifies and repeats images and ideas from an earlier passage, thus giving a circular movement to this style. This movement, which ties in with the general pattern of the first two novels of the *Quartet*, suggests that time rather than moving linearly forward, turns back upon itself. Time in this way takes on a new density and becomes another dimension of the narrative.

As Durrell continues his story of Narouz' visit to the moulid, however, he draws even more precisely upon McPherson. His magnificent description of the Magzub in action finds a close parallel in the *Moulids*. Both begin with the Magzub himself:

Durrell, *Balthazar*	McPherson, *Moulids*
p. 150: "the gaunt and terrible figure of the famous religious maniac stood, shooting out the thunderbolts of a hypnotic personality on to a fearful but fascinated crowd."	p. 314: "a gaunt and terrible creature fascinated literally an immense ring of people. He was a Magzub from Upper Egypt: in the army once, I was told, now a religious maniac: and never have I met in real life, a being with such a powerful and terrible personality."
"Narouz shuddered as he gazed upon that ravaged face, the eyes of which had been painted with crayon so that they looked glaring, inhuman, like the eyes of a monster in a cartoon. The holy man hurled oaths and imprecations at the circle of listeners, his fingers curling and uncurling into claws as he worked upon them, dancing this way and that like a bear at bay, turning and twirling, advancing and retreating upon the crowd with grunts and roars	"He hurled Jeremiads at the people and kept them entranced and terror-stricken by his voice, his fearsome gestures, and his marvellous whirling and contortions. . . . " [later comes the phrase] "fingers vibrating like claws. . . . "
	p. 314: "he himself emitted sounds which were anything but human, roars, grunts, and animal notes indescribable."

and screams until it trembled before [p. 151] him, fascinated by
his powers. He had 'come already
into his hour,' as the Arabs say,
and the power of the spirit had
filled him."

p. 315: "It was towards mid-
night that the Spirit came upon
him with unusual power, and he
came into 'his hour.' "

"The holy man stood in an island of the fallen bodies of those
he had hypnotized, some crawl-
ing about like scorpions, some
screaming or bleating like goats,
some braying. From time to time
he would leap upon one of them
uttering hideous screams and ride
him across the ring, thrashing at
his buttocks like a maniac, and
then suddenly turning, with the
foam bursting from between his
teeth, he would dart into the
crowd and pick upon some unfortunate victim, shouting: 'Are you
mocking me?' and catching him
by his nose or an ear or an arm,
drag him with superhuman force
into the ring where with a sudden
quick pass of his talons he would
'kill his light' and hurl him down
among the victims. . . . "

p. 314: "He was a born witch
doctor, and now and again smelt
out a heretic or a pious fraud, and
hypnotised him on the spot.
Sometimes the ring was like a
spot on the island of Circe, bodies
with the head bent back nearly to
earth, or circulating upside-down
on all fours and looking like scorpions, or bleating cries for mercy
in ovine voices, or in the attitude
of an ass carrying the magzub on
their backs or shoulders. . . . "

p. 314: "When he took a new
victim in hand, he generally fixed
him with fierce wild eyes, and
with fingers vibrating like claws
asked him,—'Are you laughing at
me?'. . . . Without waiting for a
reply, . . . he seized him by the
hair, nose, or any member, and
swung him into the ring. . . . "

p. 151: "A respectable-looking
sheik with the green turban
which proclaimed him to be
of the seed of the Prophet was
walking across the outskirts of the
crowd when the Magzub caught
sight of him. . . . "

p. 315: "The last occult triumph
I witnessed was the subjugation
of a highly respectable-looking
sheikh, wearing a green turban,
proclaiming him to be of the seed
of the Prophet." [pp. 315–316:
the account is continued in both
McPherson and Durrell.]

p. 152: "Narouz went back to
his tombstone to meditate on the
beauty of his surroundings . . .
the drone of the holy men from
some nearby shrine."

p. 316: "Seated on a tombstone
to meditate on the strange beauty
of the surroundings, the whisper-
ing of veiled women . . . came to
me, . . . and the singing or dron-
ing of holy men. . . . "

Although other parallels between these two works might be noted,[33] enough material has been presented to reveal how Durrell uses his source. In general outline, the descriptions are the same. But Durrell consolidates, cutting out those parts of McPherson, such as his biblical and classical allusions, which are extraneous to his recreation of the scene. Adroitly, he adds the descriptive simile—("like a bear at bay")—or the graphic detail ("foam bursting from between his teeth").

For his descriptions of Coptic Egypt, Durrell uses the little-known work by S. H. Leeder, *Modern Sons of the Pharaohs*.[34] In general, the Hosnanis and their milieu are developed from Leeder's account of "a Coptic Squire."[35] But, surprisingly enough, even the details of Narouz' and Nessim's ride to their farm are indebted to Leeder. "The bird life by the waterside," he says, "is enchanting. Here the kingfisher, whose glory of colour and sheen have never been known to those who have not seen him boldly flitting about in such sunlight as this, shows little trace of any fear of man." A little later he goes on, "Small owls, too, fly in and out of the banks, having apparently forgotten the night habits of their species; or, if they choose to sleep, we pass them on the bare boughs of the few small trees, nestling together in couples" (p. 7). Undoubtedly with this passage before him, Durrell condenses: "Brilliant kingfishers hunted the shallows like thunderbolts, their wings slurring, while here and there the small brown owls, having forgotten the night habits of their kind, flew between the banks, or nestled together in songless couples among the trees."[36] A simile, a touch of color, a verb: again a Durrellian recreation.

Leeder also helps Durrell in describing Coptic celebrations and ceremonies. Quoting one of his Coptic friends, Leeder relates in some detail the events of a three day Coptic wedding. The preparations are both costly and elaborate. The "pavilion" or "marquee" is hung with "ancient oil lamps" and with "electric chandeliers" (p. 119). Guests and "officials" are invited from all over Egypt, Cairo, Alexandria, and Assiout. Fethy Pasha, the Mudir of Assiout, is given special mention. On each day of the wedding, "local families" give "splendid displays of horsemanship," each performance ending "with a procession round the house, the horsemen beating drums and shouting." "an interesting incident took place when the leading horseman . . . rode his horse up the great flight of steps" (p. 120). In full, this description takes about two pages.

For his account of Justine and Nessim's wedding, Durrell concentrates the chief ideas of this passage into a paragraph. But at the same time, he romanticizes the incidents in the original description. Leeder's three day wedding becomes four; the single marquee becomes "a huge encampment of tents and marquees" with "carpets and chandeliers and brilliant decorations." Although Durrell's social figures are all from Alexandria, as in Leeder "local mudirs and sheiks, peasants innumerable, dignitaries from near and far had flocked in to be entertained." "The Bedouin," continues Durrell, "whose tribal grounds fringed the estate, gave magnificent displays of horsemanship, galloping round and round the house firing their guns." Leeder's procession becomes a gallop, his nameless horsemen become Bedouin, his single procession becomes repeated encircling, and his beating of drums becomes the firing of rifles. In his final incident of this description, Durrell has "old Abu Kar himself" ride "up the steps of the house on his white Arab and into the very reception-rooms with a bowl of flowers."[37] Durrell's romanticizing is obvious.

The details of Narouz' Coptic burial,[38] details which have been questioned as unrealistic,[39] are drawn mainly from Leeder's chapter on "Coptic Burial Customs."[40] The emphasis on the woman's place in the burial customs (p. 122), "the piercing *zagreet* of lamentation" (p. 125), the use of "Ma'leesh"—"Do not mind" (p. 123), the "dirtiest dark blue coverings" and "indigo" of the female mourners (p. 125), the "professional wailing women" with their "little drums" and tambourines (pp. 126–127), the breaking of "all the china and glass" in the house (p. 126), all are used by Durrell in his recreation of the Coptic funeral. And, although Leeder asserts that Coptic women "no longer blacken their faces and hands to accompany the funeral to the cemetery" (p. 128), Durrell retains the custom and his women accompany Narouz' body "with faces blackened now like furies."[41] The words spoken over Narouz' grave, "Remember me O Lord when Thou hast come to Thy Kingdom" and "From dust to dust," come from Leeder's account (pp. 128–129). Even so, Durrell, as we have begun to expect, touches the cold facts with life. The death scene is transformed into "the very picture of human failure."[42] In the breaking of the china and glass, Durrell tries to show "the systematic destruction of the memory of death itself."[43] Particular instances might be multiplied, but the point has already been well illustrated.[44]

Suggestions for some of Durrell's minor Egyptian characters are taken from studies of Egyptian life. The superstitious Hamid, Darley's comical, one-eyed servant, seems to have been drawn from some hints given in Lane's *Modern Egyptians*. In the course of his discussion of the term " 'efreet" which he defines as "an evil ginnee" (I, 287), Lane tells the story of a "humorous cook, who was somewhat addicted to the intoxicating hasheesh." One night, Lane heard him "muttering and exclaiming." Upon going to see what the trouble was, Lane found that the cook was being frightened by an 'efreet—invisible to Lane, of course.

Earlier in the same chapter on superstitions, Lane writes at length on the "Ginn" and the Egyptian people:

> It is a common custom of this people, on pouring water, &c., on the ground, to exclaim, or mutter, "Destoor;" that is, to ask the permission, or crave the pardon, of any ginnee that may chance to be there: for the ginn are supposed to pervade the solid matter of the earth. . . . They are also believed to inhabit rivers, ruined houses, wells, baths, ovens, and even the *latrina*: hence, persons, when they enter the latter place, . . . say, "Permission," or "Permission, ye blessed":—which words, in the

case of entering the latrina, they sometimes preface with a prayer for God's protection against all evil spirits. . . . (I, 282)

Lane emphasizes the connection between the Ginn and the bathroom, and the use of "destoor," permission. Durrell takes these details, adds Lane's humorous cook, and molds them into a picture of Hamid. "How tired I had become," writes Darley,

> of hearing his muttered "Destoor, destoor," as he poured slops down the kitchen sink—for here dwelt a powerful djinn and its pardon had to be invoked. The bathroom too was haunted by them, and I could always tell when Hamid used the outside lavatory . . . because whenever he sat on the watercloset a hoarse involuntary invocation escaped his lips ('Permission O ye blessed ones!') which neutralized the djinn which might otherwise have dragged him down into the sewage system. Now I heard him shuffling round the kitchen in his old felt slippers like a boa-constrictor muttering softly.[45]

Hamid, of course, is a cousin to Lane's Egyptian cook. But, juxtaposed as this scene is with the initial love-making of Justine and Darley, it serves a larger purpose in the novel than a piece of local color. Hamid represents the mundane reality of the real world. Quoting the words of the dying Amr from Forster, Darley says, "I feel as if heaven lay close upon the earth and I between them both. . . ."[46] He lies quite literally between the earthy reality of Hamid and the etherial bliss of Justine.

Discussing his "love scenes" and "underwater scenes" with an interviewer, Durrell insists that they "are really a mime about rebirth on the parable plane."[47] Of course, this comment makes clear the reason for Durrell's almost mystical attitude toward love where Justine becomes a symbol of heavenly bliss, but it also suggests—rather indirectly—a source for the rebirth scene near the end of the *Quartet*. In the notes to *A Key to Modern British Poetry*,[48] Durrell comments that one of "the most suggestive" of Francis J. Mott's books is *The Universal Design of Birth*,[49] a book concerned with birth and rebirth in all their psychological aspects. "Bizarre as it may seem," says Mott, "a number of dreams dealt with in *biosynthesis* seem to assert a memory of having been called out of a condition in which the essential ego . . . persisted prior to the existence in the mother's womb" (p. 128). This prior existence is often symbolized by an island-like structure. One dreamer said that it was a rock "in the ocean and yet up in the heavens. . . . I was on a rock in the Mediterranean" (p. 129). From the island, the dreamer goes into the sea which symbolizes the maternal womb. The dreamer here stays until he comes forth into the air, i.e., is born. Also Mott asserts that "the prenatal skin feeling . . . is felt as a cloak of light or 'electric' energy" (p. 18n).[50] Thus in the waters of the womb there is a "sense of light" (p. 121). Birth itself is felt to be a "great Fall" (p. 121), and this fall is embodied in both nursery rhymes and religious myths (p. 121). From this natal fall result the "lingering shocks of birth" (p. 64).

"The first breath," says Mott, "must often be extremely painful for the newborn child" (p. 65).

With these "suggestive" ideas in mind, Durrell built his parable of rebirth in *Clea* (Part III, Chapter 2). Clea is the first to find Narouz' island, a "granite boulder" in the Mediterranean.[51] From this rock, Darley and Clea dive into the "phosphorescent" water: "We plunged [says Darley] side by side and ranged down into the water, transformed into figures of flame, the sparks flashing from the tips of our fingers and toes with the glitter of static electricity."[52] This scene, of course, forms an obvious parallel with Mott's "cloak of light or 'electric' energy" and the sea of the maternal womb. Further, at this point Durrell introduces a reference to a myth commemorating the Fall of Birth, "A swimmer seen underwater looks like an early picture of the fall of Lucifer, literally on fire,"[53] one of Mott's ideas.

But Clea, who is being reborn, must undergo the shocks of birth. After having her hand pinned to a sunken hull by a harpoon and almost drowning, she is saved by the artificial respiration administered by Darley. "It must have hurt, as the first few breaths hurt a newly born child. The body of Clea was protesting at this forcible rebirth."[54] Nevertheless, through the pangs of rebirth, Clea emerges "an artist at last."[55]

Darley also completes the quest for artisthood, and, perhaps, in the final analysis the major theme of the *Quartet* is the growth of the artist. And molding a widely divergent group of sources into this tetralogy of artistic development is the consummate artist, Lawrence Durrell. Although certainly not all the sources are considered here, enough have been to suggest the eclectic quality of Durrell's reading. In using his borrowings, he recreates with a deft hand, revealing his romantic turn of mind. As he himself argues,[56] the artist must not be judged by the merit of the source, but by the use he makes of it. Like the true Philosopher's Stone of Paracelsus, Durrell changes base metal into pure gold.[57]

Notes

1. Lawrence Durrell, *A Key to Modern British Poetry* (Norman, Oklahoma, 1952), p. x. He gives a general outline of his reading on p. xii.

2. See pp. 3, 63, 70, 105, 109. Marais's *Soul of the White Ant* is not specifically cited, but see Winifred De Kok's translation (New York, 1937), pp. 78–79.

3. Lawrence Durrell, *Prospero's Cell and Reflections on a Marine Venus* (New York, 1960), p. 140. Both works are separately numbered. Durrell's baffling reference to "Viscount Kirkwall, 'Four Years in the Ionian,' " seems to be to Kirkwall's *Four Years in the Ionian Islands*, 2 vols. (London, 1864).

4. *Reflections*, p. 198.

5. For the personal background which merges with the literary, see *Lawrence Durrell, Henry Miller: A Private Correspondence*, ed. George Wickes (New York, 1963), pp. 179–205.

6. Two references will be given: first to the cheap but accessible Cardinal Edition,

Justine (New York, 1961), p. 259; second to the first edition by Faber and Faber, *Justine* (London, 1957), p. 253. The Cardinal Edition is the copy text.

7. *Balthazar* (New York, 1961), p. 248; (London, 1958), p. 250. See Marais, pp. 108–110. Also the image from *Balthazar*, p. 143, p. 151, "the hundred little spheres which religion or lore creates and which cohere softly together like cells to form the great sprawling jellyfish which is Alexandria," seems to come from Marais, pp. 78–79.

8. *Mountolive* (New York, 1961); (London, 1958).

9. *Clea* (New York, 1961), p. 280; (London, 1960), p. 287. For a bibliography of Durrell, see Robert A. Potter and Brooke Whiting, *Lawrence Durrell: A Checklist* (Los Angeles, 1961).

10. E. M. Forster, *Alexandria: A History and a Guide* (Garden City, New York, 1961). Until 1961, after the *Quartet* had been published, copies of this work, according to Forster, were "rare."

11. *Justine*, p. 32, pp. 40–41. John Arthos, "Lawrence Durrell's Gnosticism," *Personalist*, XLIII (1962), 360–373, discusses this aspect of Durrell, but does not seem to realize his full debt to Forster.

12. *Justine*, p. 183, p. 181: "This is no journey for the feet, however. Look into yourself, withdraw into yourself and look." Embedded in a longer quotation from Plotinus, Forster (p. 71) has the following sentences: "This is not a journey for the feet. . . . Withdraw into yourself and look."

13. *Balthazar*, p. 159, p. 166. See Forster, p. 132.

14. Many details in the *Quartet* take on added significance when read with Forster in mind; e.g., Balthazar's "small key in the shape of an *ankh*" (*Justine*, p. 90, p. 94) read in the light of Forster, p. 74, "the key-shaped 'ankh' . . . a sign of their immortality."

15. Franz Hartmann, *The Life and the Doctrines of . . . Paracelsus* (New York, 1910); there are many editions of this work with various textual changes.

16. *Justine*, p. 259, p. 253: "Caballi. The astral bodies of men who died a premature death. 'They imagine to perform bodily actions while in fact they have no physical bodies but act in their thoughts.' *Paracelsus*." Hartmann, pp. 42–43, writes: "Caballi . . . The astral bodies of men who died a premature death. . . . They imagine to perform bodily actions, while in fact they have no physical bodies, but act in their thoughts. . . . "

17. E. g., *Justine*, p. 34, p. 42, called a "quotation from Paracelsus" (without italics), is from Hartmann, pp. 121, 218, with some changes in punctuation.

18. *Justine*, p. 41, p. 49; Hartmann, p. 132, "Where the carrion is, there will the eagles assemble." Durrell makes minor changes.

19. See *Justine*, p. 45, p. 52; p. 174, p. 173; p. 190, p. 188. Hartmann, p. 288, uses the names "Melissa" and "Artemisia" in the same passage. After mentioning Melissa, he says that "Venus and Artemisia are both the products of the same essence."

20. *Justine*, p. 47, p. 54; p. 236, p. 231.

21. *Justine*, p. 236, p. 231.

22. *Justine*, p. 53, p. 60.

23. *Clea*, p. 67, p. 76.

24. Other significant repetitions link Melissa and Clea; e.g., *Justine*, p. 16, p. 25; and *Clea*, p. 90, p. 99. This passage seems to be indebted to Edward William Lane, *An Account of the Manners and Customs of the Modern Egyptians* (London, 1871), I, 93.

25. Durrell's mention of Budge's *Egyptian Book of the Dead* in *The Dark Labyrinth* (New York, 1962), p. 119, which was first published in London, in 1947, suggests that he had already begun his research at that time. See *Cefalû* (London, 1947), p. 107.

26. J. W. McPherson, *The Moulids of Egypt (Egyptian Saints-Days)* ([?Pocala, Sudan, 1940]).

27. See pp. 191, 220, 233, 236, 297.

28. *Balthazar*, p. 130, p. 138.

29. See McPherson, pp. 240–243, 44. McPherson (p. 242) says, "This is not a moulid in the typical sense of a celebration at the shrine of a local saint." Durrell changes the *Sitna Mariam* into a local celebration.

30. For simplicity, only one reference to Durrell, that of the Cardinal Edition, will be given in the text.

31. McPherson, pp. 51–73.

32. *A Key to Modern British Poetry*, p. 70: a phrase used in praise of Mott.

33. Durrell uses McPherson for Egyptian religious background. Mahmoud Manzaloui in his misguided but informative article "Curate's Egg: An Alexandrian Opinion of Durrell's [corrected] *Quartet*," EA, XV (1962), 254, suggests Durrell's debt to McPherson, but does not elaborate.

34. *Modern Sons of the Pharaohs: A Study of the Manners and Customs of the Copts of Egypt* (London, [?1918]).

35. Leeder, pp. 3–26.

36. *Balthazar*, p. 61, p. 70.

37. *Balthazar*, p. 90, p. 99.

38. *Mountolive*, pp. 286–292, pp. 314–320.

39. Manzaloui, pp. 256–257. Those details to which Manzaloui objects are cited by Leeder as authentic Coptic customs.

40. Leeder, pp. 122–135.

41. *Mountolive*, p. 291, p. 319.

42. *Mountolive*, p. 286, p. 314.

43. *Mountolive*, p. 288, p. 315.

44. A full length study of Durrell's debt to Leeder would be enlightening. The tirade of Leila's husband (*Mountolive*, pp. 29–33, pp. 40–44), for example, is obviously indebted to Leeder's Chapter 8, "The Egyptian Christians and British Rule," pp. 327–343.

45. *Justine*, p. 82, p. 87.

46. *Justine*, p. 83, p. 88. Cf. Forster, pp. 62–63: "I feel as if the heaven lay close upon the earth and I between the two. . . . "

47. Lawrence Durrell, "The Kneller Tape (Hamburg)," *The World of Lawrence Durrell*, ed. Harry T. Moore (New York, 1964), p. 166.

48. P. 209.

49. *The Universal Design of Birth (An Analysis of the Configurational Involvement of Birth and Its Relation to Emergence Generally)*, (Philadelphia, 1948).

50. See also Mott, p. 22.

51. *Clea*, p. 216, p. 224.

52. P. 239, p. 246.

53. P. 239, p. 246.

54. P. 245, p. 252.

55. P. 275, p. 281.

56. *A Key to Modern British Poetry*, p. 145.

57. Since writing this study, I have been able to identify two further sources: R. Talbot Kelly, *Egypt: Painted and Described by R. Talbot Kelly* (London, 1923) and Otto Rank, *Art and Artist: Creative Urge and Personality Development* (New York, 1932). Kelly helps Durrell to some magnificent descriptive passages: e.g., the night fishing scene which begins *Mountolive*, pp. 2 ff., pp. 12 ff. (cf. Kelly, pp. 139–140); the image of Alexandria in the sky

which begins *Balthazar*, p. 6, p. 16 (cf. Kelly, p. 5, "an hour or two later, the *real* city slowly appeared," with Durrell's "an hour later, the *real* city appeared."); the visit to the Arabs in order to obtain a horse in *Balthazar*, pp. 76–82, pp. 84–90 (cf. Kelly, pp. 199–205); and the street scene in *Clea*, pp. 24 ff., pp. 31 ff. (cf. Kelly, pp. 14, 52, 26, 162, etc.). Kelly provides Durrell with native Egyptian touches throughout, but, as we might expect, Durrell transforms his material. The night fishing scene, e.g., seems to be a combination of Kelly and of Durrell's personal experiences recorded in *Prospero's Cell*, pp. 38–41.

Rank seems to be less fully used. In *Clea*, p. 182, p. 191, Liza Pursewarden says that her brother read her "a quotation from a book." The passage, which deals with incest, comes with slight changes from a footnote in *Art and Artist* (p. 145). Rank points out, on the same page, that incest is "a symbol of rebirth," and as we have noted, rebirth is a recurrent theme in Durrell. Juxtaposed, these facts give us a clue to the reason for the incestuous love of Pursewarden and his sister: it suggests the rebirth of the artist.

Rank also provides a detail in *Clea*, p. 54, p. 63: "I felt like the Adam of the mediaeval legends: the world-compounded body of a man whose flesh was soil, whose bones were stones, . . . and whose thoughts were clouds." Rank writes: "In medieval legends Adam, the first man, is formed of seven substances: the body from the earth, the bones of stones, . . . the thoughts from clouds" (p. 217). Durrell uses the same seven elements in the same order listed by Rank.

Lawrence Durrell and the
Return to Alexandria   Robert Scholes*

Once upon a time the first words of a story used to be "Once upon a time." But these are the last words, or almost the last words, of Lawrence Durrell's *Alexandria Quartet*. Which suggests that we may have come to the end of a literary cycle, or rather to the beginning of a new loop in the spiral of literary history. You remember the passage which closes *Clea*, the last volume of the *Quartet*:

> Yes, one day I found myself writing down with trembling fingers the four words (four letters! four faces!) with which every story-teller since the world began has staked his slender claim to the attention of his fellow men. Words which presage simply the old story of an artist coming of age. I wrote: "Once upon a time . . ."
> And I felt as if the whole universe had given me a nudge!

In reading the passage we feel very strongly a kind of duality which pervades Durrell's work: we are pulled toward the primitive by those four magical words and by the description of the artist as a mere story-teller, but we are also made aware of the modernity of the work; we are pulled toward the sophisticated by the preoccupation of the passage with the art of story-telling. Like so many modern works, this is a portrait of the artist, a *Künstlerroman*, about a character in a book who is writing a book in

*Reprinted from *The Fabulators* (New York: Oxford University Press, 1967), 17–28. Originally published, in a slightly different version, as "Return to Alexandria: Lawrence Durrell and Western Narrative Tradition," *Virginia Quarterly Review* 40 (1964):411–20.

which he is a character. And the shades of Proust and Gide, among others, hover between our eyes and the page. What is new in Durrell, however, is neither the primitive nor the sophisticated but his peculiar combination of the two.

Take for example, the scene in which Pursewarden and Justine visit the house of the child prostitutes. The two visitors are surrounded by these terrible children, who in another scene nearly drive Mountolive out of his wits as they attempt to capture him in the manner of the Lilliputians against Gulliver. Pursewarden describes the way Justine tames the little creatures:

> And when the light was brought she suddenly turned herself, crossed her legs under her, and in the ringing words of the street story-teller she intoned: "Now gather about me, all ye blessed of Allah, and hear the wonder of the story I shall tell you. . . . "
>
> It was a wild sort of poetry for the place and the time—the little circle of wizened faces, the divan, the flopping light; and the strangely captivating lilt of the Arabic with its heavy damascened imagery, the thick brocade of alliterative repetitions, the nasal twanging accents, gave it a Laic splendour which brought tears to my eyes—gluttonous tears! It was such a rich diet for the soul! It made me aware how thin the fare is which we moderns supply to our hungry readers. The epic contours, that is what her story had. I was envious. How rich those beggar children were. And I was envious too of her audience. Talk of suspended judgment! They sank into the imagery of her story like plummets.

This scene is typical of the book. It is wild, exotic, romantic. Yet its main interest is not life, but art. It is really a little essay in esthetics, presented in the form of a dramatic scene. It reminds us of the moments in *Don Quixote* when there is a pause in the adventures of the Knight of the Mournful Countenance to allow for a literary discussion involving the Bachelor and the Curate or some passing stranger. And the resemblance is not a chance one. Cervantes's work was written as an anti-romance, and became, via Fielding and Smollett in English tradition, a major ancestor of a new literary form—the novel. Durrell's work, as the passage quoted above indicates, is an anti-novel in the same sense as Cervantes's work was an anti-romance. Both men were faced with a constricting literary tradition and revolted against it.

Of course, Pursewarden's point about the thinness of modern literary fare is not meant to be mere literary discussion in a vacuum, any more than the similar discussions in *Don Quixote*. We are meant to apply Pursewarden's theory to Durrell's practice. To do so we must look back, as Pursewarden suggests, to an older literary tradition than the novel. And so we shall. But before we do so we must observe that Durrell's revolt is not an isolated and magnificent gesture of defiance against an entrenched and flourishing literary tradition. The tradition he finds thin and constricting is the very one started by Cervantes—the tradition which begins as anti-romance and gradually insists on more and more scientific treatment of life: the empirical tradition which in its theoretical formulations calls itself first realism and finally naturalism. The naturalism to which Durrell is reacting is, of course, about as feeble now as the romances were in the time of Cervantes, and the new revolutionary is no more alone in his revolt than the old. A James Joyce can adapt naturalism to allegorical purposes as well as an Edmund Spenser could adapt romance. And a Marcel Proust can destroy empirical notions of characterization as thoroughly as Cervantes himself could destroy the romantic heroes. Just as Samuel Beckett is the heir of Joyce—a somewhat rebellious heir, producing anti-naturalistic anti-allegories—Lawrence Durrell is the heir of Proust. For it is Proust who explodes the empirical notions of characterization so essential to realistic and naturalistic fiction, by demonstrating the artificiality of the real and the reality of the artificial. "Even in the most insignificant details of our daily life," the narrator of *Swann's Way* tells us,

> none of us can be said to constitute a material whole, which is identical for everyone, and need only be turned up like a page in an account book or the record of a will; our social personality is created by the thoughts of other people. Even the simple act which we describe as "seeing someone we know" is, to some extent, an intellectual process. We pack the physical outline of the creature we see with all the ideas we have already formed about him . . . so that each time we see the face or hear the voice it is our own ideas of him which we recognize and to which we listen.

Proust emphasizes here the artificiality of reality. We do not see our friends, only our ideas of them. In another passage he develops this paradox further, illustrating the converse principle, the reality of artifice:

> A real person, profoundly as we may sympathize with him, is in great measure perceptible only through our senses, that is to say, he remains opaque, offers a dead weight which our sensibilities have not the strength to lift. . . . The novelist's happy discovery was to think of substituting for those opaque sections, impenetrable by the human spirit, their equivalent in immaterial sections, things, that is, which the spirit can assimilate to itself.

Proust's brilliant exposition of the paradoxical notion that we can truly experience life only through art is the death knell of the realistic-naturalistic movement in fiction, though even today, forty years afterward, neo-naturalists like James Jones continue to write frantically, headless chickens unaware of the decapitating axe. For Durrell, however, Proust's new esthetic is a release and an inspiration. In the following passages from *Justine*, we can observe him adapting the Proustian view to his own purposes. In the first we find the narrator, Darley, examining Arnauti's diary, *Moeurs*, in which Justine is a character called Claudia: "Nor can it be said that the author's intentions are not full of interest. He maintains for example that real people can only exist in the imagination of an artist strong enough to contain them and give them form. Life, the raw material, is only lived *in potentia* until the artist deploys it in his work. Would that I could do this service for poor Justine." Like Pursewarden, Arnauti longs for a different kind of fiction. He wishes to set his ideal book "free to dream." His view is different from Pursewarden's but complementary, not contradictory; and Durrell's novel embodies both views. Darley finds Arnauti's diary so vivid that he feels at times like some paper character out of *Moeurs*. And after Pursewarden's death he writes of him,

> How much of him can I claim to know? I realize that each person can only claim one aspect of our character as part of his knowledge. To every one we turn a different face of the prism. Over and over again I have found myself surprised by observations which brought this home to me. . . . And as for Pursewarden, I remember, too, that in the very act of speaking . . . he straightened himself and caught sight of his pale reflection in the mirror. The glass was raised to his lips, and now, turning his head he squirted out upon his own glittering reflection a mouthful of the drink. That remains clearly in my mind: a reflection liquifying in the mirror of that shabby, expensive room which seems now so appropriate a place for the scene which must have followed later that night.

The *Alexandria Quartet* is alive with mirrors. The prismatic facets of character glitter, unreconciled, in our imaginations. Appearance and reality are continually confused, and the line between life and art continually blurred. Darley feels like a character out of *Moeurs*. But Darley *is* a character in Durrell's novel. What we took for fact in one volume is exposed as false in another, and the exposé itself is proved incorrect in the third. Stendhal could compare his story to a mirror, strolling down a lane, reflecting the sky and the mud. But for Durrell fiction is a whirling prism reflected in a liquifying mirror. In the scene quoted at the beginning of this chapter, in which Justine tells the child prostitutes a story in Arabic, Pursewarden longs for the opportunity to tell a story of Laic splendor to an audience which is really able to suspend its disbelief. Since the modern reader cannot recapture the esthetic innocence of Justine's audience, Durrell attempts on the one hand to establish in the reader's mind his version of the new, Proustian esthetic, and on the other to blur the line between the real and the artificial in order to make it harder for the reader to begin applying his disbelief, even if he refuses to suspend it. Durrell seeks to confuse and bewilder the reader, to separate him from his habitual reliance on probability and verisimilitude, so as to offer him something better. *Behold*, he as much as tells us, *you thought you could not walk without that crutch of realism. I tell you you can fly!* And he nearly convinces us that we can. Using the modern esthetic of Proust, and a narrative technique which, with its multiple narrators and dislocations of time, seems also typically modern, Durrell takes us on a journey—a magic carpet ride not only through space but through time as well—a return to Alexandria.

For, though Pursewarden says he longs for the old "epic contours,"

what Durrell gives us is—appropriately enough—more Alexandrian than
Attic. As Moses Hadas has observed in his introduction to *Three Greek Romances*, " 'Once upon a time' is not the way the classical Greeks opened a
work of literature." But "Once upon a time" does reflect the spirit of Alexandrian literature and of the romances written in the Greek language all
over the Mediterranean world in post-Alexandrian times. Alexandria was a
Greek city on Egyptian soil. In it the East and West met as they rarely
have elsewhere. The old joke has it that when Greek meets Greek, they
open a restaurant. But when Greek meets Egyptian in ancient Alexandria,
they opened a library. From this meeting of cultures developed the first
literary critics and a new kind of literature. E. M. Forster has described this
literature for us in his *Alexandria, a History and a Guide*—a book Lawrence Durrell frequently alludes to in the *Alexandria Quartet*. Forster
points out that the distinguishing characteristic of the new literature was its
emphasis on love:

> Ancient Greece had also sung of love, but with restraint, regarding it as
> one activity among many. The Alexandrians seldom sang of anything else:
> their epigrams, their elegies and their idylls, their one great epic, all turn
> on the tender passion, and celebrate it in ways that previous ages had
> never known. . . .
>
> > Who sculptured love and set him by the pool,
> > Thinking with water such a fire to cool?
>
> runs a couplet ascribed to one of the early Librarians, and containing in
> brief the characteristics of the school—decorative method, mythological
> allusiveness, and the theme of love.

How appropriate, too, that in the twentieth century Durrell's anti-novel
should be set in this romantic spot. It is clear that Durrell's Alexandria is
as much a country of the mind as Poe's Virginia or Kafka's Germany. Some
of the place-names are real, but beyond that there is little resemblance between the fictional Alexandria of Durrell and the geographical one. Yet
Durrell's work is completely faithful to the ancient spirit of the place.

As Forster points out, the literature of Alexandria was, unlike the literature of Greece itself, a literature of love. It was in Alexandria that love
made its way into epic poetry: in the *Argonautica* of the librarian Apollonius the love of Medea for Jason was presented so dramatically that it left an
indelible mark on poetic fiction. Vergil's Dido and many of Ovid's love-
stricken females are directly derived from this Alexandrian epic. And the
prose romances that were written in Greek around the Mediterranean in
the second and third centuries A.D. (of which Heliodorus' *Ethiopica* and
Longus' *Daphnis and Chloe* are the best known examples) are also derived,
apparently, from the Alexandrian combination of Greek and Oriental literary traditions. A papyrus dating from the second century B.C. and called
"The Alexandrian Erotic Fragment" was described by its last editor as being written in Greek prose similar to the ornate rhyming prose of Arabic
narrative. In its combination of erotic subject matter and rich prose it also

exemplifies the characteristic qualities of Durrell's work, written over two millennia later.

The *Ethiopica*, richest and most elaborate of the Greek romances, stands very much in the same relation to the Homeric epics as Durrell's *Quartet* does to such great realistic novels of the nineteenth century as *Anna Karenina* and *Middlemarch*. Both the epics and the great realistic novels present events as ordered by an omniscient narrator whose controlling mind not only shapes the events but colors them and comments on them. But in Heliodorus much of the narrative is conveyed to us directly by characters in the story. Furthermore, Heliodorus is not content simply to imitate the *Odyssey* and have one man narrate much of his own tale. In the *Ethiopica* we have as many narrators as in the *Alexandria Quartet*. Indeed, one of the first stories we are told, a brief resumé of her life by the heroine, turns out to be a tissue of falsehoods designed to deceive her captors (and also the reader, who only afterwards learns the truth). In the hands of Heliodorus the romance is characterized by a multiplicity of narrators and tales within tales like a sequence of Chinese boxes; by a consequent dislocation of the time scheme, as the narrative moves backwards and forwards from its beginning in what George Saintsbury has called a "sort of cat's cradle manner"; and by a fondness for elaborate set pieces of a spectacular nature, involving such things as battles, rituals, necromancy, and celebrations.

Though the general resemblance of the *Alexandria Quartet* to the *Ethiopica* is obvious (some of the action of the ancient story even takes place on the shores of Durrell's beloved Lake Mareotis), the point is not that the resemblance indicates any direct indebtedness; rather, it is that the two works are so similar in spirit. Durrell is not so much a descendant of Heliodorus as a reincarnation of him in the twentieth century. When Durrell speaks of his characters in an interview as "puppets," he reminds us of the way in which Heliodorus manipulates his characters in a virtuoso display of sustained and integrated form. And form, for Durrell, is nearly everything. His early novel, *The Black Book*, displays many of the characteristics of his later work—everything, almost, except form. *The Black Book* was written when Durrell was very much under the influence of D. H. Lawrence and Henry Miller, writers who tend to disdain form, to think of it as a way of distorting reality. In the recently published correspondence between Durrell and Miller we can see him gradually becoming more critical of Miller's work on the grounds of its formlessness. Though traces of Lawrence and Miller remain in Durrell's mature work, there can be little doubt that the spirit which presides over the *Alexandria Quartet* is Proust's. And in turning to Proust, Durrell brought himself into contact with a tradition of sustained form which was fundamentally opposed to the "slice of life" technique characteristic of empirically oriented mimetic fiction. The tradition of elaborate form in fiction leads back through the romances of the seventeenth century to the European rediscovery of Heliodorus in the sixteenth, whose influence on the subsequent development of prose fiction can hardly be exaggerated.

The purely melodramatic side of the Greek romance has, of course, been greatly modified in its modern reincarnation. In the old romances the characters were mainly highly stylized extremes of virtue and vice, and the plot was always subservient to the decorum of poetic justice. In the *Alexandria Quartet* the characters and the prevailing ethos are as elaborate and complicated as the plot and the setting. The thinness of characterization which, for the modern reader, relegates the *Ethiopica* to that secondary level of works whose influence surpasses their interest would be inexcusable in a modern work of serious intent. But even richness of characterization, which we think of as a peculiarly modern attribute of fiction, has its roots in Alexandria. The Alexandrians and their followers, especially Ovid and the Greek romancers, introduced the arts of rhetoric into narrative literature. The combination of psychology and rhetoric, which characterizes the crucial monologue of Medea in the Third Book of the *Argonautica*, works through Dido and the Ovidian lovers into the mainstream of narrative literature. Lawrence Durrell's rhetoric, rich and evocative as it is, has been roundly criticized by the English press as some sort of wild Celtic aberration—not (in the phrase of Mr. Podsnap) English, and hardly appropriate for a novel. But one of the glories of our resurgent narrative art has been the rhetoric of Joyce, of Faulkner, of Conrad, and of Proust; though none of them are (alas) English, either. The flat prose of sociological fiction is being abandoned to the sociologists, who, God knows, have need of it; and the rich rhetoric of the Alexandrians, of Ovid and the Greek romancers, is beginning once again to return narrative literature to the domain of art. The novel may indeed be dying, but we need not fear for the future. Durrell and others are generating a renaissance of romance. The return to Alexandria should be almost as exciting a voyage as the one described by the city's greatest story-teller, Apollonius; for, like the voyage of the Argo, it will be an enchanted one.

The Protean World
of Lawrence Durrell

John Unterecker*

Lawrence Durrell is a man of infinite variety. But he's a man of marble constancy as well. The forms in which he has worked embrace the whole

---

*This essay was revised specifically for this volume and is published by permission of the author. In earlier versions it appeared as *Lawrence Durrell* (New York and London: Columbia University Press, 1964) and as "The Protean World of Lawrence Durrell," in *On Contemporary Literature: An Anthology of Critical Essays on the Major Movements and Writers of Contemporary Literature*, ed. Richard Kostelanetz (New York: Avon, 1964):322–29.

range of literary possibility. Yet the themes he has dealt with—even the images which carry those themes—display a simple kind of shining direct-ness, mark out a clear path for his developing but remarkably consistent point of view. He is consequently one of our most protean writers and at the same time one of our most predictable ones.

It is variety, however, that immediately strikes anyone who does no more than glance through a stack of Durrell's collected works. Even if one limits one's glance to works currently in print, something of Durrell's enor-mous range is bound to be suggested. He is author, for instance, of the espionage thriller *White Eagles over Serbia* (described by Durrell's Ameri-can publisher as a book "for young persons"); of intricate poems (among them the sonnet of sonnets, "A Soliloquy of Hamlet") and bawdy ballads (Dylan Thomas's favorite being "A Ballad of the Good Lord Nelson"); of a quintet of "travel books" which should perhaps more accurately be called island portraits (*Prospero's Cell, Reflections on a Marine Venus, Bitter Lemons, Sicilian Carousel,* and *The Greek Islands*); of the lovely, casual collection of letters, poems, essays, and paintings, *Spirit of Place*; of three poetic dramas, startlingly different in tone—though not in theme; of the "solipsistic," raw fictional account of prewar London, *The Black Book*; of comic interludes about life in the diplomatic corps (particularly *Esprit de Corps* and *Stiff Upper Lip*); of *The Dark Labyrinth*, a novel which Durrell accurately described to Henry Miller as "an extended morality, but written artlessly in the style of the detective story"; of literary criticism (*A Key to Modern British Poetry*); and—by far his most popular work—of the extraor-dinarily complex, expanding study of the emotional education of a hero and his friends, *The Alexandria Quartet*. He has also in his time turned out public relations copy, newspaper columns, and—presumably unavailable to the public—a whole series of confidential reports, a bulky stuffing of diplo-mats' bags and Home Office files. He has published some of his letters to Henry Miller and a smaller group of letters (to Alfred Perlès) about Henry Miller. He has acted as translator of prose (Emmanuel Royidis' novel *Pope Joan*) and poetry (Constantine Cavafy, not only in the body of *The Alexan-dria Quartet*, but elsewhere), anthologist, and magazine editor. He was for a while one of the principal script writers for the motion picture *Cleopa-tra*—and once, in his youth, a would-be composer-lyricist of popular songs. For years after the completion of *The Alexandria Quartet* he was reported as being engaged in work on "an enormous Rabelaisian comic novel," some of which may have surfaced in the double-decker novels *Tunc* (1968) and *Nunquam* (1970), now grouped as *The Revolt of Aphrodite*, and more still of which may have appeared in the fictional and intricately interwoven ex-plorations of the nature of "reality," *Monsieur* (1974), *Livia* (1978), and *Constance* (1982).

His variety is, in fact, so spectacular that one suspects that, consciously or unconsciously, somewhere along the line Durrell must have toyed with the idea of being literature's Leonardo—the master of each literary form.

So far as I know he has not as yet written the libretto of an opera—but give him time.

Give him time enough—and space—and you will have set up the space-time continuum that, from very early in his career until the present moment, operates for Durrell as a kind of subterranean metaphor—a metaphor for a literary structure that does not significantly change from work to work and on which he has draped all of the superficial variety of poems, novels, essays, plays.

To demonstrate that, however, would take a small volume. What can comfortably be accomplished in an essay is a brief analysis of the ways this obsessive material shows up in a single work. Because it has been read by more people than any other of his works, I shall settle on *The Alexandria Quartet*. When (three paragraphs back) I tried to compress *The Alexandria Quartet* into a phrase by describing it as "the extraordinarily complex, expanding study of the emotional education of a hero and his friends," I was not so much attempting to define the novel as to insist on some of its most basic elements. Its complexity is, I suppose, obvious; and, as Durrell makes clear in his headnote, it is deliberate. The work is laid out carefully in Durrell's up-to-date geometry, the first three sections constructing for us a three-dimensional "solid" Alexandria, while the fourth, adding the dimension of time, should enable us to see the book—if we are willing to see in such a fashion—as a kind of "objective correlative" for the experience of a space-time continuum. Durrell is careful to keep this structure constantly before his readers; and he is equally careful to keep before them the similar relativity-pattern discovered by modern psychoanalysis. We are therefore always aware in Durrell's book that both external and internal "truth" is constantly being modified by its observer (who is in turn modified by it).

Durrell is sometimes heavy-handed in his treatment of these relativity motifs. (Mirrors and masks obtrude so much as to be conspicuous; and the letter-writing device, as Miller pointed out in a long letter to Durrell—itself perhaps the most penetrating critical comment yet delivered on the *Quartet*—threatens sometimes to get out of control.) But it may be that in order to enjoy later subtleties, later delicacies, we need the heavy-handedness. You could write a whole book on the importance of the obvious. Yet the obvious and its importance can be missed by supersubtle minor novelists and major critics. Durrell never makes this mistake. He realizes, for example, that many of the early intrusive remarks of *Justine*—glaringly functional in a second reading of the *Quartet*—serve, the first time round, as absolutely necessary guideposts for the reader who otherwise might well be bewildered by the structure of the world he is about to enter. Less than a dozen pages into the first book and barely introduced as a character, Justine spells out for that reader what he must not miss. She sits in front of a dressmaker's "multiple mirrors" and speculates on the art of the novel: " 'Look! five different pictures of the same subject. Now if I wrote I would try for a multi-dimensional effect in character, a sort of prism-sightedness.

Why should not people show more than one profile at a time?' " This is
clearly a case of author forcing dogma into the mouth of one of his characters. Nevertheless we must have explicit statement of this sort if later we
are to be able to accept the brilliant variants Durrell's characters will play
upon it. We need, for example, to have precisely this statement somewhere in the backs of our minds if we are properly to respond to Darley's
reflections on the nature of reality in the second book of the *Quartet*. Trying to piece together the meaning of Balthazar's interlinear, Darley calls
into question the nature and the utility of truth itself: "The really horrible
thing is that the compulsive passion which Justine lit in me was quite as
valuable as it would have been had it been real; Melissa's gift was no less
an enigma—what could she have offered me, in truth, this pale waif of the
Alexandrian littoral? Was Clea enriched or beggared by her relations with
Justine? Enriched—immeasurably enriched, I should say. Are we then
nourished only by fictions, by lies? I recall the words Balthazar wrote down
somewhere in his tall grammarian's handwriting: 'We live by selected
fictions. . . . ' " We need both Justine's early statement and this one of
Darley's to coalesce back there in our unconscious if a casual remark of Justine's in the last book, *Clea*, is properly to achieve its literary function. In
that book mirrored images from *Justine* transform themselves gracefully
into *Balthazar*'s fictions. Justine is once again speaking to Darley: "We are
after all totally ignorant of one another, presenting selected fictions to each
other! I suppose we all observe each other with the same immense ignorance." For none of the millions of mirrors of the world—or the millions of
possible points of view available to a writer—present truth, though all mirrors and all points of view present reality of a kind. Truth, as this world
knows it, is finally, Darley realizes, something which can be discovered
only in relationship:

> I . . . saw that lover and loved, observer and observed, throw down a
> field about each other. . . . Then they infer the properties of their love,
> judging it from this narrow field with its huge margins of unknown. . . .
> I had only been attesting, in all I had written, to the power of an image
> which I had created involuntarily by the *mere act of seeing* Justine.
> There was no question of true or false. Nymph? Goddess? Vampire? Yes,
> she was all of these and none of them. She was, like every woman, every-
> thing that the mind of a man . . . wished to imagine. She was there for-
> ever, and she had never existed! Under all these masks there was only
> another woman, every woman, like a lay figure in a dressmaker's shop,
> waiting for the poet to clothe her, breathe life into her.

If mirrors present to us distorted images of a single face, that single
face presents its own distortion to the mirrors. And when it moves away
from mirrors, it freezes into something fixed, immobile, deceptive. Reality,
in Durrell's major work, becomes in fact something very much like a
masked ball—with the masks nothing less than our own false faces and
those false faces we project onto the faces of all men and women around

us. The difficult trick for the novelist in this sort of carnival atmosphere is to find a way of revealing the kinds of "realities" each of his major characters observes—and also as many as possible of the "selected fictions" which that major character uses to disguise the poverty of his irresolute and private self.

Durrell's solution is a little like Gide's in *The Counterfeiters* or Faulkner's in *Absalom, Absalom!*: a storyteller finds variant accounts of what ought to be a single story. Later on, in *Monsieur, Livia,* and *Constance,* novels as much about the nature of fiction as they are about the nature of reality, so many characters are other characters' "fictions" that Durrell amuses himself and some of his readers by tacking on at the end of the first volume a genealogy of its fictionalizers, himself, presumably, the D. who heads the list: "So D. / begat / Blanford (who begat Tu and Sam and Livia) / who begat / Sutcliffe / who begat / Bloshford . . . " etc. In *The Alexandria Quartet,* Darley's initial version of a set of events is corrected by Arnauti's *Moeurs* and by the diaries of Nessim and the false diaries of Justine; these versions are in turn corrected by Balthazar's interlinear; that interlinear is corrected by the objective history of events in *Mountolive* and by a number of sets of letters, most significant of which are those between Leila and Mountolive, Pursewarden and Mountolive, and Pursewarden and Liza. Finally, time itself offers a shifted perspective; and in *Clea,* the one novel that moves forward in time, each of the central characters is allowed the opportunity to reexamine and reevaluate his past and the pasts of the group of wounded survivors from the first three books.

For just as *Justine* is most conspicuously the book of mirrors, *Balthazar* the book of masks, and *Mountolive* the book of intrigue—the first two volumes offering private false faces and the third offering the public false faces of political action—*Clea* must take its place, it seems to me, as Durrell's book of wounds, the damaging but in a way life-giving wounds that strike through all of the false faces to the quick body beneath and that can be healed only by proper questions, proper concerns for others, such as those we find displayed in the tenderness of human affection. There are of course wounds, as there are mirrors, masks, and intrigues, through all four books; in one way or another, hardly a character in the *Quartet* escapes disfigurement or death. (Think of the crowds of blind or half-blind figures alone: from one-eyed Hamid, through one-eyed Scobie, one-eyed Capodistria, and one-eyed Nessim, to totally blind Liza and the whole host of minor figures—blind servants, sheiks, and priests—who fumble through the novel.) But in *Clea,* the education of the hero and his friends begins to bring rewards as well as penalties. Proper questions (not: "What can you do for me?" but instead: "What can I do for you?") begin to accomplish nearly miraculous cures, and some, at least, of the wounded are not only restored to health but actually transformed—given a new and fuller life— thanks to apparent disaster. The virtuous Semira, complete with the nose designed for her by Clea and fashioned for her by Amaril, dances trium-

phantly before the affectionate assembled Alexandrians; and Clea herself—
cured by Amaril of her troublesome virginity—is freed, tenderly, to cure
not just anyone but the bankrupt and broken doctor, Balthazar, who must
finally wound her and, aiding Darley, bring her with rough tenderness
back to life. Minor characters also experience a similar transformation: the
journalist Keats turns into a Greek god when he questions the nature of
war and discovers simultaneously that "Even the dead are overwhelming
us all the time with kindnesses." And who is not pleased to discover that
Scobie, though battered to death in his Dolly Varden, is tenderly ("How
much the city misses him") elevated to sainthood and then, thanks to Nim-
rod's delicate, ironic hint, saluted by his murderers, "the boys of H.M.S.
Milton," with a fine display of naval fireworks.

For it is, in the long run, only tenderness that illuminates for an instant the solipsistic darkness, that lonely, terrible darkness that had dominated *The Black Book* and into which all of the major characters of *The
Dark Labyrinth* had briefly, at least, plunged. Yet it is also onto this darkness that the more perceptive of Durrell's major characters see projected
the crucial figures of a private "heraldic universe." It is no accident, therefore, that Darley discovers his limitations as an artist precisely when he discovers the illusory nature of the universe he must attempt to represent.
("It was life itself that was a fiction—we were all saying it in our different
ways, each understanding it according to his nature and gift.") And it is also
no accident that at this painful moment fictive Clea, "all tenderness," drops
the mask of her reserve to step out of her fictional world and, in a transparent interval, join Darley in that bright world where, restored, he will be
able to function. It is here, too, in the last book, that the reader, if he has
been attentive, will recall that passage from *Balthazar* in which Pursewarden has set down for Clea the plan for his own "last volume": "I feel I want
to sound a note of . . . affirmation—though not in the specific terms of a
philosophy of religion. It should have the curvature of an embrace, the
wordlessness of a lover's code. It should convey some feeling that the world
we live in is founded in something too simple to be overdescribed as cosmic law—but as easy to grasp as, say, an act of tenderness, simple tenderness in the primal relation between animal and plant, rain and soil, seed
and trees, man and God."

If tenderness—an "utterly merciless" tenderness rescued from sentimentality by the distancing power of irony—is the primary lesson in the
"emotional education" the questing central characters experience, they
learn their lesson most frequently from painters and from writers, also
wounded—and some of them healed—in their efforts to transmit a vision
of the elemental processes, those processes that constitute the very design
of life.

The book, in fact, is overrun with artists of one kind or another. For
in addition to the professional writers and painters—Arnauti, Pursewarden,
Darley, Keats, and Clea—there is a battalion of casual diarists and Sunday

painters, most conspicuous among them Nessim, Mountolive, and Justine. And behind all the fictional characters are the flesh-and-blood writers and painters of the flesh-and-blood world. For not only does Durrell allow Pursewarden to give a quick two-page survey of English literature, he also has the audacity to set him corresponding with D. H. Lawrence. Some of the characters in the novel have also known Cavafy, the poet whose poems about Alexandria provided Durrell with parallels important to the action of the novels, subtle, ingenious, and psychologically accurate. And Sir Louis, Mountolive's senior in Moscow, is permitted, after his retirement to Italy, both to meet Claudel and to pass on to Mountolive one of Claudel's diplomatic stories. Like the living landscape, living and recently deceased "real" writers ground the book in reality and feed their truths to the fictional artists and writers who live only in the novel. And the artists and writers in the novel feed on each other, identify with each other, merge into each other.

By offering us this collection of interrelated artists and writers, Durrell has left himself open to the sort of criticism reviewers are fond of making: Durrell becomes his own protagonist. The problem, however, is more complex than that; for not only does Durrell play games with his reader by assigning his own initials to Darley, but he also goes on to assign his own ideas to several of the other writers and painters. Reviewers, easily confused, find this confusing. And to some extent they are justified in being confused. Pursewarden, for example, seems, in some ways, the real author-identification figure. He is by far the most intelligent person in the book; and he is even made the author of a novel famous for an asterisk that refers to a blank page. He seems, therefore, just right as "author" of *Justine*, for in the one-volume edition of the *Quartet* Durrell carefully places an asterisk in the next to the last sentence of the body of the text ("Does not everything* depend on our interpretation of the silence around us? So that . . . "), and then in his note ("See page 196") refers the reader to the only blank page of the book. Shades of *Tristram Shandy*. Yet Pursewarden, for all his likelihood as "author" of *Justine*, is unfortunately killed off half-way through the *Quartet*, and Darley himself survives until the last page where, putting pen to paper, he writes, "Once upon a time."

But I think we should not really be misled by Pursewarden's inventive asterisk, and I think we should not be seriously troubled by the whole problem of author-identification. (An author is, I suppose, never one of his characters but rather the sum of them. And so far as Pursewarden is concerned, if a model need be found for his ideas, that model is as likely to resemble Henry Miller as it is to resemble Lawrence Durrell.) Within the novel, Pursewarden's function seems obviously to be less author-spokesman than teacher. Like Faustus' teacher in Durrell's play *An Irish Faustus*, Pursewarden passes on the "slender thread" of wisdom to Darley. He also has much the same function that another one of the *Quartet's* teachers, Clea, has: he shows Darley not just how to see, but what to see; and he suggests one method—the ironist's—for capturing those figures of the "heraldic universe" who, like Capodistria's homunculi, scramble, desperate for love, out of their life-sustaining fluids into the thin air of the artist's "real" world.

For love, as Pursewarden explains in his long ironic, "imaginary" dialogue with Darley, is finally what makes—the only thing that makes—the world go round. And the great book—when it is written—"will be characterized," he goes on to say, "by a *total lack of codpiece.*" It will strip us, if not to the bone, to the flesh that drives the bone, and it will present, without editorializing, the enormous variety of love: "I mean the *whole bloody range*—from the little greenstick fractures of the human heart right up to its higher spiritual connivance with the . . . well, the absolute ways of nature, if you like." Such a book, Pursewarden argues, might allow us to "rediscover in sex the key to a metaphysical search which is our *raison d'être* here below."

And though the *Quartet* is not quite the book Pursewarden visualizes—perhaps Miller's two trilogies come close to it—it is a book that does explore in the right way the right territory. For its range is very wide: from rape to homosexual passion, from child prostitution to narcissistic masturbation, from the unrequited love of Narouz for Clea to the tender exchanges of Clea and Darley, from the random skirt-chasing of Pombal to the intricate incestuous relationships of Liza and Pursewarden, and the suppressed, but just as real, incestuous quadrangle set up by Leila and Nessim, Mountolive and his mother. Durrell's project is, if you want, mere presentation, not judgment. And it has for that reason perhaps incensed those readers who feel clear lines always must be drawn between what for each of them is "good" and what for each of them is "evil" and that the novelist's lines must be their lines of demarcation. Durrell's scheme, of course, forbids this sort of public moralizing. But yet his unjudging presentation does achieve a kind of moral end: if it neither praises nor condemns, it does reveal to us significant landscapes of the human heart.

So ambitious a project, though it may eventually reduce the world, as Pursewarden suggests, to boy-meets-girl, involves, before that reduction is accomplished, each of the world's boys and girls in extraordinarily complex designs of affection. To turn again to the physicist's metaphor, it involves each figure of the novel in a "field" of emotional entanglement. This field, radiating out from each character, in intricate ways distorts the "fields" set up around each of the other characters. No figure, therefore, is uncomplicated. Justine, for example, is caught in a tangle of loves—wife of Nessim, former wife of Arnauti, mistress of Darley and Pursewarden, lover of Clea; she is also obsessed by her childhood experience of Capodistria's rape and by her passionate desire to recover her child. Yet she experiences sexual passion only when it can be coupled with political intrigue. Virginal Clea is in some ways more complex still; for, involved in the affair with Justine, she is loved by Narouz, loves Amaril, is freed by him to love Darley, and is loved by Keats. Melissa, given so little personality as to seem at times merely an object, is nevertheless involved in her own tangle of love: for, mistress to Cohen and to Darley, she sells herself for one night to Purse-warden and bears a child by Nessim. Yet each of these lovers—pair them up as we will—sees not even the false face his beloved presents to him. He sees only something he projects onto that false face: "If you can't do the trick with the one you've got," Pursewarden tells Justine, "why,—shut your eyes and imagine the one you can't get. Who knows? It's perfectly legal and secret. It's the marriage of true minds!"

Yet, if in Durrell's world *everything* admits impediment to the mar-riage of true minds, Durrell does suggest, in his imagery of interacting fields of personality, a world not strictly private, a world which, though misunderstood by each person in it, can be understood by an outsider in terms of the interactions of those persons. And beyond persons, the imper-sonal operations of the "fields"—internal and external—seem not altogether unlike that process which is the busy happening of "nothing" within the liberating cosmology of the heraldic universe.

Sometimes the machinery of Durrell's huge novel creaks. Clea's read-ing lips through a telescope seems to me farfetched. And I think Durrell is guilty of a failure in invention in the last book when he has to have Scobie imitated by three different characters. Yet in spite of occasional gasps and grunts, the machinery does finally present us a landscape essentially believ-able, a believable landscape on which believable characters, mired in time, struggle—not only with each other but as well with themselves—toward a tender acceptance of things as they are.

"It is not peace we seek but meaning," Durrell writes halfway through "The Reckoning," a poem composed about ten years after the *Quartet* was published. In the last line, however, he qualifies that aphoristic truth: "It is not meaning that we need but sight." "Precarious," truth—like reality—balances opposites and miraculously reconciles them. Sight and insight, at least in Durrell's fiction, become conjoined.

Romantic Anachronism in
The Alexandria Quartet   A. K. Weatherhead*

I

Lawrence Durrell's Byronic speed of writing, his facility with and de-light in words, and the fertility of his imagination which overflows from the

*Reprinted from *Modern Fiction Studies* 10, no. 2 (Summer 1964):128–36. © by Purdue Research Foundation. Reprinted with permission.

novels proper into "Workpoints" have resulted in a work of which the very style obscures its own broad issues. There seem to be important advances made by certain of the characters and especially by Darley, the protagonist of the tetralogy and the narrator of three of its component novels; but the outlines have been blurred by the constant gorgeous pitch of the prose, and the author has been charged with not saying very much or at least not enough to justify the expense of the apparatus employed. Such a criticism will not be answered by the following attempt to isolate one or two strands of development in the tetralogy; the attempt is designed only to show, by comparison with another novel, how the development of the *Quartet* distinguishes it from other contemporary novels and dissociates it from the group of ideas we have got used to living with.

There is some development in the fact that at the end of the tetralogy nearly all the principals are planning to leave or have already left Alexandria. It is a fact which is not given a great deal of emphasis; or rather, since there are so many others receiving the vivid stylistic embellishment, this one is not thrown into relief. But the departure is significant, because repeatedly in the tetralogy we are made aware that this city deprives men of their wills to act. The following remark of Justine's expresses best what is felt throughout: "You talk as if there was a choice. We are not strong or evil enough to exercise choice. All this is part of an experiment arranged by something else, the city perhaps, or another part of ourselves!"[1] All the way through, as long as characters remain in Alexandria, their affairs are controlled by fate, which either prohibits their actions altogether or distorts their ends, offering such inappropriate effects as the sainthood bestowed on Josh Scobie or the murder of Toto de Brunel with the hatpin from a French diplomat's disguise. Sometimes, most noticeably in the nearly disastrous love affair of Balthazar, the influence of fate is felt as the inward, compelling "It" of Groddeck, the psychologist who believed that a man's ailments could be attributed to a choice made by his own essence and whose influence on Auden's poetry has been drawn attention to by Durrell. But more often we feel the influence of fate as an external factor, presiding over people's lives or terminating them as arbitrarily as Narouz standing on the balcony killing bats with his whip.

It is not only in the general exodus from Alexandria, however, that gains are made against fate. The last great episode of the tetralogy, the rescue of Clea by Darley, marks the assertion of human purposefulness over the haphazard operations of fate. Balthazar, it will be recalled, has inadvertently fired the harpoon gun and unwittingly nailed Clea's hand to a wreck, which rests at the bottom of a deep pool together with the upright figures of seven drowned Greek sailors. Darley releases her by amputating her hand and then by artificial respiration brings her back to life. As even this brief statement may suggest, the whole passage is symbolic; and the archetypal issues—death and re-birth by water—are thrust upon us. But we are made aware also of the strong exertion of an independent human will to counteract the workings of chance. It is most apparent during the artificial respiration: "Closing my eyes I willed my wrists to seek out those water-logged lungs. . . . I would not accept the thought that she was dead. . . . I felt half mad with determination to disprove it, to overthrow, if necessary, the whole process of nature and by an act of will force her to live" (*Clea*, p. 251).

The will is there; and the point to which attention is being drawn is not compromised by the fact that Darley does not know from what source the will comes. In the act, he has discovered his real self, and it is unfamiliar to him. His agonizing choice has given him existence: "I had, I realized, decided either to bring her up alive or to stay down there at the bottom of the pool with her; but where, from which territory of the will such a decision had come, I could not guess." A passage two pages earlier indicates the self-discovery more explicitly: "I cannot pretend that anything which followed belonged to my own volition—for the mad rage which now possessed me was not among the order of the emotions I would ever have recognised as belonging to my proper self. . . . It was as if I were for the first time confronting myself—or perhaps an alter ego shaped after a man of action I had never realised, recognized" (*Clea*, p. 249).

How seriously ought we to take this as indicating a major growth in Darley and some kind of broad development in the *Quartet* as a whole? It might be argued, for example, that these are incidental, essentially undramatic little gratuities designed merely to heighten the passing incident. But I think not. In the first place, this whole incident in *Clea* may be properly considered along with the two other long episodes which come in corresponding positions in the other two novels of which Darley is the narrator: the duck shoot in *Justine* and the Cervoni ball in *Balthazar*. In one or two important respects, these two present a contrast with the episode in *Clea*. In each of them, for instance, a man is killed, whereas in *Clea* a woman is brought back from the dead. Then, more closely relevant to the matter of will, on each of the two former occasions Darley is a guest in a party, and rather than acting as a free agent he pursues a series of activities arranged by others. This is more true of the duck shoot than of the ball. But the point is that when the tragedies occur on both occasions, his role is that of a bystander unable to take any relevant action. On the occasion in *Clea*, although technically a guest on an outing he did not sponsor, he is not, quite obviously, merely at the disposition of his hostess, and he performs the important action at the critical moment. Furthermore, he performs it, as it were, *against* fate, which, we learn, had written the scenario of the action. This aspect provides another point of contrast, although a small one, with the two earlier episodes. In each of them fate is aided and abetted: at the duck shoot, the guests draw lots for the make-up of the various parties; at the ball, the anonymity conferred by the mask and domino which each guest wears provides a special opportunity for chance and mischance. Both these actions are deliberate overtures to fate by people seeking the undesigned or the unexpected. They are of a different kind from that which left the harpoon gun cocked in *Clea*, which only in metaphor was "asking for trouble."

The contrast afforded between the last of these three episodes and the first two speaks of a large design in the novel which the brilliant details may tend to obscure. The establishment of the eminence of the human will is not only significant in itself but is related to the growth of Darley as artist. The *Quartet* is laboriously concerned with art, a fact its critics have unnecessarily demonstrated; and Darley's growing up as an artist is one of the themes Durrell has claimed for the novel. One part of Darley's growth is the discovery that "transcendental knowledge," the kind of knowledge Pursewarden had attained to, cancels out the relative knowledge of facts which are at the mercy of fate.

Transcendental knowledge deals apparently in a kind of vagueness rather than in stark facts with unblurred edges. This vagueness lends excitement and attraction to what when fully known and defined would be ordinary or worse. It is perhaps like the vagueness that Wordsworth and Coleridge had sought in order to enrich the commonplace or like Swann's uncertainty about Odette which feeds his fascination for her. Hence in the *Quartet* whereas the occasional insubstantial whiff of *Jamais de la Vie*, the mysterious perfume Justine wears, had fired Darley's imagination, it becomes merely repulsive to him when she drenches herself in it and it is fully known. It is possible, then, that the vague appearance of Clea in the underwater scene qualifies her symbolically as an object of transcendental knowledge: she is "dimly recognised" as a "convulsive, coiling movement"; her activity is misconceived: she is apparently "busy upon some childish underwater game. . . . " The water refracts and distorts: "Her long hair impeded my vision. As for her face I could not read the despairing pain which must have been written on it—for the water transforms every expression of the human features into the goggling imbecile grimace of the squid" (*Clea*, p. 248).

It may seem immoderate to interpret this episode to mean that Darley has fished up transcendental knowledge from the depths and that he has thus developed as an artist along the lines laid down by Pursewarden. On the other hand, it does seem fairly clear that the presence of the will in this episode indicates the maturing of Darley's art. The will is a faculty which makes its presence felt in the work of the mature artist, and Darley hitherto had not exercised it. His first work of art, *Justine*, consists, broadly speaking, of spontaneous memories fortuitously assembled. The writer had submitted himself to the material rather than impose himself upon it; he had not yet, in the phrase Clea uses of him later, "taken possession" of the kingdom of his imagination. But in a piece of writing of any magnitude, "an author cannot sustain a spontaneous vein of creation. . . . " He "will have to summon his will to help him abide by the plans he has resolved on. . . . Such sustained writing corresponds to certain phases of the active life. Just as the will may force a man's conduct at a particular time (for instance on an expedition of exploration) to conform to a previously adopted set of resolves, against his present inclinations, so a poet may use his will to suppress new interests and preserve a unity previously resolved on."[2]

These remarks are taken from Tillyard's prescriptions for the epic but are good of course, *mutatis mutandis*, for any work of art, just as they are good, as Tillyard suggests, for certain operations in life. It is not necessary to spell out in detail how closely Darley follows these prescriptions in his rescue of Clea. This operation is not a work of art (not in the usual sense: but there are enough paradoxical remarks in the novel in which art and life change places to justify any confusing of their natures); but the newly discovered qualities in Darley which make him capable of this operation qualify him also to create a kind of art more mature than *Justine*.

In art the will is manifest as form. And some sentiments expressed by Darley toward the end of *Clea* which show his appreciation of form contribute to the portrayal of the maturing artist. At the death of Maskelyne, the stereotyped regular soldier, Darley studies a photograph of the man's grandfather: "He seemed to lighten the picture of Maskelyne himself, to give it focus. Was it not, I wondered, a story of success—a success perfectly complete within the formal pattern of something greater than the individual life, a tradition?" (*Clea*, p. 232). The idea of "success" in "formal pattern" is surely a new one to the man over whom the memories flowed in the creation of *Justine*. But at the very end of the tetralogy Darley is in a position to write, "Once upon a time . . . "—words which are nothing other than pure and traditional form.

The fourth volume of the tetralogy deals among other things with the growing up of Clea as an artist also. At the end she too has entered into possession of the kingdom of her imagination. The circumstances under which she does so, however, may at first sight seem to conflict with the idea that the book moves toward the supremacy of human purpose over the haphazard direction of fate. In her final letter to Darley she speaks of her new ability to paint as an achievement of the hand—the steel and rubber contraption that the surgeon Amaril had created for her. "IT can *paint!*" "One day it took up a brush and lo! pictures of truly troubling originality and authority were born. . . . I know that the Hand was responsible" (*Clea*, p. 278). These passages and others like them seem at first to point to an impersonal agency as the effective creator.

On consideration, however, it seems that the artificial hand has a different symbolic significance. It was created by Amaril, the surgeon, and to this extent is linked with the earlier sexual affair between Amaril and Clea. The affair, in turn, was an experience deliberately sought out by Clea to deliver her art, as she explains, from a state of aridity. It seems that the steel hand should probably be taken not as an agent of chance but as a symbol of Clea's experience, chosen by herself. And to this extent her own will has brought forth her success in painting.

Thus Clea's part of the story is another manifestation of the development of the novel toward the idea that the human will *can* remold things nearer to the heart's desire.

II

The most interesting feature of this belief in the ability of the will is that it distinguishes the *Quartet* from a number of its contemporaries, which accept exactly the opposite premise—that the human will is finally impotent to reorganize the world. It is the latter belief, codified rather unsystematically by Camus, that has captured the contemporary imagination; and it is the novels written out of it that speak to our generation. Not the exertion of the will but its success seems to place this novel in the age of Byron rather than that of anxiety. The exertion of the will, although unavailing, is noble. Even further from the contemporary "line" is the ability of the principals of the *Quartet* to leave Alexandria—simply to remove themselves from the arena in which fate, or indeed life, exerts its absurd influence. Such a removal, according to the premises that so many of Durrell's European contemporaries have accepted, is not a possible expedient. It is impossible, for instance, in *La Peste* to leave Oran, the plague-stricken city. Camus posited only two alternatives to the process of living with the absurd: physical suicide and philosophical suicide. And the retreat from Alexandria symbolizes neither.

The way in which Durrell's novel is set apart from the dominating ideas of the last forty years may be further clarified by comparing it not with a novel of Camus but with *The Sun Also Rises*, a novel which did indeed speak for its times but which in many other respects the *Quartet* resembles not merely adventitiously. Martin Green has pointed out that Durrell's novel is related to the works of an earlier generation of expatriates, finding especial kinship between the characters and the conversation in the *Quartet* and those in Norman Douglas' *South Wind*.[3] The relationship to *The Sun Also Rises* seems to me to be even more striking. Each novel deals largely with deracinés—the cafe society insufficiently related communally to speak of as a foreign colony. In each, casual sexual unions fail to break the isolation of men and women. Lady Brett Ashley says of Robert Cohn, "He can't believe it didn't mean anything";[4] Darley records that his "most solitary movements" were "those of coitus with Justine."

A more significant similarity is the domination of each novel by a nymphomaniac (or, if this term is exceptionable, at least a *femme fatale*) and, more or less closely associated with her, a great city. In Durrell, the association of Justine with Alexandria is frequently suggested; and as we have seen the city is the place where men's wills are generally defeated. In Hemingway, the combination of Brett and her city, Paris, seems to me to be no less a symbol of the absurd world. In the early part of *The Sun Also Rises* an emphasis is given to the matter of whether one likes living in

Paris, which would be irrelevant if Paris had not some symbolic value. "You love Paris, do you not?" Francis Clyne asks the prostitute whom Jake has brought to the "dancings" (p. 18). Robert Prentiss asks Jake, "Do you find Paris amusing?" (p. 21). And Jake's anger at the question is, I think, to be attributed to the fact that a fundamental question—the question of living—is being discussed in facetious prattle. Count Mippipopolous, a good man who lives by the Hemingway code, finds Paris "a fine town."

Lady Brett Ashley belongs to Paris. When Jake toys with the idea of living in the country, she says, "It wouldn't be any good. I'll go if you like. But I couldn't live quietly in the country" (p. 55). Later she says, "I was a fool to go away"; then, "One's an ass to leave Paris" (p. 75). Of the early discussions about Paris, the one most to the point is that between Jake and Robert Cohn. Having read and assimilated *The Purple Land* by W. H. Hudson, Cohn wants to go to South America. Jake says: "Listen, Robert, going to another country doesn't make any difference. I've tried all that. You can't get away from yourself by moving from one place to another. There's nothing to that. . . . If you went there the way you feel now it would be exactly the same. This is a good town. Why don't you start living your life in Paris?" (p. 11).

The Purple Land, insofar as it endows life in South America with remoteness, and hence vagueness and excitement, is dangerous and Jake rejects it. But Cohn's projected excursion is just the romantic expedient that is permitted to Durrell's leading characters. In *The Sun Also Rises*, however, it is not the protagonist but the antagonist, Cohn, the man who fails to live by the code, who entertains the possibility of departure.

It is Cohn also who has expectations of romantic love, who can't believe, at any rate, that the affair with Brett "didn't mean anything." In Durrell, sex is certainly not meaningless, although, as we have seen, it doesn't automatically serve to make for community. What is interesting is that Durrell provides an alternative to sex which saves men and women from mutual alienation. There is, again, a way out. In a word, the possession of a common cause and the promise of action in it draws men and women, and for that matter men and men, into community where they had previously been at odds. Nessim's courtship of Justine is a case in point; it is effective only when he reveals to her that their marriage will be instrumental in advancing a common cause. Later the failure of the cause alienates them and injures the marriage; and the injury is only repaired when the cause blossoms once more. In a sense the career of Pombal, the French diplomat, is comparable: after his promiscuous affairs and then after fate has snatched away his true love he finds some kind of purpose in life in the cause he shares with Pordre, with whom he is at last in this way reconciled. In Darley's affair with Clea the common interest in art, though not exactly a cause, serves to unite them.

In *The Sun Also Rises*, on the other hand, although romantic love does not *necessarily* mean anything, there is no alternative for it. Jake pursues alternative interests, such as the fishing holiday at Burguete. But this is only a temporary escape—the whole passage only a brilliant cadenza. The world is always with him; he is bound to return to Brett and Paris. The wound that precludes him from sleeping with Brett renders this world absurd. "[I]n a universe suddenly divested of illusions and lights," says Camus, "man feels an alien, a stranger. . . . This divorce between a man and his life . . . is properly the feeling of absurdity."[5] In the final scene of *The Sun Also Rises*, having bought the train tickets for Paris, Jake and Brett, riding in a taxi, are thrown against each other when the taxi is stopped by a policeman in khaki. The incident epitomizes the absurd workings of the world. The khaki-clad policeman, recalling the war which has mutilated Jake,[6] is instrumental now in throwing him into a situation in which, because of the unbridgeable gulf his mutilation has created, his rational demands are unanswered and his desires frustrated. So the novel ends with the protagonist prepared to live with the sorry scheme of things unchanged.

If this view of the world speaks for our time as it did for Hemingway's, then Durrell is writing against the grain; and in offering a solution that simply won't do he is precluding himself from contemporary acceptance. Indeed, our century in its later decades has by no means encouraged the revival of the kind of romantic literature against which at its outset it was at pains to revolt. It calls still for objectivity and clearly defined fact rather than the allurements of the vague. And for the most part it still finds the world absurd: "once upon a time" does not predicate "happily ever after." In this climate the world's biggest marlin may be hooked but not brought home; in this climate Durrell's tremendous catch will probably not survive.

Notes

1. *Justine* (London, 1957), p. 27. Quotations from *Clea* are also taken from the London edition (1960).

2. E. M. W. Tillyard, *The English Epic and Its Background* (London, 1954), p. 10.

3. "A Minority Report," in Harry T. Moore, ed., *The World of Lawrence Durrell* (Carbondale, Illinois, 1962), p. 136.

4. *The Sun Also Rises* (New York, 1954), p. 181.

5. Albert Camus, *The Myth of Sisyphus and Other Essays*, trans. Justin O'Brien (New York, 1959), p. 5.

6. See Mark Spilka ("The Death of Love in *The Sun Also Rises*," *Hemingway: A Collection of Critical Essays*, ed. Robert P. Weeks [Englewood Cliffs, New Jersey, 1962], p. 137), who draws a different conclusion from the incident.

Durrell's Fatal Cleopatra   Jane Lagoudis Pinchin*

We are used to misogyny, accept it, covered, like our bones. Yet if we look at a work like *The Bear*, and if, as I do, we care about women and how they are viewed in the world, we rest uneasy, suspecting, with Leslie Fiedler, that had Faulkner leveled half the venom he directs at women toward any minority group, his work would meet with genuine outrage.[1] We are used to literary images of women engendered by hostility. Still we need remember what Lawrence Durrell tells us, life imitates art, women and men shape their images of themselves on fictive visions, making that acceptance frightening indeed.

Misogyny is, of course, a dangerous if euphonious word. Like Woman. We must be extremely careful when generalizing from Isaac's wife, or Francis Macomber's, even if an author explicitly invites our generalizations. And, after all, some may argue one-dimensional villains need not weaken a fictive work if their roles are small, if they move amongst full blown characters, if characterization is not central to the work at hand. But if women command the stage and our attention, as they do in Lawrence Durrell's *The Alexandria Quartet*, they must shine like visions of colored glass.

What of Durrell's Cleopatras? Clearly they are not inspired by hatred of women. One heard Pursewarden chuckle, or swear. They are, nevertheless, inspired by an outrageous view, a view in which generalizations are not only invited but writ large. *The Quartet* is of course a work without an objective perspective, for even the "facts" the third-person narration relates in *Mountolive* are altered by private visions in the novels that follow and precede it. Still, we can say that the not-so-omniscient author of the penultimate volume joins his fictive personae to talk about the virtues and vices of Woman. What is one to do with a novelist who gives us the following.

Darley on Justine:

> Whatever passed for thought in her was borrowed. . . . She had picked out what was significant in books not by reading them but by listening to the matchless discourses of Balthazar, Arnauti, Pursewarden, upon them. She was a walking abstract of the writers and thinkers whom she had loved or admired—but what clever woman is more? (*J*, 179)[2]

Balthazar:

> As for Pursewarden, he believed with Rilke that no woman adds anything to the sum of Woman, and from satiety he had now taken refuge in the plenty of the imagination—the true field of merit for the artist. (*B*, 99)

*Reprinted from *Deus Loci: Proceedings of the First National Lawrence Durrell Conference* 5, no. 1 (25 April 1980):24–39.

> Like all women, Justine hated anyone she could be certain of. . . .
> Women are very stupid as well as very profound. (*B*, 102)

> "Truth has no heart," writes Pursewarden. "Truth is a woman. That is
> why it is enigmatic. Of women, the most we can say, not being French-
> men, is that they are burrowing animals." (*B*, 157)

The narrative voice in *Mountolive* on Nessim and Justine:

> For the first time he struck a responsive chord in her by a confession of
> the heart. To her surprise, to her chagrin and to her delight, she realized
> that she was not being asked merely to share his bed—but his whole life,
> the monomania upon which it was built. Normally, it is only the artist
> who can offer this strange and selfless contract—but it is one which no
> woman worth the name can ever refuse. . . . He stared at her, thrilled
> and a little terrified, recognizing in her the perfect submissiveness of the
> oriental spirit—the absolute feminine submissiveness which is one of the
> strongest forces in the world. (*M*, 178–181)

And in *Clea*, Darley looking back on Justine:

> Nymph? Goddess? Vampire? Yes, she was all of these and none of them.
> She was, like every woman, everything that the mind of man (let us de-
> fine "man" as a poet perpetually conspiring against himself)—that the
> mind of man wished to imagine. She was there forever, and she had
> never existed! Under all these masks there was only another woman, ev-
> ery woman, like a lay figure in a dressmaker's shop, waiting for the poet
> to clothe her, breathe life into her. In understanding all this for the first
> time I began to realize with awe the enormous reflective power of
> woman—the fecund passivity with which, like the moon, she borrows her
> second-hand light from the male sun. (*C*, 49)

There is of course more. Darley: "Women are sexual robbers, and it
was this treasure of detachment she hoped to steal from me . . . " (*J*, 174).
Darley on Amaril: "For him the most splendid thing in the world was to
possess a fashionable woman, a prize greyhound, or a pair of invincible
fighting-cocks. . . . His devotion to women was the most obvious thing
about him" (*B*, 110). In books round with pregnant metaphors we have
Pursewarden's, "The evening has begun to yawn around us with the wearisome promise of girls to be ploughed" (*C*, 109). Pursewarden who suggests:
"an artist saddled with a woman is like a spaniel with a tick in its ear . . . "
(*C*, 51).

What do these snippits tell us about Durrell as a novelist? Are they
central to our vision of *The Quartet*? They tell us, many would say, that,
like God, Durrell is a Humorist. Others might argue that although banal
they are not important; women are on center stage but this is after all a
portrait of an artist as a young man.

For all the interest expressed in love and sex, the major concern of
Durrell's fiction is with writing, the real hero is the writer or the male creator: the artist or his surrogates, doctor, politician, priest. The stars in his

cast are men of the tribe, the "Real Ones," linked throughout history by their power to "Outface, defy, disprove the Oracle in order to become the poet, the darer" (C, 133). They talk to one another, like C. P. Cavafy's Theocritos and his young poet in "The First Step."

If you can forgive them for despising ordinary middle class people, the civil servant and the literary critic, his twin, a Kenilworth who drops in on James Joyce; for despising the Arab or the black—Joyce " 'was paying for his privacy by giving lessons to niggers at one and six an hour!' " (C, 118)—or for their attitudes toward blind, English, Greek, grey, and oriental Muses, you'll find them, in the main, an agreeable group. Durrell includes in their numbers Keats, Byron, Donne, Shakespeare, Pope, Eliot, Blake, Whitman, Rabelais, de Sade, and of course D. H. Lawrence, whom Pursewarden affectionately chides. They form a chain that, in the novels, leads from Arnauti to Pursewarden to Darley and includes Amaril and the brothers, Nessim and Narouz. They are extremely non-competitive; engaging in a present and an historical camaraderie, they share rooms, advice, and women. It is no accident that in an interview with Marc Alyn, discussing his poem "Elegy on the Closing of the French Brothels," Durrell compared brothels with their British cousin, the pub.[3] Prostitutes, for Durrell, function as sweet women do for Hemingway, they are places men go to play with one another.

The Quartet is after all a portrait of an artist in merry fellowship, an artist as a young man divesting himself of his codpiece—that last teacozy of Victorian morality, a young man who will unrobe, who fiercely believes that sex is "root-knowledge."

The trouble is, scared of what he'll see, he chooses his favorite mirror. And "women have," Virginia Woolf reminds us, "served all these centuries as looking glasses possessing the magic and delicious power of reflecting the figure of man at twice its natural size."[4]

The artist is interested in knowing all about sex, that dangerous, repetitive act. But, although he is after control of women, the poet's orderings, he is not interested in knowing the other sex. One other sex? one might ask. Isn't Alexandria "the great winepress of love," where "there are more than five sexes," where ordinary heterosexual coupling gives way to infinite variety? Darley tells us "The symbolic lovers of the free Hellenic world are replaced here by something different, something subtly androgynous, inverted upon itself" (J, 12). I would suggest that variety in love, while an important part of the backdrop of Durrell's canvas, is, in the main, illusory.

Certainly when one thinks of Balthazar, Scobie, and the haunting presence of C. P. Cavafy, all homosexuals compared with Tiresias in these novels, one is tempted to say that Durrell is indeed approaching more androgynous love. But ironically, with a single exception that I will discuss later, there are no important homosexual unions in *The Alexandria Quartet*. Durrell is interested only in mentors, in wise old men, who have, it would seem, not so much encompassed the male and female within them as lost, perhaps transcended, gender, who are solitary souls. Young homosexuals, Pombal's Gentlemen "of the Second Declension" (*B*, 21), are treated with a comic condescension that is close to scorn.

No. In *The Quartet* sex and hate are heterosexual. The couple is Alexandria and the artist. Cleopatra and her Adamic Antony. The woman of the pasir becomes the man's landscape and history, his time and space. Alexandria who like a madame presides over her hetairae, whose "caryatids supporting the darkness" (*J*, 166), is a city created by its women. We are reminded of Wallace Stevens' "Notes toward a Supreme Fiction," in which the poet's voice addresses an illusive reality calling her

> Fat girl, terrestrial, my summer, my night.
> You are familiar, yet an aberration.
> Civil, madam, . . . this unprovoked sensation requires
> That I should name you flatly. . . .

That difficult task—fluid not flat—ends in a naming of sorts: Reality has become "my green, my fluent mundo."

Lawrence Durrell's heroes must also order, control, and write about Reality; they must name their world. Like Stevens—whose landscapes are more abstractly placed, less clearly grounded—that world, that landscape upon which the imagination plays, is female.

For Durrell the artist, as part of the great male tribe, becomes an adventurer. Justine's chevalier, Semira's "knight in search of the Holy Grail" (*M*, 139), Leila's crusader, on what is clearly a medieval quest, a quest John Unterecker suggests is at the core of much of Durrell's important work,[5] a quest to conquer, and by conquering heal, his landscapes. He is an explorer touching territory in the only way he sees left open to the contemporary mind, unveiling and veiling "Alexandria, princess and whore," the words Darley uses to describe the "ancient city with all its cruelties intact" when he reenters her, feeling "like Adam of the medieval legends" (*M*, 55).

"Alexandria, princess and whore. The royal city and the *anus mundi*." Unlike Stevens' pliant other, Durrell's lady will not comply; she is seldom indifferent or benevolent. Durrell might have named Alexandria what he had once called the island of Rhodes, "the great dark abdominal FEMALE PRINCIPLE!!" (*S*, 87). Passive and predatory, a threatening chaos.

If writing, ordering reality, is the essential act, coupling is its metaphor in the world, and the source of strength for an artist who writes only by courting danger. His protagonist must experience *all* the women around him—Melissa, Clea, who, mirroring her mild friend, is baled up into Darley's life like a Cleopatra, and the woman from "that race of terrific queens. . . . The giant maneating cats like Arsinoe were her true siblings" (*J*, 18): Justine. Balthazar says of her first husband Arnauti "she preyed upon all that he might have kept separate—his artist-hood if you like. He is when all is said and done a sort of minor Antony and she a Cleo. . . . this is really a city of incest" (*J*, 86).

How does Alexandria's embodiment, this Justine, prey upon her sons? She is as Leila describes her[:] barren, "arid—all her milk has turned into power-love" (B, 83), frigid, for all her foreplay, checked, locked, closed since youth. Like the rubber doll that haunts Durrell's dreams she must be inflated by men, take in their vitality. Living, as Durrell would have her live, vicariously, her sole strength becomes her ability to sniff out vitality, to find the man with the most monomanical vision and, amoral, like "all women worth the name," she is interested not in the shape of that vision but in its intensity. She will therefore cuckold any artist for another of greater vitality (even lover for husband). Although she will sleep with anyone, *does* in fact sleep with others for [her] own true knight, like a prostitute for her pimp, collecting other men's metaphors, information, dreams (one thinks of Cohen and Melissa), she gives the gift of serious sex, a kind of love, as the prize for real vitality.

This might at first glance seem delicious. Its dangers are two-fold. For she may—even as you create her, fill her—defeat you, sap your energies, give you over to the chaotic abyss, the rule of Mephistopheles. She may engage you in a battle in which sex becomes death, a murder at the Cervoni's ball.

Or she may judge you unworthy, not potent enough to arouse her, to solve the riddle, release the sword, for Justine is not a whore with a heart of gold, like Melissa (who herself, one might add, however innocently, does men in).

The dynamics of Justine's judgment are fascinating. The knight wants to be first to order chaos, to win the prize, but he wants to do this in order to free other men to take their own art; he wants to lead and join his fellows. Towards them he feels neither hostility nor competition: he would in fact, in solving the puzzle of rape, make Justine accessible to all men. The enemy is not other artists. She is the critic, the intuitive judge, a Cleopatra who may, over the whole of Alexandria and throughout history, betray you.

"He is when all is said and done a sort of minor Antony and she is a Cleo. . . . this is really a city of incest." It hardly seems accidental that in one of the many works in our literature in which woman is moon to man's sun, the two readings of that last word hang in the air. Incest interests Durrell for many reasons. Perhaps most important: he is intrigued by what he perceives to be the fusion of knowledge and evil, the root-knowledge that the familial reaches. Also, as an enemy of Puritanism who, somewhat ironically, believes in evil but lives in an age that no longer does, he must invent an evil that will shock an unshockable audience, an audience still given to yawn, "Four volumes of mystery ending up with what happens in the country every wet Sunday afternoon."[6] He works hard to surprise and succeeds more often through violence and deformity than through sex.

One may, in addition, wonder whether incest fascinates the voice that shapes the novels because he is concerned with discovering that androgynous place where male and female mesh. I think not. In fact I would suggest the opposite. Knowledge and evil come together in *The Quartet*'s incestuous unions because Durrell envisions a meeting of the extremes of masculinity and femininity. When brother and sister, sharing the virtues and vices of inheritance, touch, they sculpt not the self, but the other, stripped of all that is extraneous to sex.

Thus Pursewarden meets Liza. Medusa is not a Humorist. She is the physical embodiment of an audience that can see nothing but what the poet creates, that world with which he peoples an Irish farmhouse. She gathers reflective grandeur and becomes Isis and Arsinoe, becomes the King's mythological queen whose total passivity startles us in these lines: "He converted my blindness into poetry, I saw with his brain, he with my eyes" (*C*, 166). But the passivity of this "strange, blind witch" (*C*, 145), once again, does not preclude betrayal. Liza awaits the Stranger, who will come one day, like a new generation of artists.

Liza joins Melissa, Mountolive's mother, and Leila as women who wait. But Leila, for all that she is Penelope, is also different from all the women we've examined thus far: for she could have been artist instead of Muse. We see, in fact, her possibilities as doctor, writer, priest, and politician.

Leila has incestuous links to Nessim and Narouz. But it is Mountolive with whom she lives out an Oedipal love. Durrell likes her, because she accepts limits with dignity, as Cavafy suggests we must. And because, I think, she takes on a woman's role he admires; she becomes an artist for an audience of one. As female observer who sharpens male vision, she is artist as mother, a loving teacher who is not herself interested in outfacing time and space. Like D. H. Lawrence's Gertrude Morel, she has planted sons in the world who see it for her. She has offered Mountolive a son's carnal knowledge which, once given, need not be repeated. "In the circle of Leila's arms, as if he were Antony at Actium, he could hardly bring himself to feel fear" (*M*, 224). One is tempted to say theirs is presented as a near perfect union in which woman, with "disciplined tenderness," supports man's ideas, his life, and in which there is no sex!

But of course that is not true. Sons and lover must free themselves from a mother who, while allowing sexual wandering, demands spiritual fidelity. The adventurers—Mountolive and Nessim, his true double—must not, Durrell suggests, be bound and so, to survive, must hunt rather than be preyed upon.

Thus, mating becomes conquest, and even a kind of murder. Which is why, it seems to me, Mountolive's final portrait of Leila—cheap perfume, shrill voice, exaggerated make-up, unkempt hands—is later mirrored in Darley's portrait of the new Justine, who, like Leila, in the end can come to her former lover only to beg. It is as if each Antony must pull his Cleopatra from her pedestal, must both affirm and reverse history, save and desert his queen.

We are left with the final and most important Cleopatra, a figure who slaps Darley when he suggests he'll write criticism and would seem to contradict much of what I've said. Clea does not spell danger. She is a true artist who need not be pulled from her pedestal. She would indeed even seem to belie my notion that there are no significant homosexual attractions in *The Quartet*, for like many of the novel's Antonys, Clea loves Justine. But that is, I think, the clue.

As an artist Clea must know Justine, "The great dark abdominal FE-MALE PRINCIPLE," before she can create. She must travel what Durrell has drawn as a masculine road and—for all that she is cast as a wise confidante to wounded male lovers—accept its perspectives. " 'There are only three things to be done with a woman. . . . You can love her, suffer for her, or turn her into literature' " (*J*, 19), says Clea quite early on.

Indeed, as confidante, Clea becomes what Leila did before her, an artist for an audience of one, the artist's artist, a true critic who judges vitality, not only with Justine's instincts but with a painter's eye. Although tempted, she will not sleep with a second-rate practitioner.

In fact, for a long while, although declaring "the whore is man's true darling," she will not sleep with anyone. One might even suggest that Durrell comes close to his Victorian ancestors, creating a fair lady whose face and hair bespeak the outer reflection of an inner grace, a virgin whose sexuality is therefore particularly prized as a landscape to which no one has travelled before.

Still, in an important way Clea has known as many men as Justine. She has been Pursewarden's "Clement reader," his artistic helpmeet, thanked for "being there, devoted, watchful, a true reader between the lines" (*B*, 203). And more—she has furthered the tribe. She can say to Darley, about both novelists: "Unknown to either of you, you joined hands in me! As writers" (*B*, 202). We are reminded of Pursewarden's lines: "writers at heart want to be loved for their work rather than for themselves. . . . But then this presupposes a new order of woman too. Where is she?" (*B*, 204–205).

Clea may be that new woman. But, I would suggest, Durrell does not let us rest comfortably with even such an obliging artist-Muse. He is drawn to the story of Pygmalion, as *Nunquam* makes clear, fascinated with new tellings of the tale of Adam's Rib. Theodore Reik's observation is important here: the story of creation reverses the sexuality of birth, allowing man to create woman and thus perhaps calm fears he has of her reproductive powers.[7]

The Quartet is haunted by the images of a dead foetus and a dead girl. Its births are fictive. Like Iolanthe, Sabina and Semira (along with Balthazar's homunculi) do what any good character is supposed to do; they rise off the page and come to life, motherless daughters (like the young Justine), products of the mating of science and art.

Sons of the tribe give birth to Clea too. Amaril and Darley, male doctor and writer who first make a good woman of Clea, just as surely as any

Victorian gentlemen would have, curing her of her homosexuality and her virginity.

On Timonium this Cleopatra is all but lost to the powers of fate—Narouz's call, the ghost of the aborted child—and that old Crone, the sea. But by what A. K. Weatherhead has rightly called an act of Darley's will[8] she is saved. Darley squeezes her lungs in what he describes as a "pitiful simulacrum of the sexual act" (*C*, 218). Like copulation, and like writing. Darley, who has recently had the power to defeat Justine, again orders chaos. He gives birth to Clea and can now turn her over to another member of the tribe, to Amaril who, with the new Hand, gives her new art. "It can paint!" (*C*, 242). Like the utterly blank Semira, Clea in the end becomes a perfectly sculpted figure, a breathing *objet d'art*.

Notes

1. Leslie Fiedler, *Love and Death in the American Novel* (New York: Criterion Books, 1960), p. 309.

2. The following works by Lawrence Durrell are used in the text and have been abbreviated as follows: (*B*) *Balthazar*. London: Faber and Faber, 1968. (*C*) *Clea*. London: Faber and Faber, 1969. (*J*) *Justine*. London: Faber and Faber, 1969. (*M*) *Mountolive*. London: Faber and Faber, 1971. (*S*) *Spirit of Place: Letters and Essays on Travel*. ed. Alan G. Thomas. New York: E. P. Dutton, 1969.

3. Lawrence Durrell, *The Big Supposer: A Dialogue with Marc Alyn* (New York: Grove Press, 1973), p. 130.

4. Virginia Woolf, *A Room of One's Own* (New York: Harcourt, Brace and World, 1929), p. 35.

5. *Lawrence Durrell* (New York: Columbia University Press, 1964), pp. 30–31.

6. Francis Hope, "Strange Enough: *Nunquam* by Lawrence Durrell," *The New Statesman*, 27 March 1970, p. 451.

7. Theodore Reik, *The Creation of Woman* (New York: G. Braziller, 1960).

8. A. K. Weatherhead, "Romantic Anachronism in *The Alexandria Quartet*, " *Modern Fiction Studies*, 10 (1964), 128–136.

"Intimations of Powers Within": Durrell's Heavenly Game of the Tarot

Carol Peirce*

"I'm using all this stuff for my Book of the Dead," Lawrence Durrell wrote his friend, Henry Miller, in the spring of 1945: "It is a calculus of pure aesthetic forms, a game like a heavenly chess; it brings out the meaning of the Tarot and all kindred morphologies" (*Correspondence*, 202). Towards the end of that book, *The Alexandria Quartet*, L.G. Darley, Dur-

*This essay was written specifically for this volume and is published here for the first time by permission of the author.

rell's artist-narrator, thinks about the past and "about us all moving in it, the 'selective fictions' which life shuffles out like a pack of cards, mixing and dividing, withdrawing and restoring" (*Clea*, 276–77). This is exactly what Durrell, the god behind the game, is doing as he plays the Tarot on the tables of his imagination.

Durrell is not the first modern writer to become enthralled by this strange deck of cards with its long memories going back into the past through traditions as seemingly disparate as magic and Jungian theory. Yeats feels the cards to be gigantic archetypes, figures from *Spiritus Mundi*, the cosmic storehouse of memory; he believes in their power and sees them as sources of strength within his poetry. Eliot, thinking of them as a sort of cardboard representation of the Grail quest, uses them eclectically but more intrinsically than is generally realized. Charles Williams breathes life into the cards themselves in such books as *The Greater Trumps*, and they flash the light of their magic from deep within Tolkien's *Lord of the Rings*. Durrell, however, plays them as a symbolic game, laying them out to tell his story and to define and give resonance to his characters. In return, *The Alexandria Quartet* illuminates the Tarot.

The Tarot deck itself, the Renaissance-medieval pack of cards, from which all modern playing cards originate, is in many ways an enigma. It consists of seventy-eight cards, including a group of twenty-two allegorical trump cards known as the Major Arcana and four suits (the Minor Arcana) of wands, swords, pentacles, and cups. These are related to the four elements of fire, air, earth, and water and hence to their symbols, the lion, eagle, bull, and man or Adam. The Major Arcana may or may not have been part of the original deck; indeed, they may have come later or even be of far earlier origin. Speculations on place of origin, as well, have varied widely from France, to the Valley of the Taro in Italy, to ancient China—to Alexandria, Egypt (Cavendish, 11; Douglas, 17–23). Although the Tarot as a whole formed a game and still does, the Major Arcana work less well than the Minor in this capacity and are no longer a part of Bridge and other modern games. They are very much a part of gypsy fortune-telling, however, and to many the Tarot is known mainly for this use.

More deeply intrinsic to the Tarot, and especially to the Major Arcana, is its symbolic significance.[1] Again, theories abound, and though nothing is actually documented, many have thought it a pictogram of the paths of the Jewish Cabala (Cavendish, 49–58; Case, 1–5). It has been seen as closely related to Gnostic initiation rites or possibly Knights Templar mysteries; and, most recently, it has been suggested as a design to be "followed" in the Renaissance Art of Memory (Douglas, 24–30). It seems to incorporate Celtic, Norse, and Christian myth as well; and, thus, significantly, both its symbols and symbolic figures seem to tie it to the Grail quest legend and its equally mysterious origins and symbolism (Douglas, 31–33). Both can be read to tell the tale of a journey to self-knowledge and understanding. In modern terms it can be seen as both expressing Jung's theory of archetypes and as realizing Campbell's hero myth. Thus, finally, like a touchstone it seems to draw to it many different mysteries and philosophies and somehow to reconcile the paths of the past to Illumination. One stricture of every Tarot study is that each reader must come to know and understand the Tarot for himself.

The varied decks of Tarot cards reflect this last injunction. They are as diverse as the early sixteenth-century Marseilles deck, with its woodcut figures, and the Ryder-Waite deck, created by a member of Yeats's Order of the Golden Dawn in Pre-Raphaelite style. There are, in fact, many different decks from medieval to modern. But although there are occasional differences in individual names or individual order, all contain most of the same cards representing most of the same symbolic forces. All move from The Magus to the dance of The World. Gradually the cards have accrued symbolic meaning and affiliations. Each may be related to patron deities, letters of the Hebrew alphabet, earth elements. However one looks at them, each holds accretions of symbolic meaning.

There are also certain relationships among the cards that re-illuminate or suggestively alter their values when they are laid out in varying ways. Some are closely affiliated, some almost twins, and certain groups of four have bonds of strength when placed together. In addition, every card has a different meaning when it is turned upside down (or reversed). And one card, The Fool, numbered zero, may be placed at the beginning or the end of the deck or paired with another card. Where it moves can alter all. Thus, the Tarot cards resemble Durrell's characters and character creation in their levels, their compatibilities, their shifting mythological resonances.

It is from the Major Arcana, then, that Durrell primarily draws in *The Alexandria Quartet*, although he takes from the four suits the idea of the elements. Each of his four volumes clearly emphasizes one of these; they include the fire of *Justine's* passion, the airy intelligence and reason of *Balthazar*, the earth power of Egypt in *Mountolive*, and the water world epiphany of *Clea*. He seems to draw most on the Ryder-Waite and Marseilles decks, though he turns occasionally to black magician Aleister Crowley's pack, famous (or infamous) for its unique and suggestive design.[2] Actually Durrell builds his own deck, using or neglecting features as he chooses, and sometimes introducing variants. As each player inevitably does, he evolves his own pattern, his own symbolism, his own game plan.

The cards are turned up in approximate sequence in the *Quartet*, following the Tarot story about the young initiate's striving for manhood, artistry, and vision. In this quest he is guided by many of the others—notably The Fool seeking wisdom and The Hermit seeking philosophical truth. With each volume new characters, new cards appear, and new insights grow out of associations and events, until, at the end, the artist-protagonist is a completed self. As the last card is turned, Darley achieves, in the dance of The World, his "Heraldic Universe." His fortune has been told.

The story begins with the card labeled Roman numeral I in the Tarot,

The Magus or The Juggler. He stands behind a table on which lie, in some decks, the implements of his trade and, in others, the symbols of the four suits, the four elements, the Grail quest—wand, sword, pentacle, and cup. At the beginning of his journey he approaches the rites of manhood, The Magus *in potentia*; indeed, still, "The light of the ego obscures the softer radiance of the spirit" (Douglas, 46). He is young and not yet skilled, but on the quest he will learn. Thus, the *Quartet* opens in the voice of the narrator, "I" or Darley, who must learn, in the passage of the four volumes, to master his life and to control his craft. Like Hermes, his Tarot deity, and so Hermes Trismegistus, he is the maker of language, the juggler of words, striving to achieve his artistic balance (Cavendish, 68).[3] Self-exiled from Alexandria to a Greek island, he carries with him to rebuild his life only the wand of his creative power. He must use it well, for Durrell, who sets the rules of the game, plans for him to fashion out of the four elements before him the books of the *Quartet*.

The first volume, *Justine*, takes its being from the neophyte narrator's first experience of the fiery element of romantic love. In it, through memory, he re-enacts his Alexandrian past: "We have all of us taken different paths now; but in this, the first great fragmentation of my maturity I feel the confines of my art and my living deepened immeasurably by the memory of them. In thought I achieve them anew; as if only here—this wooden table over the sea under an olive tree, only here can I enrich them as they deserve" (17).

As Darley metaphorically lifts the wand of his rough magic, sets pen to paper on the wooden Greek table, he begins the Tarot journey. By "all of us" he connects with himself his two loves, Melissa and Justine, and his friend, Nessim, Justine's husband and briefly Melissa's lover. Durrell intertwines their lives deeply: "The four of us were unrecognized complementaries of one another, inextricably bound together" (203). It is not coincidental that the first four cards of the Tarot—the Magus, High Priestess, Empress, and Emperor—may be laid in an interlocking rectangle. Each ineluctably affects all the others. Their story forms the first book of the *Quartet*.

Darley enters that first book and begins his initiation with the card of The High Priestess (II). She guards the Mysteries of the Tarot, the portals of life, its white and black columns carved, in the Ryder-Waite deck, with the first letters of the Hebrew words, Jachin and Boaz, meaning Affirmation (or Beginning) and Negation (Butler, 118). They emphasize the strength of contraries joined. And fascinatingly, they are, as well, the first letters of *Justine* and *Balthazar*, the first two books of the *Quartet*, that are both twin and opposite.[4]

Darley's first love is Melissa Artemis, the pale, young, paradoxically virginal prostitute. Like The High Priestess, who is both virgin and prostitute, she sits waiting for him, solitary and dreaming, whereas he is active and outgoing (Cavendish, 71). Twice she tells Pursewarden, Durrell's alter-ego, the wise novelist of the *Quartet*, *"Monsieur, je suis devenue la solitude meme"* (*Justine*, 201; *Mountolive*, 167). Like Melissa, The High Priestess is identified in symbolism with the Greek goddess of the moon Artemis, through her head-dress and the crescent moon at her feet. (These are also symbols of the Egyptian Isis, patron of the dead and dying, as is in a sense Melissa.) In addition she is associated with the Eleusinian Mysteries (Butler, 118): " 'Melissa' I said again, hearing the lovely word echo in the silence. Name of a sad herb, name of a pilgrim to Eleusis" (*Clea*, 41). Finally she seems to symbolize the Virgin Mary, with her blue cloak and sign of the Cross.

Behind The Priestess hangs a light curtain, appearing in changing perspective as either a screen painted with pomegranates and palms or as an open doorway into a luxuriant garden: "I think of Melissa once more: *hortus conclusus, soror mea sponsor . . .* " (*Justine*, 39). This is the garden of the Song of Songs (Chapter 4, "A garden inclosed is my sister, *my* spouse; A spring shut up, a fountain sealed. / Thy plants *are* an orchard of pomegranates with pleasant fruits . . . "). It is also the Mary garden of the medieval world, which "Bore the medicinal flower of Grace"; and there bloom "The Lillies: Virginitie, Humilitie, and Charitie" (Stewart, 31). Darley's first introduction to Melissa speaks of her "charity, in the Greek sense of the word" (*Justine*, 18). Melissa is the little sister, the fountain sealed, the "patron of sorrow," the solitude itself. Clothed in the metaphor of Mary, she dwells in—and is—that garden.[5] By contrast, Justine "does not slide from kisses into sleep—a door into a private garden—as Melissa does" (*Justine*, 136).

Justine, the dark, passionate woman who supersedes Melissa in Darley's affections, is The Empress (III), "a woman clothed with the sun, and the moon under her feet, and upon her head a crown of twelve stars" (*Revelation*, Chapter XII). Beside her lie a field of ripe wheat and a winding river. She possesses a scepter of earthly power and a shield bearing the outline of a heart or an eagle. Often identified as a Byzantine ruler, she derives originally from the ancient Triple Goddess and is the heiress of all her power. Thus she is also Venus, "Many-throned, many-minded, many-wiled, daughter of Zeus" (Crowley, 75). She can be seen as the *femme fatale* of legend, "The Empress or the Temple Prostitute" (Gardner, 19). Like the many-breasted Diana of Ephesus, she gives to all but is herself never sated: "It was as if men knew at once that they were in the presence of someone who could not be judged according to the standards they had hitherto employed in thinking about women. . . . But of course our friend is only a shallow twentieth-century reproduction of the great *Hetairae* of the past, the type to which she belongs without knowing it, Lais, Charis and the rest . . . " (*Justine*, 77).

She is like Cleopatra or Theodora, and we see her revealed over and over again in Justine, a "mistress, who resembled one of those ancient

Goddesses in that her attributes proliferated through her life and were not condensed about a single quality of heart which one could love or unlove" (*Justine*, 166). Also written of The Empress, the phrase, "lust and loneliness, a nymphomaniac, overindulgence or extravagance," could be one of Durrell's own (Butler, 124). If one adds that her perfumes are enveloping, her drugs aphrodisiacs (Butler, 122), one can almost catch the haunting scent of *Jamais de la vie*.

The Empress is, however, also the goddess of abundance, Ceres; and, in reverse, she is the *mater dolorosa*. Though Justine is far from motherly, she does relive the ancient myth of the mourning goddess, who laments and seeks her daughter, kidnapped from beside a lake by Hades, the god of death.

Her final identification comes toward the end of the *Quartet* when, love and power gone, she and Nessim live almost in banishment. Darley brings them Melissa's child by Nessim: "It was all as it should be—the coloured playing card characters among whom she could now number herself! If Justine remained a somewhat withdrawn and unpredictable figure of moods and silences it only added, as far as I could see, to the sombre image of a dispossessed empress" (*Clea*, 196).

Nessim Hosnani, Justine's husband, the leader of a secret Coptic plot to regain power in the Middle East, relates to the fourth card. He is The Emperor, characterized by temporal power, will power, and the domination of intellect over passion: "an adventurer, a corsair, dealing with the lives and deaths of men" (*Mountolive*, 200). He is sometimes seen as a modern captain of industry (Butler, 127). Yet Nessim's "was a Byzantine face such as one might find among the frescoes of Ravenna" (*Mountolive*, 17)—worthy to have been that of a Justinian or a Constantine. "*Chevalier sans peur*, etc.," Clea says of him (*Mountolive*, 194). Actually his affiliations go further back in history. In his plot and in his relationship to Justine as Cleopatra and Venus, Nessim becomes Antony and, in a sense, Mars, one of The Emperor's patron deities. He also is connected to Alexander, the founder of the city; and in his series of historical dreams, he relives Alexander's time in Egypt.

Like Alexander too, Nessim is on his weaker side tied to his mother, who nourished the plot and him in its undertaking. Eden Gray sees The Emperor in reversal as characterized by "Emotional immaturity, bondage to parents." He adds, "Possibility of injury to body or household, of being defrauded out of inheritance" (81). In some decks he seems to rule a waste land. So too, in time does Nessim, defeated in his great enterprise, deprived of an eye and a finger in World War II, wounded in his sexual spirit like the fisher king of the Grail legend. Justine puts it: "You see, when he does not act, Nessim is nothing. . . . When a sense of destiny consumes him he becomes truly splendid" (*Clea*, 58). When the little girl enters their playing card realm, "almost ravenous to take up her own place in the gallery of images I had painted for her," she finds herself in "a world peopled by those presences—the father, a dark pirate-prince, the stepmother a swarthy imperious queen . . . " (*Clea*, 15).

"Inextricably bound together," these characters play out their love game in *Justine* (203). "I am accustoming myself to the idea of regarding every sexual act as a process in which four persons are involved," Durrell quotes Freud as writing (Epigraph). In a corollary that could almost be a comment on the *Quartet*, Richard Gardner writes on the Tarot, "These first four cards are a representation of magical love making. That is love making of so high a quality that it transforms the parties, instead of leading to conception" (23).

Two of the most important cards in Darley's progress are played out of order by Durrell. Or rather, the first, The Fool (0), has no order, appearing at the beginning and end of the deck and relating to all the other cards. The other card, The Hermit (IX), comes early to aid the quester and take the lead in his own book, *Balthazar*. These two characters are Darley's exemplars, his guides, and both challenge and strengthen him in his quest.

The Fool, identified originally by Carl Bode as Pursewarden (Moore, 211), is often considered the most important and mysteriously profound card in the deck.[6] As he jauntily steps over a cliff to suicide, dressed in motley, pursued by a yelping dog or a scratching cat, he laughs in knowledge of the world. In his hand he carries the white rose of Neo-Platonism. In his shoulder pack he carries all wisdom, though sometimes the purse becomes a net to catch butterflies—or the wind (Cavendish, 64). Pursewarden's very name defines his Tarot affiliation, and Durrell early provides an explicit reference: " 'I cannot fall in love', he [Pursewarden] made a character exclaim, 'for I belong to that ancient secret society—the Jokers!' " (*Justine*, 201). And later, sharing his secrets with children, he showed them "some card tricks" and then asked them "to write down three things in their notebooks":

1. Each of our five senses contains an art.

2. In questions of art great secrecy must be observed.

3. The artist must catch every scrap of wind.

                                        (*Balthazar*, 114)

The Fool is, of course, a medieval jester, with the jester's lusty vigor. But his card is also that of the "superconsciousness," of the Creator, who comes before and after; his laughter is jovial, for he is affiliated with Zeus or Jupiter. "I was born under Jupiter, Hero of the Comic Mode!" says Pursewarden, speaking of follies (*Clea*, 142). Indeed, he represents laughter, detachment, and madness, for "When in any of these three states we are closer to God." The card also suggests genius, as "Genius is akin to the Creator" (Gardner, 86–87). The Fool is thus Osiris, the resurrected Egyptian deity, the god of death who was also god of the sun, wedded to his sister, Isis, goddess of the moon. One thinks of Pursewarden's sister, Liza, and of their study together as children of that "one book there, a Plutarch, which we knew by heart" (*Clea*, 190).[7] The Fool is also the Greek Dionysus, god of wine and sex, ecstasy and joy, dead and reborn. The leap of suicide encompasses folly, wisdom, sacrifice, and godliness. So Pursewarden's suicide is at once "the sacrificial suicide of a true cathar" (Moore, 168), the "enigmatic leap" of the great artist "into the heraldic reality of the poetic life" (*Clea*, 153), and the putting on of the godly by the man. Indeed, Balthazar feels that Pursewarden's most profound statement is on the nature of man and the God within. He speaks of it as "the real secret which lay hidden under the enigma of his behavior" and quotes him: " 'You see, Justine, I believe that Gods are men and men Gods; they intrude on each other's lives, trying to express themselves through each other—hence such apparent confusion in our human states of mind, our intimations of powers within or beyond us . . . ' " (*Balthazar*, 124).

Pursewarden leads Darley toward understanding and artisthood, his wise and ribald laughter sounding even from beyond the grave. "Here," indeed, "lies an intruder from the East" (*Balthazar*, 241). He is The Fool: Dionysus and Osiris, great novelist and poet, trickster and buffoon, the Creator beginning and ending the Tarot, and above all Durrell himself as master of the revels and the game.

The young initiate's other guide and teacher, The Hermit, directs him in his search for the truth. Like The Fool, he too is questing, standing tall and thin, holding a lantern high, gripping a staff, a very old Magus, searching still. In fact, the card may originally have signified Time. He is connected with the Hebrew letter symbolizing the hand, and the quality attached to his card is Work (Cavendish, 57). Diogenes-like, he walks in a solitude of thought, not unrelated to philosophers like Plotinus, Bruno, or the Wise Men (Cavendish, 99; Butler, 145). He strives toward spiritual perfection and intelligence. In reversal he represents rashness and lack of prudence. Gray puts it well, "Immaturity, foolish vices, refusal to grow old, the perpetual Peter Pan" (86).[8]

Durrell's Hermit, Balthazar, doctor and teacher of Hermeticism and Gnosticism, bears the name of one of the Wise Men. He is tall and thin, stoops slightly, and has a deep, beautiful voice, large ugly hands, and a spur of hair under his chin like one on the "hoof of a sculptured Pan" (*Justine*, 91). In his own moment of Tarot identification, "He was looking, he said, for the key to his watch—the beautiful gold pocket-watch which had been made in Munich. I thought afterwards that behind the urgency of his expression he masked the symbolic meaning that this watch had for him: signifying the unbound time which flowed through his body and mine, marked off for so many years now by this historic timepiece" (*Justine*, 94).

The old philosopher, who has been seeking for the key to time, voices for Darley one of the central questions of the journey: " 'Fact is unstable by its very nature. Narouz once said to me that he loved the desert because there "the wind blew out one's footsteps like candle-flames." So it seems to me does reality. How then can we hunt for the truth?' " (*Balthazar*, 102). And he makes explicit his identification as the Hermit seeker when, in his parting words to Darley, he calls himself "The Wandering Jew" (*Clea*, 271).

Other cards cluster and form combinations as Durrell plots Darley's Alexandrian journey. *Balthazar*, the second book of the *Quartet*, in addition to reflecting the questionings of the old philosopher, introduces and centrally involves another group of cards.

The card of The Lovers (VI), thematic in nature, looks back to the lovers already encountered but forward as well to new complications. The Hierophant (V), twin card to The Emperor, bearing the sign of Taurus the Bull, is revealed in Narouz, Nessim's strange, demonic, yet godly brother, whose dual nature reflects the changing interpretation of the cards, from Waite's benign, holy image to Crowley's sinister, almost obscene figure. It is not without significance that in the apotheosis of Narouz beneath the Holy Tree, his great whip has "got coiled round his body in some manner" (*Mountolive*, 305), as the figure of the bull coils round the body of The Hierophant on Crowley's card. He comes to hate his mother's lover, David Mountolive, who is also his brother's best friend, a member of the British foreign service, eventually ambassador and knighted—Sir David or "Sir Mountolive" (*Clea*, 18). The Charioteer (VII) enters the novel in his form, driving the horses of British colonial power. Fascinatingly, whether by chance or not, the Marseilles card bears the initials S.M. on his chariot. He loves their mother, Leila, but cannot forget his duty. Leila, who in turn cannot forget her Coptic heritage, even in her love for Mountolive, is the eighth card, Fortitude or Strength. "One day we will find our way back to the center with or without your help! We have long memories," she tells him (*Mountolive*, 45). She can, in fact, almost pry open the lion's mouth, as she does upon the card. Again, a four-card love trick is played.

Halfway through the Tarot and the *Quartet* The Wheel of Fortune (X) turns. Mountolive picks up and twirls "the old Tibetan prayer wheel," which his father had given him as a boy (*Mountolive*, 98). His love turns too. Justice (XI), which is sometimes reversed with Fortitude (XIII) in the deck, may represent Mountolive's new love Liza, Pursewarden's sister. But Fortitude and Justice are also qualities of life, and, at the halfway point of the Tarot, cards representing people yield to cards representing abstractions, forces, or life events.

And in *Mountolive*, Durrell turns his third volume, the book of earthly values, over to an omniscient narrator to play out the discovery of Nessim's Coptic power plot and the identification with it of the suicide of Pursewarden and the murder of Narouz. In these events can be seen the epiphany of The Hanged Man (XII)—or god—sacrificed on the World Tree of Norse mythology (and in some sense the Cross of Christian), reborn in visionary experience (*The Elder Edda*, 56–60).[9] Its companion card (XIII) represents the trial of Death. This card symbolizes "not only the frontier between

Time and Eternity, but that between the Future and the Past" (Ussher, 30). It is a sign not only of endings but of transformation, and certainly in the *Quartet* the card of Death waits beyond The Hanged Man. Darley too, the seeker, must gain vision and courage to endure the death of the old self and attain rebirth.

Always there is the temptation of The Devil (XV). He has rampaged his lust through all the volumes; in *Balthazar*, for instance, Capodistria wears his costume, and his characteristics suit Da Capo well (*Balthazar*, 207–209). In *Mountolive* and then in *Clea*, on his own ground, in his own Tarot position, he tries to—and perhaps does—destroy Narouz: "The meeting with The Devil is the most dangerous encounter of all, because he embodies the energy of the inner self. If he triumphs, then consciousness is flooded with his dark force and the seeker may become a megalomaniac. Reasserting his egocentricity, he will be possessed by a sense of his own power and wisdom. He will believe himself to be the recipient of all knowledge, the divinely appointed messenger of God—even the incarnation of God himself. He will be like one possessed as he grasps the attributes of divinity to himself" (Douglas, 91).

Each force or challenge must be confronted and survived by the potential Magus if he is to achieve his destiny. Darley has lacked strength, and it has been prophesied that in a moment of great need Clea, his deepest love, will turn to "one near at hand who might aid you if he could. But he will not be strong enough" (*Clea*, 207). Darley, however, is learning and growing; he has himself been reworked on the slow wheel of reality and Fortune (12). Pursewarden again comes to his aid, speaking from beyond Death to "Brother Ass": "I am only suggesting that you have not become desperate enough, determined enough. . . . So for people like me I would say: 'Force the lock, batter down the door. Outface, defy, disprove the Oracle in order to become the poet, the darer!' " (*Clea*, 153–54).

Darley, then, a stronger man, of deeper power and understanding of life, having endured his island exile and pursued the truth, returns to Alexandria and begins to speak again in his own voice. As he moves into the final element, the water world of the fourth volume, *Clea*, he is gaining both self-knowledge and artistic power. The cards now begin to include a series of universal, cosmic symbols. Temperance (XIV) represents transformation; she is also Tempus, the herald of Time. Her angel figure is sometimes seen as Iris, the goddess of the rainbow, symbol of hope and love (Cavendish, 116). With a sunburst or star on her forehead, she is closely related to The Star (XVII), the card of Clea. So, in the beautiful morning prayer scene, Darley sees woman, woman's personality, and especially Clea as "a rainbow of dust" (*Clea*, 98–99).

She pours the liquid of time and transformation from past to future. But in the world of the Tarot it may flow both ways: "One of the cups the angel holds is the past, the other is the future. The rainbow stream between the cups is the present. You see that it flows both ways. . . . Men think that all flows constantly in one direction. They do not see that every-thing perpetually meets and that Time is a multitude of turning circles" (Ouspensky, 56).[10] *Clea*, of course, is Durrell's book of Time, in which, coming full circle, Darley learns much of the nature of time, the ever-moving. But he learns even more of its still spirit, of the "continuous pres-ent which is the real history of that collective anecdote, the human mind" (14).

Obstacles, however, remain. The card of The Tower (XVI) also marks the end of *Mountolive* and the opening of *Clea*. Nessim and Justine's plot fails, and all involved in it fall from power, as the figures on the card dra-matically fall to earth. Darley approaches this Dark Tower, too, as the bombs of World War II fall on the waste land city. But Clea, his Star "of the shining possibilities of the future" pours her silver into the sea—the last element on the tables of Darley's imagination (Cavendish, 125). And here too is Darley's last and lasting love, long present but now truly visible: "I see the bright figure travelling like a star across this twilit firmament, its hair combed up and out in a rippling whorl of colour" (228). She is both herself and the card of the spirit and imagination, both the city's and Dar-ley's "grey-eyed Muse" (245), who will redeem both. For him at last three women, three cards have "arranged themselves as if to represent the moods of the great verb, Love: Melissa, Justine, and Clea" (177).

But before Darley can attain Clea, he must face the trial of saving her, passing the sinister card of The Moon (XVIII). On it two dogs or wolves bay at a troubled moon above a mysterious pool from which a sea creature crawls. Beyond, two baleful towers appear. It is the card of eerie dreams and superstition (Cavendish, 128). The Moon may represent the abode of the Dead; and in another version, in which a harpist serenades a young girl, the symbolism is that of Death calling the maiden (Cirlot, 207). Doug-las lists among its divinatory meanings, "A situation in which one has only oneself to rely on" and, reversed, "Failure of nerve" (101). The card signi-fies Narouz's powerful call to Clea from the underworld, and the pool is that below Narouz's island. Darley must dive into the "still waters of pain" (*Justine*, 247) of the Chapel Perilous under the sea, cutting Clea free from her own hand pinioned by Narouz's old harpoon gun to an ancient wreck. The sentence, "Yet we hit the sky with a concussion that knocked the breath from me—as if I had cracked my skull on the ceiling of the uni-verse" (*Clea*, 250), defines the episode; it leads directly to his coming of age. Clea, Darley's star, is, indeed, like the Hebrew letter tzaddi (the fish-hook) written on her card, the force "which pierces the soul and draws it up out of its accustomed element to a higher level" (Cavendish, 127).

Beyond The Moon's dark towers, however, gleams The Sun (XIX), both companion card to The Moon and its opposite, characterized by joy and happiness as The Moon is by nightmare and despair. It may be a card of wrestling children (Marseilles), of twin winged spirits dancing on the green of a rising hill crowned by a wall (Crowley), or of a naked child riding a great horse bareback (Waite). Over all The Sun glows radiantly, realized in all its meanings—"to combine, to unify, to embody, to synthesize"—the card of spiritual achievement, of the rider who "fares forth free and joyous on his journey home" (Case, 181, 186).[11] Pursewarden has foreseen it all long before, looking towards "his" conclusion in which he says he wants above all "to combine, resolve and harmonise the tensions so far created . . . to sound a note of . . . affirmation—though not in the specific terms of a philosophy or religion." So he foresees with the card that man may some-day live within the true terms of " 'joy unconfined' " (*Balthazar*, 238–39). As Durrell approaches his own conclusion in *Clea*, he pauses to allow Pursewarden another moment of ecstatic prophecy, for Pursewarden's Ideal Commonwealth is practically a verbal realization of Crowley's glorious card (140–41).

And the quester's way leads on to Judgment (XX), the call to rebirth. Alfred Douglas phrases it: "The trumpet-call, the summons from the Eternal, announces that the arduous search is about to reach its fulfilment. The individual elements of the psyche have reached full integration and are being reborn. The last shadow of illusion is about to melt away, bringing the Great Work to its consummation" (106). So Durrell brings his hero towards the end of his way. When Douglas adds that this card symbolizes "the meeting place of all opposites . . . the great conjunction, the still heart of the Wheel of Fortune which has now ceased its motion; the timeless hub of the cosmos," we may well feel that Durrell has brought Darley at last to maturity at the great crossroads of Alexandria, the meeting point between the Gates of the Moon and the Sun. There is one more pertinent sentence: "In the outer world this card refers to the creative impulse in man which calls forth the highest within him; the strains of divine discontent that keep him striving upwards to new heights of endeavor" (106). This too is Darley.

The last card Durrell turns is The World (XXI); it celebrates the cosmic dance. The dancer moves in space within a mandala or mandorla, an image of psychic wholeness, of perfected achievement. An end has been reached, but an end that is to Durrell a "continuous present." The dancer turns "at the still point where past and future, evolution and involution, action and inaction all intersect and interact" (Douglas, 108). Truth, love, or poetic consciousness—even the great globe itself dances in harmony and joy. Each who achieves the quest becomes the dancer. So Darley achieves the heraldic reality that Pursewarden already knew: "It came on a blue day, quite unpremeditated, quite unannounced, and with such *ease* I would not have believed it" (*Clea*, 282). For the last card of the Tarot is that of Durrell's own Heraldic Universe.

In one version of the card two angel children hold up a circle of the world in which a white-towered city shines over the sea like Darley's first vision of Alexandria, in Pursewarden's words, "luminous and trembling, as if painted on dusty silk" (Cavendish, 143; *Balthazar*, 16). He now knows that the city, once more regained, "half-imagined (yet wholly real), begins and ends in us, roots lodged in our memory" (13). Pursewarden phrases it, "My spirit trembles with joy as I contemplate this city of light which a divine accident might create before our very eyes at any moment" (*Clea*, 141).

Around the edge of Waite's version of Card XXI the signs of the four elements appear once more. Darley, the juggler of words, has sought his fortune and his world and found it, a true Magus at last. Pursewarden calls it exactly: "—you might try a four-card trick in the form of a novel; passing a common axis through four stories, say, and dedicating each to one of the four winds of heaven" (*Clea*, 135). And The Fool, speaking through Pursewarden, adds his voice: "The object of writing is to grow a personality which in the end enables man to transcend art" (*Balthazar*, 141).

Durrell, past master of novel and Tarot, has come full circle and played his game. An interview after the publication of *Justine* reiterates his purpose: "I'd like to hope that seen from the other end of the continuum my characters seem not just 'people' but symbols as well like a pack of Tarot cards. But I'm still not sure if I can build the books the way I want. *Espérons*" (Moore, 157). He has built *The Alexandria Quartet* as he hoped—and in the conjunction of game and art he illuminates both.

Notes

1. There are many books on the Tarot approaching it from different points of view. Among the most comprehensive are Cavendish and Douglas. Paul Foster Case especially emphasizes its relationship to the Cabala and the Hebrew alphabet. Bill Butler collates and compares both the principal decks of cards and their main treatments.

2. References in this paper are to the Ryder-Waite deck when not specified otherwise.

3. For a further discussion of the merging of the Greek gods Hermes and the Egyptian Thoth into the Renaissance magus figure who authored the *Hermetica*, see Frances A. Yates, *Giordano Bruno and the Hermetic Tradition*, 2, 6–8, *et passim*.

4. Durrell wrote to Henry Miller, "The ground plan, if I can do it, is four books of which the first two fit into each other—different but the same book—Giordano Bruno" (*Correspondence*, 314).

5. One of Mary's titles in the Middle Ages was *hortus conclusus*. A passage using all the symbolic details of fount and garden was that of Adam of St. Victor (Stewart, 41). Her garden merges with the garden of Venus into the Botticellian picture of eternal spring in the Renaissance. Melissa relates to all of these.

6. Carl Bode is the first scholar to consider Durrell's use of the Tarot. He begins to explore the subject in "A Guide to Alexandria," where he devotes four pages to "the most remarkable source of symbols, the Tarot deck of cards." He explains, "Eliot used them in the *Waste Land* but his use was slight compared to Durrell's. For him they are the chief source of symbolic suggestions." Bode begins to make tentative identifications but adds, "He uses the cards loosely but freely" (Moore, 211). Durrell, in a letter to Richard Aldington, refers specifically to Bode's article, which he says, "has bracketed the Tarot references" (*Literary Lifelines*, 201–202).

7. The Plutarch referred to is *De Iside et Osiride*, dedicated to a Delphic priestess, Clea. It is an important source of symbolism in Durrell's development of Pursewarden and Liza.

8. The full description of The Hermit here could, in fact, be read almost as a character sketch of Balthazar.

9. "Gallows, rood, and tree are all Yggdrasil, the World Tree" writes Butler; "the tree is a place of sacrifice, of safety, a gallows, and a place of visionary experience" (153–54). Odin for "nine long nights" hanged himself on it, "Offered, myself to myself," to gain wisdom and words of power (*The Elder Edda*, 56–60). The card of The Hanged Man is closely related to that of The Fool and his sacrifice: "By sacrificing his life the Hanged Man opens the way to his rebirth into the immortality of the spirit" (Douglas, 82). Thus the card can be closely identified with Pursewarden as well.

Narouz, however, is also identified with a Holy Tree, the great "*nubk* tree" (*Mountolive*, 305), beneath which he is found dying, in a symbolic crucifixion. The *nubk* or *nabk* is called Christ's Thorn Tree in Egypt, and Narouz's vision and tragedy are also connected with The Hanged Man.

10. This quotation is remarkably close in spirit to Pursewarden's definition of his—and Durrell's—" 'n-dimensional novel' " (*Justine*, 248).

11. Case is quoting Waite here.

Works Cited

Butler, Bill. *The Definitive Tarot*. London: Rider, 1975.

Case, Paul Foster. *The Tarot: A Key to the Wisdom of the Ages*. Richmond: Macoy, 1947.

Cavendish, Richard. *The Tarot*. New York: Harper and Row, 1975.

Cirlot, J. E. *A Dictionary of Symbols*. Translated by Jack Sage. New York: Philosophical Library, 1962.

Crowley, Aleister. *The Book of Thoth: A Short Essay on the Tarot of the Egyptians*. 1944; reprint. New York: Samuel Weiser, 1969.

Douglas, Alfred. *The Tarot: The Origins, Meaning and Uses of the Cards*. Harmondsworth: Penguin Books, 1972.

Durrell, Lawrence. *Balthazar*. New York: E. P. Dutton, 1958.

_____. *Clea*. New York: E. P. Dutton, 1960.

_____. *Justine*. New York: E. P. Dutton, 1957.

_____. *Mountolive*. New York: E. P. Dutton, 1959.

_____ and Henry Miller. *A Private Correspondence*. Edited by George Wickes. New York: E. P. Dutton, 1963.

_____ and Richard Aldington. *Literary Lifelines: The Richard Aldington–Lawrence Durrell Correspondence*. Edited by Ian S. MacNiven and Harry T. Moore. New York: Viking, 1981.

The Elder Edda: A Selection. Translated by Paul B. Taylor and W. H. Auden. New York: Random House, 1970.

Gardner, Richard. *Evolution through the Tarot*. London: Rigel, 1970.

Gray, Eden. *The Tarot Revealed*. New York: Inspiration House, 1960.

The Holy Bible. King James Version. London: Eyre and Spottiswoode, n.d.

Moore, Harry T., ed. *The World of Lawrence Durrell*. New York: E. P. Dutton, 1964.

Ouspensky, P. D. *The Symbolism of the Tarot: Philosophy of Occultism in Pictures and Numbers*. Translated by A. L. Pogossky. 1913; reprint. New York: Dover, 1976.

Plutarch. *De Iside et Osiride*. Edited and translated by John Gwyn Griffiths. Cambridge: University of Wales Press, 1970.

Stewart, Stanley. *The Enclosed Garden: The Tradition and the Image in Seventeenth-Century Poetry*. Madison: The University of Wisconsin Press, 1966.

Ussher, Arland. *The Twenty-two Keys of the Tarot*. Dublin: Dolmen, 1953.

Yates, Frances A. *Giordano Bruno and the Hermetic Tradition*. New York: Random House, 1964.

Voluptia
Malcolm Bradbury*

In my mind, I was thinking. Alexandria, Queen of Cities, gathered round me as if it were a violet dusk. Mauve clouds like sheered seaweed filtered across the sky. Somewhere, over boxes of nougat, ambassadors wrangled. I scratched a love-bite on my shoulder and gazed down at my pallid body, clad in its tartan underdrawers, stretched out before me, a long, sad groan of fate. O, how lonely I felt. I called Ali, in my best Greek, to bring me a nectarine of Scythian *krash*. I was so subtracted I forgot he was deaf, and probably knew no Greek anyway. But he KNEW, even as I held up a finger which hung in the velvet air like a tendril of verbena.

Then Voluptia was there. She laid a hand over my ears, and whispered softly. I could not hear her. I gazed upon her dank lips, rubbed with old kisses, those obfuscating osculations suspended there, recalled on the instant she reappeared. That her words were endearments of love (L-O-V-E) I was sure. Then, with a brisk chattering snatch of laughter, she sat: as delicately as a mushroom on the green sward.

"Darley!" she whispered.

"Voluptia!" I murmured.

"Darley!" she said.

Then I noticed she had lost her nose! I stared spellbound at the hole like a fox's hide which lay gaping between her eyes. A long moment wound itself away; I knew she would tell me. "I've had a tiresome day," she began. Ali came in with my *krash*, and I signalled one for her in my second-best Greek. "First," she whispered, "let us drink to . . . love!" "Life!" I said.

She arranged herself into a pattern of Byzantine order, her clothes fighting for their colour with the grass. "I lost an ear this morning," she uttered at last. "Hamid cut it off in pique. Then the left eye Memlik dashed out at lunchtime, because I wouldn't take him on Mountolive's spider-shoot." But it was still the nose that took me by surprise. I looked at her, trying to fathom the labyrinths of her silence. What can I give you, I cogitated with myself, but sympathy? (As Pursewarden—the devil—wrote: TO ALL WHO SUFFER SHALL COME . . . SUFFERING.)

The heat popped and eddied in my eardrum; I watched lazily as a bead of sweat formed on the skin of my baggy, shapeless hand. "Let us make love," I outspake at last, "even on a punt, even on Mareotis, which by now must be the colour of gunmetal, the texture of boiled offal. Now!" I feared that she would feel unwanted.

"No," she responded, vivid in grass, "I must tell you the story, and without obfuscation. There are three versions so far, as many as there are

*Reprinted from *The Faber Book of Parodies*, ed. Simon Brett (London: Faber, 1984), 140–43. Originally published in *Who Do You Think You Are?* (London: Curtis Brown, 1976).

persons, and there might be more if we wait. If we have time to wait. You
see, it is so cruel, not really knowing WHY!"

"Yes," I muttered. My heart was drenched in brilliants of violet love.
But before she could even begin her first explanation, there was the sound
of footfalls, many footfalls. Scobie dashed in on us, his glass lips blubbering.
Behind, the soft-footed Ali beat out his lighter yet fundamentally arrogant
note. He stood protective as Scobie, disagreeably abnormal, spoke in a tot-
tering voice.

"Sorry, Darley," he said, avoiding looking directly at the nipples on
my chest, "but I've got to cart Voluptia off to chokey. She's been interfer-
ing down in the circumcision booths. There've been complaints."

Voluptia, to give her credit, resisted.

"YA SCOBIE," I yelled, "are you sure you're not under the influence?"
After a moment he nodded, closing his eyes. Then musingly he *loquitur*:
"Sometimes the mind strays further than life allows. It is easy to excuse,
but one's duty is in the end to judge. Alas, our pitiless city demands. . . ."

Voluptia rose. I glanced at her warningly. There was a terrible mêlée.
I became another person, utterly different from the person I'm usually talking to. In the frantic struggle, Scobie sweated, and Voluptia had her foot
pinned to the floor by a Bimbashi's dagger. I was aghast!

Then she had all her clothes pulled off. UNDERNEATH SHE WAS
DRESSED AS A MAN! "Voluptia!" Scobie cried out, his voice stark, nude.
"She eschews definition," he finally said. Voluptia, wax pale, moaned on
the note of a distant sirocco. Then she broke from Scobie's grip and her
lips touched my ankle. She murmured, brokenly, half a dozen lines from
Cavafy, their spirit untranslatable. Scobie watched and uttered: "Sex
speaks rapidly between unbridgeable cultures." Then Scobie took her, not
as a lawgiver takes a lawbreaker but as a dragoman leads a spirited horse.
"Allah be praised!" said Ali by dumb-sign as he left with his prisoner. Prisoner! (As Pursewarden writes: we are all prisoners.) I heard her go, soft-
footed to the last.

"Another Scythian *krash*," I signalled, my head askew on my shoulders. Mareotis grinned back at me under the puce moon. I felt almost sick.
Alexandria! Her voice came again from below, swept up on the hot airs of
the city. "*Chéri!*" she cried, and I could sense the vibration of those firm
slashing breasts, "We must all go back."

Sweaty, my tartan undershorts clung coldly to my alabaster thighs.
Again I was lonely. I wanted to press someone's elbow, but there was only
Ali; and after some thought I simply pressed my own. Outside smugglers
drove past in old cars; somewhere, over boxes of nougat, ambassadors still
wrangled. A smell of decay, the smell that goes indeed with perfection,
came up from the city. Excited, my nostrils quivered. For then it came to
me, throbbingly out of the desert, over Mareotis, over minaret and palm,
through the circumcision booths, through the pierced cheeks of the demon

dancers, straight as a glinting arrow through the musk and maze of what we think of as reality. As Pursewarden said: Love is a four-letter word! In a feeling of exultation, I rubbed my hands together, thankful that, despite the company I mixed with, I still had them to rub.

Tunc-Nunquam:
The Quest for Wholeness   Tone Rugset*

G.S. Fraser, in a chapter on the "Tunc-Nunquam Problem," confesses that "What I have failed to grasp, I suppose, or to grasp properly, is what he [Lawrence Durrell] has ultimately to say. . . ."[1] This statement strikes me as a fitting epitome of a bewildered *Tunc-Nunquam* criticism. It may also explain why *Tunc* and *Nunquam*, unlike *The Alexandria Quartet*, seems to have been avoided by literary critics.

After my first reading of *Tunc-Nunquam* I could not have been more in agreement with Fraser. I felt I was dealing with an animal refusing to lie down for dissection—changing appearances, always looking back at you with a new and different face. I was chasing *Tunc-Nunquam* like Charlock chases Julian, who refuses to manifest himself. This is what makes the structure of the books so important. It gives a clue to the "scattered utterances" on the verbal level, providing a framework for an overall interpretation. I shall here view *Tunc-Nunquam* as a triplex expression of the same underlying concept, more specifically the concept of wholeness, unity, harmony. This basic concept comes to the fore through three different derived concepts: the music of the spheres, the circle and the square, and the doctrine of opposites. Firmly rooted in the history of ideas, these are in fact three different versions of the quest for wholeness. Towards the end of this article I shall attempt to bring them together, and, drawing on Jung's theory of archetypes, offer an integrated interpretation of *Tunc-Nunquam*.

As I have suggested above, the structure of the books offers a convenient starting-point for an analysis. Just a glance is enough to discover that both books are divided into seven chapters. It is also easy to note that each chapter is subdivided into sections. What is not so obvious at first glance, however, is that these simple facts should give any indication of circular structure. But they do.

All in all *Tunc-Nunquam* consist of 14 chapters and 44 sections. If the 44 sections are divided by the fourteen chapters, the result is 3.14, in other words, π. The formula of the circumference of a circle is π multiplied by the diameter, which means that in this connection the 44 sections constitute the circumference and the 14 chapters the diameter. The result is an all-embracing circle, knitting *Tunc-Nunquam* together as a whole.

*Reprinted from *Labrys* (England) 5 (July 1979):155–62.

Durrell's construction in terms of π indicates a careful design, and this impression is confirmed when the structure of the narrative itself is subjected to closer scrutiny. By following Charlock from beginning to end, we can see a pattern emerging from his journeys. Besides, by using Charlock's memory as a structuring principle, Durrell echoes the π-notion with a circular structure in the narrative. We first meet Charlock in Athens, "off the map," where he is doing "a little occupational therapy in the form of these autobiographical notes" (T16). Going back in memory, he has a flashback to London just before [he] broke away, then he goes further back to the Athens of the days before he collided with the Firm. From Athens he goes to Turkey, and from there to London. From London he embarks on a journey to Athens, Turkey, and back to London. After a stay in London, he goes to Paris, back to London, and finally leaves for Athens, where we first met him. So the end is the beginning: the circle has been connected. In *Nunquam* he wakes up in Paulhaus, a mental hospital, and from there goes to Paris and London. From London he sets out on a new journey to Athens, Turkey, and back to London, where the narrative ends in St. Paul's. The connection between St. Paul's and Paulhaus connects the circle in *Nunquam*. Charlock even refers to St. Paul's as "this Paulhaus of ours" (N278). The result of this is that we are left with three circles,[2] one encompassing *Tunc-Nunquam* as a whole, and two smaller ones for the novels individually.

Circularity, however, is not the only structural indication of balance, symmetry and harmony. The places visited by Charlock in *Tunc* are counterbalanced by the places he visits in *Nunquam*. Events that take place *en route* do also correspond to each other on different sides of the axis. The symmetry starts with the London period of the wedding between Charlock and Benedicta. This is balanced on the *Nunquam* side by the London period culminating at St. Paul's, at Jocas' funeral, where both Julian and Iolanthe are killed. The counterbalancing points are made up by the beginning and end of Charlock's and Benedicta's nightmare, *Nunquam* ending up with harmony between them. The next counterbalancing points are the journeys, one a honeymoon resulting in pregnancy, one a "pilgrimage" to visit a dying man, Jocas, who unfolds to his friends the wisdom of the Eastern attitude towards death. The crucial points thus, are birth and death. Next follows a London period in both *Tunc* and *Nunquam*. One point of connection here is Iolanthe, who in *Tunc* opens the exhibition as a walking symbol of the mob-culture, and in *Nunquam* is built as an artefact of beauty. Finally, Paris in *Tunc* and Paris in *Nunquam* are connected in that the latter is a memory of the first.

It seems that the points on each side are balanced almost like counterpoints in music, and this impression of musical balance comes out clearer still if the structure of *Tunc-Nunquam* is compared to the Musica Mundana, or the music of the spheres—a Pythagorean concept belonging within the framework of the ancient universe. According to ancient tradition, the universe consisted of concentric spheres with the earth as their centre. Pythagoras developed the concept of the music of the spheres from an assumption that the musical intervals corresponded to those between the celestial bodies, thus reflecting the harmony of the cosmos. The notion of a divinely ordered universe was, of course, central both to the ancient and Renaissance mind. Man was seen as part of a greater whole, and his task was to imitate this harmony and order. This quest for harmony is precisely the structuring principle of *Tunc-Nunquam*.

The Pythagorean concept of harmony, described as concord in music, and as health in the human body and the body politic, derives from the doctrine of the fusion of opposites. This doctrine reflected a dualistic outlook, and the dualism could be overcome only by a fusion of opposites in the mean: wholeness arises out of a synthesis of opposite elements. In *Tunc-Nunquam* several features can be seen in this perspective. First, the books themselves seem to represent opposites: they balance each other as opposite sides of an equation. In fact they remind me of a psychiatric case report, *Tunc* representing the illness, *Nunquam* the cure. The characters in *Tunc* are strained, suffering from some kind of neurosis. Both Charlock and Benedicta are examples of this. In Charlock's case, *Tunc* culminates in a breakdown. He reappears in a mental hospital. As *Tunc* represents enigma, strain and frustration, so *Nunquam* represents explanations, relief and resolution of conflicts. Benedicta unfolds her childhood; when they come back to Athens, past mysteries are explained to Charlock, and Benedicta and Charlock go to Cathay to exorcise their memories. Charlock, who is desperately chasing Julian in *Tunc*, meets him in *Nunquam*: conflicts are resolved, and in the end Charlock takes over the Firm. To use Durrell's own words, "*Tunc* represents the questions and *Nunquam* the answers."[3]

The Persons are also opposites of each other; thus Charlock: "The two women, one dark, one graven fair; two brothers, one darkness and one light" (T15). Moreover, the positions are changed in *Nunquam*. The Benedicta of *Tunc* is different from the Benedicta of *Nunquam*. The same is true of Iolanthe, of course. And then there is the East-West polarity, embodied in Jocas and Julian respectively. It is significant, however, that all these polarities are dissolved into harmony in the end. Charlock's taking over the Firm brings unity between its east and west branches. Their respective representatives, Jocas and Julian, are dead: the "east" Jocas is buried in the "west" St. Paul's; the "west" Julian has agreed to be buried in the "east" family mausoleum. Out of the antitheses emerges the synthesis—embodied in Charlock.

Having thus established that *Tunc-Nunquam* consists of two opposite or antithetic circles embedded in an all-embracing circle, we may now go back to Musica Mundana, and look at its details. The Musica Mundana scale has 14 intervals; *Tunc-Nunquam* has 14 chapters. The fourteen intervals of Musica Mundana are circumscribed by a large circle, the Diapason. Embedded in this circle are two smaller circles, dividing the scale in two

halves. These two circles, the Diapason formalis and the Diapason ma-
terialis, express opposite concepts, just as do the two circles in *Tunc-
Nunquam*. Again, however, the point is that they are united or synthesised
in the larger circle to form a harmonic whole.

In *The Big Supposer* Durrell relates the Pythagorean concept of health
and wholeness to the concept of the circle and the square: "One must try
to fit the rectangle inside the square, which represents health in the Pythagorean sense. Health equals balance."[4] The problem of squaring the circle
was well-known in the Renaissance, as shown, for example, by Don Parry
Norford in his article on "holy mathematics."[5] The circle represents the
conceptual world of unified perfection, whereas the square represents the
material world. So the problem of squaring the circle is essentially a "geometrical formulation of the incongruity between the world of concept and
the world of matter."[6] The concept of the circle and the square and what
they emblematised was carried over into human geometry. The reason
must obviously be sought in the Renaissance view of man as a microcosm,
a "compendium of creation," as Heniger puts it.[7] Thus man epitomises the
incongruity between the conceptual and the material world, "serving as
nexus between the world of spirits and the world of matter."[8] Man was thus
standing in the middle, being the place where the two worlds meet. On
the basis of this, a geometry of the human body was set up, showing its
symmetry and proportion. The *locus classicus* for this doctrine was Vitrivius in his treatise *De architectura*. Norford refers to a famous Vitrivian figure, stating that ". . . when the figure is considered in relation to the circle, his navel is the centre of the diagram; but when considered in relation
to the square, his sexual organs become the centre."[9] It is interesting to
note that the same Vitrivius is also cited by Durrell in the words of Caradoc, in his speech on the Parthenon: "Now Vitrivius, in common with the
whole of classical opinion, describes the navel as the central point of the
human body. For my part the argument that the genital organ forms
the real centre has more appeal to one who has always kept a stiff prick in
an east wind" (T75). This is not the only place Caradoc refers to Vitrivius.
In the same speech he describes how human proportions were built into
the Doric and Ionian columns. According to Caradoc it is Vitrivius who has
told us this story (T73). Later in the speech Caradoc talks about the shanty
towns growing up in Athens: "Though they are unplanned in our sense of
the word these settlements are completely homogenous and appropriate to
their sites and I shall be sorry to see them vanish. They have the perfection
of organism, not of system" (T77).

According to Durrell himself, the rectangle is the system and the circle the organism.[10] In other words, "these shanty towns" have the perfection of the circle, not of the rectangle. Caradoc says in his speech that all
cities were built in his mother's image, and continues: "They have no more
than the four gates necessary to symbolise integration. The quaternary of
resolved conflicts—even though it is harder to construct creatively upon a

rectangle than upon the free flow of curve or ellipse!" (T72). The rectangle and other geometrical figures, such as the circle, are known as archetypes of integration and wholeness, which brings us to Jung's theory of archetypes. This theory is closely connected with the alchemical tradition, where the squaring of the circle is seen as the fusion of opposites—effected by a Mediator. In *Tunc-Nunquam* there are several implicit and explicit references to alchemy. The incestuous relation between Benedicta and Julian, between brother and sister, is connected with alchemy, and Julian is seen as a Black Prince treading the black path with an urge to know. The fusion of opposites, the alchemist's quest for the lapis Philosophorum is a quest for wholeness—or a quest for "self," in Jungian terms. In the foreword of his *Mysterium Coniunctionis*, Jung states that for the alchemist "there was first of all an initial state in which opposite tendencies or forces were in conflict; secondly there was the great question of a procedure which would be capable of bringing the hostile elements, once they were separated, back to unity again."[11] Jung goes on to draw a parallel to the psychic sphere, the therapist being the one who is supposed to bring the opposites to a unity. "The images of the goal which then appear in dreams often run parallel with the corresponding alchemical symbols."[12] More specifically, Jung points out that a *lapis*, or a stone, often appears in dreams as a symbol of the self.

In Jung's psychological terms the Self is the centre where the conscious and the unconscious unite. The experience of the Self is archetypal. As pointed out above, its images often appear in dreams in the form of alchemical symbols. More specifically, such archetypes of the Self often take the form of something that is hard to achieve, so that the achievement involves a quest. Frieda Fordham describes it as unconsciously "seeking a goal, which eventually defined itself as the quest for wholeness—that mysterious entity 'the whole man'—and which necessitated the forging of a link between the conscious and the unconscious aspects of the psyche."[13] Among these various archetypes, then, are geometrical figures—mandalas—such as the circle and the square. It is, by the way, interesting to note that mandala, which simply means "magic circle," is hinted at by Durrell at the end of *Nunquam*, when Charlock "kills" Iolanthe: "I crawled into the magic circle she was tracing with that lovely body of hers . . ." (N281–82). Furthermore, mandala may also be a dance, and at the very end of *Nunquam* Benedicta and Charlock ". . . have been dancing, dancing in complete happiness and accord. And it will keep on this way even though Rome burn" (N283). This, then, is another expression of harmony and concord. In Jungian terms *Tunc-Nunquam* represents a quest for wholeness, a struggle to integrate contradictory elements, both on the personal and cultural level. The quest theme, moreover, is underlined by the numerous allusions to the Legend of the Holy Grail. Durrell himself has said that *Tunc-Nunquam* is a struggle for happiness,[14] which, I am tempted to add, is a consequence of achieved wholeness.

It is evident that Durrell has been strongly influenced by Jung. In fact, Durrell has mentioned Jung among those who have biased his thinking.[15] It is a well known fact that Jung was preoccupied with the spiritual poverty of Western civilisation, which lacks the more profound wisdom of the East. Durrell is obviously thinking along the same line. Charlock's role is that of the Mediator, reconciling and integrating East and West. In Durrell's own words, we are caught between the circle and the square, we need them both: "The struggle for our culture is played out between the two forms. And the tragedy is that we need them both. We are caught."[16] I take this to mean that we need the riches both of the East and the West: the West has to integrate the wisdom of the East to become fertile. The same is true on the personal level, East and West here symbolising the unconscious and conscious aspects of the psyche. It is a question of integrating the unconscious, of coming to terms, to become the whole man. Charlock realises that he cannot escape the Firm. He becomes the leader of it, integrating it. In short, he comes to embody the Self.

Seen in this perspective, *Tunc-Nunquam* is an expression of the human predicament in general. Man is in a constant dilemma, torn between the "eastern" and "western" aspects of his psyche and culture. Western culture as we know it is biased in the direction of excessive intellectualism. This has created a spiritual crisis providing fertile soil for a different bias: that towards oriental mysticism and the occult. However, man cannot choose between these two spheres. Neither of them are self-contained. His only hope lies in uniting them, integrating them into a personal and cultural Self:

> One cannot simply abandon the intellect and all the riches that we have amassed throughout history. That would be absurd. On the other hand there is always the threat of an excess of intellectualism. We must add something better than second-rate mysticism; I don't know what. This is a thing that inevitably happens: once a civilisation begins to secrete too much intelligence, you find the same sort of lunatics springing up as you had in the Middle Ages. I am against that, too. Man requires nourishment for both sides of his nature.[17]

Thus, the goal of Durrell's "struggle for happiness," is Wholeness.

Notes

1. G.S. Fraser, *Lawrence Durrell: A Study* (1973), p. 167.

2. The concept of the circle is of further significance in *Tunc-Nunquam*. First, there are more indicators of circularity than those mentioned here. Secondly, the circles point to central elements in the works simply by the location of their centres. The details of this fall outside this essay's scope.

3. Lawrence Durrell, *The Big Supposer: A Dialogue with Marc Alyn*, p. 135.

4. *Big Supposer*, p. 42.

5. Don Parry Norford, "Marvell's Holy Mathematicks," *Modern Language Quarterly*, 38, no. 3 (1977), pp. 242–261.

6. S.K. Heniger, *Touches of Sweet Harmony: Pythagorean Cosmology and Renaissance Poetics* (1974), p. 111. Quoted by Norford, p. 242.

7. Heniger, p. 191.

8. Heniger, p. 191.

9. Heniger, p. 142, note 93. Quoted by Norford, p. 243.

10. *Big Supposer*, p. 42.

11. C.G. Jung, *Mysterium Coniunctionis*, 2nd ed. (1970), p. xiv.

12. Jung, p. xv.

13. Frieda Fordham, *An Introduction to Jung's Psychology* (1972), p. 76.

14. *Big Supposer*, p. 137.

15. Lawrence Durrell, *A Key to Modern British Poetry* (Oklahoma 1970), p. xii.

16. *Big Supposer*, p. 42.

17. *Big Supposer*, p. 42.

The Counterlife of Heresy   Reed Way Dasenbrock*

Lawrence Durrell has never suppressed the presence of death in the world of his fiction. The "living English death" of *The Black Book* (1938), the natural disaster in *The Dark Labyrinth* (1947), the political violence in *White Eagles over Serbia* (1957), and the deaths and dismemberments that punctuate *The Alexandria Quartet* (1957–60) underscore this. But in Durrell's late fiction this concern with death has deepened and become a significant theme in its own right. The aim of this essay is to consider the theme of death in some of Durrell's recent fiction, particularly in the second part of *The Revolt of Aphrodite*, *Nunquam* (1970), and *Monsieur* (1974), the first novel in a projected "quincunx" of which three volumes have been published, *Monsieur, Livia, or Buried Alive* (1978), and *Constance* (1982).

Akkad, Durrell's gnostic spokesman in *Monsieur*, reminds us that "death sets in with conception."[1] This truth may be unpalatable but it is also irrefutable, and characters in Durrell's late fiction reveal a great deal—everything, really—about themselves according to how they respond to this truth. The plot of *Nunquam* revolves around an attempt by Julian and his firm Merlin to deny the inevitability of death. Julian has become obsessed with the image of a dead film star, Iolanthe, who in *Tunc* (the first novel in *The Revolt of Aphrodite*) was the lover of Julian's brother-in-law Felix, the inventor. Julian's obsession leads him to devote Merlin's resources to

---

*This essay was originally published as "Death and the Counterlife of Heresy in Wyndham Lewis and Lawrence Durrell" in *Deus Loci: Proceedings of the First National Lawrence Durrell Conference* 5, no. 1 (25 April 1980):306–27. It has been revised by the author specifically for this volume.

the creation of a new Iolanthe, a mechanical imitation of the dead Iolanthe. This new being has been given all of Iolanthe's memories so that she is unaware that she is not Iolanthe, and she is so perfect a simulacrum that even Felix and Julian on occasion lose their awareness that she isn't Iolanthe.

Of course, this raises a question: what is the difference between Iolanthe and Iolanthe? (Durrell is cunning in the way he prevents us from distinguishing them verbally.) Durrell is pushed to the conclusion that there is none, for all practical purposes. The robot is as lifelike as the rest of us: Iolanthe is a perfect imitation of a human, and most humans are perfect imitations of robots. As Felix says to Julian,

> "But Marchant [Felix's collaborator on the project] insists they are so perfectly adapted from the point of view of responses that they could, according to him, be turned loose in the real world without danger of being discovered for what they are."
>
> "Why not, Felix? They will probably be more real than most of the people we know."[2]

Marchant himself makes this point in more explicitly political terms: "While society is happily creating a slave class of analphabetics, 'les visuels,' who have forgotten how to read and who depend upon a set of Pavlovian signals for their daily bread and other psychic needs—surely we have the right to build a model which will be at least as 'human' as these so-called human beings? . . . What is to prevent her taking her place with all the other dummies and pushing a lever for her living, her Pavlovian living?" (N, 128–29). And in fact this dummy would probably not pass as human if those she is designed to resemble were themselves less like dummies. "We've photocopied the daily life of about twenty women to work out the range of situation responses for Iolanthe. It's really amazing how monotonous the ordinary range of movements, conversations, stock responses, can be" (N 131).

Felix alone seems disturbed by the project and what it reveals about man and society. He warns Marchant at one point that Iolanthe's successful "resurrection" has potentially explosive implications: "It's quite a consideration if the things you make get up off the operating table and start being MORE real than you? You will be forced to reassess your . . . dirty word . . . culture?" (N 141; Durrell's emphasis and ellipses). Not long after Felix's warning, Iolanthe does get up and start being more real than anyone else. She escapes from the control of the firm Merlin in a parallel to earlier flights from Merlin's control in *Tunc*. But her flight is much more resolute than Felix's or Caradoc's in *Tunc*. She is truly more human, more uncontrollable and spontaneous, than the humans.

Further ironies result from the fact that the mechanical imitation of the dead Iolanthe is more alive than her creators. After her escape, she is tracked down in St. Paul's, and in a macabre scene she tries to "kill herself." Julian falls to his death attempting to save her, but after her fall she is still live electrically—if not fully alive in the sense she had been before—so Felix has to stab her. Iolanthe's second life ends in a second death. Thus, Julian's attempt to cheat death, to turn the clock back to the time when Iolanthe was alive, is ultimately a failure, and it is fitting that it is Iolanthe herself who brings the fact of death home to Julian. One can delay one's recognition of the fact of death, but it cannot be denied.

Yet for a long time Julian's attempt to cheat death succeeds and its relative success, more interesting than its ultimate failure, shows up the opposition between life and death we take for granted as something less than absolute. This life that Julian wants to perpetuate—how much of a life is it? Iolanthe can pass as alive, though she is dead (or has no life in her), because everyone else in the world of the novel is essentially dead, though unaware of the fact. Julian, the character most fascinated by Iolanthe, is called a mummy by Felix (N 141), and Julian himself confesses at one point to feeling only vicariously alive (N 151). Marchant informs us in a marvellous detail that embalming has become the rage among the avant-garde in Paris: "They don't really want to live, the young. They want to be embalmed so that they can impress their friends" (N 132).

The world of *Nunquam*, thus, is a world of living death, and in exposing everyone's deadness the project of Iolanthe can be seen as a kind of protest against that living death. But if a protest, it is a protest of the wrong kind, a futile holding action that does not strike at the root of the problem. It is as futile as embalming, as helpless a protest against death and decay. Appropriately, Merlin is also involved in the embalming business. Felix and Marchant spend a good deal of time in the studio of the master embalmer Goytz (N 167), as they find that there is an "affinity of attitude" (N 177) between his work and their own.

The affinity lies, as Felix says, in their "attitude toward Beauty" (N 177). Both embalming and the construction of Iolanthe are characterized by a certain aesthetic attitude, which is that the artistic ideal is to approach life as closely as possible. The beautiful is the lifelike. Goytz himself compares the problem of his art, as he calls it, to that of portraiture, and he cites Singer Sargent as his authority (N 177). In its lifelikeness, a Sargent portrait is about as far from one of Goytz's corpses as a corpse is from Iolanthe, but all exemplify an aesthetic of imitation. Furthermore, each of these imitations arises from a desire like Julian's to cheat death. The notion that art serves as a defense against death, a protection against the encroachments of time, is familiar to us from Shakespeare's *Sonnets* and Keats's *Ode on a Grecian Urn*. And the artistic tradition of the West arises out of Egyptian culture's attempt to deny death: portraiture originally had a very close relation to mummification. Both are (or have often been presented as) attempts to make man survive death, to deny the passage of time. Iolanthe's construction represents the triumph of this conception of art as a defense against death. But such a triumph also puts this aesthetic into question:

what is the point of laboriously reproducing human appearances in a work of art if engineers can manufacture things that look and behave just like human beings? Who needs a portrait of someone if after she dies she can be "reborn" again?

So the value of art as well as the value of life is put into question by Iolanthe's construction. What is the point of living if a machine can do just as well? What is the point of art if engineers can do better? But it is important to recognize that what is being questioned is a kind of life and a kind of art: Durrell is not rejecting (or suggesting that we reject) life and art; he is questioning what we have come to regard as art and life. We have already seen Felix speaking of how the existence of Iolanthe should force a reassessment of culture (of what it means to be human), and the contrast between the alive robot Iolanthe and all of the (living) dead around her forces Felix at least to that reassessment of which he speaks.

Of course, Felix's reassessment is also Durrell's, and the scope of Durrell's reassessment is far clearer in *Monsieur* (1974), Durrell's next novel after *Nunquam*. In *Monsieur*, a way of being in the world and a way of making art are sketched which revolt against the living death of *The Revolt of Aphrodite* in the right way, not in the doomed way attempted by Julian. It is of course Iolanthe's ultimately unsuccessful revolt, her spontaneous escape from Merlin's control, that gives *The Revolt of Aphrodite* its title. And the path of revolt found in *Monsieur*, though not exactly that of Aphrodite, has some common features with Iolanthe's revolt. If one needs a label for that path, the label one finds in *Monsieur* is gnosticism. *Monsieur* does warn us that it is not a gnostic tract; as Pia says, "If one really deeply believes something one shuts up and never dares to speak of it" (*M* 225). But readers of *Monsieur* should understand and be prepared to entertain the gnostic vision (as Durrell presents it) and its stance towards the world.[3]

According to that vision, the world is under the domination of evil, the spirit of matter. The gnostic feels a "sense of inner estrangement and alienation from the so-called real world" (*M* 137). Deeming that world a facade that must be seen through and punctured, the gnostic voluntarily chooses death to expose ordinary life as worse than death. The world is a great lie that the gnostics refuse to accept; instead, they make what Akkad calls "the great refusal," the refusal of this life under the rule of Monsieur, the Prince of Darkness. This leaves one only with death, but death is as debased and in need of redemption as life: "The key to the whole [gnostic] stance was the redeeming of death. . . . Today death is a limbo peopled by the living" (*M* 224).

Hence, gnosticism is a total and uncompromising rejection of the conditions of existence. The role of the gnostic, as Akkad says, "is to hold the pass, to fight a Thermopylae of the psyche" (*M* 224). By facing the truth about the world, the gnostic tries to live a counterlife (*M* 196), totally against the grain. This permanently antagonistic and heretical stance distinguishes it from Platonism and other forms of philosophic Idealism. The world is a facade, but one to be resisted, not transcended, or more precisely to be transcended through resistance. Gnosticism sets itself against all forms of orthodoxy: religious, sexual, and political. The world has been usurped, and heresy is the only appropriate response.

This notion of an heretical counterlife is at the center of *Monsieur*, but the difficulty of being a heretic in our century is worth a moment's reflection. The orthodoxies of the present are not religious but social and political ideologies. Julian Benda argues in *La Trahison des clercs* (1927) that it was the natural role of the intellectuals to be heretics, to oppose all forms of orthodoxy, though contemporary intellectuals were castigated by Benda for not living up to the role he had assigned them. Artists have been more enduring and persistent heretics in the modern era, and Renato Poggioli has argued that an antagonistic stance (or moment, as he calls it) has been the basic attitude of the modern artist. It certainly needs no documentation that modern writers have tended to be antagonistic toward both the past (or tradition) and the public, and Poggioli argues that these "two antagonisms are merely complementary forms of the same opposition to the historical and social order."[4] Such a stance is not revolutionary, as it does not seek to replace the old order with a new and different order. It is instead a stance of permanent opposition, *a rebours*, which resembles what Durrell calls the counterlife of gnosticism in its free choice of and deep commitment to heresy. It has even been suggested, by Kenneth Cox, that the "modern or modernist movement in art, which arose in France about the middle of the nineteenth century and is now in its last throes, may be seen as a recrudescence of gnosticism."[5]

I doubt if this claim could be substantiated, nor need it be for my purposes. A reasonable analogy between the modern artist and the gnostic suffices to bring together the two themes of *Monsieur*, gnosticism and the art of fiction, which seem to compete for our attention. Durrell himself seems to be working with such an analogy, as the novel's oscillation between the themes of heresy and art finally serves to link the two. Artists and gnostics alike are heretics whose heresy is the acceptance of death, though neither commits suicide: they kill their friends instead, though the artist murders only vicariously through the agency of his art.

Monsieur begins with the death of Piers, and the first part, "Outremer," is his brother-in-law Bruce's rather anguished narrative of the aftermath of this death which he cannot comprehend. The fundamental movement in this chapter is Bruce's slow realization that Piers is indeed dead, and it closes with the arrival of the death-mask. With Piers transformed into art, Bruce then tries to explain that death, which he does by going *outre-mer*, to Egypt, and narrating his and Piers's exposure to gnosticism there. For it seems as if Piers may have chosen to die because of his involvement in a gnostic cult.

"Macabru," part two, is concerned primarily with Akkad, who introduced Piers, Bruce, and his wife Sylvie to gnosticism, and his exposition of the gnostic heresy to them. But at the end it turns back first to Bruce and his struggles in writing this story down, and then to his brother-in-law, the novelist Rob Sutcliffe, and Sutcliffe's struggles in his last novel, which survives only in notebooks. Part of Sytcliffes problem, as he obliquely indicates in the story of Tobor the poet (*M* 279), is that, instead of dying and turning into art, his wife simply left him. We have already heard of these notebooks, in "Outremer," and of his novel about Piers, Bruce, and Sylvie, which Bruce has quoted as a source. But now Sutcliffe dominates the novel and, in the third part, "Sutcliffe, the Venetian Documents," he seems to be writing the earlier part of the novel. He composes the first paragraph (*M* 193) and summarizes the plot (*M* 195), even though he is dead by the time of the beginning of the novel. From this point on, the novels within the novel proliferate inordinately and confusingly, while summaries of the story of Piers, Bruce, and Sylvie return us periodically to more material on gnosticism and Akkad.

"Life with Toby," the next section, moves forward to the time of the novel's opening, and Sutcliffe's narration in the previous section is revealed to be what Bruce is reading in Avignon after Piers's death while living with Sutcliffe's friend Toby. Bruce is reading, sifting, and deciphering these documents in an attempt to get to the bottom of Piers's death. Toby is also working with documents, continuing his life-long investigation into the mystery of the Templars. As the first famous ancestor of Piers and Sylvie was involved in the downfall of the Templars, Toby's interpretive labor is curiously parallel to Bruce's. One is studying the appearance of the family, the other its disappearance. The theme of deciphering texts and mysteries which dominates this section of *Monsieur* contributes to the novel a sense that everything must be scrutinized, as all appearances are misleading and the truth of any matter is obscure. But texts and heresies need the most deciphering, and Toby, the model historian, thinks that by stripping away illusory facades he has discovered the truth about the Templars, which is (naturally) that they were gnostics. The end of *Monsieur* is such a stripping away: "Dinner at Quartilla's" reveals all that has come before to be part of a novel written by Aubrey Blanford. Then, in the "Envoi," Durrell steps in and acknowledges Blanford as *his* creation.

But this stripping away and "truth-telling" should be distinguished from the truth of gnosticism and art, which read everything antagonistically and heretically. One never gets to the bottom of anything, but only chooses out of fatigue to stop at something which one calls the bottom, though it is surely a false one. Nothing demonstrates this more clearly than Akkad's ceremony of initiation which Piers, Bruce, and Sylvie undergo. Afterwards, Akkad makes sure that Piers sees an article exposing the initiation as a fake. But this, too, is a fake, as Akkad reveals in turn. Then, when Piers's belief in the initiation is restored, Akkad points out that the article is correct in some respects and that the initiation would not really stand up to critical scrutiny.

Akkad's initiation is a lie and the very fact that it is a lie helps one to realize the truth, which is that the acceptance of any ordering or system of explanation, even a heretical one, produces the fatal quiescence of orthodoxy. Akkad's disturbance of Piers's easy acceptance of his initiation into gnosticism is, therefore, Piers's real initiation into gnosticism; what Akkad tells Piers at that point deserves extended quotation: "You see quite clearly that the stability of the gnostic universe is quite inadvertent; the conformity of matter to models or modes is very precarious and not subject to causality as they imagine. Once this dawns on you the notion of death is born and gathers force so that you start, not to live according to a prearranged plan or model, but to *improvise*. It is another sort of existence, at once extremely precarious, vertiginous, hesitant—but truthful in a way that you never thought you could be" (*M* 168).

At the end of *Nunquam*, inspired by the spontaneity showed by Iolanthe, Felix has grasped the same idea, and his projected burning of all of Merlin's contracts is a truly gnostic act of improvisation. The gnostic acceptance of death, therefore, is above all a way to challenge and transform life, our lives, as death is the only guarantor of change, the best goad to complacency. If we live with a full awareness of death, we will not settle into the static and unchanging patterns that can turn life into a living death. Art, too, has a role to play in this acceptance of death: great art never conforms to a model, but is a precarious but truthful improvisation. New art always questions and subverts the pre-existing order of art, yet it knows that in turn it will be questioned and subverted.

But this causes problems for the artist, whose work is an ordering, even if a re-ordering. Bruce defines this dilemma succinctly: "It has done me good to put so much down on paper, though I notice that in the very act of recording things one makes them submit to a kind of ordering which may be false, proceeding as if causality was the real culprit" (*M* 173). The real culprit, however, is not causality but the acceptance of any single causal explanation, the belief that any ordering is solid and true. The process of reading *Monsieur* is a continuous dislocation of such assumptions. The reader cannot settle into the quiescence of an orderly, orthodox reading, for he remains in a state of confusion as to what this novel is really about, when it takes place (if it does take place), and who ultimately is telling the story. Durrell plays with our belief in the reality of what is being narrated just as Akkad plays with Piers's belief in his own initiation. And this constitutes our initiation into the counterlife of art, a creative improvisation which refuses the world even as it redeems it. One never knows where one is in *Monsieur*, and that is the right place to be.

Notes

1. Lawrence Durrell, *Monsieur* (New York: Viking, 1975), p. 143. All subsequent citations will be incorporated parenthetically in this form: (*M* 143).

2. Lawrence Durrell, *Nunquam* (New York: Dutton, 1970), p. 155. All subsequent citations will be incorporated parenthetically in this form: (*N* 155).

3. I should point out here that I have not been concerned in this essay with the accuracy of Durrell's presentation of gnosticism, with the relationship between Durrell's gnosticism and the historical phenomenon of gnosticism. For a study of this question, see James P. Carley, "Lawrence Durrell's Avignon Quincunx and Gnostic Heresy," *Malahat Review* 61 (1982), 156–67.

4. Renato Poggioli, *The Theory of the Avant-Garde*, trans. Gerard Fitzgerald (Cambridge, Mass.: Harvard University Press, 1968), p. 30.

5. Kenneth Cox, "Dualism and les autres," *Agenda* 7, No. 3–8, no. 1 (Autumn-Winter 1969–1970), 136.

The Avignon Quintet and Gnostic Heresy

James P. Carley*

Throughout his fiction Lawrence Durrell has shown an interest in mystical and heretical traditions; it is not surprising, therefore, that gnostic themes become articulated as one of the principal motifs in his new *Avignon Quintet*. On the most obvious level, Durrell shares with the gnostic writers a fascination with evocative and recondite language; he uses gnostic terminology as a means of capturing the decadent medieval feel of Avignon and the overbred heretical temperament of his characters. For Durrell, as for the gnostics, traditional symbols are constantly, and sometimes literally, reversed: the epigram prefacing *Livia*—"In the name of the Dog the Father, Dog the Son, and Dog the Wholly Ghost, Amen"—is immediately relevant to the theory and spirit of gnosticism. Like the gnostics, moreover, Durrell shows a metaphysical interest in the structure of the *word*. The gnostic systems all visualize a hierarchical universe whose workings are understood only through a complex arcane verbal knowledge. Both *The Alexandria Quartet* and *The Avignon Quintet* take physical models of the universe and explore their linguistic ramifications: in each series, the form is a logical—or at least psychological and philosophical—manifestation of contemporary theories of knowledge.

Monsieur, the first volume in the *Quintet*, is—as Durrell pointed out when he first completed it—"a sketch for a city that I haven't built yet. It's a ground plan. . . . The first volume itself is a terrible muddle because it's got all the themes in it, it's an old suitcase full of all themes I intend to develop."[1] As such, it plays a key role in the *Quintet*; the gnostic themes it sets out will reverberate through the remaining four books. *Monsieur*, as Blanford (the "author" and presumably Durrell's own persona) calls the book, or *The Prince of Darkness*, as Sutcliffe (Blanford's created voice and

*This essay was written specifically for this volume and is published here for the first time by permission of the author.

alter ego) calls it, takes its very title from the name of the usurping ruler of our world, the creator of the blind mechanistic Darwinian structure which is generally perceived as reality. According to gnostic doctrine, as Durrell interprets it, the created world is a giant trap, attractive on the outside, but in fact evil, corrupt, and, on closer inspection, self-devouring. As the Judeo-Christian tradition asserts, this world is the result of a Fall. The gnostics, however, disagree radically about the origin and consequences of this Fall. According to the orthodox version, God first created the world and, as Genesis relates, saw that it was good. Through the proddings of Lucifer, the Serpent, Eve ate fruit from the Tree of Knowledge and persuaded Adam to do the same. This led to the Fall from Grace and brought death into the world. The gnostic doctrines violently repudiate this cosmology. This world in its state of stinking corruption could never have been good; it must be the result of an earlier and more dramatic fall. Our world is not the perverted image of something formerly perfect; it is itself the manifestation of an earlier imperfection. Originally, so the Ophites claim, there was only the Supreme One, unfathomable and inscrutable in nature; he was known as *Bythos* or "The Primal Man": "The Beginning of Creation . . . was the 'thought' *Ennoia*, of Bythos, who also bears the significant name of *Sige*, 'Silence.' Ennoia is the consort . . . of Bythos, and she produced *Pneuma*, 'the Spirit,' who . . . is entitled . . . *Sophia*. . . . Sophia produced two new Emanations—the one perfect, *Christos*, the other imperfect, *Sophia-Achamoth*."[2] Later, Achamoth's son *Ildabaoth* (known to the uninitiated as Jehovah of the Old Testament),[3] prompted by ambition and pride, "fell" and then created the lower world and man. His mother took pity on man and intermingled Divine Light with his lower form; but this enraged Ildabaoth, the Demiurgus, who in revenge created the viciously imperfect kingdoms of Nature—that is the Animal, the Vegetable, and the Mineral worlds. Ildabaoth also glanced at his own image in the abyss and it came to life as *Ophiomorphos*, the embodiment of evil and cunning.[4] To keep man confined and to separate him from Achamoth, Ildabaoth forbade man to eat of the Tree of Knowledge. Achamoth then sent Ophis, the serpent, to persuade man to break this prohibition. The first pair listened to Ophis and disobeyed the command; in fury Ildabaoth then shut them in the prison-house of matter, that is the body. Ophis was also contaminated by matter and was converted into the exact image of Ophiomorphos, and produced an antitype of his former self (and also, as it happens, the third dualism in the course of creation). In his new form Ophis has joined with Ildabaoth and his son and is continually seeking to chain man to the body with all kinds of corrupt desires and ambitions. Man's only hope of redemption lies in an increased consciousness of his nakedness, that is of the misery of his imprisonment in the charnel house of the body and Ildabaoth's world.

The pre-Edenic world was one of bliss, a world of pure spirit; Akkad describes it as "a sort of nougat-land." Ildabaoth's machinations, however, have brought about a shift "which pushed the balance over from the domain of spirit into matter. Hints of this can be traced in the old mythologies. The whole axis of the human sensibility was altered—as if somewhere out of sight an Ice Cap had melted."[5] As a result, human consciousness has been permanently traumatized; as Blanford puts it, "our whole civilization could be seen as a tremendous psychic mishap."[6] The most fundamental and dire consequence of the shift has been the awareness of, and therefore submission to, the concept of dualism, which now pervades every aspect of our world. The philosophical and psychological problems of dualism are insoluble and catastrophic; they lead to a completely destructive either / or bind. In the matter / spirit struggle, moreover, the Judeo-Christian system has committed itself to matter (which is actually illusory according to the gnostics); as a result man has become subject to death—matter automatically decays through time—and civilisation has been impelled forward by an ever accelerating death drift:

> The presiding demon is the spirit of matter, and he springs fully armed from the head of classical Judaism of which all European religions are tributaries. The Prince is usury, the spirit of gain, the enigmatic power of capital value embodied in the poetry of gold, or specie, or scrip. . . . Jesus, like so many Jews, belongs to our persuasion. . . . His end was poetic and not theological; the cosmogony from which his spirit issued was not one of the four Ms—which characterise our own age with such a great depth of focus. I mean Monotheism, Messianism, Monogamy, and Materialism. But you can illustrate this simple thesis at every level— whether you take Marx's great analysis of our culture or the Freudian analysis of absolute value as based upon infantile attitudes to excrement. Gold and excrement, that is poetic indeed![7]

Through a pernicious anti-alchemy brought about by the materialist Midas touch of Jehovah's teaching, excrement has replaced the philosophic (that is, spiritual) gold as a cultural value; blood has supplanted sperm.

The formulation of a theory of an individual ego (which entails the concept of death on a personal level as an unspeakable but inevitable calamity) is also a consequence of Jehovah's plan: "It's a sign of our intellectual abjectness that psychology with its miserly physical categories and positivist bias should prove liberating and enriching as it does. . . . The real seed of the neurosis is the belief in the discrete ego; as fast as you cure 'em the contemporary metaphysic which is Judeo-Christianity manufactures more I's to become sick Me's."[8] Freud is, of course, the immediate villain in this particular sham, but the origin of this concept dates back to Aristotle and his unquenchable need to "name parts": "The day when Aristotle decided (malgré lui) that the reign of the magician-shaman was over (Empedocles), was the soul's D-Day. The paths of the mind had become over-grown. From that moment the hunt for the measurable certainties was on. Death became a constant, the ego was born."[9] To distinguish individual entities and name them one by one, the agent has first to exist separately as "I," clearly and distinctly autonomous in selfhood.

In Jehovah's scheme, then, the individual and society are both doomed. What, however, about the world in which they live? Here, too, the outlook is grim. Presumably the universe is a closed system and is, therefore, subject to the laws of entropy, that is, to a constant and irreversible process of dying, or more precisely of disintegration into inert waste. In the late nineteenth century Henry Adams pointed out that higher powers of energy tended to fill lower and that "all nature's energies were slowly converting themselves into heat and vanishing in space, until, at the last, nothing would be left except a dead ocean of energy at its lowest possible level . . . incapable of doing any work whatever."[10] In the face of this phenomenon, which permeates the world of communication as well as the material world, what should we do? Or, as the character Schwarz asks Constance: "To what extent have we the right to interfere with the principle of entropy, the cosmic submission which subsumes everything—the death-drift of the world?"[11]

For the Gnostic, as for the modern existentialist with whom on the surface he would appear to have little in common, there is a way out of the above series of deadends.[12] The first step involves a conscious awareness of personal alienation, which comes only through careful scrutiny of the allurements of the so-called real world: "As for man—we are protected from the full consciousness of our own natures—and consequently from that of the real world—by a hard scaly integument, a sort of cataract, a lamination covering the actual soul. It is a coating of rubberoid hardness, difficult if not impossible to pierce. It insulates us against reality, this skin. Hence unless we make a special effort we can only see the truth indistinctly—as we see the sun, through smoked glass."[13] Awareness leads inevitably to the refus, an unconditional refusal to accept the terms of life as they are offered in Jehovah's world: "The poets have shown us the way. For those, in every age, who feel the deeply humiliating condition of man and nourish any hope, I won't say of ever changing it, but even ameliorating it . . . they sense the great refusal as necessary. . . ."[14] Naturally the refusal ultimately raises the question of suicide, which acts as a release for the soul (a spiritual entity trapped in matter's grip) from the material world and from the mechanistic laws of Jehovah's universe. Death, moreover, can be seen as a positive, expanding, even creative, factor: "The basic fear which drives us towards an insight into ourselves or an enquiry into the world around us is death; the irreversibility of process, the lunge towards dissolution, towards rotting and melting."[15] Nevertheless, death must be made conscious and articulated; suicide for the initiate becomes both an acte gratuit (and therefore a free act of defiance) and a calculated step. The suicide cult in *The Avignon Quintet* is conscious improvisation. It is a matter of chance selection since the name of the next initiate to be killed is chosen randomly; the "victim," however, receives a letter telling him to prepare for his imminent death and therefore he has the opportunity to make his end conscious and calculated as well as random and contingent. It becomes a moment of heightened consciousness, of revelation: "What really dies is the collective image of the past—all the temporal selves which have been present in a serial form focused together now in an instant of perfect attention, of crystal-clear apprehension which could last forever if one wished."[16] In the suicide pact lies an acceptance of the ultimate meaningful rhythm of nature: that by an active espousal of chance and coincidence one places oneself into the workings of a higher order. What the gnostics perceive of this pattern, what Jung in another context calls acausal orderedness, also accounts for the meaningful coincidence of the I Ching, of astrology, and of alchemy.[17]

Suicide, for the initiate, is a poetic act: a return to wholeness and an actualization of all the threads of one's past. Moreover, in refusing, in dying, one participates in the redemption of nature. One defeats entropy.[18] The ultimate and transcendent meaning of nature in this context lies in a rediscovery of, or re-adaptation to, an archetypal rhythm: "Yet when we say nature we really mean rhythm, and the basic rhythm is oestrus, the beating egg in its primal pouch. Naturally having lost the marvellous amnesia of sexual periodicity we live by a time-pining, time-bound, chronology."[19] Interestingly, this description of nature comes very close to the one put forward by Jung in his *Symbols of Transformation* and later elaborated by Marie-Louise von Franz, the most important of Jung's disciples, in *Number and Time*. For van Franz the only way to move beyond a desperate solipsism is to recognize the symbolic connection of psychic number patterns (as expressed in dreams) and physical number (expressed in world structures). When one pierces the barriers of limited time-bound empirical experience one discovers that these two coalesce in a *unus mundus* and that spirit and matter, the microcosm and macrocosm, can be reconciled, time understood in the context of eternal pulsating energy: ". . . one assumes that the energy rhythms of atoms remain constant. This postulate has led to a widely accepted hypothesis that *the universe possesses one single fundamental rhythm*, on which our whole concept of physical time might possibly be based. . . . Our measurement of time is founded on the temporal periodicity of a quantum-specified structure, and if we consider this structure in four dimensions, periodicity becomes a lattice structure in time. Periodicity, however, is nothing but a rhythm. The modern rhythmical view of time also seems to have a biological foundation. . . . Introspective observations on the flow of thought also lead to findings of a similar nature."[20] Both the Jungians and Durrell use gnostic symbols of reconciliation and integration in their attempt to describe the world.

In Durrell's imagined gnostic world, as in Jung's psychoanalytic world, consciousness (that is, fully realized selfhood) is a key term. If the ego alone dominates, internal forces are projected outward and it becomes impossible to separate legitimate perception from subjective imaginings, paranoia, or even psychosis. As just pointed out, for death to be valid in Akkad's gnostic sense, it must be consciously articulated. This, however, is not the only area where consciousness must be extended in the process of the redemption of nature. Sex is perhaps the most obviously rhythmic of man's activities and one of the least articulated on all levels. Lower man perceives it as a purely physical activity. The gnostic—like Durrell himself who has stated that "I am convinced that there is a profound link between sexual and psychic energies"[21]—knows that there is a deep symbolic, highly spiritual aspect to this function. Not surprisingly, then, one of Akkad's major preoccupations is to make the orgasm conscious as a means of recovering the hitherto repressed potential of the sexual act:

> . . . our world is a world not of repression and original sin but of creation and relaxation, of love and not doubt. This is what sets us apart from the others who today rule everything in the name of death. . . . Self-realisation is an imperative. . . . As far as death is concerned one must develop a certain discretion about choosing one sort from another. All questions of sorrow, fear, illness, for example, must be drained away until only the pure precipitate, like calc, of the gnostic death remains. This style of mind once achieved redeems all nature for a second or two, re-establishes that self-perpetrating cycle of joy which was the bliss of yesterday—the ancient mode of yesterday. . . . We are making the orgasm more and more conscious. . . . There is a way to comprehend the gnostic's giant onion of a world, the concentric circles, with the Pleroma beckoning there, the white heart of light, the source of that primal vision which for a second or two can recapture paradise. We can make amends by loving correctly.[22]

By making sex more conscious one also improves the quality of sperm; as in ancient times it will again become richly oxygenated; as Lacarrière points out: "Nous manquons de tout, de l'oxygène divin, du feu hyper-cosmique, et surtout de la vérité, demeurée solitaire dans les hauteurs de l'hyper-monde."[23] Because the orgasm has been neglected, our present civilization has become "poorly documented": "When the quality of the sperm deteriorates a whole culture can be put at risk—which is what is happening now in the Hegelian West! And the first sign, the first signal of alarm comes from the woman who is biologically more vulnerable and more responsible than the man for the future which they literally weave like a tissue with their kisses and caresses."[24] Through articulated sex, too, man returns briefly to the original blissful pre-Edenic state, where there was one integrated androgynous primal man, whose subsequent division represents one of the destructive dualities of the Fallen world: "when the couple was created out of the original man unit, clumsily divided into male and female parts, the affective distribution did not correspond at all with the biological. The sex of the man is really the woman's property, while the breasts of the woman belong to the man. . . . The male and female commerce centres around sperm and milk—they trade these elements in their love-making.

The female's breasts first gave him life and marked him with his ineradicable thirst for creating—Tiresias! The breasts are prophecy, are vision!"[25]

At every level, then, the gnostic world involves recognition of an earlier, purer state, making conscious repressed material, articulation, coming to know what is already there buried in the depths of the mind, the shining philosopher's stone hidden in darkest earth. In other words, once we know how to observe it correctly, even in our fallen world the microcosm can indeed be made to reflect the macrocosm. Symbolism, properly interpreted, is the key. The art of interpretation, moreover, lies in the hands of the *vates*—the inspired prophet who is one with the poet. Here, we come up against Durrell's own romantic vision of the writer, and his concept of heraldic reality: "In the genetic make-up of things lies the 'signature' of their ultimate form. . . . Everything begins 'in potentia' and gradually actualizes. Meanwhile, at every stage everything is changing into everything else. When a man sharpens his intuition enough, becomes enough of a poet, he can read the signature inherent in things and in people; he can reach behind appearances to divine their ultimate form. He reaches the Heraldic Reality where art has its roots."[26] The poet, of course, must express his insights, and this raises the question of form. So far in this paper I have looked at Durrell's intellectual, as it were, articulation of a number of gnostic themes, many of which appear particularly resonant in the context of modern civilization. I should now like to see how they relate to the formal structure of the *Quintet*.

Although the gnostic systems are replete with symbols of reconciliation, gnosticism itself cannot be taken as a panacea for the problems of western society. Durrell himself points out that the gnostics are an antithesis, in the Hegelian sense, to the excesses of orthodox Christianity.[27] As he states, pure gnosticism "defeats its own end and I think if one examines in detail Hindu philosophy and Chinese philosophy for example, one can see how the refusal can be operated without taking it so far as to die. It's a good deal saner way of dealing with this problem of dissent than the gnostic way which is so extreme."[28] Gnostic lore, for the most part, is a Judeo-Christian development of earlier eastern thought.[29] Ultimately, the *Quintet* leads back to pure Eastern wisdom (which is why, I think, one finds so many resonances of Jungian psychology in it), but it gets there through the gnosticism / Christianity opposition: "I wanted to do a book about people but under the people I wanted the city to convey some of the unease, some of the despair and some of the disgust that I feel about Christianity."[30] In other words, gnosticism is a reaction, not an absolute. Beyond its own world of mirrors and antitypes gnosticism must be evaluated by means of the reflections of yet another looking glass.

In this context, the primacy of the serpent symbol—always used as an antithesis to the Biblical story (and all the repressive sexual connotations which the Genesis account has accrued)—is particularly relevant. Durrell describes an Ophitic form of gnosticism in his portrayal of Akkad's rite.

There is an actual snake at the initiation which becomes a focus for the revelations. When Bruce watches the snake Ophis he becomes aware of an unexpected poetic symbolic plane in the ceremony: "Looking so fixedly at this strange machine-like animal-bird insect I felt as if it were talking to me, felt it had the sort of significance which one cannot render clear by words, a deep symbolic significance of something which has by-passed causality. The alchemists apparently have to deal with this sort of symbol in their work. . . ."[31] To the gnostic the serpent is good not evil, a purveyer of gnosis, the means of infinitely expanding consciousness.[32] At a lower level it stands as a symbol of sexual powers,[33] and at the highest level as a symbol of time itself. For as Uroboros (or as the Orphic egg), devouring its tail it forms a perfect mandala, reconciling time with eternity and forming the highest symbol of the *unus mundus*, the unity of nature which underlies the apparent duality of psyche and matter. Alchemical, gnostic, and dream symbolism meet in this figure of reconciliation.[34]

Durrell picks up on another common gnostic theme in discussions of incest and inversion in the *Quintet*.[35] The brother-sister variation is of particular relevance here since in gnostic lore the act of original creation is often seen as the result of this union. In alchemy, too, it is the divine marriage of the brother and sister which accomplishes the *opus*. The split into male and female, as we have seen, mirrors the basic spirit / matter split of the universe. When the masculine spiritual quality espouses his material sister, then a new, all encompassing, and fully integrated fusion results.[36]

The situation of Piers, Sylvie, and Bruce is equally apposite: "Old Hippolytus has spoken of you in his tract on the refutation of all heresies. The Myth is as follows: There were three unbegotten principles of the universe, two male and one female. One male principle is called Good, who takes forethought for the course of things; the other male is called Father of the Begotten, but he is without the foreknowledge and invisible. The female is without foreknowledge, wrathful, double-minded, double-bodied, a virgin above and a viper below. She is called Eden, she is called Israel. These are the principles of the universe, the roots and springs from which everything came."[37] Like the product of brother-sister incest, this trinity comes to represent a movement beyond the original duality of the world. The three become a symbol of a new self.[38] Here, the symbolism of number comes into play: "With three something new in the concept of number makes its appearance. In the I-You situation the ego is still held in tension with the You, but that which is above it, *it*, the Third, the Many is the world. This thesis, in which the psychic, the linguistic, and the numerical come together, might serve as a rather vague paraphrase of early man's concept of number. One—two—many, is it not mirrored exactly in the numerical forms of the substantives singular, dual, plural?"[39]

Next comes the question of the discrete ego, a phenomenon which—as has already been pointed out—the gnostics rejected even if they lacked the terminology to label it in modern jargon:

> Car cette communion qui mêle les semences, les désirs et les êtres en brisant tout lien de nature . . . aboutit à une sorte de fusion, première victoire sur ce monde dont la nature profonde est la séparation, la division, l'éparpillement dans la pesanteur matérielle. . . . A ce stade, en effet, les individualités disparaissent avec la première de toutes les prisons, celle du Moi. Briser le Moi, se fondre dans le Toi, dans le Lui (et l'on retrouve ici l'importance que Simon donnait précisément à la grammaire dont les catégories rigides étaient l'un des milliers d'exemples révélateurs de la séparation aliénante des elements du monde), supprimer ces catégories du Moi, du Toi, du Lui, *devenir Nous*, tel devait être le sens des soi-disant "mysteres des Simoniens."[40]

A number of the characters in the *Quintet* also doubt the "real existence" of the discrete ego: Constance, the Freudian analyst, likens the hypothesis of an individual ego to an "unconscious hallucination." But if there are no individuals of the type which Judeo-Christian culture has posited and Freud has dissected and categorized, what then happens to the novel—whose job traditionally has been to chart the progress of the individual through time? Surely the form of the *bildungsroman* is the basic model for modern fiction. Blanford, Durrell's alter ego, addresses this problem: he plans to write a novel where the characters are, as the Biblical injunction exhorts us, "members of one another" or even spare parts:

> "The old stable outlines of the dear old linear novel have been side-stepped in favour of soft focus palimpsest which enables the actors to turn into each other, to melt into each other's inner lifespace if they wish. Everything and everyone comes closer and closer together, moving towards the one. . . . By the same token the people also, and even pieces of them, spare parts which are not as yet fully reincarnated. One must advance to the edge of the Provisional, to the very precipice. . . . Yes, a book like any other book, but the recipe is unusual, that is all. Listen, the pretension is one of pure phenomenology. The basic tale which I have passed through all this arrangement of lighting is no more esoteric than an old detective story. The distortions and evocations are thrown in to ask a few basic questions like—how real is reality, and if so why so? Has poetry, then, no right to exist?"[41]

This discussion, of course, reflects many of the questions Durrell has posed and the techniques he has used to mirror the problems: the story within a story within a story, the overlapping of fictional characters with their own fictions, the rewriting of the same material (and same individuals) from a variety of perspectives, and so forth. Individuals in the *Quintet* are indeed highly provisional, discrete only in a most unorthodox sense. Marc Alyn points out that "In your novels, of course, everything is double. The story of the characters in search of an author is carried to extremes, stirred up to a frenzy. First you have the characters, then you have an author, who is also a character, and then the characters who in their way are all the authors."[42]

If the literary consequences of gnostic "refus" of the ego premise lead to essential reformulations of the concept of character in the novel, they also lead to variations in plot and style. As the importance of discrete characters diminishes, so does the dominance of chronology and the acceptance of causality. On occasion in *Quinx*, for example, we escape from the "sullen monorail of story and person" and are given "poetic substance detached from the narrative line," where "the undeveloped germs of anecdote . . . dissolve in the mind."[43] The compressed aphoristic style of parts of the *Quintet* also arises in part from a rejection of the traditional convention of a strict narrative flow linked to the voice of an individual character. Like the gnostic priest, the poet / writer becomes an inspired seer. He has inklings about the nature of the world, inklings which can flash out in any given situation. These inklings resemble the koans of Zen Buddhism, "those sublime paradoxes that light up, as with a flash of lightening, the inscrutable interrelations between ego and self."[44] In many places narrative in the *Quintet* is replaced by groups of inklings; sometimes they masquerade as the writer's notebook, sometimes they simply insert themselves, almost randomly, into the text.

Finally, we come to Durrell's most obvious formal departure from the traditional novel: the use of a quincunx of books. Why, one might ask, is there a need for five books? In what sense is this a quintet? What is the meaning of the gnostic / Templar quincunx of trees? Five is a sacred number for the Pythagoreans; they were fascinated by the physical mechanism of musical fifths and, in terms of metaphysics, associated the number with the music of the spheres. Durrell's *Quintet* reflects this; like Sutcliffe Durrell produces a "whole book arranged in diminished fifths from the point of view of orchestration. A big switchy book, all points and sidings."[45] In gnostic lore five is the number of the Hieros gamos, the divine marriage of the anthropos (three) and the anima mundi (two). The symbol of five in its beneficent form is the pentangle, the endless knot, movement through eternity. Five related to man as microcosm reflecting the universe: his four limbs and the head which controls them. As such it often appears in alchemy, where it is associated also with Aristotle's quintessence as philosopher's stone. This ties in with the whole question of the Templar treasure. In *Livia* Quatrefages—whose very name suggests "the eating of the four"—says: "But I think there is no treasure; I think Philippe Le Bel got it all. I have not mentioned this to anyone because I am not absolutely sure—but our search for the quincunx of trees concerns another sort of treasure." And Blanford links this with the alchemists' enterprise: "I do understand a little bit. You mean the Philosopher's stone, don't you?"[46] The Philosopher's stone solved the problem of the imperfect four elements (earth, air, fire, water) and their qualities (moist, dry, hot, cold). The need for a redeeming quintessence is a result of the gnostic fall into matter, at which time "The table of essences gave place to the table of elements. The Philosopher's Stone, the Holy Grail of ancient consciousness gave place to the usurping values of the gold bar; it was the new ruler of the soul. . . ."[47]

Soon after he began the construction of the *Quintet* Durrell compared his form to the linking sections of a telescope or a cluster of tables:

> I was intending to go over five books this time . . . and I was going to do a telescopic form, what the French call gigogne—you know, those clusters of tables, you open one and it opens another and so on and so forth. And I didn't want to do it in continuum form this time, I wanted to do it straight like a telescope, not fleuve you understand. For example, in the second volume it emerges that the first volume is not by me at all, it's by a character, one of the characters in the first. . . . And gradually the thing should become on the one hand more flou, that is to say more dispersed apparently, and much tighter in its inner organization and lie anchored on Avignon and a very small group of people.[48]

Certainly, this explains why Durrell needed to construct a series of novels, the various members of which intersect at all sorts of strange places and fit one into the other. It does not, however, completely explain the choice of five. Moreover, if one of the accomplishments of the *Quintet* is to challenge the existence of the discrete ego, what can be meant by "a small group of people"? Sutcliffe—an imagined novelist's imaginary character—suggests that there is a negative side to the Fifth Substance, which, as far as he can see, makes all persons the same person and all situations identical: "The universe must be dying of boredom."[49] His creator Blanford elaborates: ". . . history is simply gossip from an eastern point of view—the five senses, the five arts, are its plumage. For after relativity and the field-theory bleakness sets in and the universe becomes cosmically pointless."[50] Here, the question of the quincunx, that is the structural form of the pattern of five which Durrell is using, becomes of paramount significance. We are not dealing with a pentagon but with a quincunx, quite a different geometric shape.

> Whereas the pentagon with its five angles geometrizes the number five in its quantitative and additive form, the quintessence is represented by the quincunx as the center of four. Jung says of the quincunx: "The four (forms), as it were, a frame for the one, accentuated as the centre. . . . By unfolding into four it acquires distinct characteristics and can therefore be known. . . . So long as a thing is unconscious it has no recognizable qualities and is consequently merged with universal unknown, with the unconscious All and Nothing, with what the Gnostics called a "nonexistent all-being." But as soon as the unconscious content enters the sphere of consciousness it has already split into the "four," that is to say it can become an object of experience only by virtue of the four basic foundations of consciousness. . . . The splitting into four has the same significance as the division of the horizon into four quarters, or the year into four seasons. That is, through the act of becoming conscious the four basic aspects of a whole judgment are rendered visible.[51]

Toward the end of *Quinx* this quinary kind of understanding of selfhood, a reconciliation of east and west, an alternative to Sutcliffe's bored entropic universe, seems to be put forward as the goal of Blanford's great literary opus, the *Quintet* itself. What Blanford plans to do is "To celebrate the mystical marriage of four dimensions with five skandas." According to Buddhism, personality as we define it is an empty convention, a label whose true referant is not a unified stationary ego but rather five amorphous heaps or skandhas—physical actions, feelings, perceptions, volitions, and consciousness—dynamically arranged in the form of the quincunx. Human reality, then, consists of a set of aggregates of conditioned dharmas. By a creative application of the quincunx as reconciling symbol, moreover, eastern wisdom can be brought to bear on the western world, which is one number short of wholeness;[52] the east can teach us to transcend our despair, overcome our fear at the loss of ego, and to end the terrifying death drift which seems to be leading to total annihilation of human civilisation. Quatrefages, so it appears, discovered a similar kind of truth during his researches into the secrets of the Templars: "In architecture the quincunxial shape was considered a sort of housing for the divine power—a battery, if you like, which gathered into itself the divinity as it tried to pour earthward, to earth itself—just like an electrical current does. This magical current was supposed to create an electrical "field" around the treasure and protect it from being discovered until its emanations were fully mastered and could be used in the alchemical sense to nourish a sort of world bank which might enable man to come to terms with matter—his earthly inheritance, so to speak."[53]

Philosophically, in context, this sounds both revolutionary and immensely important. Blanford / Durrell, however, does not necessarily have the last word. Sutcliffe reminds him (and us):

> "If you had seen a Kashmiri merchant or a Bengali bunia or a Hindu business man you would realise that the West has no monopoly in materialism and ego-worship. So there!"
> It was true, of course, and Blanford knew it in his heart of minds. His version was too pat.[54]

Our situation as readers is similar to that of Piers after the episode of the magazine article in *Monsieur*—do we know for certain that the whole opus might not be a fake, a glittering sham to delight the ear and tickle the intellectual fancy? By nature, there is no answer; all that can be observed is that Durrell—with whatever degree of authority he might possess above that of his character—has recently stated that the *Quintet* is Tibetan.[55]

As he was beginning work on *Sebastian*, Durrell produced the following formula to describe his literary evolution:[56]

an	a	an
Agon	Pathos	Anagnorisis
◯	◯	◯
The Black Book	*The Quartet*	*The Quinx*

In literary terms, at least, the pattern seems complete.[57]

Notes

1. See James P. Carley, "An Interview with Lawrence Durrell on the Background to *Monsieur* and its Sequels," *Malahat Review* 51 (1979), 46.

2. See C. W. King, *The Gnostics and Their Remains* (2nd ed.; London, 1887), pp. 95ff. The material comes from Hippolytus's reconstruction of the Ophite system. Although there has been much new research since King's day, and caches of lost gnostic documents have been found, I have used his book wherever possible because he is sympathetic to the gnostics and does not get bogged down in narrow points of scholarship. More specifically, Durrell knows and admires his work.

3. In *The Decline of the West* Spengler, a strong influence on Durrell, suggests that the recognition of Jehovah as evil and opposed to the goodness of Jesus is one of the most important discoveries of Western culture. In this context see also Durrell's comment in his interview with Marc Alyn in *The Big Supposer: Lawrence Durrell, A Dialogue with Marc Allyn* (New York, 1974), p. 136: "[*The Decline of the West*] contained some astonishing foresights, including Caesarism (which culminated in nazism) and gold, a notion which heralded Freud's theories."

4. The mirror image predominates in the gnostic systems. In this context, C. G. Jung's elucidation of the myth of Narcissus—who needed to look into the mirror to find his own spiritual nature—should be consulted. See also Durrell's own poem "For a nursery mirror."

5. *Monsieur or the Prince of Darkness* (London, 1974), p. 217. In his exposition Akkad has extrapolated from the gnostic systems and is giving his own formulations of the material. Durrell, however, warns against taking his literary reconstruction of gnostic dogma too seriously: "I'm just making free use of the material which is lying about all over the field." (See James P. Carley, "Lawrence Durrell and the Gnostics," *Deus Loci* 2 [1978], 7.)

6. Lawrence Durrell, *Quinx or the Ripper's Tale* (London, 1985), p. 35. See also Jacques Lacarrière, *Les Gnostiques* (Paris, 1973), pp. 39–40: "Indiscutablement, les gnostiques eussent été fascinés par les découvertes de Freud et des freudiens car toute leur cosmologie et leur anthropologie portent l'empreinte de ce traumatisme cosmique que fut l'apparition *Avant Terme* d l'homme" ("Undoubtedly the discoveries of Freud and the Freudians would have fascinated the Gnostics, for all their cosmology and their anthropology bear the imprint of this cosmic trauma caused by man's *premature* appearance on earth"). Durrell wrote a preface to *Les Gnostiques* and paraphrases it in various parts of the *Quintet*.

7. *Monsieur*, pp. 140–41. In his comparative analysis of Eastern and Western religions, C. G. Jung comes to a very similar conclusion, expressed in similar terminology. Jung points out that for Western man God is safely outside, "totaliter aliter": "If you shift the formula a bit and substitute for God some other power, for instance the world or money, you get a complete picture of Western man—assiduous, fearful, devout, self-abasing, enterprising, greedy, and violent in his pursuit of the goods of this world: possessions, health, knowledge, technical mastery, public welfare, political power, conquest, and so on. What are the great popular movements of our time? Attempts to grab the money or property of others and to protect our own. The mind is chiefly employed in devising suitable 'isms' to hide the real motives or to get more loot." *Psychology and Religion: West and East. The Collected Works of C. G. Jung*, vol. 11 (2nd ed.; Princeton, 1969), pp. 482–83.

8. Lawrence Durrell, *Constance or Solitary Practices* (London, 1982), p. 304.

9. *Quinx*, p. 27. This contrasts absolutely to Eastern wisdom:

> The Tao that can be told of
> Is not the Absolute Tao;
> The Names that can be given
> Are not Absolute Names.

The Nameless is the origin of Heaven and Earth
The Names is the Mother of All Things.

(Ling Yutang, *The Wisdom of Laotse* [New York, 1948], p. 41.)

10. Quoted in Zbigniew Lewicki, *The Bang and the Whimper* (Westport, Conn., 1984), p. 72. As Lewicki shows, entropy as a philosophical concern has found its way into much modern literature, especially among contemporary American writers. The structure of Thomas Pynchon's *The Crying of Lot 49*, for example, is based on an application of the principles of entropy; it shows in literary terms, as Lewicki suggests, the breakdown of all communication systems. Interestingly, Pychon shares both themes and techniques with Durrell: the mingling of real and imaginary landscape, the assimilation of a "fictional" Jacobean play into the plot, the use of names interchangeably as personal indicators and as symbols, plays on the form of acronyms (W.A.S.T.E., K.C.U.F.), and so forth. Indeed, the whole Trystero plot and Oedipa's confusion between objective reality and paranoia are superficially similar to what we find in Durrell, although the two writers are very different in their ambitions and accomplishments. Lacarrière suggests that the gnostics had an instinctive perception, almost like the awareness of an unpleasant odour, of the existence of entropy: "Il est curieux de voir que, d'une façon évidemment imparfaite et sommaire, les gnostiques ont entreve que le destin du monde materiel tendait vers l'inertie" (*Les Gnostiques*, p. 20; "Curiously enough, the Gnostics perceived, albeit in an imperfect and incomplete manner, that the tendency of the material world is towards inertia").

11. Lawrence Durrell, *Sebastian or Ruling Passions* (London, 1983), p. 175. Schwartz is, of course, a naive and charmingly optimistic materialist (and a dedicated Freudian analyst), committed as such to the "real" world. Rather than face the evil consequences of the dominant philosophy of our Judeo-Christian civilisation (in the form of the return of his wife from the concentration camps) he commits suicide—a despairing suicide which is the antithesis of the positive gesture of refus of the gnostic initiates.

12. Sartre's play *Huis Clos* has been translated into English as *No Exit*. There are many similarities of concept, and even overlappings in language, between gnosticism and existentialism: the sense of the absurd, a feeling of alienation, the centrality of the refus, and the vertiginous sense of freedom generated by the realization of the randomness of Nature.

13. *Monsieur*, p. 166. Using a different metaphor Lacarrière makes the same point: "Et du fond de cette mer obscure, l'homme ne percoit, de la surface lumineuse du monde supérieur, que des formes éphémères, des reflets fugitifs, des fantômes évanescents à l'image de ces poissons phosphorescent qui seuls illuminent l'obscurité millenaire des grands fonds" (*Les Gnostiques*, p. 20; "And from the bottom of this dark sea, man perceives from the luminous surface of the upper world only ephemeral forms, fleeting reflections, evanescent phantoms which are like those phosphorescent fish that alone illuminate the age-old darkness of the great ocean depths").

14. *Monsieur*, p. 139. See also Durrell's preface to *Les Gnostiques*: "Eux, ils ont refusé de protéger un monde qui a été imparfait et eux, ils ont affronté le grand mensonge de Lucifer et de Mammon avec la splendeur sans espoir des trois cents Spartiates" (p. 7; "They refused to countenance a world which was imperfect and confronted the great lie of Lucifer and Mammon with the splendor without hope of the three hundred Spartans"). On the gnostics as poets see Elaine Pagels, *The Gnostic Gospels* (New York, 1979), pp. 3ff.: "Like circles of artists today, gnostics considered original creative invention to be the mark of anyone who becomes spiritually alive."

15. *The Big Supposer*, p. 143. Interesting in this context is Durrell's own feeling about salvation from suicide through the creative act: "What I can say for certain though is that either I start a novel or I commit suicide" (*The Big Supposer*, p. 97).

16. *Monsieur*, p. 14. This is quite similar, it seems to me, to Norman O. Brown's interpretation of Eastern thought; see, for example, *Life Against Death: The Psychoanalytical*

Meaning of History (Wesleyan University, 1959), p. 106: "The Nirvana-principle regulates an individual life which enjoys full satisfaction and concretely embodies the full essence of the species, and in which life and death are simultaneously affirmed, because life and death together constitute individuality, and ripeness is all."

17. The law of causality is, for the gnostic, the ultimate mechanistic trap, the greatest illusion perpetrated by Jehovah. In *The Avignon Quintet* the death cult becomes an active commitment to chance. On one level, then, it is a parallel to the existentialist's "acte gratuit," which serves as a means of affirming free will by denying determinism. On a metaphysical level, however, it moves beyond this to an acceptance of a symbolic and meaningful transcendent chance and involves an assumption that there is a metaphoric and reconciling reality hidden behind the false world of causality.

18. "Nous vivons dans le monde de la mort, une mort à la fois matérielle et cosmique, dont la matière, inerte est le signe le plus tangible. Et ce n'est qu'en la partageant, en l'émiettant, en la dissolvant peu à peu, en consommant en quelque sorte toute la substance de ce monde que l'homme parviendra à s'arracher aux cercles de l'Erreur. 'Il faut vous partager la mort afin de l'épuiser,' dit Valentin à ses disciples, 'afin de la dissoudre pour qu'en vous et par vous meure la mort' " (*Les Gnostiques*, p. 80; "We live in the world of death, a death which is both material and cosmic, of which inert matter is the most tangible sign. And it is only by parceling it out, scattering it, dissolving it little by little, by consuming all the substance of this world in one way or another that man will succeed in tearing himself from the circles of Error. 'You must share death among yourselves in order to exhaust it and cause its dissolution,' says Valentinus to his disciples, 'so that in you and through you death may die' ").

19. *Monsieur*, p. 142.

20. Marie-Louise von Franz, *Number and Time*, trans. Andrea Dykes (Evanston, 1974), p. 250; see also pp. 252ff.

21. *The Big Supposer*, p. 33.

22. *Monsieur*, pp. 141–43. The history of literary puns on dying as a sexual metaphor is also relevant in this context.

23. *Les Gnostiques*, p. 80; "We lack everything: divine oxygen, hyper-cosmic fire and above all truth, which has remained alone in the upper regions of the hyper-world."

24. *Constance*, p. 288.

25. *Constance*, p. 284. See also Lacarrière on the Simonians: "Faites l'amour, dit Simon, pour lutter contre le désordre du monde, rétablir le désir dans ses droits essentiels, entretenir le feu générateur qui est aussi sang, lait, semence" (*Les Gnostiques*, p. 58; "Make love, says Simon, as a means of struggling against the disorder of the world, of restoring desire to its essential rights, of maintaining the generative fire which is also blood, milk, and semen.")

26. *The Big Supposer*, p. 150. The concept Durrell articulates here links up closely with neo-Platonic thought, with Jung's collective unconscious, and with Eastern mysticism. As Affad points out, "Einstein's non-discrete field, Groddeck's 'It,' and Pursewarden's 'heraldic universe' seem all and the same concept and would easily answer to the formulations of Patanjali" (*Sebastian*, p. 28).

27. Ironically, Christianity's excess consists of a blind refusal to acknowledge the existence of evil—articulated by St. Augustine in his theory of evil as a "privatio boni." Jung sees this blindness to evil to be one of the chief causes for the "decline of the west," and a key factor in our western dualism, our serious split in consciousness. And, as Durrell himself points out: "[reading the gnostic texts] seemed to suggest that there was some other Christ apart from the orthodox statutory hellenistic view of our Christ, who had been sort of drummed out, Luciferian wise, and was trying to fight his way back. . . . And I wondered . . . whether we hadn't overweighed the frail bark of Christianity by denying totally the real-

ity of evil." ("An Interview with Lawrence Durrell," pp. 42–43.) In some ways, nazism and other terrifying regimes act as compensations in a psychological sense for the repressed Christian position: "We [the Nazis] are not washed in the blood of the Christian lamb, but in the blood of inferior races out of which we shall fashion the slaves which are necessary to fulfil our designs. It is not cupidity or rapacity which drives the Führer but the desire for once to let the dark side of man have his full sway, stand to his full height. Seen in this way Evil is Good, don't you see?" (*Constance*, p. 237).

28. "An Interview with Lawrence Durrell," p. 45.

29. King articulates this point over and over again and gives many examples to substantiate the thesis.

30. "An Interview with Lawrence Durrell," p. 43. Avignon itself, as Durrell points out in *Livia*, p. 48, is "a cathedral to Mammon. It was here our Judeo-Christian culture finally wiped out the rich paganism of the Mediterranean! Here the great god Pan was sent to the gas-chambers of the Popes." The Palace of the Popes represents the nadir of Christian idealism, the real expression of just how materialistic the Christian world had become. Petrarch called it the Babylon of the West and gazed with amazed horror at the "poor fishermen of Galilee" who were now "loaded with gold and clad in purple." And, of course, the very existence of two papacies caused extraordinary tension in the Christian West: it represented a cataclysmic split for Western Christian consciousness. On the other side, Avignon is associated with the Cathars, with gnostic heresy. The Templars and their connections with Avignon provide a thematic link between the gnostics of Egypt and modern Europe. In their frenzied desire for self-destruction they show the culmination of the death drift implicit in Western civilisation. *Livia* ends with a description of Avignon's pompe a merde and the citation of St. Augustine's aphorism: Inter faesces et urinam nascimur, followed by Blanford's realization of the ironic fact that "It had been, after all, Augustine's 'City of God,' transplanted once upon a time to this green and innocent country." Avignon, then, becomes a metaphor (or rather a realized symbol) for the development of the "signature" contained in Judeo-Christian thought.

31. *Monsieur*, p. 124.

32. "Hippolytus, giving an account of the doctrine of the Naassenes, says that the serpent dwells in all thing and creatures. . . . 'They say, too, that all things are subject to her, the serpent, that she is good and something of everything in herself. . . . She imparts beauty and ripeness to all things' " (*Psychology and Alchemy. The Collected Works of C. G. Jung*, vol. 12 [2nd ed.; Princeton, 1968], p. 449).

33. "For us it is, of course, a symbol of the caduceus of Aesculapius, of the spinal column, of the kundalini-serpent of the Indians—you will be able to trace the ancestry of the idea through many continents and many religions. It is also the sacred phallus of Greece and Egypt and India, as well as the coiled intestines from which one can perform a divination by entrails as our ancestors did" (*Monsieur*, p. 133).

34. For Jung's interpretation of the various levels of symbolism of Uroboros (who figures on the cover of Lacarrière's book) see *Aion. The Collected Works of C. G. Jung*, vol. 9.2 (Princeton, 1968), pp. 259, 264. On the *unus mundus*—"the unitary world, towards which the psychologist and the atomic physicist are converging along separate paths"—see *Civilization in Transition. The Collected Works of C. G. Jung*, vol. 10 (2nd ed.; Princeton, 1970), pp. 409, 411, 452.

35. Incest played a role in the *Quartet* as well, most notably in the case of Pursewarden and Liza. For a detailed discussion of various literary implications of incest as well as for a most useful general bibliography, see Frank Whigham, "Sexual and Social Mobility in *The Duchess of Malfi*," *PMLA* 100 (1985), 167–86.

36. As Durrell points out, there is a connection here with the hermaphrodite prophet Tiresias.

37. *Monsieur*, p. 139.

38. "'In further meditations upon the unholy trinity they form, I had a sudden small gleam of light. I suddenly saw the underlying unity of the three children as a total *self*, or the symbol of such an abstraction. Against the traditional duality-figure of our cosmology I place a triune self, composed of two male and one female partner—a gnostic notion, if I remembered correctly" (*Monsieur*, p. 214).

39. Karl Menninger, *Zahwort und Ziffer; Eine Kulturgeschichte der Zahl* (Gottingen, 1958), pp. 27ff. Quoted in von Franz, pp. 105–106.

40. *Les Gnostiques*, pp. 59–60; "For this communion which mixes together seed, desires and beings, while breaking all ties of nature . . . leads to a sort of fusion, the first victory over this world whose deep nature is separation, division, dispersal through the weight of matter. . . . At this stage, in fact, individualities disappear with the first of all prisons, that of the I. To break down the I, to melt into the Thou, into the He (and here one rediscovers the importance which Simon attributed to grammar, whose rigid categories were among thousands of revealing examples of the alienating separation of the elements of the world), to suppress these categories of I, Thou, He, and *to become We*, such must have been the meaning of the so-called 'mysteries of the Simonians.' "

41. *Quinx*, pp. 99–100.

42. *The Big Supposer*, p. 19.

43. *Quinx*, p. 32.

44. *The Structure and Dynamics of the Psyche. The Collected Works of C. G. Jung*, vol. 8 (2nd ed.; 1969), p. 225.

45. *Constance*, p. 123.

46. *Livia*, p. 163. *Quinx*, of course, ends just as the group is about to enter the caves where the treasure was supposedly hidden and bring it forth; this is, then, the "precise moment that reality prime rushed to the aid of fiction and the totally unpredictable began to take place."

47. *Monsieur*, p. 217.

48. "An Interview with Lawrence Durrell," p. 46.

49. *Constance*, p. 123. Here, we are back to the question of entropy.

50. *Quinx*, p. 139.

51. *Number and Time*, p. 121.

52. Von Franz (*Number and Time*, pp. 120ff.) points out that in eastern thought five possesses the same significance as a number of wholeness that four does in the West. The eastern five represents a centred four—that is a quincunx—Westerners have neglected the centering process. In Tantric mythology the five Jinas, which constitute the body of the universe, correspond mystically to the various aspects of the universe. "Five elements correspond to the five Jinas, five senses and sense-objects, five cardinal points (the centre being the fifth). At the same time there are further correspondences with letters of the alphabet, with parts of the body, with the various kinds of 'vital breath,' with colours, sounds, etc." (Edward Conze, *Buddhism. Its Essence and Development* [New York, 1965], p. 190).

53. *Quinx*, p. 131.

54. *Quinx*, pp. 41–42.

55. *Égoiste* 8 (1984), 52: "Moi, j'ai un individuel flou qui correspond au tibétain."

56. Unpublished letter in my possession. See also *Égoiste*, 52.

57. It is interesting, too, that Durrell is threatening to make life imitate art; like Blanford, who vaguely imagined monastic life at some point in the future, Durrell claims to be contemplating a retreat to the lamasery at Chateau de Plaige, with which he is already actively involved.

INDEX